Char.

C000131737

Manchester University Press

Series editors: Anna Barton, Andrew Smith

Editorial board: David Amigoni, Isobel Armstrong, Philip Holden, Jerome McGann, Joanne Wilkes, Julia M. Wright

Interventions: Rethinking the Nineteenth Century seeks to make a significant intervention into the critical narratives that dominate conventional and established understandings of nineteenth-century literature. Informed by the latest developments in criticism and theory the series provides a focus for how texts from the long nineteenth century, and more recent adaptations of them, revitalise our knowledge of and engagement with the period. It explores the radical possibilities offered by new methods, unexplored contexts and neglected authors and texts to re-map the literary-cultural landscape of the period and rigorously reimagine its geographical and historical parameters. The series includes monographs, edited collections, and scholarly sourcebooks.

Already published

The Great Exhibition, 1851: A sourcebook   Jonathon Shears (ed.)

Interventions: Rethinking the nineteenth century   Andrew Smith and Anna Barton (eds)

Charlotte Brontë

Legacies and afterlives

Edited by Amber K. Regis and
Deborah Wynne

Manchester University Press

Published by Manchester University Press
Altrincham Street, Manchester M1 7JA
www.manchesteruniversitypress.co.uk

British Library Cataloguing-in-Publication Data
A catalogue record for this book is available from the British Library

ISBN 978 1 7849 9246 0 hardback

ISBN 978 1 5261 3948 1 paperback

First published by Manchester University Press in hardback 2017

This edition first published 2019

The publisher has no responsibility for the persistence or accuracy of URLs for any external or third-party internet websites referred to in this book, and does not guarantee that any content on such websites is, or will remain, accurate or appropriate.

Typeset by Out of House Publishing
Printed in Great Britain
by TJ International Ltd, Padstow

Contents

List of figures   vii

Notes on contributors   viii

Acknowledgements   xii

Introduction: picturing Charlotte Brontë   1
Amber K. Regis and Deborah Wynne

**Part I: Ghostly afterlives: cults, literary tourism
and staging the life**   **41**

1   The 'Charlotte' cult: writing the literary pilgrimage, from
    Gaskell to Woolf   43
    Deborah Wynne

2   The path out of Haworth: mobility, migration and the
    global in Charlotte Brontë's *Shirley* and the writings of
    Mary Taylor   59
    Jude Piesse

3   Brontë countries: nation, gender and place in the literary
    landscapes of Haworth and Brussels   79
    Charlotte Mathieson

4   Reading the revenant in Charlotte Brontë's literary
    afterlives: charting the path from the 'silent country'
    to the seance   96
    Amber Pouliot

Contents

5 Charlotte Brontë on stage: 1930s biodrama and the
   archive/museum performed   116
   Amber K. Regis

Part II: Textual legacies: influences and adaptations   **143**

6 'Poetry, as I comprehend the word': Charlotte Brontë's
   lyric afterlife   145
   Anna Barton

7 The legacy of Lucy Snowe: reconfiguring spinsterhood
   and the Victorian family in inter-war women's writing   164
   Emma Liggins

8 Hunger, rebellion and rage: adapting *Villette*   182
   Benjamin Poore

9 The ethics of appropriation; or, the 'mere spectre' of Jane
   Eyre: Emma Tennant's *Thornfield Hall*, Jasper Fforde's
   The Eyre Affair and Gail Jones's *Sixty Lights*   197
   Alexandra Lewis

10 'The insane Creole': the afterlife of Bertha Mason   221
   Jessica Cox

11 *Jane Eyre*'s transmedia lives   241
   Monika Pietrzak-Franger

12 'Reader, I [shagged/beat/whipped/f****d/rewrote] him': the
   sexual and financial afterlives of *Jane Eyre*   258
   Louisa Yates

   Appendix: Charlotte Brontë's cultural legacy, 1848–2016   280
   Kimberley Braxton

   Index   294

Figures

1 George Richmond, *Charlotte Brontë* (1850). Image
   © National Portrait Gallery, London   4

2 *Charlotte Brontë: From an original painting by Chappel*
   (1870s). Henry W. and Albert A. Berg Collection of
   English and American Literature, the New York Public
   Library, Astor, Lenox and Tilden Foundations   8

3 Cover illustration from Maurice Clare, *A Day with
   Charlotte Brontë* (c.1911). Courtesy of the University of
   Sheffield Library Special Collections   11

4 Illustration from Maurice Clare, *A Day with Charlotte
   Brontë* (c.1911). Courtesy of the University of Sheffield
   Library Special Collections   12

5 Charlotte Cory, *Her Portrait by Richmond* (2013).
   © Charlotte Cory   22

6 Blue plaque on rue Terarken, Brussels, Belgium   92

Contributors

Anna Barton is a senior lecturer in Victorian literature at the University of Sheffield where she also co-directs the Centre for Nineteenth-Century Studies. Her work on nineteenth-century poetry includes *Tennyson's Name: Identity and Responsibility in the Poetry of Alfred, Lord Tennyson* (2008) and *In Memoriam: A Reading Guide* (2012) as well as articles and chapters on Blake, Clough, Edward Lear, Swinburne and Barrett Browning. She is currently writing a book on liberal philosophy and nineteenth-century poetry. With Andrew Smith she edits the series 'Interventions: Rethinking the Nineteenth Century' for Manchester University Press. She also co-edits the Victorian literature section of *Literature Compass*.

Kimberley Braxton is a Ph.D. student in English literature at Keele University. Her thesis focuses on the textual and writing community of the Brontë family. She identifies cases of individuality and similarity and explores the disintegration of their communities in pursuit of establishing the presence or lack thereof of a family connection within their writing. She has delivered papers on the Brontë relics, the life-writing of Anne and Emily Brontë, the erotic retellings of *Jane Eyre* and the influence of Byron on the writing of Brontë siblings. In addition, she has worked as a reviewer for the *Brontë Studies* journal and as chief editor for the postgraduate journal *Under Construction @ Keele*.

Jessica Cox is a senior lecturer in English literature at Brunel University London. She has research interests in Victorian sensation fiction, the Brontës, neo-Victorianism and the cultural history of breastfeeding. She is the author of a short biography of Charlotte Brontë (2011) and several articles on the Brontës, editor of the Penguin edition of Charlotte Brontë's *Shirley* (2006) and contributor to the BBC Two documentary

Being the Brontës (2016). She is editor of a collection of essays on Mary Elizabeth Braddon (2012) and co-editor of a major anthology on *Women and Belief* (2010). Her current work examines the legacy of the Victorian sensation novel in contemporary culture and the history of breastfeeding in the long nineteenth century.

Alexandra Lewis is a lecturer in English literature and associate director of the Centre for the Novel at the University of Aberdeen. She was a Cambridge Commonwealth Trust Scholar at Trinity College and has taught English literature at the universities of London (Goldsmiths) and Warwick and several Cambridge colleges. Her publications on the Brontës include chapters in *Acts of Memory* (2010), *The Brontës in Context* (2012), *Picturing Women's Health: 1750–1910* (2014) and *Feminist Moments* (2016). Alexandra is editor of *The Brontës and the Idea of the Human: Science, Ethics, and the Victorian Imagination* (forthcoming) and has been invited to produce the next Norton critical edition of *Wuthering Heights*. She is currently completing a monograph on trauma in nineteenth-century literature and psychology. Alexandra serves on the executive committee of both the British and the Australasian Associations for Victorian Studies.

Emma Liggins is a senior lecturer in English literature at Manchester Metropolitan University. She has recently published *Odd Women? Spinsters, Lesbians and Widows in British Women's Fiction, 1850s–1930s* (2014). She has a chapter on modernist women's ghost stories in Emma Young and James Bailey (eds.), *British Women Short Story Writers* (2015) and a chapter on May Sinclair and women's war work in Rebecca Bowler and Claire Drewery (eds.), *May Sinclair: Body and Mind* (2016).

Charlotte Mathieson is a lecturer in nineteenth-century English literature at the University of Surrey. She gained her Ph.D. in the Department of English and Comparative Literary Studies at the University of Warwick in 2011. Her research focuses on mobility and space in Victorian literature by authors including Charles Dickens, Charlotte Brontë and George Eliot. Her publications include *Mobility in the Victorian Novel: Placing the Nation* (2015) and the edited collection *Sea Narratives: Cultural Responses to the Sea, 1600–Present* (2016).

Monika Pietrzak-Franger is a visiting professor at the University of Hamburg, Germany, having previously taught in Mainz, Siegen, Braunschweig and St Louis. She received a Volkswagen Foundation scholarship for her postdoctoral project on syphilis in Victorian literature and culture (forthcoming as a monograph), for which she was awarded the BritCult Award by the German Association for the Study of British Cultures. She has published widely on Victorian and neo-Victorian Studies, gender, medicine, visual culture and adaptation. She is the author of *The Male Body and Masculinity* (2007) and editor of *Women, Beauty, and Fashion* (2014). She is also co-editor (with Antonija Primorac) of a 2015 special issue of *Neo-Victorian Studies*, 'Neo-Victorianism and Globalisation'; (with Martha Stoddard Holmes) of a 2014 special issue of the *Journal of Bioethical Inquiry* on 'Disease, Communication and the Ethics of (In)Visibility'; (with Eckart Voigts and Barbara Schaff) of *Reflecting on Darwin* (2014); and (with Martin Middeke) of the forthcoming *Handbook of the English Novel, 1830–1900*.

Jude Piesse is a lecturer in English at Liverpool John Moores University. Her book *British Settler Emigration in Print, 1832–1877* was published in 2016. She completed her AHRC-funded Ph.D. on the literature of Victorian settler emigration at the University of Exeter in 2013.

Amber Pouliot is a teaching fellow at Harlaxton College, the UK study-abroad centre of the University of Evansville. Originally from the United States, she has a master's degree in Victorian literature and a Ph.D. from the University of Leeds, where she wrote her thesis on the development of Brontë biographical fiction in the inter-war period. This interdisciplinary work on early neo-Victorian biographical fiction led to the co-convening of *Re-imagining the Victorians, 1901–2010* (2010), a conference on neo-Victorian fiction, as well as the more recent *Placing the Author: Literary Tourism in the Long Nineteenth Century* (2015). Her reviews and reports have appeared in *SHARP News* and *Neo-Victorian Studies*. She has written on literary tourism and digital pedagogies for the *Journal of Victorian Culture Online* and is associate editor of the Charlotte Brontë bicentenary issue of *Victorians: A Journal of Culture and Literature*. She is currently writing on the novels of Henry Siddons for *The Cambridge Guide to the Eighteenth-Century Novel, 1660–1820*.

Benjamin Poore is a lecturer in theatre at the University of York. Ben's research interests include stage and screen adaptations of nineteenth-century fiction, contemporary historical theatre and the cultural legacies of the Victorians. He is the author of *Heritage, Nostalgia and Modern British Theatre: Staging the Victorians* (2012) and *Theatre and Empire* (2016). An edited collection, *Neo-Victorian Villains*, and a monograph on Sherlock Holmes stage adaptations are forthcoming in 2017.

Amber K. Regis is a lecturer in nineteenth-century literature at the University of Sheffield. She is the editor of *The Memoirs of John Addington Symonds* (2016) and has published essays and reviews in *Life Writing*, *English Studies*, *Journal of Victorian Culture* and the *Times Literary Supplement*. Her current book project explores tradition and experiment in nineteenth-century auto/biography.

Deborah Wynne is professor of nineteenth-century literature at the University of Chester. Her current research projects emerge from an interest in textile cultures in Victorian and Edwardian Britain, for which she received an AHRC Fellowship in 2013–14. She is the author of *Women and Personal Property in the Victorian Novel* (2010) and *The Sensation Novel and the Victorian Family Magazine* (2001). Her latest book project examines Charlotte Brontë, Elizabeth Gaskell and the textile industries of Yorkshire and Lancashire. She has also published on Victorian and Edwardian literature and culture in journals such as *Dickens Studies Annual*, *Journal of Victorian Culture*, *Literature Compass*, *Textile History* and *Women's Writing*.

Louisa Yates is director of collections and research at Gladstone's Library in Hawarden, Wales, and a visiting lecturer in English at the University of Chester. Louisa is co-director of the Gladstone Centre for Victorian Studies, and she was previously a Gladstone fellow at the University of Chester. Her research examines literary engagements with the nineteenth century, in particular neo-Victorian novels published between 1990 and 2010. Her publications on this topic are found on traditional print as well as digital open-access platforms. Her most recent work includes book chapters on the British contemporary novelist Sarah Waters and the financial afterlives of Charlotte Brontë as well as an entry on Sarah Waters' *The Paying Guests* for the online Literary Encyclopedia and a case study for Gale Cengage's new *Punch Historical Archive 1841–1992*. She is also festival director of GLADFEST, hailed in the *Huffington Post* as a 'great small literary festival'.

Acknowledgements

We are grateful to all our contributors for their energy and unfailing commitment to this project. We'd particularly like to thank Emma Liggins and Jude Piesse for their helpful comments on our own chapters. Anna Barton and Andrew Smith, the series editors, have been encouraging throughout. Thanks are also due to the staff at Manchester University Press, who have been helpful and patient. Kimberley Braxton has cheerfully taken on the job of compiling the appendix at short notice and Katie Baker has willingly helped with the index; we are grateful to both of them. Thanks to Simon Grennan for creating the book's cover image and to Charlotte Cory for permission to reproduce her 'Visitorian' artwork; we appreciate their interest in this project. The staff at the Brontë Parsonage Museum, particularly Sarah Laycock, have been very helpful, and we would like to thank them for their invaluable work in promoting the legacy of the Brontës. Finally, to the ghosts of Charlotte Brontë that inhabit our literary, visual and performance cultures: you haunted this project throughout, and we hope we have done justice to the continuing presence of your past.

Introduction: picturing Charlotte Brontë

Amber K. Regis and Deborah Wynne

In response to the centenary of Charlotte Brontë's birth in 1916, the Brontë Society commissioned a volume of essays entitled *Charlotte Brontë, 1816–1916: A Centenary Memorial* (1917), with contributions by some well-known literary figures, including G. K. Chesterton and Edmund Gosse. It opened with a foreword by the then president of the Brontë Society, Mrs Humphry Ward, in which she explained that the book set out to offer 'fresh impressions and the first-hand research of competent writers who have spoken their minds with love and courage' (Ward, 1917: 5). One hundred years later, the current volume of essays, *Charlotte Brontë: Legacies and Afterlives*, also strives to offer 'fresh impressions' based on the 'first-hand research' of 'competent writers'; equally, most of the contributors can claim that a love of Brontë's work motivated this project. However, while the contributors to the 1917 volume considered courage to be required to assert Charlotte Brontë's importance, the writers in this book show no inclination to defend her reputation or argue for the significance of her work. Her 'genius', a term emphasised repeatedly, often anxiously, in the 1917 collection, can now be taken for granted, and for that comfortable assumption we have generations of feminist scholars to thank. The current volume instead charts the vast cultural impact of Charlotte Brontë since the appearance of her first published work, *Poems by Currer, Ellis and Acton Bell* (1846), highlighting the richness and diversity of the author's legacy, her afterlife and the continuation of her plots and characters in new forms.

Although the centenary and bicentenary collections share an aim to celebrate Charlotte Brontë's achievements, there are unsurprisingly

1

significant differences between the two projects. A glance at the chapter titles of the *Centenary Memorial* indicates that many are personal reflections, such as 'Some Thoughts on Charlotte Brontë' by Mrs Humphry Ward; 'Charlotte Brontë: A Personal Sketch' by Arthur C. Benson, an anecdotal account by one who knew people who knew the author; and Edmund Gosse's 'A Word on Charlotte Brontë'. Others are impressionist essays focusing on her indebtedness to the Romantics, such as Halliwell Sutcliffe's 'The Spirit of the Moors' and G. K. Chesterton's 'Charlotte Brontë as a Romantic'. Some contributors to this earlier volume trace the real people and places that Brontë drew upon in her novels, incorporating evidence from the aged population of Haworth. These contributors also share a sense that Charlotte Brontë, for all her literary achievements, was a flawed genius, her work being inferior to that of her sister Emily.[1] Indeed, the early twentieth century can be read as a turning point for Charlotte's reputation, when a temporary decline set in. She was dismissed as irretrievably Victorian by modernist writers who valued the ambiguity of Emily's work as speaking more effectively to twentieth-century readers. Ward is typical of the contributors in the *Centenary Memorial* in asking, 'Which was the greater, [Charlotte] or Emily?', to which she answers: 'To my mind, Emily, by far', while Anne is not even mentioned (Ward, 1917: 37). Ward emphasises Charlotte as having a specifically 'Victorian' personality: 'a loving, faithful, suffering woman, with a personal story which, thanks to Mrs Gaskell's *Life*, will never cease to touch the hearts of English folk' (Ward, 1917: 30). The centenary essays share Ward's confidence in 'knowing Charlotte', assuming that Elizabeth Gaskell's version of her friend offers an accurate picture of the woman and her place in the world of letters. Two hundred years after the author's birth, academics are considerably less confident about their ability to 'know' Charlotte; significantly Claire Harman's recent biography is entitled *Charlotte Brontë: A Life* (2016), in contrast to Gaskell's *The Life of Charlotte Brontë* (1857).

The impulse motivating the current volume of essays stems from the following questions: Why does Charlotte Brontë continue to be so widely read? What are the qualities that have made her a household name? Why do her characters endure in so many different cultural contexts? 'Charlotte Brontë' is a cultural phenomenon which continues to evolve, as do her literary legacies both in terms of her influence on later authors and the extraordinary afterlives of her plots and characters. Contributors to *Charlotte Brontë: Legacies and Afterlives* evaluate more than 150 years of cultural engagement with Charlotte Brontë, considering fluctuations in her literary reputation; innumerable adaptations of her novels for film, television, radio, theatre and the Internet; biographies and fictional biographies; the development of an author cult and the growth of literary tourism; neo-Victorian reworkings of Charlotte Brontë's works; the legacy of her poetry; her influence on subsequent writers; the afterlives of her characters; and the evolution of critical approaches to her work. While the contributors to the 1917 collection attempted to offer a definitive image of the author and an evaluation of her genius, *Charlotte Brontë: Legacies and Afterlives* is engaging with current interests in Victorian afterlives with the aim of demonstrating the richness, variety and complexity of Charlotte Brontë's cultural impact.

This book focuses exclusively on Charlotte Brontë, not only because her bicentenary in 2016 has offered our contributors an occasion to reflect on her achievements and legacies but also because we wanted as much as possible to set her apart from her associations with the collective entity known as 'The Brontës'. The family's mythic status has resulted in the idea of shared attributes relating to Yorkshire and Englishness, genius and femininity, the Victorian family and rural life, passion and sexuality, feminism and liberation, working women and female mobility. However, this tendency to see the sisters as a collective has sometimes blurred their differences, leading to distortions which do not necessarily do full justice to each sisters' individual achievement. The most well known and well regarded of the three sisters during the Victorian period, Charlotte Brontë bequeathed a legacy which is more extensive and more complex than the legacies of Emily and Anne. Charlotte Brontë outlived her sisters, going on to develop relationships outside the family circle which have been recorded in extant letters and journal entries; she became the friend of fellow female writers Elizabeth Gaskell and Harriet Martineau, sharing with them her experiences of literary endeavour and public life. She also socialised with other key literary figures of the day, including William Thackeray and G. H. Lewes. She was the only sister to marry, and her death in 1855, possibly from the effects of pregnancy, singles her out as different from her siblings – all of whom underwent early deaths from consumption in the late 1840s. Unlike Emily and Anne, Charlotte became the subject of many obituaries, journalistic sketches and biographies during the Victorian period. The archive of material on Charlotte is, then, more extensive and more diverse. Whether we accept Gaskell's representation of 'the wild little maiden from Haworth' (Gaskell, 1997: 78) or accommodate Edward Fitzgerald's view that she was the 'Mistress of the Disagreeable' (quoted in Ward, 1917: 22), or consider her as an early feminist, or take seriously a twenty-first-century view of her as 'a filthy minx' (Gold, 2005), it is evident that focusing upon Charlotte Brontë has afforded the contributors to this volume a wealth of material to consider.

The *Centenary Memorial*, then, had a limited archive with which to work; nevertheless, its contributors felt confident in 'knowing Charlotte'.

1 George Richmond, *Charlotte Brontë* (1850)

Some of them refer to George Richmond's 1850 portrait (Fig. 1), well known from Gaskell's *Life*, and from this image they attempt to read the author's personality, presuming it to be an authoritative likeness and source. By contrast, examining Charlotte Brontë's life and work from the perspective of 2016, we feel more tentative about what we can know of the author's life. She died in her late thirties in 1855 and left relatively few autobiographical traces behind her. Our uncertainty is nowhere more apparent than in our inability to know what she looked like, prompting paradoxical desires to recover and re-read the mutable text of her invisible, ineluctable face. The convoluted, unfinished story of Charlotte's likenesses, portraits and visual depictions, therefore, provides an apt introduction and starting point for this new volume, speaking to our persistent fascination and creative engagement with the Brontës' life and work.

Charlotte Brontë, icon

In late July 1850, two parcels arrived at Haworth parsonage. Each contained a portrait, gifts from George Smith, Charlotte's publisher. The smaller parcel was intended for Charlotte and contained an engraving of Arthur Wellesley, Duke of Wellington. The larger parcel was intended for her father, Patrick, and contained her own image: a chalk portrait on brown paper, the work of George Richmond and commissioned by Smith at the cost of thirty guineas. Charlotte sat for the artist while in London the previous June, but from the first it was a contested likeness.[2] According to Smith, on first seeing the portrait Charlotte 'burst into tears, exclaiming that it was so like her sister Anne, who had died the year before' (Smith, 1900: 794). She had glimpsed a memory: the lines of a sister's face reflected in her own, both self and other. Tabby, the Brontës' servant, proved another unseeing audience (doubly so, when one considers she was nearing eighty and her eyesight was failing):

> our old servant [...] tenaciously maintains that it is not like – that it is too old-looking; but as she, with equal tenacity, asserts that the Duke of Wellington's picture is a portrait of 'the Master' (meaning Papa), I am afraid not much weight is to be ascribed to her opinion.
>
> (Brontë, 1995–2004: II, 434)

The Brontë sisters had adopted pseudonyms at the insistence of Emily, or Ellis Bell, but Charlotte clung to anonymity long after she revealed her authorship to her publishers in 1848 (and despite becoming known in literary circles during the early 1850s). She continued to publish as Currer Bell, and, crucially, no authorial image was permitted to circulate in newspapers and periodicals or to accompany her works. 'What author would be without the advantage of being able to walk invisible?' (Brontë, 1995–2004: II, 4), she had once remarked. It is hardly surprising, then, that from 1850 until her death in 1855, Charlotte's only professional portrait taken from life hung upon the dining-room wall at the parsonage, a private image to be gazed at by family and friends. All this changed in 1857. Elizabeth Gaskell's *Life of Charlotte Brontë* was unequivocal: Currer Bell was Charlotte Brontë, and a copy of Richmond's portrait was reproduced as an illustration. Gaskell fought hard to have the portrait accompany the biography – a work she was commissioned to undertake at the request of Charlotte's father.[3] At first, Arthur Bell Nicholls withheld permission for his late wife's likeness to be copied (Gaskell, 1966: 393). Charlotte's friend, Ellen Nussey, sympathised with Gaskell but not without qualification: 'I am very sorry about the refusal of the portrait. Though there would always have been regret for its painful expression to be perpetuated' (Wise and Symington, 1932: IV, 205). Undeterred, Gaskell enlisted the help and bluster of Sir James Kay-Shuttleworth who appealed to the father and forced the hand of the widower (Gaskell, 1966: 399). Permission was secured in late July 1856 and by December she was in possession of a good-quality photograph (Gaskell, 1966: 423).[4] Nussey need not have worried: the engraving by J. C. Armytage, placed opposite the biography's title page and rendered greyscale in the printing, softened Charlotte's countenance. Likeness or not, Richmond's portrait was now a public image; though dead, Charlotte would never walk invisible again.

Taking her cue from Erving Goffman's work on *The Presentation of Self in Everyday Life* (1956), in which he identifies 'social front' as an effect produced by performative elements that 'define [a] situation for those who observe' (Goffman, 1956: 13), Shearer West contends that portraiture renders visible and legible both sitter and 'front': '[p]ortraits are filled with the external signs of a person's socialized self', thus the portraitist must balance competing representational demands of inner and outer, individual and type (West, 2004: 30). In Charlotte, Richmond was faced with a subject doubly situated: two 'fronts', public writer and private woman, with competing signifiers attached to each identity. When the

finished portrait arrived at the parsonage, Patrick saw the writer first and
foremost:

> Without ostentatious display, with admirable tact and delicacy, he has
> produced a correct, likeness, and succeeded, in a graphic representation
> of mind, as well as matter […] I may be partial, and perhaps, somewhat
> enthusiastic, in this case, but in looking on the picture, which improves
> upon acquaintance, as all real works of art do – I fancy I see strong indica-
> tions, of the Genius, of the Author, of "Shirley", and "Jane Eyre".
>
> (Brontë, 1995–2004: II, 435)

Patrick admired the portrait's writerly 'front', reading and elucidating
outward signs of interiority and intellect – the same features that Nussey
considered her 'painful expression', perhaps. Likewise, in a late essay-
memoir by George Smith, the extraordinariness of Charlotte's head
comes in for scrutiny. Though he offers no direct comment upon the portrait, merely noting its commission and execution, Smith provides a lens
through which to view the picture. He reproduces a phrenological report
by T. P. Browne, the result of an examination undertaken for amusement
while Charlotte was in London in 1851, just a year after sitting for her
portrait:

> In its intellectual development this head is very remarkable. The forehead is
> at once very large and well formed. It bears the stamp of deep thoughtful-
> ness and comprehensive understanding. It is highly philosophical. It exhib-
> its the presence of an intellect at once perspicacious and perspicuous. […]
> This lady possesses a fine organ of language, and can, if she has done her
> talents justice by exercise, express her sentiments with clearness, precision,
> and force – sufficiently eloquent but not verbose.
>
> (Smith, 1900: 787)

By the time Smith published the report, copies of Richmond's portrait
had circulated far and wide. Readers would not have struggled to bring
the image before their mind's eye, projecting the phrenologist's conclusions. But significantly, neither father nor publisher lose sight of the
woman behind the writer. Patrick's language, his diction and register,
strike an appropriately feminine note. His praise for the artist blends with
approbation for the manner of Charlotte's presentation: Richmond's tact,
delicacy and lack of ostentation stand as proxy for his subject – these
features become her, signifying production, '[to] come into being', and
correspondence, to 'suit, befit, grace' (*OED*) – and the portrait serves,
paradoxically, as evidence of demure, retiring femininity. Smith too
ensures that Charlotte's difference – her 'Genius', as Patrick would have

From an original painting by Chappel in the possession of the publishers.

Johnson, Wilson & Co. Publishers, New York

Entered according to act of Congress AD 1873 by Johnson Wilson & Co in the office of the Librarian of Congress at Washington.

2 *Charlotte Brontë: From an original painting by Chappel* (1870s) it – is safely accommodated within domestic ideology, the phrenologist's report equally emphasising the importance of duty and the 'warm and affectionate' conduct of her 'domestic relations' (Smith, 1900: 786). Richmond's portrait, read variously as indicative of writerly profession and womanly duty, was a singularly fitting image to accompany *The Life of Charlotte Brontë*. Gaskell divides her subject into 'parallel currents – her life as Currer Bell, the author; her life as Charlotte Brontë, the woman', and seeks to recount the 'separate duties belonging to each character' (Gaskell, 1997: 258–9). Biography and portrait thus sustain a dual iconography: made public together, they set an enduring and ineluctable precedent, a pattern for subsequent accounts and portrayals of Charlotte Brontë to adopt, adapt and contest.

Richmond's portrait soon began to proliferate, reproduction upon reproduction. Remarkably, this process began before *The Life of Charlotte Brontë* established the image as icon: George Smith appears to have arranged for a copy to be made before sending the original to Haworth (Brontë, 1995–2004: II, 430), and Arthur Bell Nicholls allowed (or indeed, commissioned) J. H. Thompson, Branwell Brontë's friend and fellow student of portraiture at Leeds, to make use of the picture as a template for a new portrait of his late wife.[5] During preparations for the biography, three photographs were taken to enable Armytage to execute his engraving, permission granted on condition that two photographs were returned (Gaskell, 1966: 421). Following publication, demand for and access to Charlotte's image could no longer be controlled: portrait, via engraving, crystallised her public image and prompted the circulation of countless copies. With Richmond as urtext, Jane Sellars notes the strong family likeness exhibited by these reproductions: 'Richmond's portrait established a kind of pictorial symbol for the face of Charlotte Brontë that persists to this day' (Sellars, 2012: 123). It was then, as now, a recognisable commodity. This fact was not lost upon Ellen Nussey when in 1868 she sought permission from Smith to reproduce the image (presumably Armytage's engraving, since she sent her request to the publishers, Smith, Elder) upon *cartes-de-visite* to sell at a church bazaar (Brontë, 1995–2004: I, 34). And yet, if Richmond established a 'pictorial symbol' for Charlotte's face, it has proved mutable, polysemic. This is not a question of in/fidelity to an original, for the subject of portraiture is always already absent – in this case, a living woman who may or may not have been 'like' (the term is vague) the figure depicted in chalk, a sitter who lived apart from its dead, flat paper. From the first, therefore, Richmond's portrait has been reimagined variously.

Charlotte's two 'fronts', writer and woman, established and explored through the pages of Gaskell's biography, have endured in the afterlife of Richmond's icon – sometimes the one, sometimes the other is ascendant. These variations and manipulations prove the testing ground for iconographic engagements with Charlotte's posthumous legacy and reputation. An 1870s engraving of a portrait by Alonzo Chappel (Fig. 2) reveals this to be a complex, contradictory process. Chappel follows Richmond's pattern in his depiction of the head and features, but he also supplies the absent body. Charlotte's figure is glamorous, sexualised, with a narrow waist and full skirts. But the implied presence of a corset also suggests strict regulation, her body conforming to nineteenth-century moral and medical strictures. As Birgitta Berglund reminds us, the corset was 'considered essential for back support and good posture', and 'a woman who did not wear a corset was considered indecent, "loose", as if the structural firmness of the corseted body equalled a moral firmness' (Bergland, 2012: 319). Likewise, Chappel's portrayal of Charlotte's hands sustains different readings. In her left, Charlotte holds a book, a clear symbol of authorship. But the volume is half closed, held casually, carelessly, tilted away from her gaze. In her right, Charlotte holds the lace-trimmed fabric of a handkerchief. This second symbol picks up and repeats the lace of her collar and sleeves, appropriately feminine (lacework being a suitable accomplishment and domestic pursuit). Gaskell's 'parallel currents' are clearly in evidence, but maintaining the visibility of both identities has proved a perennial problem for artists appropriating the Richmond portrait. Chappel struggles to marry the woman and writer: authorship, explicitly invoked, is overwritten by multiple signifiers of idealised femininity. An alternative strategy can be found in Maurice Clare's *A Day with Charlotte Brontë* (c.1911), illustrated by C. E. Brock. In contrast to Chappel's palimpsest, Brock separates woman from writer, turning twice to Richmond for inspiration. He produces two appropriative images to fit each 'front': a cover portrait in colour (Fig. 3) and a simple line drawing following the front endpaper (Fig. 4). The first portrays the woman; it is indebted to J. H. Thompson's reworking of the image, where Brock's light pastel shades (in watercolour, not the rich tones of Thompson's oils) extend his idealisation of Charlotte's femininity. The second, however, returns to the writer; it is a far more accurate copy of Richmond's portrait and technique, where the features emerge through the contrast between paper, line and hatching. Unlike Chappel, there is no book to symbolise Charlotte's writerly 'front', for Brock achieves this indirectly. In 1906, the National Portrait Gallery acquired Richmond's chalk original.[6] By

3 Cover illustration from Maurice Clare, *A Day with Charlotte Brontë* (c.1911)

4 Illustration from Maurice Clare, *A Day with Charlotte Brontë* (c.1911)

the time Clare's brief biography was published, it had been on public display for five years. So often reproduced and adapted, the portrait was now enshrined within a public institution dedicated to 'the appreciation and understanding of the men and women who have made and are making British history and culture' (NPG, 2016). Though ideal femininity and domestic duty are integral to Charlotte's posthumous reputation, her place upon the gallery's walls was earned by the labour of her pen. Brock's return to Richmond, his stripping away of details supplied by later artists like Thompson and Chappel, speaks to a reclamation of the image as writerly icon, granted official status as the portrait of a sitter who 'made' history and culture.

Contested images

From 1914 it was possible to picture Charlotte differently. In March that year two rediscovered Brontë portraits were put on display at the National Portrait Gallery. Both were the work of Branwell: a surviving fragment from a lost group portrait, known as the Gun Group, from which Emily's likeness had been cut and preserved (c.1833–34), and *The Brontë Sisters* or Pillar Portrait (c.1834).[7] The paintings had been found in a wardrobe by Arthur Bell Nicholls' second wife, Mary. Nicholls had evidently not much cared for Branwell's efforts. Having cut Emily from the Gun Group, he destroyed the remaining canvas; and the Pillar Portrait was damaged when removed from its frame and folded.[8] Reframed and rehung, the portraits caused a minor sensation. *The Times* approved of the gallery's arrangements, noting the fitness of the sisters' illustrious company: 'effigies of the three sisters of genius, of their biographer [Elizabeth Gaskell], and of the man who made them known to the world of both hemispheres [George Smith] are placed in fortunate juxtaposition' (Anon., 1914).

These portraits were known before their rediscovery, though their lines and likenesses were lost to the vagaries of memory and poor quality reproduction. Gaskell twice describes the Pillar Portrait in *The Life of Charlotte Brontë* (Gaskell, 1997: 101–2, 412), and a rare photograph was sometimes reproduced.[9] Likewise, an engraving of the Gun Group was used to illustrate J. Horsfall Turner's *Haworth: Past and Present* (1879), with no comment upon its provenance beyond the following: 'Our picture of the Brontë group is a faithful reproduction of Mr Branwell's painting of himself and sisters' (Horsfall Turner, 1879: 170). Acquisition by the National Portrait Gallery revived these images in the popular imagination, but the act of restoration was partial. The Gun Group could never be fully restored, of course; and, contrary to usual policy, the gallery decided to preserve, not repair, the damage to both paintings. For Christine Alexander and Jane Sellars, this decision accords with something illusive (and elusive) in the Brontës' posthumous legacies, an incompleteness that fascinates: the folds and frayed edges, cracks and holes, 'signified an important aspect of the poignant Brontë story, namely Nicholls' simultaneous act of preservation and censorship which speaks of his sensitivity to the preying biographers' (Alexander and Sellars, 1995: 311). The spectacle of their damage certainly enthralled the press. Coverage in the *Daily Graphic* and *Sphere* focused upon the 'romance' of their rediscovery, while prominent photographs concentrated attention upon their poor condition.[10] And though the *Saturday Review* considered it a 'great pity that one should have been ruthlessly folded and the other as ruthlessly cut', this pity soon commutes to reverence: the pictures '[look] more like tattered relics than works of art' (W. J. W., 1914: 337).

Branwell's artistry was not, it seems, a primary matter for concern; it was the paintings as family possessions, crafted by Brontë hands within the space of the parsonage, that captured the imagination. Looking upon the Pillar Portrait seemed to hold little promise of greater acquaintance with Charlotte's face. Gaskell had politely (but not convincingly) conceded that 'the likenesses were, I should think, admirable'. But she undermined her own claim, describing the work as 'not much better than sign-painting, as to manipulation', being merely a 'rough common-looking oil-painting' (Gaskell, 1997: 101, 412). By contrast, Richmond's chalk drawing had shaped Charlotte's posthumous legacy for fifty-seven years, and it would continue to serve as her writerly icon. Branwell's Pillar Portrait provided a private, amateur counterpart to this professional image: painted before the sisters achieved fame, poorly executed and poorly treated. And yet, the image has proliferated just as widely as Richmond's portrait, its fascination (and 'romance') increasing over time with the gradual re-emergence of Branwell's painted-out figure from behind the fading pillar.[11]

Branwell's portraits reveal the Brontës' likenesses to be persistent loci of desire. The Pillar Portrait and Gun Group pose unsolvable puzzles, seeming to conceal more than they reveal; and yet, we continue to seek for their lost faces. The Pillar Portrait has been subject to infra-red photography and x-ray examinations in the hope of revealing Branwell's figure, and various theories have been proffered to explain his erasure.[12] Likewise, individual and institutional collectors of Brontë relics and remains have sought to reconstruct the obliterated Gun Group. The engraving in

Horsfall Turner's *Haworth: Past and Present* was a constant though inexact reminder of what had been lost, but in 1932 C. Mabel Edgerley (honorary secretary of the Brontë Society) reported the existence of 'three old tracings of half length female figures' formerly in the possession of John Greenwood, the Haworth stationer, and thought to be the work of his hand (Edgerley, 1932: 29). The tracings were labelled with the Brontë sisters' names and ages, and Edgerley was permitted to try them against the Gun Group fragment at the National Portrait Gallery: the tracing labelled 'Emily' was a perfect fit. And so, suddenly, here were three more likenesses, though the tracings lack detail: pencil on waxed paper, they are but crude outlines of clothing, coiffure and facial features. The tracings were acquired by the Brontë Parsonage Museum in 1961, but in 1989 another exciting discovery was found in the museum collection: a photograph of the Gun Group, copied from an earlier daguerreotype.[13] The photograph is in poor condition. Branwell's eyes shine out from the centre-right of the frame, but it is difficult to discern the features of his sisters. Juliet Barker, who discovered the photograph, notes how the copying of a copy has increased this indistinctness: '[t]he heightening of the contrasts […] effectively blanks out the features of the sitters and darkens the shadows around them' (Barker, 1990: 9).[14] Paradoxically, then, the irrecoverable Gun Group remains with us, a revenant recalled through its ghostly traces. But these survivals elide and unsettle our ability to recognise the Brontës; they refuse to offer a pattern or template comparable to Richmond. Charlotte's painted image, like those belonging to her brother and sister, destroyed after her death by her widower, is reduced to an imprecise outline in a pencil tracing, a faceless figure in a fading photograph and a type of cartoonish womanhood in a second-rate engraving.

With so few surviving portraits taken from life, a host of images have sought to supply this lack, contesting their place within the Brontë portrait canon. Charlotte's archival traces have been co-opted in the process. Two claimed self-portraits, both executed in 1843 during her second sojourn in Brussels, have been discovered among her papers and books. The first, an ink sketch forming part of the postscript to a letter to Ellen Nussey, depicts Charlotte waving goodbye to Ellen, separated by a stretch of water, as the latter departs with a suitor (Brontë 1995–2004: I, 311–12 and plate 3).[15] The second, a pencil drawing on the reverse of a map in *Russell's General Atlas of Modern Geography*, has recently been identified by Claire Harman as a self-portrait, though the provenance in this case is less certain (Harman 2016: 178–9).[16] Both images have been viewed as manifestations of Charlotte's belief in her own ugliness: a '[c]omic sketch showing a grotesque stunted little female figure' in the case of her letter to Nussey (Alexander and Sellars, 1995: 261); and in the case of the atlas sketch, a real-life counterpart to Jane Eyre's self-discipline: 'tomorrow, place the glass before you, and draw in chalk your own picture, faithfully, without softening one defect […]; write under it, "Portrait of a Governess, disconnected, poor, and plain"' (Brontë, 2008: 161; Harman, 2016: 179). These readings respond to or project exaggeration; they identify ugliness and excess as a means to punish or satirise. As such Charlotte's self-portraits are more readily categorised as caricatures – that 'less exalted art' (West, 2004: 35) – for they do not adhere to forms of portraiture founded upon reference and moderation in the signification of 'front'. Just like Branwell's portraits, surviving and destroyed, these images excite rather than ease our desire to look upon Charlotte's face.

Satisfaction has been sought elsewhere. Misattributions, fakes and doubtful claims have found ready audiences and willing advocates: more than ever, we are driven to imagine Charlotte's face anew, hoping to recognise within the lines of a portrait or photograph the very person, or personality, that we feel we know. Representatives of the Brontë Parsonage Museum receive regular requests to comment upon and authenticate newly claimed or disputed likenesses. In an interview with the local press, principal curator Ann Dinsdale remarked that she had 'lost count' of the number of pictures received at the parsonage (Knights, 2015); and she has offered words of caution to accompany stories in national newspapers: 'You've got to think, why would there be a picture of them? […] Everybody wants to know what the Brontës looked like […]. We do what we can, but if the image has got no provenance and it's not documented anywhere, it's really difficult' (Sutherland, 2015). Dinsdale draws upon the relative obscurity of the Brontës during their lifetime to encourage a healthy scepticism, but it has proved difficult to counter the 'romance' of rediscovery. Since 2009 there have been three high-profile claims, their notoriety achieved on account of the large sums changing hands at auction or effective advocacy campaigns. In 2009 James Gorin von Grozny purchased a group portrait of three female figures for £150. He claimed it was a painting of the Brontë sisters by Edwin Landseer, executed c.1838. Despite a sceptical press reception (BBC News, 2009), the painting resold at auction in May 2012 for £14,000.[17] Auctioneers, J. P. Humbert, claimed the painting had been 'attributed' by the National Portrait Gallery (Anon., 2012b), prompting the Australian Brontë Association to report, enthusiastically, that the gallery had 'confirmed its link to both

Landseer and the renowned literary sisters' (Burns, 2012). But not all is as it seems. Enquiries at the National Portrait Gallery reveal their records to be equivocal at best: 'the image has been filed among "doubtful" portraits of the Brontë sisters and labelled as "possibly" by Edwin Landseer'.[18] Photographs in particular have been coveted and contested, while online platforms and social media have been used to disseminate images and their claimed attributions. Perhaps the most visible of these sites is *The Brontë Sisters: A True Likeness?* (www.brontesisters.co.uk), founded by Robert Haley to communicate his research into a photograph held by a Scottish archive, inscribed upon the reverse 'Les Soeurs Brontës'. In 2011 the photograph was presented to the Parsonage Museum, but in the absence of clear provenance the image was not deemed to be authentic. By way of response, the website seeks to crowdsource opinion and evidence to support the claim, and it questions the likenesses and attributions of other Brontë images. Likewise, a photograph purchased on eBay in 2015 for just £15, with 'Bells' inscribed upon the reverse, has been the subject of a short-lived Twitter campaign (@realbrontes) led by the photograph's owner, Seamus Molloy. These photographs have spread online, going viral and provoking debate among online communities of Brontë devotees.[19] More than other media, perhaps, photography holds the greatest allure, seeming to promise that longed-for surrogate encounter with a once-living face.

It is tempting to smile at the popular faith shown in the most unlikely (and unlike) of Brontë portraits. And yet, professionals working at the Parsonage Museum and National Portrait Gallery have not proved themselves immune: both hold images with contested or disproved attributions in their collections. Certain objects at the Parsonage Museum reveal the intricacies of interpersonal archives, where attributions become uncertain and confused as a result of complex paper trails and sustained correspondence between friends and acquaintances – where sitters and subjects become indistinct, interchangeable figures within the historical record. In 2004 the museum purchased a small chalk portrait believed to be of Charlotte and drawn by her friend, Mary Dixon, while they were together in Brussels in 1843.[20] The drawing's provenance can be traced to Martha Brown, the Brontës' servant, and is believed to have been a gift from Charlotte. Claire Harman, however, contests this attribution. Turning to the evidence of Charlotte's correspondence with Dixon, it appears they exchanged portraits (Brontë, 1995–2004: I, 336). Therefore, the likeness retained in Charlotte's possession and later gifted to Brown could just as likely – more likely, for Harman – be of Dixon herself

(Harman, 2016: 162). Trickier still is the museum's possession of two similar *carte-de-visite* photographs with contradictory inscriptions and attributions.[21] Both entered the collection in 1896 as part of a bequest from Elizabeth Seton-Gordon, George Smith's granddaughter. One photograph bears an ink inscription on the reverse, 'Within a year of CB's death', and seems to confirm the provenance of a glass negative held by the National Portrait Gallery, part of the Emery Walker collection and indexed as being 'from a *carte-de-visite* of Charlotte Brontë, taken within a year of her death' (Barker, 1986: 27).[22] An accompanying letter reveals the negative was made sometime before January 1918 and that the sitter was assumed to be Charlotte (Barker, 1986: 27–8), but this was long after George Smith (who could have verified the likeness) had died. The other photograph bears a pencil inscription on the reverse: 'Miss Ellen Nussey friend of Charlotte Brontë circa 1860' (Harman, 2016: 340). Some hold that the first *carte-de-visite* does indeed portray Charlotte, photographed shortly after her marriage to Arthur Bell Nicholls, possibly while on honeymoon (Foister, 1985; Barker, 1986). Others, however, consider the presence of Nussey among Smith's papers to be the more likely scenario; some claim that she is the sitter in both photographs, the items being in Smith's possession on account of Nussey's failed negotiations to bring out an edition of her Brontë letters (Harman, 2016). The Parsonage Museum does not hold a definite position on the chalk drawing or *cartes-de-visite*: they 'remain open minded about the possibility that [the photograph] could be Ellen and that the chalk portrait is likely to be Mary Dixon'.[23] The provenance for each item, though failing to reveal absolutely the sitter's identity, does successfully associate the material with the Brontë family and their close associates. This in itself justifies a place in the museum collection. But there does appear to have been a quiet withdrawal from the *carte-de-visite* photograph claimed as Charlotte. Until recently, the image formed part of the Brontë Society's online picture library – captioned '*Carte-de-visite*, likely to be Charlotte's only known photograph' – but in 2016, Charlotte's bicentenary year, it was removed.[24] It is possible that this change reflects a shift in the general weight of opinion, a tacit acknowledgement that the photograph and its history cannot be disentangled from a mass of interrelated lives and likenesses.

Our willingness to see Charlotte's face in the features of another is grist to the forger's mill, while the money changing hands for Brontë portraits, with or without provenance, is a constant temptation. Most famously, in 1906, the National Portrait Gallery purchased what it considered to be a painting of Charlotte executed in 1850 by an artist signing themselves 'Paul Héger'.[25] Esther Chadwick records that the purchase was arranged by Smith, Elder: Charlotte's former publishers were approached by Alice Boyd Green, whose family (it was claimed) acquired the painting from a friend of the Heger family (Chadwick, 1914: 396). The portrait depicts a woman wearing a green dress reading from an open book: the title page reveals this to be *Shirley* (1849) and gives the author's name as 'C. Brontë'. Upon the reverse of the canvas two inscriptions reaffirm the sitter to be Charlotte. In late September 1906 the painting was hung upon the gallery's walls and a photograph published in Smith, Elder's *Cornhill Magazine* (post-dated October 1906). The accompanying editorial declared it was the work of 'M. Paul Heger', hastily explaining away the discrepancy between the artist's name and that belonging to Charlotte's Brussels teacher (Constantin): 'M. Heger is accepted as having sat for the character of Paul Emanuel of *Villette*' (Anon., 1906). Almost immediately Brontë scholars and devotees spoke out against the image and denounced the gallery's acquisition policy. Clement Shorter was invited by the gallery director, Lionel Cust, to examine the portrait. Writing publicly in the *Sphere*, Shorter described it as 'an obvious forgery' and listed his many objections (to name but a few): the artist's name was signed with an acute accent, whereas Heger was unaccented; M. Heger did not see Charlotte again after she left Brussels in December 1843, so the portrait could not be 'from life'; *Shirley* was published under the Currer Bell pseudonym, not Charlotte's name, and the Hegers did not then know of her authorship (Shorter, 1906: 82). Moreover, Shorter reproduced a letter in French from Heger's surviving son that denied all connection between his family and the portrait. Such was the vehemence of Shorter's account, Cust put pen to paper, writing a letter to the editor of *The Times* and firmly standing his ground:

> The tone of this attack is such that it might be more seemly for the Trustees [of the National Portrait Gallery] to take no public notice of it. As, however, silence might be taken to mean assent, it would be an advantage to the public to know that the attack was by no means unexpected, and that the evidence at present in the possession of the Trustees justifies them, at all events for the present, while giving all attention to the important details of the attack, in not regarding it as in any way convincing.
>
> (Cust, 1906: 10)

Over the next few days, Shorter and Cust wrote letters back and forth in *The Times*: Shorter repeated his criticisms and Cust continued to censure his 'tone' (while studiously avoiding his objections). The matter was revived in February 1907 when *The Times* reported the gallery's recent acquisition of the Richmond portrait, used as an occasion to announce the findings of a 'searching investigation' into the provenance of the claimed Heger painting: it was declared 'an authentic likeness of Charlotte Brontë' (Anon., 1907: 22). Incensed, Shorter wrote again to *The Times* demanding proof: 'I shall be glad [...] to acknowledge my error in sackcloth and ashes when the Trustees have left the region of mere assertion and have furnished the public with something in the shape of evidence' (Anon., 1907: 23).

Shorter was vindicated in the sequel. In 1913, Esther Chadwick convinced the new gallery director, C. J. Holmes, to re-examine the case. She claimed success in persuading him that Charlotte's teacher 'always used the signature "C. Heger," and his son, Dr. Paul Heger, was only a boy of four in 1850'.[26] As a result, the plate attached to the frame, which read 'Signed Paul Heger 1850', was 'removed in [her] presence'; soon after, 'the officials of the National Portrait Gallery found an impression of an inscription in large hand across the back of the painting "Portrait of Miss Mary Vickers"' (Chadwick, 1914: 397, 399). The picture was eventually taken down from the gallery's walls, but it remains in their collection and continues to be associated with the Brontë name, albeit at one remove. Now entitled *Unknown Woman, Formerly Known as Charlotte Brontë*, the gallery's website links the painting to other images where Charlotte is sitter, including Richmond's chalk drawing and Branwell's Pillar Portrait. The story of its acquisition, the public disagreements and slow unravelling of its provenance means the picture is an object of interest in its own right. It might not be able to show us what Charlotte looked like, or how her dual 'social front' as woman and writer was conceived and negotiated by the Heger family, but it can tell us volumes about Charlotte's posthumous legacy: an object of desire, a commodity of value, a persistent enigma. By maintaining the link to Charlotte's name, the National Portrait Gallery recognises the forged portrait as an integral part of these contested constructions of Brontë iconography, celebrity and mythology – histories that continue to be written.

Recent reimaginings

The proliferation of Charlotte's image, the muddling of attributions and spurious claims, has reached its acme and apotheosis with the Internet and our digital age. Nothing represents this better than a Google Images search under Charlotte's name: thousands of results; reproduction upon appropriation of Richmond's drawing and Branwell's painting; stills from film and TV adaptations of the sisters' works; book covers and illustrations; cartoons and cosplay. There has been a democratising of Charlotte's image in a culture of file-sharing and image manipulation, testing to the limit those laws of copyright and licensing that can be employed to monetise Brontë portraiture, where the interest in a surrogate is protected (such as a photograph or other duplicate) rather than the original. It would be impossible to trace or stop the spread of an accessible image file of a Brontë portrait, recognised likeness or not; and it would be impossible to prevent creative engagements with these images via Photoshop and other graphics software. Fan-art appropriations abound. The same Google Images search will reveal Charlotte Brontë memes, her face (typically a version of the Richmond portrait) accompanied by an inspirational quotation from her work, most often those famous lines from *Jane Eyre* (1847): 'I am no bird; and no net ensnares me: I am a free human being with an independent will' (Brontë, 2008: 253). Similarly, the *Wall Street Journal* recently illustrated a bicentenary article surveying rewrites, mash-ups and spin-offs with a Brontë photocollage. The 1870s engraving of Chappel's portrait, based upon Richmond (see above), was transformed into colourised pop art: Charlotte, complete with sunglasses and carrying a satchel, cuts an appropriately postmodern figure (Maloney, 2016).

Charlotte's accepted portraits have been reimagined and made to speak to new audiences and situations. The Richmond portrait and its derivations have proved particularly durable and adaptable, with amateur and professional artists alike returning to this foundational image to commit repeated acts of iconoclasm or icon renewal. If Richmond could be accused of flattering his subject by emphasising and moulding her features to fit ideals of beauty (Bostridge, 1976), more recent artists have paid homage by returning to the portrait as an icon of Charlotte as writer. The Parsonage Museum as an official site dedicated to the lives, work and legacies of the Brontë family has been at the forefront of these imaginative engagements. A reproduction of the Richmond portrait hangs upon the chimney breast in the dining room, the very place occupied by the original during Patrick Brontë's lifetime. But this is not a house museum in slavish pursuit of an impossible authenticity in the recreation of space. Such tendencies are held in check, and interrogated, by the museum's contemporary arts programme. In 2013, the photographic artist Charlotte Cory was invited to explore the heritage and tourist industries built upon the Brontës' lives and work. Cory is best

5 Charlotte Cory, *Her Portrait by Richmond* (2013)

known for her work in surrealist collage and 'Visitoriana', an alternative nineteenth century imaginatively located in '[a] post-Darwinian universe of reworked, recycled, collaged and montaged Victorian photography and taxidermy in which the animals are clearly in charge' (Cory, n.d.). Cory's exhibition, entitled *Capturing the Brontës*, transformed the parsonage into a 'Visitorian' museum: images and artefacts portraying the Brontës as animals were installed throughout the parsonage, drawing upon human-animal encounters and animal representations documented in their writings and other accounts.[27] During the exhibition, the museum's reproduction of Richmond's portrait was replaced by a 'Visitorian' reimagining (*Her Portrait by Richmond*, Cory, 2013: 137; see Fig. 5). The head and features were those of dog, with Cory taking her inspiration from a letter to W. S. Williams, first published in Gaskell's biography, in which Charlotte mused upon the gendered expectations of authorship:

> The original of Mr Hall [a character in *Shirley* (1849)] I have seen; he knows me slightly; but he would as soon think I had closely observed him or taken him for a character – he would as soon, indeed, suspect me of writing a book – a novel – as he would his dog, Prince.
>
> (Brontë, 1995–2004: II, 260)

Having constructed a *carte-de-visite* photograph of Charlotte-as-woman-writer-come-dog (*An Unswerving Conviction*, Cory, 2013: 121), Cory made use of the same canine head, rendered in brushstrokes, for her 'Visitorian' portrait.[28]

Cory's work and its treatment of Brontë iconography is irreverent. This playfulness, though grounded in Charlotte's and her siblings' words, was perceived by some visitors to the museum to be an act of desecration, one committed within and legitimised by the very authority and site established to preserve the Brontës' posthumous legacy. TripAdvisor reviews bear witness to this dissatisfaction: one visitor thought the museum had been 'vandalised by a bizarre, ill-judged initiative', while another noted that the exhibition had proved 'much to the distaste of most contributors to the visitors' book'.[29] But the provocation posed by Cory's work prompts us to question how Brontë relics and remains can and have been read and employed variously. Richmond's public icon had been a private portrait in the family home until the publication of Gaskell's *Life of Charlotte Brontë* ensured the celebrity of both the image and its sitter. Cory's erasure of Charlotte's face returns the human subject to the obscurity she enjoyed while alive, prompting the viewer to reconsider Charlotte's own words concerning anonymity ('the advantage of being able to walk invisible') and the incredulity that often accompanies a woman's entrance into the literary public sphere. One further TripAdvisor review complained that *Capturing the Brontës* '[muddled] the authenticity of the rest of the exhibits'.[30] Here too is a provocation. In the case of Richmond's portrait, Cory's canine reimagining did not replace the original artefact but a reproduction, a counterfeit revealed only to those who take time to scrutinise interpretation cards and souvenir guides. And so we are prompted to question the reconstructed space of the house museum and whether Cory's image is any less authentic than a reproduction of a portrait that has itself been copied, adapted and disseminated *ad infinitum*.

Charlotte's bicentenary year, 2016, has provided the cue and occasion to reflect upon her legacies and afterlives, the appropriation and transformation of her life and work. Reimagining her image forms an integral part of this process, ongoing since the publication of Gaskell's biography in 1857. This has proved particularly true of media and museum contributions to the bicentenary celebration. On screen, Charlotte's face and figure have been imitated and performed, reimagined through embodiment. For a BBC documentary entitled *Being the Brontës*, broadcast in March 2016, actors and volunteers restaged Charlotte's wedding to Arthur Bell Nicholls.[31] Sophie Trott was corseted, bonneted and dressed in a bridal gown that matched, as far as possible, eyewitness accounts and Charlotte's surviving clothing. Likewise, *To Walk Invisible*, a recent feature-length BBC drama written and directed by Sally Wainwright, saw actress Finn Atkins in the role of Charlotte. Filmed partly in and around Haworth, the production required the building of a replica parsonage on Penistone Hill. Atkins' styling, her costuming, make-up and hair design have set new televisual patterns for contemporary conceptions of Charlotte's visual appearance – just as the replica parsonage, when viewed on screen, was largely indistinguishable from its stone original.

Museums have also turned to Charlotte's face and features to conceptualise or brand, through her recognisable iconography, their bicentenary events and exhibitions. The Parsonage Museum has set up a network of *Brontë 200* webpages dedicated to forthcoming bicentenaries, from Charlotte in 2016 to Anne in 2020. The banner for 'Charlotte 2016' is a photocollage combining four distinct images: a colour photograph of the moors is overlaid by a black-and-white photograph of the parsonage before the Wade extension was built during the 1870s; and a page of Charlotte's handwriting is overlaid by J. H. Thompson's portrait (BPM, 2016). 'Official' bicentenary events, organised or endorsed by the Parsonage Museum, join together and cohere under this banner. Visitors to the webpage encounter a visual reminder of Charlotte's profession and the importance of place to her work and subsequent legacies. But there is, undoubtedly, a marketing subtext: her face and words blend with the Yorkshire landscape and Haworth locale, the suggestion being that 'authentic' engagements with both the woman and writer are tied to a visit, or pilgrimage, to the sites, sights and spaces she occupied and traversed during her lifetime.

If recognisability has been key to the Parsonage Museum's visual approach to the bicentenary, the Sir John Soane's Museum in London, in direct contrast, has turned to anonymity and unknowing. Exploiting the absence of any claim to Brontë biography, the curatorial team were freed from any too exacting imperative to reconstruct the past. Charlotte did not visit the museum on any of her trips to London, and so, for their bicentenary exhibition, the Soane invited Charlotte Cory to turn her attention once more to the Brontës and 'Visitoriana'. The resulting collaboration, *Charlotte Brontë at the Soane*, was comprised of objects from the Soane collection or on loan from the Parsonage Museum set alongside Cory's original artwork.[32] The exhibition explored Charlotte's time in the capital and sought to 'bring her to the Museum at last' (Cory, 2016a). Portraiture, both real and imagined, played an important role in this (re-)locating of the subject. Cory's 'Visitorian' reimaginings of the Richmond portrait were again in evidence: her 2013 canine revision hung upon the gallery's walls, and in a nearby cabinet there were cut and collaged versions of the same icon, including one that imagined what Charlotte's likeness and iconography could have been if she had accepted John Everett Millais as her portraitist (Cory, 2016b: item 10c).[33] Displayed alongside these imagined likenesses were 'genuine' drawings by Anne Brontë, sketched upon the pages of a family book and possibly depicting her sisters. The centrepiece was a dress considered by many to have been worn by Charlotte while attending a dinner at William Thackeray's house.[34] Illustrations on display boards, reproduced in the exhibition guide and on the webpage, depicted a colourful, cartoon-like Charlotte wearing this dress and timidly exploring the Soane. Next to the dress was a portrait set upon an easel, an unknown woman taken by Cory as cipher for the lost image of Charlotte in Branwell's Gun Group painting (*The Missing Charlotte?*, 2015; Cory, 2016b: item 11). That the face of an unknown woman in a space unvisited by the purported subject could be made to signify meaningfully as a portrait of Charlotte Brontë challenges us to consider the contingencies of our received iconography, passed down through more than 150 years of adaptation and appropriation. Picturing Charlotte Brontë in the year of her bicentenary, and beyond, remains a provocative activity, one productive of new engagements with her life and work. We continue to see her anew.

Legacies and afterlives

Charlotte Brontë: Legacies and Afterlives explores, among other things, readers' desires to 'see' and 'know' the author. Analysing Brontë's evolving legacy, varied afterlife and impact on cultures at home and abroad, the twelve essays in the current volume together cover the period from Brontë's first publication in 1846 to her work's presence in the early twenty-first century. Contributors examine a range of topics: Victorian responses to Brontë's life and work in the forms of obituaries, essays and the biographies which appeared shortly after her death, along with evaluations of the importance of her poetry to her later prose writings, and her influence on later female writers. Some contributors consider the radical transformation of the parsonage at Haworth from the incumbent's home to a literary museum and major tourist attraction, while the creation of a Brontë heritage site in Brussels, the model for the city of Villette, is also explored. Other contributors consider how Brontë's life and work have been adapted across different media: theatre, film, radio, television and internet sources, emphasising how valuable her life and work have been to many cultural industries. Some contributors demonstrate how the emerging genre of neo-Victorian fiction has drawn upon her literary legacy for many of its plots, themes, characters and motifs. This book shows how these influential and commercially powerful uses of 'Charlotte Brontë' have kept the author at the forefront of Western, indeed global, literary and screen cultures. It assesses Brontë's legacy in terms of literary genre, narrative style, language, national and regional identities, sexuality and gender identity, adaptation theories, Cultural Studies, post-colonial and transnational readings, as well as analyses of her reception across the century and a half since her death.

The first section of the book, 'Ghostly Afterlives: Cults, Literary Tourism and Staging the Life', focuses on the myths associated with Charlotte Brontë's life. Many of these originated in Gaskell's biography, her careful presentation of her friend living an isolated life in rural Yorkshire and suffering bereavements, disappointments and self-denial. Gaskell's descriptions of Brontë's physical frailties and femininity prompted a myth of female genius that helped to propel literary pilgrims to visit Haworth and its parsonage after the author's death. Indeed, Gaskell was also responsible for a widespread belief that Charlotte haunted Haworth, so much so that some Victorian visitors travelling to Yorkshire were disappointed *not* to experience a ghostly encounter with the author. Deborah Wynne's chapter, 'The "Charlotte" Cult: Writing the Literary Pilgrimage, from Gaskell to Woolf', examines the origins of the impulse to seek 'Charlotte' in Haworth. Treating such tourism as a symptom of 'author love', a concept identified by Helen Deutsch as an emotional response to a dead author who has suffered in life and deserves our pity and protection (Deutsch, 2005), Wynne argues that Gaskell's presentation of Charlotte as frail, dutiful and unhappy was the catalyst for the late-Victorian 'Charlotte' cult. Its original devotees were instrumental in forming the Brontë Society in 1893 and the first museum of Brontë relics in Haworth's Yorkshire Penny Bank in 1895. They also worked tirelessly towards the establishment of the Brontë Parsonage Museum in 1928. Wynne examines diaries, letters, obituaries, poems and published accounts written by visitors to Haworth from 1855 to the turn of the twentieth century, tracing from these the shifts in perceptions of the author after her death. In 'Haworth, November 1904', an essay written following a visit to the village, Virginia Woolf expresses impatience with emotional tourism redolent of Victorian sentimentality. Questioning the value of the literary pilgrimage, Woolf wonders what impact these tourist encounters might have upon an author's literary reputation. Nevertheless, as Wynne demonstrates, Woolf herself succumbed to 'author love', recording her feelings on seeing Charlotte Brontë's relics on display. Wynne charts some of the misconceptions engendered by the Victorian cult of 'Charlotte', while recognising the achievements of its devotees in preserving Brontë heritage and successfully promoting her legacy.

Charlotte Brontë's association with Haworth has sometimes obscured the fact that she was the most adventurous and well-travelled member of the Brontë family, as Jude Piesse's chapter, 'The Path Out of Haworth: Mobility, Migration and the Global in Charlotte Brontë's *Shirley* and the Writings of Mary Taylor', shows. Piesse highlights Brontë's interest in travel, demonstrating the limitations of those who have seen the author as physically and imaginatively bound to her native village. Examining 'Brontë's topical fascination with labour migration for single, middle-class women' in *Shirley*, Piesse analyses this in relation to her friendship with Mary Taylor, the model for the novel's intrepid Rose Yorke (p. 59). Taylor's significance for Brontë has sometimes been overlooked. An emigrant to Wellington, New Zealand, where she established her own shop, and always an outspoken feminist, Mary Taylor had previously worked as a teacher in Germany, while in later life she became a writer. She offered Charlotte Brontë a model of a successful, well-travelled, single woman. Yet as Piesse shows, Brontë's work also had a considerable influence on 'Taylor's own powerful fiction and travel writing, shaped by her experiences of emigrating to New Zealand and touring the Alps' (p. 60). This body of writing can be viewed 'as one of Brontë's most radical legacies; one which has been obscured by Gaskell's more famous memorialisation' (p. 60). Through detailed close readings of Taylor's published work, and the surviving letters she exchanged with her friend, Piesse shows that *Shirley* challenges the 'Brontë myth' which has obscured her fascination with travel and the global.

Charlotte Brontë's sojourn abroad is the subject of Charlotte Mathieson's essay, 'Brontë Countries: Nation, Gender and Place in the Literary Landscapes of Haworth and Brussels', which emphasises the importance of Brussels in Charlotte's life. The author's relationship to Belgium offers an alternative way of situating her within a broader paradigm of gender and nation. Like Piesse, Mathieson argues that Charlotte Brontë's connection with Haworth has created a myth which limits her to concepts of Englishness, the local and rural. For Mathieson, 'Brussels offers a space where an alternative narrative unfolds' (p. 80), and she analyses the accounts written by literary tourists who visited the Pensionnat Heger in Brussels' Quartier Isabelle before its demolition in the early twentieth century. The late nineteenth century saw increasing interest in Brontë tourism in the city, with literary pilgrims often determined to collect relics and buy souvenirs. *Villette* (1853), set in a Belgian school, has been considered by many readers as a thinly disguised autobiography, a reflection of the author's own experiences as a pupil-teacher in Brussels between 1842 and 1843. The earliest published account of literary tourism to Brussels appeared in *Scribner's Magazine* in 1871, while the surprising publication in 1913 of Charlotte Brontë's passionate, even desperate letters to her teacher, Constantin Heger, stimulated even more interest in Brussels as a Brontë shrine, further intensifying the blurring of Charlotte's life and *Villette*. Through her readings of the accounts of literary tourists to Belgium, Mathieson reveals a key aspect of Charlotte Brontë's afterlife which removes her from the domestic stasis central to the mythology of Haworth and places her within another story of 'female independence through cosmopolitan interactions' (p. 80).

Brontë tourists in Brussels sought to locate the site of the Pensionnat Heger, its garden and the pear tree where *Villette*'s ghostly nun is thought to have appeared to the heroine, Lucy Snowe. Finding this garden was the aim of Marion Harland, the American novelist and biographer, who visited Brussels in the 1890s and published an account of her journey in a book entitled *Where Ghosts Walk: The Haunts of Familiar Characters in History and Literature* (1898). Victorian visitors to Haworth also looked for the ghosts of the sisters, and some recorded feeling their ghostly presence in the vicinity. Amber Pouliot's chapter examines commemorative poetry and fictional biographies to trace how the idea of the ghostly frames understandings of Charlotte Brontë's afterlife. In her chapter, 'Reading the Revenant in Charlotte Brontë's Literary Afterlives: Charting the Path from the "Silent Country" to the Séance', Pouliot identifies Gaskell's biography, with its repeated references to folk tales and superstitions, and the uncanny qualities of the Brontë home, as stimulating the idea of Charlotte Brontë as haunted and haunting. The craze for seances and spiritualism even resulted in the publication in 1893 of a 'spirit photograph' purporting to be of Charlotte's ghost. Gaskell's account of the author as a fey spirit continued to inspire the writers of fictional biographies in the early twentieth century; however, as Pouliot shows, while Victorian accounts presented the Brontë sisters as 'mute and inaccessible spirits', later stories became more playful in tone, depicting them as 'listening, noisy poltergeists, striving to communicate with the living' (p. 108).

The Victorian 'Charlotte' cult, with its powerful mythologising of the author, began with Gaskell's *Life* and gained momentum in the decades after her death. By the early twentieth century traces of the myth had surfaced on the stage in the form of biodramas. Dramatisations of the Brontës' lives became particularly fashionable in the 1930s, as Amber Regis demonstrates in her chapter, 'Charlotte Brontë on Stage: 1930s Biodrama and the Archive/Museum Performed'. Plays with suggestive titles, such as *Empurpled Moors* (1932) and *Stone Walls* (first performed 1933; published 1936), reinforced ideas of the sisters' isolation and the Yorkshire landscape as integral to an understanding their lives. The opening of Haworth parsonage as the Brontë Parsonage Museum in 1928 provided access to a new archive of Brontë material and relics. Additionally, playwrights were inspired by the publication of hitherto unknown Brontë texts, such as the juvenilia and unfinished novels, in the Shakespeare Head edition of their works (1931–38), as well as new letters continually coming to light. As Regis demonstrates, playwrights sought 'to construct and authenticate a particular account of the family's interconnecting lives: actors speak lines extracted from the Brontë corpus as they perform on stages filled with reproduction copies of their former possessions, prop relics that find their counterpart in the objects on display at the Parsonage Museum' (p. 117). Brontë biodramas thus constituted 'a critically reflexive art: a notable example of popular culture in dialogue with scholarship, heritage and tourism' (p. 117). Focusing on two plays which take Charlotte's life as their main subject, Alfred Sangster's *The Brontës* (1932), a popular melodrama, and Rachel Ferguson's more self-reflexive comedy *Charlotte Brontë* (1933), Regis analyses how each playwright balances long-established myths about Charlotte with new evidence from the developing archive of materials collected by museum curators and literary editors. Through a detailed analysis of both plays, Regis shows how each biodrama presents a different version of Charlotte's life. Sangster draws on well-known biographical information about the sisters, such as their habit of pacing around the dining table each evening to discuss their writing, but he also exploits newly available letters, such as those Charlotte wrote to Heger, to construct a heightened, melodramatic version of her emotional life. Ferguson, by contrast, pokes fun at the popular desire to find out everything there is to know about Charlotte Brontë, even down to the small objects she owned, exposed to full view in display cases at the Brontë Parsonage Museum. Ferguson sets out to debunk the emotional excess and importunate curiosity that renders Charlotte 'the infuriating subject of myth' (p. 139). However, the world was not yet ready for a deflation of the Brontë myth, for Ferguson's play failed to find its way to the professional stage.

Rachel Ferguson, like Virginia Woolf, was impatient of the tendency to mythologise famous authors, especially when the myths distorted their literary achievements. The essays in the second part of this collection, 'Textual Legacies: Influences and Adaptations', focus on how Charlotte Brontë's literary works have endured and been adapted. Anna Barton's chapter, ' "Poetry, as I Comprehend the Word": Charlotte Brontë's Lyric Afterlife', shows how Brontë's poetry, which appeared in print before any of her novels and is often dismissed as of negligible importance, haunts her later fiction in the form of 'an ongoing and revisionary internal exchange', a process Barton describes as a 'kind of self-encounter', whereby some of her poems become literally incorporated into her later prose narratives (pp. 147, 149). Barton identifies Charlotte as working within the Romantic tradition, self-consciously incorporating her own poetry into her later literary productions 'in a way that might both grant it a marketable posthumousness and secure the survival of the (feminine) lyric voice for the printed page' (p. 152). Through close readings of *The Professor* (published posthumously, 1857), *Jane Eyre* and *Shirley*, Barton uncovers an afterlife for Brontë's juvenilia and the poetry she wrote in early adulthood. Read in this way, her early lyrics find a new significance, revealing a hitherto unacknowledged dimension to Charlotte Brontë's creative praxis.

Barton is one of the few critics to consider the significance of Charlotte Brontë's poetry. Other contributors to this collection are also keen to move beyond the overwhelming dominance of *Jane Eyre* in Charlotte Brontë Studies. A number of chapters explore the important cultural influence of *Villette*, a novel not widely read by general readers, unlike *Jane Eyre*. *Villette*'s depiction of the maturation of a single working woman, Lucy Snowe, striving to achieve a radical independence as a teacher, inspired a generation of feminist writers born in the late Victorian period, such as Virginia Woolf, Vera Brittain and Winifred Holtby. Emma Liggins, in her chapter, 'The Legacy of Lucy Snowe: Reconfiguring Spinsterhood and the Victorian Family in Inter-War Women's Writing', highlights how many women publishing fiction and political writing between 1910 and 1940 valued Brontë's model of a working woman offered by Lucy Snowe as they reinterpreted and reworked the oblique feminist message of *Villette*. While these writers felt that Charlotte Brontë's life story offered only a partial inspiration for working women, the achievements of her heroine Lucy Snowe presented a more valuable role model for twentieth-century working women. In her chapter Liggins analyses the political and auto/biographical writing of Virginia Woolf, May Sinclair and Vera Brittain, as well as the new spinster heroines of modernist novels such as Sinclair's *The Three Sisters* (1914) and Winifred Holtby's *The Crowded Street* (1926). Inter-war women writers in rebellion against the Victorian family and domineering fathers were inspired by *Villette*'s depiction of a woman free of domestic ties and able to travel and earn her own living. Liggins argues that these writers created an alternative mythology around Charlotte Brontë, uncovering a more radical image of the author which had failed to register in Gaskell's biography. For them, Brontë's emergence from the Victorian myth of dutiful daughter revealed her to be a 'revolutionary thinker' whose work spoke to modern working women (p. 179).

Villette has been overshadowed by *Jane Eyre* in popular culture, possibly because it lacks a cinematic presence; nevertheless, it has long been an important novel for other forms of adaptation. Benjamin Poore's chapter, 'Hunger, Rebellion and Rage: Adapting *Villette*' focuses on its popularity for stage and radio adaptations. He identifies *Villette* as a problem novel in that its heroine's extreme reticence and complex interior life offer challenges to adaptors. *Villette* has also suffered from the common presumption that it is an autobiographical account of Brontë's life as a pupil-teacher in a Brussels girls' school. The novel's depiction of an irascible older professor befriending a retiring young English teacher inevitably suggested to some readers the story of Charlotte's love for Heger. Highlighting the inadequacies of such readings, Poore shows how alternative readings of Lucy Snowe's story have led to successful, often experimental adaptations for the stage and radio. Whereas the numerous stage and screen adaptations of the better-known *Jane Eyre* inevitably reference each other, the lack of a screen tradition based on *Villette* has allowed greater freedom for playwrights in interpreting Brontë's most enigmatic and ambiguous novel.

In contrast to the relative obscurity of *Villette*, there have been no shortages of film and television adaptations of *Jane Eyre*. Indeed, the novel has also figured extensively in neo-Victorian fiction, ranging from reworkings, prequels and sequels to stories that echo the characters and plot. Alexandra Lewis's chapter, 'The Ethics of Appropriation; or, the "Mere Spectre" of Jane Eyre: Emma Tennant's *Thornfield Hall*, Jasper Fforde's *The Eyre Affair* and Gail Jones's *Sixty Lights*', examines the impact of *Jane Eyre* on writers of neo-Victorian fiction. She asks how *Jane Eyre* 'has been reflected upon and invoked in twentieth- and twenty-first-century novels about the Victorians, and with what range of textual and wider cultural effects?' (p. 197). Lewis's close reading of *Jane Eyre*-based novels by Tennant, Fforde and Jones reveals how Brontë's text has simultaneously generated a sense of nostalgia and enabled reflections upon current cultural concerns. One of these concerns is the 'ethics of appropriation', and Lewis demonstrates how Tennant, Fforde and Jones each 'grapple with issues of intertextuality and originality; fidelity and creativity', considering 'the way the allusive power (or broad communal meaning) of an archetypal text can be contingent upon the oversimplification of literary and cultural complexities' (p. 199).

A concern with the 'ethics of appropriation' beset Jean Rhys when she wrote her ground-breaking prequel to *Jane Eyre*, *Wide Sargasso Sea* (1966). In a letter she expressed her doubts about rewriting Bertha Rochester as 'Antoinette', her main protagonist, wondering whether it was right 'to get cheap publicity' by using Brontë's novel (Wyndham and Melly, 1984: 263). As Jessica Cox demonstrates in her essay '"The Insane Creole": The Afterlife of Bertha Mason', Bertha, the 'madwoman' confined to the third storey of Thornfield Hall, had a complex afterlife even before Rhys's novel. Bertha has been prominent in many critical accounts of *Jane Eyre*; she is the personification of female rebellion in Sandra M. Gilbert and Susan Gubar's influential feminist reading of Charlotte Brontë's work in *The Madwoman in the Attic* (1979), and she was interpreted as the disruptive force of racial difference in Gayatri Chakravorty Spivak's 1985 post-colonial reading of *Jane Eyre*, 'Three Women's Texts and a Critique of Imperialism'. In her chapter, Cox analyses Bertha's afterlife 'as object of pity, femme fatale, proto-feminist figure, and Gothic monster' (p. 221), a character who has long haunted readers' and critics' imaginations, as well as being present in neo-Victorian writing, theatre, screen adaptations and art. Cox shows that the impulse to bring Bertha from the shadows of *Jane Eyre* has a long history, and her analysis of a range of adaptations, from early plays such as John Courtney's melodrama *Jane Eyre; or, The Secrets of Thornfield Manor* (1848) and Charlotte Birch-Pfeiffer's *Jane Eyre; or, The Orphan of Lowood* (1870), through films such as Christy Cabanne's 1934 *Jane Eyre* and Cary Fukanaga's version released in 2011, to the web series, *The Autobiography of Jane Eyre* (2013–14), demonstrates how representations of Bertha reflect changing responses to female sexuality and mental health. As Cox argues, increasing sympathy for Bertha in more recent reworkings and adaptations inevitably impinge on Rochester's heroic status: if Bertha is wrongly incarcerated and inhumanly treated, then Rochester must be the novel's villain rather than its hero, rendering Jane's marriage to him a problem rather than a happy point of closure for the heroine.

The afterlife of *Jane Eyre* and its characters in film and recently developed media is the subject of Monika Pietrzak-Franger's chapter, '*Jane Eyre*'s Transmedia Lives'. She examines a range of adaptations and media explorations of Brontë's work, particularly the newly emerging form of the web series. Pietrzak-Franger shows how *Jane Eyre* and its protagonist 'have loosened themselves from their literary form to become veritable transmedia phenomena' (p. 241). In her analysis of *The Autobiography of Jane Eyre*, she discusses the effects of the heroine's liberation from the novel's romance plot when she is placed in other relationships. This, she argues, has resulted in more radical versions of the story than those offered by most film-makers. Web series have generated different forms of reading and online community engagements with *The Autobiography of Jane Eyre* complicate traditional notions of authorship. Like Lewis, Pietrzak-Franger also explores the issues of the ethics of transmedia adaptation, pointing out that while young audiences are now able to 'appropriate the Victorians in ways hitherto unheard of', this may have created the side-effect of promoting the belief that Victorian texts 'have become our property – to be adapted, exchanged, and refurbished' in a way that risks obliterating the original novel (p. 254).

Ethical issues relating to Charlotte Brontë's textual afterlife are also discussed by Louisa Yates in her chapter '"Reader, I [Shagged/Beat/ Whipped/F****d /Rewrote] Him": The Sexual and Financial Afterlives of *Jane Eyre*'. Analysing E. L. James's *Fifty Shades of Grey* (2011) and other erotic makeovers alongside more 'legitimate' neo-Victoriana in the form of D. M. Thomas's *Charlotte* (2000), Yates argues that all 'blend cultural capital with financial potential' to render Brontë's celebrity 'as much a commodity as her text' (p. 261). Tapping into the cultural cachet associated with canonical Victorian authors can reap enormous financial benefits, Yates contends, and simply by referencing Charlotte Brontë authors have boosted sales. 'Charlotte Brontë' is increasingly exploited by acclaimed authors, as well as unknowns writing for commercial publications such as erotic makeovers. The implications of this trend, Yates argues, have not been sufficiently debated in neo-Victorian scholarship. And, as we can see from this book's appendix, compiled by Kimberley Braxton, the long list of texts drawing upon her life and work shows that Charlotte Brontë's legacy is extensive and ongoing. Her writing has now been adopted/adapted within so many commercially lucrative ventures that her commodification is both a wonder and a worry. While *Charlotte Brontë's Legacies and Afterlives* takes stock of the basis of Charlotte Brontë's allure and welcomes the diversity of her afterlives, it still hopes to celebrate the author herself and her achievements.

Acknowledgements

We would like to thank Sarah Laycock and Ann Dinsdale at the Brontë Parsonage Museum, Erika Ingham at the National Portrait Gallery, and the staff at the Women's Library, LSE, for their patience and assistance when responding to queries about Brontë portraits and likenesses in their collections.

Notes

1 To avoid confusion between the many Brontës that feature in this book, and to relieve readers from the repetition of the family name, editors and contributors alike will often refer to individuals by their first names.
2 For an account of the commission and execution of Richmond's portrait, see Foister (1985).
3 Gaskell began this fight before she was commissioned to write the biography. In May 1855, she expressed a desire to have the portrait copied for a private memento (Gaskell, 1966: 345).

4 The first print Gaskell received from Mr Stuart, the photographer, was ruined when glass covering the image 'got smashed in the post' (Gaskell, 1966: 421).

5 Held in the collection at the Brontë Parsonage Museum (BPM P25). Esther Chadwick claimed that Branwell began this portrait and Thompson completed it (Chadwick, 1914: 485).

6 Richmond's portrait was bequeathed to the National Portrait Gallery by Arthur Bell Nicholls (NPG 1452).

7 *Emily Brontë* (NPG 1724) and *The Brontë Sisters* (NPG 1725).

8 For an account of the discovery of Branwell's portraits, see Alexander and Sellars (1995: 307–12).

9 For example, Clement Shorter's 1897 article on 'Relics of Emily Brontë' reproduced a photograph of the Pillar Portrait sent to him by an unnamed 'correspondent'. The image is mislabelled: Charlotte is listed as 'Aunt Branwell'. Shorter also records Arthur Bell Nicholls' response to the photograph: 'while the one on the extreme left has some small resemblance to Anne, not one has the least resemblance to Emily or to his wife' (Shorter, 1897: 911) – this despite his being in possession of the original painting at his home in Banagher, Co. Offaly, Ireland!

10 Cuttings from the *Daily Graphic* and *Sphere* are reproduced on the National Portrait Gallery website as part of an article exploring the acquisition history of Branwell's portraits (NPG, n.d.).

11 Branwell's painted-out figure was first spotted in 1957 by Jean and Ingeborg Nixon. For the latter's account of the discovery, see Nixon (1958).

12 In most cases, commentators assume that Branwell removed himself from the group portrait; see Nixon (1958) and Barker (2010). Christopher Heywood, however, argues that Charlotte could have been responsible, forming 'part of her effort to eliminate her disgraced brother from her family's history' (Heywood, 2009: 17).

13 Greenwood tracings (BPM P69:1–3) and the Gun Group photograph (BPM Ph118). For reproductions of these images, see Alexander and Sellars (1995: 307–8) and Barker (1990).

14 Barker also notes the photograph proved, beyond doubt, that the surviving Emily fragment was cut from the Gun Group (Barker, 1990: 10). Previously many commentators assumed it had been taken from a third group portrait, see Edgerley 1932: 28–9) and Nixon (1958: 233).

15 See also Alexander and Sellars (1995: 261–2). Held in the collection at the Brontë Parsonage Museum (BPM BS50.4).

16 See also Alexander and Sellars (1995: 430), where the drawing is identified as 'possibly a sketch of a fellow pupil in Brussels'. Held in the collection at the Pierpont Morgan Library (PML Bonnell: MA 2696).

17 The painting was originally scheduled to go under the hammer in April 2012 but was withdrawn at the last minute pending further research (BBC News, 2012).

18 E. Ingham, personal communication, 13 April 2016.
19 Haley's website links to extensive debate in the comments below a *Brontë Blog* article ('Are these the Brontës?', 2012). For one blogger's response to the Molloy photograph, see Ross (2015). Emily Ross's blogsite, *The Brontë Link* (www.emilyeross.wordpress.com), is dedicated to her research into Brontë portraiture, photography and the siblings' physical appearances.
20 Chalk portrait of Charlotte Brontë (BPM P191). Before its acquisition, this drawing had been on loan at the museum. For a reproduction of this image, see Terry (2002: 259–60).
21 *Carte-de-visite* photographs (BPM SG109 and SB3045).
22 Material in the Seton-Gordon bequest proved the glass negative had been made using the *carte-de-visite*. But as Claire Harman explains, this merely confirmed that Emery Walker's studio index followed (and perhaps misread) the photograph's inscription (Harman, 2016: 340).
23 S. Laycock, personal communication, 4 August 2016.
24 The Internet Archive's Wayback Machine reveals that the *carte-de-visite* was part of the online picture library as late as March 2016: https://web. archive.org/web/20160324113323/https://www.bronte.org.uk/museum-and-library/picture-library (accessed 3 August 2016).
25 *Unknown Woman, Formerly Known as Charlotte Brontë* (NPG 1444).
26 In an ironic twist, Chadwick explains the forger's error with reference to Clement Shorter. His *Charlotte Brontë and Her Sisters*, part of Hodder & Stoughton's Literary Lives series, had been published in 1905 – just one year before the forgery was purchased by the National Portrait Gallery. This book mislabels a photograph of Heger: 'M. Paul Héger, The Hero of "Villette" and "The Professor"' (Shorter, 1905: 198). But Chadwick was not free from error herself: she confused the publication date of *Charlotte Brontë and Her Sisters* with that of Shorter's earlier work, *Charlotte Brontë and Her Circle* (1896).
27 *Capturing the Brontës*, Brontë Parsonage Museum, 4 October to 31 December 2013: www.bronte.org.uk/whats-on/52/charlotte-cory-capturing-the-brontes/53 (accessed 8 August 2016).
28 Cory's 'Visitorian' portrait can be seen, in situ, hanging upon the chimney breast in the dining room at Haworth parsonage, in her YouTube video tour of the exhibition: www.youtube.com/watch?v=kis0H-B42lE (accessed 4 August 2016).
29 'robprior' (2013) 'Go, but not till after Christmas', www.tripadvisor.co.uk/ShowUserReviews-g186409-d211789-r183164483-Bronte_Parsonage_Museum-Haworth_Keighley_West_Yorkshire_England.html (accessed 4 August 2016); 'Michael K' (2013) 'A moving insight into the conditions that created passionate novels', www.tripadvisor.co.uk/ShowUserReviews-g186409-d211789-r183416170-Bronte_Parsonage_Museum-Haworth_Keighley_West_Yorkshire_England.html (accessed 4 August 2016).

30 'Cassini'(2013) 'Superb museum, silly exhibition (but it's over soon)', www.tri-padvisor.co.uk/ShowUserReviews-g186409-d211789-r182953913-Bronte_Parsonage_Museum-Haworth_Keighley_West_Yorkshire_England.html (accessed 4 August 2016).

31 Aired on BBC Two, 22 March 2016: www.bbc.co.uk/programmes/p03kcd3l (accessed 8 August 2016).

32 *Charlotte Brontë at the Soane*, Sir John Soane's Museum, 15 March to 7 May 2016: www.soane.org/whats-on/exhibitions/charlotte-brontë-soane (accessed 8 August 2016).

33 Sidney Lee records Charlotte's refusal of Millais in his account of 'Charlotte Brontë in London' (Lee, 1909: 116).

34 Recent research has cast doubt on this being the dress worn by Charlotte at Thackeray's dinner, see Houghton (2016).

References

Alexander, Christine and Jane Sellars (1995) *The Art of the Brontës*, Cambridge: Cambridge University Press.

Anon. (1906) 'A new portrait of Charlotte Brontë', *Cornhill Magazine*, October, 28.

Anon. (1907) 'A disputed portrait of Charlotte Brontë', *Brontë Society Transactions*, 4.16, 17–23.

Anon. (1914) 'The Brontë sisters', *The Times*, 5 March, p. 7.

Anon. (2012a) 'Are these the Brontës?' *Brontë Blog*, 18 February, http://bronteblog.blogspot.com/2012/02/are-these-brontes.html (accessed 2 August 2016).

Anon. (2012b) 'Brontë sisters portrait goes under the hammer', *The Telegraph*, 17 April, www.telegraph.co.uk/culture/art/art-news/9209281/Bronte-sisters-portrait-goes-under-the-hammer.html (accessed 2 August 2016).

Barker, Juliet (1986) 'Charlotte Brontë's photograph', *Brontë Society Transactions*, 19.1–2, 27–8.

—— (1990) 'The Brontë portraits: a mystery solved', *Brontë Society Transactions*, 20.1, 3–11.

—— (2010) *The Brontës*, London: Abacus.

BBC News (2009) 'Man claims Brontë portrait find', *BBC News*, 12 August, http://news.bbc.co.uk/1/hi/england/bradford/8196844.stm (accessed 2 August 2016).

—— (2012) 'Brontë painting withdrawn from sale in Northamptonshire', *BBC News*, 25 April, www.bbc.co.uk/news/uk-england-northamptonshire-17838190 (accessed 2 August 2016).

Berglund, Brigitta (2012) 'Dress', in Marianne Thormählen (ed.), *The Brontës in Context*, Oxford: Oxford University Press, pp. 318–27.

Bostridge, Mark (1976) 'Charlotte Brontë and George Richmond: idealisation in the sitter', *Brontë Society Transactions*, 17.1, 58–60.

Brontë, Charlotte (1995–2004) *The Letters of Charlotte Brontë*, ed. Margaret Smith, 3 vols., Oxford: Clarendon Press.

—— (2008) *Jane Eyre*, ed. Margaret Smith, Oxford: Oxford University Press.

Brontë Parsonage Museum (2016) 'Charlotte 200', *Brontë 200*, www.bronte.org.
    uk/bronte-200/charlotte-2016 (accessed 8 August 2016).

Burns, Sarah (2012) 'New Brontë portrait', *Australian Brontë Association Newsletter*,
    30, http://maths.mq.edu.au/~chris/bronte/docs/news30.pdf (accessed 2 August
    2016).

Chadwick, Esther (1914) *In the Footsteps of the Brontës*, London: Isaac Pitman.

Clare, Maurice (c.1911) *A Day with Charlotte Brontë*, London: Hodder &
    Stoughton.

Cory, Charlotte (n.d.). 'Biografical note', www.charlottecory.com/Home/View/
    Biografia (accessed 4 August 2016).

—— (2013) *Capturing the Brontës*, London: Colville Press.

—— (2016a) 'Charlotte Brontë and New Babylon', www.soane.org/features/
    charlotte-brontë-and-new-babylon (accessed 8 August 2016).

—— (2016b) *Charlotte Brontë at the Soane*, London: Sir John Soane's Museum.

Cust, Lionel (1906) 'Charlotte Brontë at the National Portrait Gallery', *The
    Times*, 31 October, p. 10.

Deutsch, Helen (2005) *Loving Dr. Johnson*, Chicago, Ill.: University of Chicago
    Press.

Edgerley, C. Mabel (1932) 'Emily Brontë: a national portrait vindicated', *Brontë
    Society Transactions*, 8.1, 27–32.

Foister, Susan R. (1985) 'The Brontë portraits', *Brontë Society Transactions*, 18.5,
    339–54.

Gaskell, Elizabeth (1966) *The Letters of Mrs Gaskell*, ed. J. A. V. Chapple and
    Arthur Pollard, Manchester: Manchester University Press.

—— (1997) *The Life of Charlotte Brontë*, ed. Elisabeth Jay, London: Penguin.

Gilbert, Sandra and Susan Gubar (1979) *The Madwoman in the Attic: The
    Woman Writer and the Nineteenth-Century Literary Imagination*, New Haven,
    Conn.: Yale University Press.

Goffman, Erving (1956) *The Presentation of Self in Everyday Life*, Edinburgh:
    University of Edinburgh Social Sciences Research Centre.

Gold, Tanya (2005) 'Reader, I shagged him: why Charlotte Brontë was a filthy
    minx', *The Guardian*, 25 March, www.theguardian.com/books/2005/mar/25/
    classics.charlottebronte (accessed 20 May 2014).

Harman, Claire (2016) *Charlotte Brontë: A Life*, London: Viking.

Heywood, Christopher (2009) 'The Column in Branwell's "Pillar" Portrait
    Group', *Brontë Studies*, 34.1, 1–19.

Horsfall Turner, J. (1879) *Haworth: Past and Present*, Brighouse: J. S. Jowett.

Houghton, Eleanor (2016) 'Unravelling the mystery: Charlotte Brontë's
    1850 "Thackeray Dress"', *Costume*, 50.2, 194–219.

Knights, David (2015) 'Haworth expert's sceptical reaction to claims [of] a new
    Brontë sisters photograph', *Keighley News*, 30 July, www.keighleynews.co.uk/
    news/13508263.Haworth_expert_s_sceptical_reaction_to_claims_a_new_
    Bront___sisters__photograph (accessed 2 August 2016).

Lee, Sidney (1909) 'Charlotte Brontë in London', *Brontë Society Transactions*, 4.19, 95–120.

Maloney, Jennifer (2016) 'Charlotte Brontë turns 200', *Wall Street Journal*, 16 March, www.wsj.com/articles/charlotte-bronte-turns-200-1458149190 (accessed 4 August 2016).

National Portrait Gallery (n.d.) 'Acquisition histories: acquiring portraits for the National Collection', www.npg.org.uk/research/archive/archive-journeys/acquisition-histories/the-bronte-sisters-by-patrick-branwell-bronte-npg-1724-and-1725.php (accessed 29 July 2016).

Nixon, Ingeborg (1958) 'The Brontë portraits: some old problems and a new discovery', *Brontë Society Transactions*, 13.3, 232–8.

Ross, Emily (2015) 'The "other" Brontë photograph', *The Brontë Link*, https://emilyeross.wordpress.com/2015/09/25/the-other-bronte-photograph/ (accessed 2 August 2016).

Sellars, Jane (2012) 'Portraits of the Brontës', in Marianne Thormählen (ed.), *The Brontës in Context*, Oxford: Oxford University Press, pp. 123–33.

Shorter, Clement (1897) 'Relics of Emily Brontë', *The Woman at Home: Annie S. Swan's Magazine*, August, pp. 906–12.

—— (1905) *Charlotte Brontë and Her Sisters*, London: Hodder & Stoughton.

—— (1906) 'A literary letter', *The Sphere*, 27 October, p. 82.

Smith, George (1900) 'Charlotte Brontë', *The Cornhill Magazine*, December, pp. 778–95.

Spivak, Gayatri Chakravorty (1985) 'Three women's texts and a critique of imperialism', *Critical Inquiry*, 12.1, 243–61.

Sutherland, John (2015) 'If this is a real picture of the Brontës, then I'm Heathcliff!' *The Guardian*, 20 July, www.theguardian.com/news/shortcuts/2015/jul/20/photograph-of-bronte-sisters (accessed 2 August 2016).

Terry, Rachel (2002) 'Additions to the Brontë Society collections: further details and new items', *Brontë Studies*, 27.3, 251–60.

Ward, Mary (1917) 'Some thoughts on Charlotte Brontë', in Butler Wood (ed.), *Charlotte Brontë, 1816–1916: A Centenary Memorial*, London: Fisher Unwin, pp. 13–38.

West, Shearer (2004) *Portraiture*, Oxford: Oxford University Press.

Wise, T. J. and J. A. Symington (eds) (1932) *The Brontës: Their Lives, Friendships and Correspondence*, 4 vols., Oxford: Shakespeare Head and Basil Blackwell.

W.J.W. (1914) 'The Brontë portraits: the full story', *Saturday Review*, 14 March, pp. 336–7.

Wood, Butler (ed.) (1917) *Charlotte Brontë, 1816–1916: A Centenary Memorial*, London: Fisher Unwin.

Woolf, Virginia (1979) 'Haworth, November 1904', *Books and Portraits*, London: The Hogarth Press, pp. 194–7.

Wyndham, Francis and Diana Melly (ed.) (1984) *Jean Rhys's Letters, 1934–1966*, London: André Deutsch.

Part I

Ghostly afterlives:
cults, literary tourism and
staging the life

1

The 'Charlotte' cult: writing the literary pilgrimage, from Gaskell to Woolf

Deborah Wynne

This chapter analyses how writers and literary tourists imagined Charlotte Brontë during the fifty years after her death. It is framed by the accounts of two writers, Elizabeth Gaskell and Virginia Woolf, both of whom travelled to Yorkshire to find evidence of Charlotte Brontë's life and to assess her legacy as an author. Gaskell returned to Haworth shortly after Brontë's death in March 1855 to research the biography, and the publication of *The Life of Charlotte Brontë* in 1857 unleashed the 'Charlotte' cult, whose devotees became instrumental in the establishment of the Brontë Society in 1893 and the opening of the first Brontë museum in Haworth's Yorkshire Penny Bank in 1895 (Miller, 2001: 107). Many Victorian visitors, inspired by Gaskell's biography, sought traces of Charlotte's ghostly presence in Haworth, often writing emotional accounts of their experiences in books, articles, poems, letters and diaries. This body of writing contributed to the creation of Haworth as a literary shrine, prompting Virginia Woolf to visit in 1904. The resulting essay published in *The Guardian* in December, 'Haworth, November 1904', expresses her sense of weariness with the enduring image of the ladylike 'Charlotte', initiated by Gaskell and perpetuated by subsequent writers and literary pilgrims (Woolf, 1979). Woolf's journey to Yorkshire occurred at a time when she was planning her own entry into the literary marketplace; indeed, 'Haworth, November 1904' was her first publication. Woolf's career, then, began with a journey to Charlotte Brontë's home, a literary pilgrimage described in an ironic register, a distinct break with the emotional and reverential accounts of her predecessors. Woolf also introduced a note of concern that the Victorian love of 'Charlotte' had distorted Brontë's achievements as a writer.

The distorting lens of the literary pilgrim continues to intrigue and trouble academics today. Deirdre Lynch, Claudia L. Johnson and Helen Deutsch have each asked how academics might reconcile the need for rigorous scholarship and their own feelings of 'author love', a term coined by Deutsch to describe the longing experienced by devoted readers towards a revered writer. In her book, *Loving Dr. Johnson*, she identifies 'author love' as an amalgam of 'desire, fantasy, narcissistic misrecognition and unsettling confrontation with the alien', and central to her study is the challenge of remaining objective in the face of this strong emotional response (Deutsch, 2005: 16–17). Lynch raises the same question in her book *Loving Literature* when she asks whether 'the English professor's affective life is supposed to slop over onto her job', and she concludes that because literary study is characterised by 'boundary confusion', textual analysis and the love of texts and authors are inevitably intertwined (Lynch, 2015: 3). Johnson also ponders this point in *Jane Austen's Cults and Cultures*, noting that academics work to 'historiciz[e] the canonization of authors' while being susceptible to the same feelings of reverence and longing they are studying (2012: 13). From the eighteenth century onwards, as Lynch has shown, 'lovers of literature' became less inclined to 'treat literature as a thing but as a person [...] construct[ing] the aesthetic relation as though it put them in the presence of other people' (2015: 8). This relation emerged from an understanding that geniuses were 'a breed apart', existing within 'an aesthetic realm positioned at a distance from worldly conflicts' (Lynch, 2015: 9). Gaskell drew upon this myth in her biography, which presented Charlotte Brontë as an otherworldly genius (Regis, 2009: 126). As Linda H. Peterson has noted, 'The word "genius" appears sixteen times in Gaskell's *Life*' (2009a: 63). Unlike Woolf and more recent academics, however, Gaskell was untroubled about presenting her friend as vulnerable, ladylike, even fey, as she depicted Brontë as 'faithful to both her womanly duty and her literary gift' (Peterson, 2009a: 66, 68). The love she felt for her subject unleashed powerful emotions; for her, a primary aim was to make her readers feel a similar love for Charlotte Brontë, and she achieved this with remarkable success.

Gaskell's 'wild little maiden from Haworth'

Indeed, *The Life of Charlotte Brontë* remains compelling today because of Gaskell's emotional investment in her subject: an investment which she presumes her reader is also willing to make. This is most evident towards the end of the biography when she bequeaths the reputation of her friend to those readers capable of appreciating 'extraordinary genius', proclaiming: 'to that Public I commit the memory of Charlotte Brontë' (Gaskell, 2001: 457). 'Commit' is an interesting choice of verb, a performative that is associated with burial rites and is defined in the *OED* as 'to give to someone to take care of, keep, or deal with; to give in charge or trust, entrust, consign to'. The majority of definitions relate to concepts of trust or risk; one can commit crimes, marriage, goods, people, bodies to the ground, or battles, and many of the *OED*'s examples tend to come from the Bible, religious texts or legal documents. Using a formal statement and the present tense, Gaskell thus gives 'Charlotte Brontë' to her readers as a legacy, and in doing so understands the riskiness of the action she performs. Like a lawyer, she defends her dead friend from the accusations of coarseness and 'moral perversity' that had beleaguered 'Currer Bell', the pseudonym under which Brontë published her work; like a priest, she offers up a prayer to potential followers of the 'Charlotte' cult, those pilgrims who, after reading the biography, would travel to Haworth as to a shrine; like a guardian, she presents Charlotte Brontë as a vulnerable figure whose reputation will continue to need protection in the future.[1] It is hard to imagine a more effective strategy for securing Charlotte Brontë's reputation as someone to be simultaneously revered as a genius and pitied as an unfortunate woman. The biography thus effected the transformation of the controversial 'coarse and grumbling' Currer Bell, to quote the reviewer Ann Mozley, into 'Charlotte', the dutiful clergyman's daughter and loving companion to her sisters (quoted in Wilkes, 2010: 99). The *Life*, demonstrating to Victorian readers that 'female authorship posed no threat to feminine virtue', was thus instrumental in inspiring a devoted group of readers to act upon, and express, their love for the dead author (Hughes and Lund, 1999: 136).

Part of the power of Gaskell's *Life of Charlotte Brontë* was its ability to shame those who had condemned Brontë as coarse and immoral during her life. Charles Kingsley, for example, confessed in a letter to Gaskell: 'How I misjudged her! [...] Well have you done your work, and given us the picture of a valiant woman made perfect by sufferings' (quoted in Delafield, 1935: 260). Anne Mozley, who had reviewed Brontë's work negatively, acknowledged that the biography offered a 'partial solution to a mystery', for denied 'tender maternal watchfulness' throughout her childhood, it was now clear why Brontë had produced 'unfeminine' novels (quoted in Wilkes, 2010: 102). Gaskell had to some extent effected this change of heart by fictionalising her friend, as though she were the tragic heroine of a novel (Showalter, 1995: 106).[2] Meghan Burke Hattaway has suggested that Gaskell also called upon the aid of 'surrogate sisters', Ellen Nussey and Mary Taylor, to make the *Life* 'read as the collaborative work of a female community and self-styled family, through whose efforts a fallen, unfeminine genius is rehabilitated into the more socially acceptable image of a proper woman, who happened to write' (Hattaway, 2014: 677). Charlotte's positioning within this surrogate 'family' of protective female friends helped to raise Currer Bell from 'his' unfavourable image into someone resembling the familial feminine figures of sister, daughter and wife. This strategy was effective: Gaskell's emphasis on Charlotte's sororal qualities and motherless condition resembles the way Matthew Arnold had written about her two years earlier, when he also framed Charlotte Brontë as a sister. In his 1855 poem 'Haworth Churchyard' he imagined her as one of a 'Loving, a sisterly band' (reprinted in Kambani, 2004: 378–81, l. 147).

Gaskell's biography also presented the novelist as needing special protection because of her bodily oddities, and this was echoed by others who had known her. Thackeray, for example, referred to Charlotte Brontë's 'trembling little frame' (reprinted in Delafield, 1935: 254); Harriet Martineau stated that she was a 'frail little creature' (reprinted in Allott, 1974: 304), while Gaskell herself noted that Brontë's 'hands and feet were the smallest I ever saw; when one of the former was placed in mine, it was like the soft touch of a bird in the middle of my palm' (Gaskell, 2001: 76). Charlotte was thus rendered childlike and vulnerable, a woman who, for all her genius in the world of letters, was somehow, even after death, in need of care and protection. As Deutsch has shown, lovers of Samuel Johnson chose to 'cling to their hero's aberrations', such as his disabling bouts of mental anguish, his facial tics, his 'bodily difference' and physical bulk, loving him all the more because he was freakish and vulnerable (Deutsch, 2005: 25). Charlotte Brontë's Victorian following also felt that the author's 'abnormal' stature, physical weakness, melancholy and painful death were important reasons to bestow love on her, perhaps because her reputation as a writer had suffered considerably from the attacks of hostile reviewers. Elizabeth Rigby, for example, had deplored 'Currer Bell's' coarseness in 'his' powerful narratives of rebellion, and Rigby was not alone in her assessment of the author's 'unfeminine' desires (reprinted in Allott, 1974: 105–12). Mozley, when the sex of Currer Bell was known, argued that Charlotte Brontë must have been split into two opposing sides, her mind being 'masculine, vigorous, active, keen, and daring', while her body was 'feeble, nervous, suffering under exertion' (quoted in Wilkes, 2010: 104).

Gaskell's presentation of Brontë as a tiny, frail woman, a domestic and dutiful daughter who was also strong in moral probity and a boldly free spirit associated with the moors, helped readers to negotiate these apparent contradictions after her death. One literary pilgrim, who signed himself 'W.P.P.', visiting Haworth in 1856, summed up these oppositions when he wrote: 'Those tiny fingers, those small hands, were to wield a sceptre more potent than any of their predecessors. That delicately formed head was to be the fountain of thoughts that should revolutionize the whole world of letters' (reprinted in Delafield, 1935: 252). While Brontë's literary legacy ostensibly provided the rationale for the 'Charlotte' cult, her texts did not actually seem to be sufficient for many of her devotees. As Deutsch has noted, the 'power of the printed text' is often of limited significance for those committed to 'author love', for literary cults usually depend 'upon the sublimation of an author's distinctive artifice in order to render him or her commonplace and communal property' (2005: 17, 22). In other words, the author's craft in skilfully manipulating language is rarely the primary reason for loving an author. Although Dr Johnson and Charlotte Brontë share little in common as writers, their afterlives are characterised by many similarities, perhaps because both writers soon after their deaths were tamed and made familial in public memory by the work of friends who produced remarkably persuasive biographies (see Boswell, 1934–50).

While Gaskell's biography ensured that Charlotte Brontë was seen in the domestic context of her family and the parsonage home, she also carefully managed her reputation as 'wild', making it clear that her subject did not warrant condemnation as a radical who overstepped society's mores but rather resembled a small wild creature who only understood the world from the context of her native habitat. Her use of the image of a fluttering bird to describe Brontë's hand was only one of Gaskell's references to the author as related to the untamed and natural world. Amber Regis has suggested that the 'domestic rhetoric' of Gaskell's biography 'has an excessive fairy-tale quality', and this is particularly apparent when she describes her friend as uncanny, untamed, bird-like or fairy-like (2009: 126). Aunt Branwell emerges in the biography as a distant and eccentric spinster, unqualified to guide her young charges through the vagaries of polite society. Gaskell describes Charlotte at Roe Head School as 'the wild little maiden from Haworth' who did not fit in well with her schoolfellows, while at the Pensionnat Heger in Brussels she and her sister Emily were remembered as 'wild and scared-looking' young women 'with strange, odd, insular ideas about dress', thus rendering them gauche and vulnerable (2001: 81, 177). Even as 'a pale white bride, entering on a new life with trembling happy hope', Gaskell images Charlotte as a snowdrop, a delicate wild flower (2001: 456). The fact that her father failed to accompany her to the altar adds to this image of an unprotected maiden. Few brides with a parent living would have relied on their old spinster schoolmistress to adopt the parental role during the ceremony, for it was Miss Wooler who stood at the altar to 'give her away' when her eccentric father refused to do so. It comes as no surprise that so many members of the 'Charlotte' cult expressed an impulse to mother this motherless 'creature', or adopt the role of protective sister or brother.

Gaskell's image of Charlotte as both wild and vulnerable was accompanied by evidence of her strong sense of duty. Quoting Brontë's close friend, Mary Taylor, who had told her that Charlotte 'thought much of her duty, and had loftier and clearer notions of it than most people. […] All her life was but labour and pain', Gaskell promoted this image of a self-sacrificing woman existing in mental and physical pain, an image which had featured in many obituary notices (2001: 457). Harriet Martineau's 1855 tribute to her fellow author in the *Daily News* provided the main ingredients of this myth; while emphasising Brontë's 'feeble constitution', she added that she also had 'the strength of a man' (reprinted in Allott, 1974: 302). Simultaneously canonising and domesticating Brontë, Martineau suggested that she was 'a saint' and a 'perfect household image […] as able at the needle as at the pen' (reprinted in Allott, 1974: 304). Similar references to Brontë's domestic skills featured in Gaskell's biography, but the image of her as untamed and unschooled in social skills did most to establish the tone of the literary criticism of her work which appeared throughout the late Victorian period.

An admirer of Brontë's writing, Algernon Charles Swinburne argued in his 'A Note on Charlotte Brontë' (1877) that she was 'a woman of the first order of genius', and he compared her favourably to the intellectual, and in his opinion less talented, George Eliot (2004: 397). For Swinburne, Brontë's work was valuable precisely for its 'wildness', and he praised her ability to convey the 'occult inexplicable force of nature'

(2004: 395). Leslie Stephen's analysis of Charlotte Brontë's work, also published in 1877, similarly perpetuated the image of Brontë as 'wild' and, like Gaskell and Martineau, he tempered it with references to her strong sense of duty and her personal misfortunes. He maintained that her 'fiery soul' was 'imprisoned in too narrow and too frail a tenement. The fire is pure and intense. It is kindled in a nature intensely emotional, and yet aided by a heroic sense of duty' (reprinted in Allott, 1974: 420). This interpretation of the author was highly influential. Mary Ward, in her Introduction to the Haworth edition of *Jane Eyre* in 1899, also referred to Charlotte's 'fiery' qualities; however, she attributed these to the author's Celtic background. According to Ward, who published under her married name Mrs Humphry Ward, Brontë was 'first and foremost *an Irishwoman*', a heritage which Gaskell had chosen not to emphasise in her biography. Ward considered this Irish background responsible for that 'quality of exuberance, of extravagance, which her contemporaries called "bad taste"' (reprinted in Allott, 1974: 449–50). Ward suggested that Brontë was not to blame for the 'curious vein of recklessness, roughness' in her writing, for this emerged from her Celtic ancestry and existed 'side by side with an exquisite delicacy and a true dignity' (reprinted in Allott, 1974: 450). A product of Ireland, Brontë had later imbued an equally foreign 'roughness' from Yorkshire, 'the hard, frugal, persistent North', as Ward expressed it. This 'Brontë' energy, she suggests, can be felt by anyone travelling to Haworth: 'One has but to climb her Haworth hills to feel it flowing around one' (reprinted in Allott, 1974: 451). Ward's assessment of Brontë's work, while drawing on the imagery of popular myth, takes readers beyond the image of the frail, ladylike author in her emphasis on the power and originality of the 'roughness' in her writing. Nevertheless, in the decades following Brontë's death there was an assumption that her life, as represented by Gaskell, rather than her novels, provided the key to Charlotte Brontë's achievements in the world of letters.

Charlotte's ghost, grave and things

By the time the Haworth edition of *Jane Eyre* appeared in 1899, literary tourists travelling to Charlotte Brontë's home had for decades been seeking the ghostly 'Brontë' energy that Ward claimed was a hybrid mixture of Irish exuberance and Yorkshire wildness. As a ghostly presence, Charlotte Brontë haunted Victorians in the nicest possible way, for most literary pilgrimages to Haworth appeared to have been undertaken in the hope of encountering a ladylike and melancholy spirit in the vicinity of the parsonage rather than finding a wild banshee on the moors. W. H. Cooke's description of his journey to the Brontë home in January 1867, published serially in *St James's Magazine* from December 1867 to March 1868 as 'A Winter Day at Haworth', opens with his heightened expectation of seeing the ghosts of the sisters. As he approached Haworth, he saw in the distance 'the small quiet figures of two young ladies clad in mourning' and exclaimed, '"Surely these must indeed be they!"' despite the fact that twelve years had elapsed since Charlotte Brontë's death (reprinted in Kambani, 2004: 386). The main purpose of the journey for Cooke and his companion was to follow the visitor's trail mapped out by Gaskell in the *Life*. Visiting Charlotte's grave, they paused to reflect: 'she now lies buried, almost on the very spot where her feet must have stood during the performance of the marriage rite' (reprinted in Kambani, 2004: 390). They signed the visitors' book, noticing that 'it contained the names of persons from all quarters of the globe' (reprinted in Kambani, 2004: 391). At the parsonage Cooke saw the room in which the sisters paced as they discussed their writing, and where Charlotte had later paced alone; this prompted him to imagine her 'thinking mournfully of those sisterly voices that were stilled for ever in death'. Stimulated further by the scene before him, he 'saw' in his mind's eye Charlotte Brontë 'in a very agony of tears, listening shudderingly to the wind from the desolate moors'. For Cooke, her 'agony' rendered the parsonage 'almost consecrated ground' (reprinted in Kambani, 2004: 392).

Indeed, pilgrims to Haworth frequently sought the 'consecrated ground' of her burial place, but for some this was erroneously believed to be in the churchyard next to the parsonage rather than inside Haworth church. For early visitors the desire to remember Charlotte, the woman who had been presented as a product of the moors, prompted them, perhaps understandably, to mourn at the wrong place. Matthew Arnold was one of the first to be mistaken. In 'Haworth Churchyard' he reflected on Charlotte's grave: 'In a churchyard high mid the moors / Of Yorkshire, a little earth / Stops it [i.e. her ear] for ever to praise' (ll. 83–5). He imagines the grave surrounded by those of her sisters: 'Round thee they lie; the grass / Blows from their graves towards thine' (ll. 154–5). This imaginary cluster of moorland graves became the most appropriate place for the dead sisters to rest and consequently took on its own reality, despite the evidence. The American poet Emily Dickinson wrote in a similar vein, although her 'visit' to Haworth was a textual and imaginative one rather than an actual encounter with Charlotte Brontë's home. In her short tribute to Brontë in 1860, Dickinson followed Arnold in placing the author in her 'natural' resting place:

All overgrown by cunning moss,
All interspersed with weed,
The little cage of 'Currer Bell'
In quiet 'Haworth' laid.

(Dickinson, 1999: 73, ll. 1–4)

Yet, for Cooke, Charlotte's indoor burial place had its own drama, suggesting the Gothic blend of marriage and death which Gaskell's *Life* had described so powerfully. He noted that her body lay immediately beneath the place where she stood with Arthur Bell Nicholls as they made their marriage vows. The Brontë sisters' indoor burial place thus offered only a temporary setback to those who travelled to Haworth. For many later pilgrims the emotional value of their journey came from the knowledge that they were walking the 'consecrated' ground of Haworth itself, where the dead Charlotte had once trod. By treading in her footsteps, pilgrims could 'read' another version of her life via place, space and the material world, a form of 'reading' that relied purely on affect rather than rational understanding.

Literary tourism, according to Nicola Watson, involves 'the haunted' seeking the 'haunter', although for the inhabitants of Haworth parsonage, the haunted swiftly turned into the haunters as each subsequent incumbent received endless requests for access to his home from followers of Charlotte's cult (Watson, 2006: 123). Watson has suggested that Gaskell's biography provided a 'mid-Victorian guidebook' to the newly discovered 'Brontë Country' (Watson, 2006: 115). Certainly, the biography had stimulated William Cory, a poet and schoolmaster, to travel on a pilgrimage to Haworth in 1867 with two friends, also schoolmasters, and he recorded this journey in his diary. As the men approached the parsonage, they 'had been talking school shop so incessantly up the street that it was hard to remember the sacred dead, but I did, at the right time and in the right way' (reprinted in Kambani, 2004: 407). Cory considered the parsonage to be a 'miserable homestead', which evoked for him the melodramatic image of an imprisoned heroine: 'Out of that prison the little Charlotte put forth a hand to feel for the world of human emotion', which, when represented in her work, gave her readers 'new souls' (reprinted in Kambani, 2004: 407). Yet these grandiose claims did little to overwrite the prevalent image of Charlotte's littleness and frailty which Gaskell had put in place. Indeed, the 'Charlotte' cult continued

for decades to focus on the author's physical vulnerability and femininity. Marion Harland, the American author of *Where Ghosts Walk: The
Haunts of Familiar Characters in History and Literature* (1898), in which
she described her visit to Brussels to identify the places fictionalised in
Villette, tended to picture Charlotte as abnormally tiny. In her later biography, *Charlotte Brontë at Home* (1899), which depicts Harland's experience of visiting Haworth, Charlotte is referred to as having 'wee fingers',
while as a thirty-eight-year-old bride she 'looked absurdly small and
young' (Harland, 1899: 20, 263).

Harland had arranged with the incumbent of Haworth parsonage to
look around his home, 'the sacred precincts' where the sisters had lived,
and she admits to a personal investment in Charlotte, who:

> had come closer to my heart than many of my living friends. The most
> commonplace description of her appearance or habits, the most meagre
> detail of her personal history had fascination for me that did not abate as
> mature years brought disillusion to many other dreams. My approach to
> the scenes among which she had lived, laboured, suffered, and died, was
> as to a shrine.
>
> (Harland, 1899: 279)

Scorning 'the throng of sight-seers who troop thither from all parts
of the world' (Harland, 1899: 295), Harland distanced herself from
these curious tourists as she gained privileged access to the parsonage. On the doorstep she found an apparition of the woman she
sought, for, by 'some occult process', Charlotte Brontë rose up before
her 'spiritual vision', and she experienced a 'sensation that thrilled
me almost to pain in crossing the worn doorstep where Charlotte
must have sat or stood times without number' (Harland, 1899: 297,
292). Entering the parsonage the ghostly Charlotte 'seemed to glide
to my side and accompany me through the house her genius had
consecrated', a 'tiny, delicate, serious little lady, pale, with fair straight
hair and steady eyes' (Harland, 1899: 297). Harland also visited the
nearby Yorkshire Penny Bank to examine the collection of 'mementos
infinitely touching to the tender-hearted visitor', all indicative of the
'frugal simplicity of a life that ran parallel with the brilliant literary career' (Harland, 1899: 298). Harland's encounter with the 'relics'
offers an example of what Claudia Johnson identifies as the desperation felt by literary tourists 'for any material shreds that can connect
us with' an author (2012: 175). Discussing the establishment of the
Jane Austen museum at Chawton, Johnson suggests that possessions

displayed in the museum come to stand as substitutes for the author herself: 'The treasures we contemplate are calculated to create a space of presence and authenticity so that the absent beloved […] lives again before us in a particularly idealized form' (2012: 172). The love Harland expresses in *Charlotte Brontë at Home* is easy to mock as an excessive and sentimental response, her feelings towards the Brontë memorabilia often appearing as an inability to measure their significance. Nevertheless, Harland's reaction to Haworth, its famous parsonage and the makeshift museum housed in the Yorkshire Penny Bank, stands as testimony not only to the power of Charlotte Brontë's writing but also to the impact of Gaskell's *Life*. However, it was the inability of literary tourists to disentangle the significant from the trivial that particularly concerned Virginia Woolf when she wrote 'Haworth, 1904'.

Woolf in Haworth

Many Victorian pilgrims, like Harland, recorded feeling a thrill of presence and friendly connection to Charlotte Brontë in Haworth. Acknowledging this impulse to feel 'near' to a dead author, Deutsch questions 'what the love of authors has to do with the love of literature', and this seems to have been a question raised by Virginia Woolf when she visited Haworth in 1904 (2005: 12). Interestingly, Woolf initiates a departure from the reverent and emotional accounts of Victorian seekers after Charlotte in Haworth when she sought to understand why people needed to visit literary shrines. Like many later academics, Woolf was powerfully moved at the sight of Charlotte Brontë's things on display at the museum, her dresses, shoes, letters and drawings, but she was also anxious to keep a distance between the emotional force of 'author love' stimulated by these traces and critical scrutiny of the author's texts.

In an attempt to maintain this distance, Woolf adopts a dual discourse in 'Haworth, November 1904': the voice of the pilgrim is tempered by the scepticism of the critic. Irony and comedy strike the keynotes for the first part of this short essay when she refers to the inauspicious weather:

A real northern snowstorm had been doing the honours of the moors. It was rash to wait fine weather, and it was also cowardly. I understand the sun rarely shone on the Brontë family, and if we chose a really fine day we should have to make allowance for the fact that fifty years ago there were few fine days at Haworth.

(Woolf, 1979: 194)

Arriving in Keighley, 'the big town four miles from Haworth', Woolf imagines Charlotte visiting the shops fifty years earlier 'to make her more important purchases – her wedding gown, perhaps, and the thin little cloth boots which we examined under glass in the Brontë Museum'. She 'picture[s] the slight figure of Charlotte trotting along the streets in her thin mantle, hustled into the gutter by more burly passers-by' (Woolf, 1979: 195). This is a very different vision of Charlotte from those recorded by Victorian visitors, many of whom saw or imagined a ghostly Brontë gliding before them, and Woolf no doubt had such accounts in mind when she offers her deflationary image. The verb 'trotting', and the slapstick image of the 'burly' chaps 'hustling' the dearly loved author into the gutter, mock the reverent language usually employed by Victorian members of the 'Charlotte' cult. Brontë's diminutive stature and vulnerability are de-sentimentalised, rather than presented as primary reasons for loving her. Haworth, too, is cut down to size as a 'dingy and commonplace' settlement, while the 'little sparse parsonage […] built of the ugly, yellow-brown stone' quarried nearby, is for Woolf equally disappointing and uninspiring (1979: 195, 197). The museum in the Yorkshire Penny Bank, Woolf notes, offers 'rather a pallid and inanimate collection of objects. An effort ought to be made to keep things out of these mausoleums' (1979: 196).

This tone does not accurately reflect her experience, however. Although she sets out to produce a measured, revisionary account of the literary pilgrimage, Woolf abandons this in the second half of her essay from the moment she succumbs to the allure of the objects on display, reflecting on how 'we must be grateful for the care which has preserved much that is, under any circumstances, of deep interest'. Her initial irony cannot be maintained, and she finally admits to feeling an intense emotion on viewing the case containing Brontë's clothes:

> The most touching case – so touching that one hardly feels reverent in one's gaze – is that which contains the little personal relics, the dresses and shoes of the dead woman. The natural fate of such things is to die before the body that wore them, and because these, trifling and transient though they are, have survived, Charlotte Brontë the woman comes to life, and one forgets

the chiefly memorable fact that she was a great writer. Her shoes and her thin muslin dress have outlived her.

(Woolf, 1979: 196)

Woolf's recognition of the power of relics pinpoints the problem she faced on her visit to Haworth: wanting to critique the sanctification of a dead author and focus on 'the chiefly memorable fact that she was a great writer', she cannot help but succumb to the common feeling of reverence on seeing Brontë's 'little personal relics'.

Charlotte's afterlife in Haworth

T. Wemyss Reid in *Charlotte Brontë: A Monograph*, first published in *Macmillan's Magazine* in 1876, referred to Charlotte's death as 'that Easter-day tragedy which had been enacted to the bitter end among the Yorkshire hills' (1877: 183). This tragedy had originally been dramatised by Gaskell in her biography; as Peterson observes, '*The Life of Charlotte Brontë* does not end with a triumphant literary career but with a wedding and a funeral', suggesting a melancholy narrative of genius thwarted by cruel fate (2009b: 149). The image employed by Reid of the 'lonely authoress' finding companionship and 'developing into the trustful happy wife' was typical of Victorian interpretations of Charlotte's final year, where a blending of the 'lonely authoress' and the 'happy wife' helped to establish the tone of 'the cultural myth of the "Brontë" country' (Reid, 1877: 183). As Richard Salmon has suggested, Haworth's role as the site of literary pilgrimage ensured that 'the "private" space of the author's home became, paradoxically, the preeminent signifier of her public fame' (2013: 186). This amalgamation of the public figure and private woman was troublesome for her husband and father who survived her, Arthur Bell Nicholls being acutely aware of the disjunction between his wife, Mrs Nicholls, and Currer Bell, the author. Patrick Brontë found himself dealing with increasing numbers of literary tourists, autograph hunters and curious journalists, seemingly willing to oblige those who wanted a sample of his daughter's handwriting. Gaskell found him on a visit to the parsonage cutting up Charlotte's letters into strips to satisfy those fans who had requested memorial tokens (Gordon, 2010: 363). Nicholls, by contrast, was determined that no traces of Charlotte should fall into the clutches of importunate cult followers who demanded fragments of his wife's possessions. In 1861, when Patrick Brontë died, Nicholls left Haworth for Ireland, and, as Lyndall Gordon states, he carried with him 'his wife's dresses, her drawings, her portrait by Richmond which he had been the first to see, and a heap of Brontë manuscripts' (2010: 367). For decades, these objects were hidden from the world in his Irish home, inaccessible to curious members of the 'Charlotte' cult (Gordon, 2010: 368). Not suspecting the cache of treasures in Ireland, the cult followers relied upon the displays of memorabilia in the museum in Haworth, as well as the ghostly ambience of the village itself. Yet the myth, set in motion by *The Life of Charlotte Brontë*, swiftly overtook the reality of the author. As Lucasta Miller suggests, by the late twentieth century '"Brontë" has come to stand for an all-purpose cosy nostalgia with no connection at all to literature' (2001: 107). Although this is a slight exaggeration, the literary connection informs the myth as a residual trace, there is indeed a disconnection between Charlotte Brontë's writing and her mythic status.

At the beginning of the twentieth century, as we have seen, Woolf had attempted, with limited success, to shift Brontë away from her image as the vulnerable Victorian lady genius and emphasise her work as a professional writer. Her later *A Room of One's Own* (1929) builds upon earlier feminist interpretations of Charlotte Brontë's writings, such as the suffragette Millicent Fawcett's book, *Some Eminent Women of Our Times: Short Biographical Sketches* (1889). Woolf suggests that Charlotte Brontë should be viewed as both an inspiration to educated women and a warning against the snare of self-sacrificing domesticity.[3] Yet Woolf's attempt to undo the emotionally charged work of the Victorian 'Charlotte' cult was a long time in taking effect. In a centenary address delivered in Haworth in 1916, Bishop Welldon summarised the seventy years since Charlotte Brontë's death as a long and continuous period of mass mourning, 'our feelings are so deep', he insisted (1917: 67). He also doubted 'whether any votaries in the history of literature have pursued their cult with more passionate or pathetic feelings' than have the followers of Charlotte Brontë (Welldon, 1917: 66). Reid had made a similar point in 1876 when he referred to the nation's 'cry of pain and regret' on reading the news of her death (1877: 184). The Victorian followers of the 'Charlotte' cult were haunted by Brontë's image as presented in the emotional accounts of writers of obituaries, biographies and diaries, each of whom unleashed a licence to mourn and acknowledge their feelings of love. Charlotte Brontë's afterlife in the twentieth century, particularly after the purchase of the parsonage in 1927 and its conversion into the Brontë Parsonage Museum, became considerably more complex than the unselfconscious worship of Victorian cult followers. Nevertheless, even the most sceptical of contemporary visitors to Haworth are unable to ignore how the legacy of author love continues to shape and dominate one small Yorkshire settlement. Welldon's summary of the mood in 1916, 'our feelings are so deep', is applicable to many literary tourists in Haworth today.

Notes

1 Anne Mozley accused Currer Bell, Charlotte Brontë's pseudonym, of 'moral perversity' in a review of 1853 (quoted in Wilkes, 2010: 99).
2 Deirdre d'Albertis (1995) sees Gaskell's presentation of Brontë in the biography as reductive, framing Brontë as 'odd' as a way of containing her; however, her narrative of Gaskell's sense of rivalry and covert tactics is unconvincing.
3 See Liggins, Chapter 7 in this volume.

References

Allott, Miriam (ed.) (1974) *The Brontës: The Critical Heritage*, London: Routledge & Kegan Paul.

Boswell, James (1934–50) *The Life of Samuel Johnson, LLD*, ed. George Birkbeck Hill, 6 vols., Oxford: Clarendon Press.

D'Albertis, Deidre (1995) 'Bookmaking out of the remains of the dead: Elizabeth Gaskell's *The Life of Charlotte Brontë*', *Victorian Studies*, 39.1, 1–31.

Delafield, E.M. (1935) *The Brontës: Their Lives Recorded by Their Contemporaries*, London: The Hogarth Press.

Deutsch, Helen (2005) *Loving Dr. Johnson*, Chicago, Ill.: University of Chicago Press.

Dickinson, Emily (1999) *The Poems of Emily Dickinson*, ed. R. W. Franklin, Cambridge, Mass.: Belknap Press of Harvard University Press.

Fawcett, Millicent (1899) *Some Eminent Women of Our Times: Short Biographical Sketches*, London and New York: Macmillan Press.

Gaskell, Elizabeth (2001) *The Life of Charlotte Brontë*, ed. Angus Easson, Oxford: Oxford University Press.

Gordon, Lyndall (2010) *Charlotte Brontë: A Passionate Life*, London: Virago.

Harland, Marion (1899) *Charlotte Brontë at Home*, London and New York: Knickerbocker Press.

Hattaway, Meghan Burke (2014) '"Such a strong wish for wings": *The life of Charlotte Brontë* and Elizabeth Gaskell's fallen angels', *Victorian Literature and Culture*, 42.4, 671–90.

Hughes, Linda K. and Michael Lund (1999) *Victorian Publishing and Mrs Gaskell's Work*, Charlottesville, Va.: University Press of Virginia.

Johnson, Claudia L. (2012) *Jane Austen's Cults and Cultures*, Princeton, NJ: Princeton University Press.

Kambani, Mariana (ed.) (2004) *Lives of Victorian Literary Figures II: The Brontës*, London: Pickering & Chatto.

Lynch, Deidre Shauna (2015) *Loving Literature: A Cultural History*, Chicago, Ill.: University of Chicago Press.

Miller, Lucasta (2001) *The Brontë Myth*, London: Jonathan Cape.

Peterson, Linda H. (2009a) 'Elizabeth Gaskell's *The Life of Charlotte Brontë*', in Jill L. Matus (ed.), *The Cambridge Companion to Elizabeth Gaskell*, Cambridge: Cambridge University Press, pp. 59–74.

—— (2009b) *Becoming a Woman of Letters: Myths of Authorship and Facts of the Victorian Market*, Princeton, NJ: Princeton University Press.

Regis, Amber K. (2009) '"The loose, drifting material of life": experiments in nineteenth- and twentieth-century life writing', unpublished Ph.D. thesis, Keele University.

Reid, T. Wemyss (1877) *Charlotte Brontë: A Monograph*, London: Macmillan.

Salmon, Richard (2013) *The Formation of the Victorian Literary Profession*, Cambridge: Cambridge University Press.

Showalter, Elaine (1995) *A Literature of Their Own: From Charlotte Brontë to Doris Lessing*, London: Virago.

Swinburne, Algernon (2004) 'A note on Charlotte Brontë', in *Major Poems and Selected Prose*, ed. Jerome McGann and Charles L. Sligh, New Haven, Conn.: Yale University Press, pp. 395–9.

Ward, Mary (1917) 'Some thoughts on Charlotte Brontë', in Butler Wood, *Charlotte Brontë, 1816–1916: A Centenary Memorial*, London: Fisher Unwin.

—— (1974) 'Introduction to *Jane Eyre*, Haworth edition [1899]', in Miriam Allott (ed.), *The Brontës: The Critical Heritage*, London: Routledge & Kegan Paul, pp. 448–60.

Watson, Nicola J. (2006) *The Literary Tourist: Readers and Places in Romantic and Victorian Britain*, Basingstoke: Palgrave Macmillan.

Welldon, J.E. (1917) 'Centenary address at Haworth', in Butler Wood (ed.), *Charlotte Brontë 1816–1916: A Centenary Memorial*, London: Fisher Unwin, pp. 63–80.

Wilkes, Joanne (2010) *Women Reviewing Women in Nineteenth-Century Britain*, Farnham: Ashgate.

Woolf, Virginia (1949) *A Room of One's Own*, London: The Hogarth Press.

—— (1979) 'Haworth, November 1904', *Books and Portraits*, London: The Hogarth Press, pp. 194–7.

2

The path out of Haworth: mobility, migration and the global in Charlotte Brontë's *Shirley* and the writings of Mary Taylor

Jude Piesse

> Caroline was limited once more to the grey Rectory; the solitary morning walk in remote bypaths; the long, lonely afternoon sitting in a quiet parlour.
>
> Charlotte Brontë, *Shirley* (1849)

Following Elizabeth Gaskell's defence of her friend's posthumous reputation in *The Life of Charlotte Brontë* (1857), Brontë has frequently been associated with ideas of static and feminised local place – the dutiful daughter at home who, after death, haunted Haworth. The 'grey Rectory', 'quiet parlour' and 'remote bypaths' which constrain Caroline Helstone in *Shirley* have similarly limited conceptions of Brontë and her wider cultural legacy (Brontë, 2006: 368). By focusing closely upon this novel, however, the present chapter will reveal that Brontë was deeply preoccupied with the movement of people and capital across global space, as well as with visions of restrictive local place. Like the sea-stained pages of her aunt's magazines, which Caroline reads in the rectory library (Brontë, 2006: 368), *Shirley* is in fact saturated with traces of movement within and across a global sphere of action – a sphere to which female, as well as male, characters are afforded a significant degree of access. Following a brief exploration of the novel's sophisticated understanding of global space and mobility, this chapter moves on to focus upon Brontë's topical fascination with labour migration for single, middle-class women in the light of the friendship and correspondence with Mary Taylor, the model

59

for *Shirley*'s Rose Yorke, which informed *Shirley*'s production and conception. I will conclude by showing how Taylor's own powerful fiction and travel writing, shaped by her experiences of emigrating to New Zealand and touring the Alps, can be viewed as one of Brontës' most radical legacies, one which has been obscured by Gaskell's more famous memorialisation. Taking the path out of Haworth through what Taylor termed in an 1850 letter to Brontë the characteristic 'life & stir' of her friend's most globally engaged novel enables us to both reconceptualise the nature of Brontë's creative vision and to trace the extension of this vision within Taylor's writings (reprinted in Brontë, 1995–2004: II, 439). This chapter thus both seeks to restore critical attention to elements of mobility and global awareness within Brontë's writing which have not survived into what Lucasta Miller has termed the 'Brontë myth' and to show how recognising these dimensions illuminates Brontë's intersections with and influence upon later feminist writing (Miller, 2002).

Shirley's 'furrin' parts'

While Gaskell's vision of Charlotte as the cloistered daughter of the house continues to hold cultural sway, much recent criticism has challenged the strong association between Brontë and static local place that underpins this myth. Carl Plasa's analysis goes far beyond the well-established post-colonial readings of *Jane Eyre* (1847) to consider the ways in which Brontë's 'colonial imagination' shaped the breadth of her literary output, including juvenile writings about Africa, colonially oriented poetry such as 'The Letter', and coded references to the Irish Famine and Irish migration in *Shirley* (Plasa, 2004: x). Sally Shuttleworth makes a similar case about the extent of Brontë's preoccupation with exotic, foreign locales from Angria onwards, arguing that in the mature novels 'elements of foreign culture are placed within an English setting' in order to 'measure indigenous social and gender relations' (1996: 341). Charlotte Mathieson's chapter in this volume extends our understanding of Brontë's interest in the foreign by showing how Brontë's cultural afterlife has also been marked by a broad geographical range in her consideration of Brontë-related literary tourism in Brussels.

I aim to add to this growing body of work by bringing to light the extent of Brontë's interest in migration and mobility between places, as played out in her most globally oriented novel, *Shirley*. Though Brontë was undoubtedly fascinated by particular foreign locations in Europe, Africa and beyond, her writing also reveals a strong interest in migration and movement that transcends the boundaries of any particular place and which instead operates across a modern global spatial formation that exceeds local, national and colonial borders. Despite recent efforts to extend our understanding of the geographical range of Brontë's cultural legacy, this fascination with global space and mobility has not been the focus of sustained critical attention. Mobility and migration, after all, do not afford the same commemorative opportunities that are attached to concepts of rooted 'place', defined by ideas of memory, meaning and affective experience. Linking Brontë to particular locations – however globally dispersed those places may be – allows us to honour the writer's memory by experiencing her haunting presence, performing various site-specific rituals, and even purchasing souvenirs to aid our process of memorialisation.[1] By recognising Brontë's engagements with mobility and the global in *Shirley*, this chapter aims to reveal a breadth of creative vision and understanding in the Brontë oeuvre which has not always been recognised by either early proponents of the 'Brontë myth' such as Gaskell, or by those critics who have recently sought to extend the boundaries of this myth. As I shall show in subsequent sections of the chapter, this in turn opens up possibilities for tracing the ways in which Brontë's preoccupations with mobility were in dialogue with those of her friend Mary Taylor and subsequently reformulated and developed within Taylor's own feminist writings.

Foregrounding the global dimensions of *Shirley* should not, however, entail neglecting to recognise the strength of its preoccupation with the local. Though the novel is set amid the relative bustle and stir of the neighbouring Gormersal-Birstall district (Stevens, 1972: v), visions of local rootedness are present in the novel from its very first sentence. Here the curious image of 'an abundant shower of curates' falling 'thick on the hills' of the novel's 'north of England' locality suggests a strong blurring of the relationship between people and place which is continued throughout the text (Brontë, 2006: 5). The Yorke family bear the earthy weight of their defining locality in their names, while Shirley Keeldar and Caroline find a point of connection in their sense of a shared identity as 'Yorkshire girl[s]' (Brontë, 2006: 200). Moreover, the novel also pairs its strong invocation of the local with a penetrating analysis of enforced female stasis and confinement within domestic spheres. Caroline's life of tortured inertia after experiencing Robert Gerard Moore's initial rejection is highly concordant with the ideas of feminine sacrifice and domestic constraint perpetuated by Gaskell's biography. Indeed, Caroline increasingly merges with the haunting vision of Charlotte which is central to the 'Brontë myth' – reduced for large portions of the narrative to a state in which she is 'scarcely *living*' (Brontë, 2006: 354) and consumed by the same 'starved, ghostly longing' experienced by the novel's 'Old Maids' (2006: 174).

Yet, while *Shirley* is preoccupied with local place and domestic confinement, these concerns are also consistently paired with a much broader vision of global space. Indeed, the resolutely local image of curates falling 'thick on the hills' is swiftly reformulated and retracted when the line is repeated a few paragraphs later: 'Of late years, I say, an abundant shower of curates has fallen upon the north of England; but in eighteen-hundred-eleven-twelve that affluent rain had not descended' (Brontë, 2006: 5). The novel signals its movement away from the static local present by focusing upon the dramatic era of the Anglo-French wars, revealed by a mobile, omniscient narrator who bids the reader 'step into' the first sustained portrait of dinner at one of the curate's houses in Whinbury (Brontë, 2006: 6). *Shirley* soon proceeds to reveal the darker, destabilising forces which were 'heaving under the hills of the Northern counties' at this time (Brontë, 2006: 30): bad harvests, unemployment, food-riots and the machine breaking and violence associated with the Luddites. What is noticeable, however, is the way in which these local concerns are consistently situated within the broadest global framework. 'Condition of England' problems in the novel are in fact never the exclusive concern of the nation. Rather, Brontë is careful to plot her understanding of economic failures and successes within a far broader terrain, informed by a comprehension of the importance of the circulation of capital within global markets to British prosperity. The catalyst for the economic downturn which shapes much of the novel's plot is the lack of access to American markets after America ceased trade with Britain following its embroilment in the Anglo-French wars. Robert frequently reflects upon his desire for a change which would 'open our way in the West' (Brontë, 2006: 158), and it is these wider circumstances that ultimately inform his decision to court Shirley rather than Caroline. It is only upon the repeal of the Orders in Council in June 1812 that prosperity returns and that Caroline and Robert can finally marry alongside Shirley and Robert's brother, Louis Gerard Moore. Moreover, the novel is also deeply aware of the presence of the new settler world and of its economic potential. Numerous characters in the novel, including Robert, Louis, William Farren and, as I shall discuss below, Rose Yorke, Jessie Yorke and Shirley, consider emigrating to the southern hemisphere or to the American West in order to improve their prospects. These are both spaces which James Belich has shown were becoming available to British migrants during the 1810s (2009: 88–94) and that had become increasingly important within 'Condition of England' debates by the 1840s.

This awareness of modern global space informs the novel's linguistic and imagistic qualities as well as its take on economics. Local people and places are often described in a globally aware language that throws the local into broader relief. Mr Malone is an Irish man with a 'North-American-Indian sort of visage' (Brontë, 2006: 8), local women gossips are described as having 'tomahawk tongues' (2006: 166), and the 'West-Riding-clothing-district-of-Yorkshire rioters' yell' sounds as fearful to the narrator's ears as a Native American war cry. The language of emigration in particular repeatedly shapes the deeper textures of the novel, as when Shirley dreams of 'the green wilderness' (Brontë, 2006: 453) in her girlhood essay on 'Genius and Humanity' (2006: 457) or the novel's recurrent vision of the future is conceptualised as a distant 'land' to be 'reached': an 'Elf-land' with 'shores […] yet distant' (2006: 94). Thus, *Shirley*'s apparently staunchly local register breaks open to reveal far more polyphonic vocabularies and frames of reference, just as conversation at the curate's house in the novel's opening scene breaks into a 'confusion of tongues' akin to that issuing from 'three presumptuous Babylonish masons' (Brontë, 2006: 12).

It is within the parameters of this global spatial framework and sensibility – spanning European, British, American and settler distances and vocabularies – that Brontë gives range to her strong interest in migration and mobility.[2] Characters in *Shirley* frequently move across national boundaries, particularly when it suits their economic interests to do so. Most notably, Robert, as his name suggests, is 'but half a Briton' and marked by an over-determined foreignness that exceeds the parameters of his Anglo-Belgian identity (Brontë, 2006: 27). Like their brother, Hortense and Louis are also Belgian migrants with emphatically foreign characteristics. Even Hiram Yorke's local affiliations are complicated by his experiences of travel, which leave their trace in the pictures of Canadian and Italian views that adorn his home. As discussed above, numerous characters in the novel are associated with emigration to either America or Australasia, and these central references to migration are also echoed across a wider cast of minor characters in the novel. These include the rioters whose transportation to Australia Robert ultimately brings about, the dismissed workmen who Hiram Yorke helps to 'remove with their families' to districts in which work will be available (Brontë,

2006: 47), and 'the Antwerp girl' who Robert offers to employ as a servant for Hortense (2006: 84).

Despite the nostalgia for local place portrayed in the novel's concluding vision of the 'oak trees and nut trees' of Fieldhead Hollow (Brontë, 2006: 607), *Shirley* is ultimately more energised than hampered by its vision of global space and mobility. Robert's cosmopolitan understanding of foreign markets, shared by his ally, Shirley, is celebrated in contrast to the weaker understanding of his poor opponents. Indeed, the machine-breakers' understanding is linked to a marked provincialism that views even Belgium as what the Luddite Moses Barraclough terms 'a distant coast, another quarter and hemisphere of this globe' (Brontë, 2006: 115). Rather, it is the mobile, migrant and cosmopolitan characters Robert and Louis who succeed in consolidating their economic fortunes and personal happiness through their commitment to going 'Forward' (Brontë, 2006: 29). Though Brontë pays lip service to the plight of the Luddites, she is ultimately on the side of the masters whose awareness of global markets is contrasted with the fiercely local understanding of workers who refuse all dealings with 'furrin' parts' (2006: 123).

Shirley's characters can thus be viewed as inhabiting a highly mobile terrain that contrasts with the model of cloistered, feminine, local place – also apparent within the novel – which has become a dominant component of the 'Brontë myth'. Through pairing the local and the global in this way, Brontë reveals a sharp understanding of the ways in which local life was increasingly being shaped by its relationship to a new form of global space that encompassed both hemispheres. Furthermore, through her focus upon and ultimate celebration of characters who move across global space, Brontë reveals her understanding and acceptance of the importance of mobility within expanding global capitalist markets. These were, of course, developments of which Brontë had a deeply personal as well as intellectual comprehension through her long-standing friendship with the emigrant Mary Taylor.

'Wandering alone in strange countries': women on the move

In plotting *Shirley* within a global arena and demonstrating the necessity for the circulation of people and capital across this enlarged sphere, Brontë sets the stage for highly topical explorations of the extent to which women might have access to these same augmented fields of action. The novel's investigations of the plight of confined women such as Caroline repeatedly lead not only into explorations of the need for women to find work in order to sustain themselves, but also into an explicit recognition of their need to move in order to secure it. *Shirley* thus reveals an early propensity to view labour migration as a source of empowerment for women which was also evident within emerging feminist debates at mid-century. From the 1850s onwards, debates about emigration for single middle-class women in particular played an important part in the discussions of the Langham Place group, several of whose members countered ideas about shipping out 'redundant' women to become colonial wives by emphasising the opportunities for employment and independence that emigration to the settler world could bring (Piesse, 2016: 127–42).

In order to understand these trains of thought in *Shirley*, it is instructive to consider the novel in the light of Brontë's close friendship with the emigrant feminist Mary Taylor. Taylor first met Brontë and Ellen Nussey at Roe Head School where the three were to forge their lifelong friendships (Stevens, 1972: 9).[3] Raised in a politically radical household in Gomersal which Brontë often visited, Taylor was highly intellectual, personally intrepid and a firm proponent of women's rights. After working as a teacher in Germany, Taylor emigrated to Wellington, New Zealand, in 1845. As Brontë wrote in a letter to Emily Brontë in 1841, 'Mary has made up her mind that she can not and will not be a governess, a teacher, a milliner, a bonnet-maker nor housemaid. She sees no means of obtaining employment she would like in England, so she is leaving it' (Brontë, 1995–2004: I, 251). Taylor went on to lead an active and successful life in Wellington, building and renting out her own house and running a flourishing general store. During her time as a settler, she also wrote much of her novel *Miss Miles*, eventually published in 1890, and appears to have further developed the ideas about women's work, independence and experience of restrictive cultural expectations which were published as a series of essays in the feminist *Victoria Magazine* from 1865 and collected as *The First Duty of Women* in 1870 (Horowitz Murray, 1989: 142). Through her own emigration, Taylor was also a significant pioneer and shaper of feminist ideas about female labour emigration to New Zealand which flourished within *Victoria Magazine*'s precursor, the *English Woman's Journal*, through the writings of the Langham Place feminist Maria S. Rye in the late 1850s and early 1860s. Though Taylor moved back to England in 1859, she remained a frequent traveller and went on to co-write a collection of fascinating sketches based on her journeys through the Alps, *Swiss Notes by Five Ladies* (1875).

Taylor not only produced fiction, feminist essays and travel writing, but she was also a prolific writer of lively and engaging letters. Indeed, Taylor wrote several letters about Brontë at Gaskell's request which are widely excerpted in the *Life*, including a letter in which Taylor recalls Brontë's tearful but resolute refusal to join her in New Zealand (Stevens, 1972: 161). It is, however, the letters which Taylor wrote to Brontë herself that throw most light on the global, mobile elements of *Shirley* – dimensions of the novel which I am suggesting serve to complicate the more famous myth of rooted locality propagated by Gaskell. The earliest surviving New Zealand letter dates from July 1848 (Stevens, 1972: 62), when Brontë was in the process of writing *Shirley*. Letters winged their way between Haworth and Wellington until Brontë's death in 1855, forming a bridge between the Yorkshire parish and what most British people then perceived to be the very furthest reaches of the globe. Taylor's letters are consistently punchy, packed and full of the language of commerce. Thus, in July 1848, Taylor writes as follows: 'I think I told you I built a house. I get 12/- a week for it. Moreover in accordance with a late letter of John's I borrow money from him & Joe & buy cattle with it' (Brontë, 1995–2004: II, 88). She proceeds to speak of her hope that future prosperity would lead to even greater personal freedoms: 'If I could command £300 & £50 a year afterwards, I would "hallock" about N.Z. for a twelve-month then go home by way of India & write my travels which would prepare the way for my novel' (Brontë, 1995–2004: II, 88).

Though it is well known that Brontë had reservations about Taylor's emigration, Brontë's own letters to Taylor reveal a firm respect for her friend's decision. As Brontë wrote to Ellen Nussey as early as March 1845, 'Mary is in her element now – she has done right to go out to New Zealand' (1995–2004: I, 387). She repeats the same point to Ellen in a letter written just one week later: 'Mary Taylor finds herself free – and on that path for adventure and exertion to which she has so long been seeking admission [...] I repeat then, that Mary Taylor has done well to go out to New Zealand' (Brontë, 1995–2004: I, 388). Increasingly, Brontë seemed wistfully aware of the contrast between what she termed Taylor's 'active, happy and joyous life' in a letter to Margaret Wooler of August 1848 and her own feelings of confinement at Haworth (1995–2004: II, 107). Indeed, Taylor's letters appear to have directly inspired Brontë to increase the levels of her own activity and mobility. As Joan Stevens notes, it was Taylor's apparent pity for her friend's cloistered life in Haworth that led Brontë to write a full account of her exciting nocturnal railway journey to London with Anne Brontë in order to confirm their separate identities to publisher George Smith (Stevens, 1972: 61). Given Taylor's capacity to galvanise her friend into action, it is probable that the incident was itself inspired by Taylor – and telling that, as Stevens notes, Brontë's related letter was the only one which Taylor kept (Stevens, 1972: 61).[4]

Written as it was during 1848 and 1849, when the Taylor–Brontë correspondence was flourishing, it is evident that *Shirley*'s preoccupations with female work, migration and mobility were shaped by the friends' ongoing, long-distance dialogue. Just as Taylor's letters inspired Brontë to increased levels of activity, so too did the experiences and ideas they conveyed embed themselves deeply within the fabric of the novel she was writing at the time. This is most evident in the novel's portrayal of the sisters who emigrate to 'some region of the southern hemisphere' (Brontë, 2006: 145), Rose and Jessie Yorke. Indeed, Rose and Jessie were close portraits of Taylor and her cousin Martha, one of a number of Taylor family portraits in *Shirley* which Taylor deemed in a letter to Brontë of August 1850 to be very recognisable (Brontë, 1995–2004, II, 439). Rose and Caroline's meeting in Chapter 10 can therefore be viewed as a fairly faithful fictionalisation of Taylor and Brontë's debates about migration, female employment and women's rights. Like Taylor, Rose delivers powerful arguments against what her mother deems to be 'all womanly and domestic employment' (Brontë, 2006: 378) and is characterised by a strong desire to go 'wandering alone in strange countries' (2006: 377). Though Caroline expresses anxieties about the emigrant's life, her objections to Rose's powerful vision of female freedom gained through migration and active employment derive primarily from fear. The debate between them is itself won by Rose, just as Taylor's case for emigration appears to have persuaded Brontë at an intellectual level.

Beyond this most obvious engagement, *Shirley* also returns to themes of female mobility, migration and work in subtler and more peripheral ways. Though it is tempting to dismiss Hortense Moore as a comic character, she is also a single migrant woman who succeeds in securing a fulfilling life for herself in England. Far from being a redundant spinster, equivalent to the novel's English 'Old Maids' in Chapter 10, Hortense is 'ever breathlessly busy' (Brontë, 2006: 77) and secure in a strong sense of her own usefulness and self-worth. Similarly, Shirley, though a 'Yorkshire girl', is a boyish, mobile character who displays a marked facility with foreign parts through her perusal of the foreign sections of the newspaper and through her own personal experiences of travel. Shirley is also frequently associated with exotic or foreign attributes or possessions. Adorned in ornaments of gold and bright gems and possessing 'mobile […] speaking' features which cannot be 'interpreted all at once' (Brontë, 2006: 170), Shirley at her most powerful is mysterious, 'fair and imperial' (2006: 568). Like Rose, Shirley also frequently dreams of emigration. This is apparent both in the playful vision of emigrating to the Far West which she shares with Louis and in the wider imaginative life revealed in her girlhood essay. Though set in ancient England, the 'savage' inhabitants, 'burning sun' and thick, virgin forest that characterise her 'green wilderness' are very much the stuff of mid-Victorian settler narratives (Brontë, 2006: 453–4).

Even the novel's most rooted character, Caroline, frequently strains at the limits of the nation in her pursuit of activity and occupation. Her desire to 'to go to some very distant place' (Brontë, 2006: 180), while never realised, repeatedly surfaces in her shared imaginative life with Shirley. Upon the 'breezy walk over Nunnely Common' which cements their friendship (Brontë, 2006: 198), Caroline and Shirley create a vision of a wild and romantic landscape that blends Shirley's experiences of travelling in mountainous regions in the Scottish borders with Caroline's experiences of the Yorkshire moors. This vision of freedom of mobility is later extended into plans to voyage 'out into the North Atlantic' towards the Faroe Islands (Brontë, 2006: 230).

In keeping with Brontë's own personal views and decisions, *Shirley* ultimately restores more traditional forms of power to its central female characters. Thus, in the last chapter, the long-promised sea voyage that has been winding its course throughout the novel is finally repudiated as Robert decides to marry Caroline and give up his plans to emigrate to Canada. That Caroline's final words in *Shirley*, in answer to Robert's schemes for extensive improvement of the land, are 'Stilbro' Moor […] defies you, thank Heaven!' (Brontë, 2006: 606) suggests a final reunion of femininity and ideas of local, rooted place after their periods of trial separation in the novel. Similarly, Shirley's exotic fantasies of emigration to the Wild West or to the 'green wilderness' recede after she assumes the more passive role of Louis's tame 'leopardess' following their courtship (Brontë, 2006: 586). Caroline and Shirley's earlier dreams of mobility and freedom are ultimately warped into frightening images of unlocatable women who haunt the text from its margins: fleeting images of 'monstrous' mermaids in Shirley's imagined North Atlantic (Brontë, 2006: 232), terrifying 'foam-women' in Martin Yorke's book of fairy tales (2006: 532), or Caroline and

Shirley's own short-lived transformation into secret nocturnal rioters on the moor.

And yet, despite the novel's ultimate refusal to combine visions of mobility with the traditional feminine roles of wife and mother for which Shirley and Caroline are destined, it never entirely precludes this possibility for its single female characters. Indeed, it is the mobile, single women who choose alternative paths in the novel who are ultimately most rewarded. Hortense, as I have argued above, remains a successful migrant characterised by self-confidence and activity. Similarly, some futurity is permitted for both Rose and Jessie following their emigration. Though the narrator presciently records Jessie's death overseas, Rose lives, and is last envisaged sitting on the banks of a river, 'thinking' (Brontë, 2006: 145). The fate of both emigrant sisters is thus arguably preferable to Caroline and Shirley's sudden extinction from the plot following their marriages in the novel's hasty conclusion. Despite its predominant conservatism, the novel's ending in fact suggests that the stance of fierce localism which both Shirley and Caroline increasingly adopt as they renounce their girlish freedoms and hopes is not entirely satisfactory. Like the Luddites with whom they are linked in the riot scene, the reader is led to conclude that Shirley and Caroline are ultimately doomed for not embracing the wider prospects and facility with 'furrin' parts' they originally hoped for. Like the mermaids, rioters and leopardesses with which they are compared – and like Brontë herself – they become mythic, haunting figures who strain against boundaries but never break free.

Even as it affirms traditional bastions of female power, the novel thus also points towards the opening of new pathways for women which might take them beyond the limits of the local and the domestic. Shirley and Caroline's vibrant fantasies and memories of free movement and travel are carried forward by the novel's minor characters, who escape marriage plots in order to find activity, occupation and mobility in new worlds. Indeed, these are the dimensions of the novel which are likely to have inspired the feminist writer Phyllis Bentley to draw upon *Shirley* as inspiration for her 1932 novel *Inheritance*, adding further weight to Emma Liggins' case, made in this volume, for recognising Brontë's strong influence on the development of a feminist literary tradition.[5] Despite its conservative ending, the novel thus registers an early interest in the new modes of female mobility and feminist freedom which Brontë was aware of through her friendship and correspondence with the pioneering emigrant Mary Taylor.

What Rose did next: the writings of Mary Taylor

Brontë's friendship and correspondence with Taylor had a marked impact upon *Shirley*'s preoccupation with female mobility, emigration and work. This section will explore how this dialogue also deeply informed and shaped Taylor's own writing. Indeed, while it would be inaccurate to claim that influence always ran in a unilateral direction from Brontë to Taylor, Taylor's letters to Brontë reveal a playful competitiveness with her friend that spurred her on to reach her own creative potential. Thus, in April 1849, she writes of her authorial ambitions in the following characteristically witty and confident terms: 'I write at my novel a little & think of my other book. […] It is my child, my baby & I <u>assure you</u> such a wonder as never was. I intend him when full grown to revolutionise society & faire époque in history. In the meantime I'm doing a collar in crochet work' (Brontë, 1995–2004: II, 199). Here, the underlined 'assure you' and the scale of assertion itself is suggestive of Taylor's ambition to approach the level of Brontë's success following *Jane Eyre* – a success which, as Taylor told Ellen Nussey in March 1855, was gaining Taylor 'a great literary reputation' by proxy even in settler New Zealand (Brontë, 1995–2004: II, 586). Taylor's published writing eventually works through her preoccupation with Brontë both by fictionalising the dynamics that underpinned their friendship and by developing many of the ideas about female mobility and employment which are evident in earlier but less radical form in *Shirley*. Reading *Miss Miles* and *Swiss Notes* in the light of their relationship to *Shirley* and Taylor's personal and creative dialogues with Brontë highlights a productive reciprocity between the two writers.

Telling the story of four protagonists, the working-class Sarah or 'Miss Miles', and the more genteel Maria, Dora, and Amelia, *Miss Miles* has been described by Janet Horowitz Murray as an innovative form of '*feminist* bildungsroman' that emphasises the importance of education in women's development and the power of female friendship over heterosexual romance (Horowitz Murray, 1990: xx). Drawing upon the ideas outlined in Taylor's *First Duty*, the novel is centrally concerned with its female characters' difficulties in finding opportunities for work and activity, plotting the trials faced by each woman in their pursuit of a living and the support networks formed between them. The novel thus owes much of its power to the mature feminist perspective and concerns of Taylor, who did not publish the novel until near the end of her life in 1890.

And yet, despite its radical agenda and late publication date, parts of the novel are contemporaneous with *Shirley*. One of Taylor's letters to Brontë indicates that one and a half volumes of *Miss Miles* had been written in New Zealand by as early as 1852 (Stevens, 1972: 109, 145). As Horowitz Murray observes, the early parts of the novel are in fact clearly shaped by Taylor's friendship and dialogue with Brontë during the 1840s and 1850s (Horowitz Murray, 1990: xii). This is most evident in Taylor's depiction of Dora and Maria, whose friendship develops during childhood and sustains them throughout adult life. Dora – feisty, difficult, affectionate and physically unattractive – lives a life of terrible confinement in her stepfather's house following her mother's death. Left to effectively 'die by slow atrophy' (Taylor, 1990: 347) and eventually faced with abuse by her stepbrothers, she is supported only by her correspondence with Maria, who has relocated in order to set up a school following her own parents' death. These letters, incorporated into *Miss Miles*, strongly echo the dynamics of Taylor's friendship with Brontë following her emigration to New Zealand. Indeed, the language used to describe Dora and Maria's separation by only ten miles often seems hyperbolic in this reduced context. Thus, Dora feels that Maria's letters 'were all that held her mind fast to the actual world', despite appearing only 'at intervals of a month at least' (Taylor, 1990: 342) and describes Maria as inhabiting a 'new world' (1990: 111). The imagery of emigration and the ocean voyage that winds through *Shirley* also consistently seeps into Taylor's account of Dora and Maria's lesser degree of separation, as when Maria asks Dora: 'If I sink in the deep sea […] why should I call you after me? You at least are on land, though but a barren land' (Taylor, 1990: 109). Indeed, such are the striking parallels between these elements of the novel and the Brontë–Taylor correspondence that Stevens suggests that *Miss Miles* may have drawn upon real letters written by Brontë which Taylor is known to have later destroyed (Stevens, 1972: 145). Glimpses of Brontë are also visible in the portrait of the intelligent but fearful Amelia, who refuses the opportunity of work proposed to her by her former servant and friend Sarah Miles upon her family's bankruptcy, and soon afterwards dies.

Clearly reflecting on Taylor's friendship with Brontë, and commenced and largely executed in tandem with *Shirley*, *Miss Miles* is also a remarkably similar novel in terms of its themes and setting. Like *Shirley*, it is set in the Gomersal-Birstall district during a period of political unrest and poverty – in this case taking its 1890s readership back sixty years into the era of Chartism and Taylor and Brontë's own Yorkshire girlhoods. As in *Shirley* also, the 'Condition of England' dimensions of the text are largely usurped by the novel's deeper interest in the economic and social condition of women and their attempts to secure independence through paid employment. Migration, in another echo of *Shirley*, is key to success in this respect. Thus, Maria leaves her 'native town' for the 'thriving place' of neighbouring Repton to open a school (Taylor, 1990: 79–80). Similarly, Sarah moves to Baumforth to learn singing in order to support herself. Dora, following her long domestic tribulations, finds refuge with Maria before launching a career as a touring lecturer, planning to eventually speak on women's rights. The recurring motifs of the novel are in fact girls on the move: Sarah's memory of herself as a 'girl sliding down the hill' with friends in the snow (Taylor, 1990: 290), or Maria's recollection of Dora as a 'girl running across the fields' to meet her (1990: 100).

Unlike *Shirley*, however, even married women in *Miss Miles* are able to find fulfilling employment. While both Sarah and Maria marry towards the end of the novel, marriage remains a peripheral part of their stories and does not impact upon their levels of activity. By the novel's conclusion, Dora, Maria and Maria's elderly genteel friend Miss Everard are all 'energetic and busy' (Taylor, 1990: 453) in running a new boarding school and 'bound by a tie' (1990: 447) of friendship that far surpasses that between the more peripheral suitors and their brides. Sarah goes so far as to punch her suitor Sam upon his first indication of romantic interest in her and is decidedly in control of the relationship to the end. Significantly, *Miss Miles*'s female characters also share a commitment to doing any kind of work in order to succeed, a level of flexibility modelled by the novel's highly intelligent and adaptable working-class heroine, Sarah. Only Amelia, who both chooses to stay within the confines of her relatively comfortable but stifling home and to protect her own class status by refusing the dressmaking work proposed by Sarah, fails to prosper and accordingly fades away from the novel in a comparable way to Shirley and Caroline in Brontë's *Shirley*.

Given *Miss Miles*'s radical stance on female work, mobility and independence, it is initially surprising that the novel does not take its female characters into the global terrain with which Taylor was herself so familiar. Indeed, *Miss Miles* is a more deeply provincial novel than *Shirley* and does not share the full range of its global horizons. To some extent this may link to Taylor's commitment to portraying accurately the real pressures of confinement and limited opportunity faced by the majority of women in the early Victorian period. Like *Shirley*, *Miss Miles* ends on a somewhat pessimistic and realistic note, observing that the central characters 'had many changes and sorrows, so we had better leave them in sight of that paradise which never comes but at the end of a novel' (Taylor, 1990: 466). However, closer consideration reveals that Taylor's

global awareness nevertheless operates as a crucial driving force in the
novel, albeit in subtle ways. While Taylor's commitment to representing
the 'narrow circle' of women's opportunities in the 1830s does not permit
her to take her characters much further than Baumforth in their pursuit
of work and freedom (Taylor, 1990: 334), the conceptual flexibility that
permits her to counter social conventions and normative representations
of gender more deeply than Brontë appears to be shaped by the sense
of shifting perspectives and enlarged horizons that Taylor herself was
experiencing during the period of the novel's conception and composition. Written largely from the very furthest reaches of the British empire,
Miss Miles in fact perfectly embodies the radical outsider's perspective
often associated with New Zealand at this time.[6] Indeed, the novel frequently draws connections between radical ideas and the radical reori-
entations in space that are evocative of the migrant's experience. Thus, in
one fascinating scene, the narrator addresses the reader as follows:

> Were you ever quite at your ease with all the world against you, not merely
> some one person, or even many, but the whole world?
>   Did you ever try not to fall out of your armchair? Did you ever grasp the
> arms in terror, and strive with all the might of your trembling limbs to keep
> yourself in the middle of it? You have never done this because you thought
> it would be impossible to fall out if you tried. Yet this is what you would do
> if, looking round, you saw that the earth was gone, sunk far away beneath
> you, and your fall would be fearful.
>
> (Taylor, 1990: 294)

This passage describes the dawning of Sarah's new consciousness, as she
begins to question the values of her close-knit community and to challenge the forms of control which men exert over women through sex and
marriage.

Elsewhere, the novel makes similar links between a shift in location
and original, counter-cultural thought – what Sarah terms the quest 'to
widen her horizon' (Taylor, 1990: 242). Thus Maria's future husband, Mr
Branksome, continually attempts to persuade her to marry him by asking her not to be held hostage to the 'customs of the country' (Taylor,
1990: 159) in refusing his unconventional, largely epistolary suit. Other
sections of the novel read from a perspective akin to that of a practitioner
of ethnographic participant observation, as Sarah casts her alienated and
penetrating eyes as a 'looker-on' (Taylor, 1990: 202) upon the customs of
idleness and atrophy that characterise middle-class female domestic life
in Amelia's home; pondering 'the mysterious rites of gentlefolks visiting'

(1990: 210) or the puzzle of Amelia's father standing 'on his native hearthrug' (1990: 211).

In one particularly resonant scene, Sarah and a group of friends go so far as to enact a version of the settlement process experienced by Taylor herself. This is significantly after Sarah has become involved in a Chartist rally, finding herself inspired by the speakers and eager to try her own oratorical skills:

> She had raised her clenched fist in the face of the authorities. All the girls applauded. […]
> 'Look,' she said, 'at that grass; how straight up it grows! Let's build a house round it!'
>   It was a square yard or two of level ground by the waterside. Near it were some elder bushes, with their thick buds just burst. They gathered boughs of them, and enclosed the bit of level with a fence about a foot high.
>
> (Taylor, 1990: 186)

The house built by women orators stands in marked contrast to the restrictive domestic spaces that stifle Amelia or *Shirley*'s Caroline. Rather, the sequence and the energy invoked is strongly reminiscent of the power and agency that Taylor was experiencing as she built a house and ran a business in Wellington. While Sarah and the other female protagonists of the novel are ultimately subject to local limits in their pursuit of work and freedom, the novel thus incorporates mobility and the global perspective deep within the fabric of its conceptual framework – using it to explode the 'customs of the country' that Taylor had left behind her and allowing her characters to reap some of the rewards of freedom and self-empowerment which are denied to *Shirley*'s heroines.

The links between female mobility and female empowerment which are present in *Shirley* and developed within *Miss Miles* are, however, perhaps most fully realised in Taylor's *Swiss Notes*. Published in 1875, *Swiss Notes* constitutes a co-authored collection of journal entries written by Taylor and four young female friends who she led on an expedition to the Alps: Grace Hirst, writing as 'Grace', Frances Maria Richardson ('Fanny'), Marion Pollock Ross ('Marion') and Marion Sellers Neilson ('Minnie').[7] Writing as 'Frau Mutter', Taylor is the 'moving spirit' of the book and of the party, frequently interjecting in what appears to be an editorial capacity and taking charge of her companions on a series of adventurous travels and mountain ascents (Taylor, 2003: 7). In emphasising female friendship through both its content and collaborative form, the text is in many ways a continued exploration and extension of the themes that Brontë initially addressed in *Shirley* and Taylor then extended in *Miss Miles*. Indeed, in the Alps of *Swiss Notes*, women are finally permitted access to the sublime, romantic landscapes that Brontë could ultimately only allow Caroline to imagine and require Shirley to forget. Thus, chasms in *Swiss Notes* are transformed from the symbols of desperate disempowerment visualised by Caroline when she pictures the distance separating herself and Robert into stimulating practical challenges. Likewise, mountains become exciting new terrains to be mastered rather than inaccessible regions of fantasy or memory.

Far removed from the limitations of local place that restrict the paths of characters in both Brontë and Taylor's novels to different extents, however, the Alps in *Swiss Notes* also constitute a testing ground in which women can fully realise their capacities for heroism and independence through intense activity and mobility. Clad in mountain boots, the five 'heroines of the story' (Taylor, 2003: 41) are consistently dynamic and energetic as they travel in pursuit of adventure and pleasure. Thus, 'Minnie' is described as 'equal to anything – except sitting still' while Fanny is described as 'never known to be out of breath on the steepest ascent' (Taylor, 2003: 6). The pace of the narrative is fast, encompassing a series of climbs that culminate in the ascent of Mont Blanc, stays in hotels and conversations with other travellers and locals. The women consistently depict themselves as undertaking feats of extreme mobility and exertion as they go about 'jumping almost impossible crevasses' (Taylor, 2003: 39) or navigating 'steep ice slopes, sweeping away into unfathomable depths' (2003: 38). Though the authors are tourists rather than workers, Taylor also remains notably fixated upon employment and commerce and is often more interested in the working arrangements for mountain guides than in describing Alpine landscapes.

As in *Miss Miles* and *Shirley*, this preoccupation with mobility, activity and work is also paired with a playful inversion of traditional gender roles. Invigorated by her journey through what has historically been viewed as the 'male zone' of the Alps (Colley, 2010: 110), Frau Mutter delights in taking issue with a male traveller who 'demurred to the propriety of ladies making ascents' (Taylor, 2003: 16) while Grace describes the women's moment of 'revenge' (2003: 57) when a disapproving guide himself slipped down an ice slope. Indeed, *Swiss Notes* is frequently fascinated by confined or disempowered men, including a man who becomes sick following a climb, a group of young male musicians who play to a small audience, and are therefore inadequately remunerated, and a group of monks whose 'privation and solitude' (Taylor, 2003: 48) Marion deeply pities following the women's stay in a mountain refuge. By taking its middle-class heroines into the Alps, *Swiss Notes* thus comes close to finally exorcising the ghostly figures of Caroline, Shirley, Amelia and even Brontë herself, compounding their release by projecting images of confined men in their place.

Yet, while *Swiss Notes* realises the possibilities of female mobility to a greater extent than both *Shirley* and *Miss Miles*, it is telling that even this predominantly optimistic text ends on a non-committal and ambiguous note. After its joyous romps through the mountains, *Swiss Notes* concludes with a return to England and Taylor's account of a strange dream in which the women become lost in a Glasgow alleyway and are ultimately separated: 'We are still wandering about the world apart. Shall we ever find each other again?' (Taylor, 2003: 105). The mournful, inconclusive endings of all three texts thus suggests, to varying degrees, the impossibility of fully realising the freedoms envisaged for their female protagonists within the context of the social, cultural and economic constraints that dictated many women's lives even by the 1890s. Upon returning from the utopian realm of the Alps, Taylor loses confidence in the visions of freedom and sorority which *Swiss Notes* has promoted. Rather, it was the younger generation – that of the four young women who co-wrote *Swiss Notes* – who would be the true beneficiaries of the pathways carved out by Brontë and Taylor. Indeed, Marion Sellers Neilson went on to become a suffragette, Grace Hirst a global traveller and Frances Richardson's sister, Katharine, a leading mountaineer. As Taylor predicted in *The First Duty of Women*: 'It will soon be impossible to find an "unprotected female." The next generation will wonder to hear of a woman – perhaps forty years old – being unable to perform the operation of getting a railway ticket and seating herself in a carriage without some one to help and guide her' (1870: 131). For women of Brontë and Taylor's generation, access to the wider horizon, whether via a nocturnal flight to London or a trailblazing, exceptional voyage to New Zealand, too often remained intermittent or altogether out of reach.

Conclusion

This chapter has argued that *Shirley* reveals a side of Brontë that has not survived into the dominant 'Brontë myth'. The novel's 'remote bypaths' (Brontë, 2006: 368) consistently lead into a mobile, global field of action about which Brontë was evidently curious, and to a significant extent enthusiastic. Moreover, this is a field of action within which female characters – albeit to varying extents – are permitted to operate. Recognising this dimension of *Shirley* makes it possible to map Brontë's understanding of place, work and gender relations within a global and migratory, as well as a European or colonial framework. Understanding the global dimensions of *Shirley* also enables us to assess how this novel intersected with and influenced the writings of Mary Taylor. Drawing significant inspiration from Brontë, Taylor's writings took her friend's explorations of links between female mobility, work and independence to more radical conclusions and in turn helped pave the way for the greater feminist freedoms experienced by a new generation of female friends.

Notes

1 See Mathieson, Chapter 3 in this volume.
2 This interest in mobility and migration may well help to explain *Shirley*'s popularity with Victorian and early twentieth-century feminist writers, such as Vera Brittain and Phyllis Bentley.
3 Unless otherwise indicated, all details of Taylor's life are sourced from Stevens (1972).
4 As Janet Horowitz Murray notes, Taylor's letters had previously provided the impetus for Charlotte and Emily to go to school in Brussels. Taylor also prompted Charlotte to return to England when she was pining for the married professor Monsieur Heger (Horowitz Murray, 1990: xi).
5 See Chapter 7.
6 See Piesse (2016: 135). See also pp. 139–42 for an earlier reading of Taylor's *Victoria Magazine* essays in the light of her emigration to New Zealand.
7 See Marshall and Brown (2003). All references to *Swiss Notes* and all biographical information about its authors are sourced from this edition.

References

Belich, James (2009) *Replenishing the Earth: The Settler Revolution and the Rise of the Anglo-World, 1783–1939*, Oxford: Oxford University Press.
Brontë, Charlotte (1995–2004) *The Letters of Charlotte Brontë*, ed. Margaret Smith, 3 vols., Oxford: Clarendon Press.
—— (2006) *Shirley*, London: Penguin.
Colley, Ann C. (2010) *Victorians in the Mountains: Sinking the Sublime*, Farnham: Ashgate.
Gaskell, Elizabeth (1997) *The Life of Charlotte Brontë*, ed. Elisabeth Jay, London: Penguin.

Horowitz Murray, Janet (1989) 'The first duty of women: Mary Taylor's writings in *Victoria Magazine*', *Victorian Periodicals Review*, 22.4, 141–7.

—— (1990) 'Introduction', in Mary Taylor, *Miss Miles*, ed. Janet Horowitz Murray, Oxford: Oxford University Press, pp. vii–xxiv.

Marshall, Peter A. and Jean K. Brown (2003) 'The identification of the five ladies', in Mary Taylor, *Swiss Notes by Five Ladies: An Account of Touring and Climbing in 1874*, ed. Peter A. Marshall and Jean K. Brown, Lancaster: Peter A. Marshall, pp. 107–46.

Miller, Lucasta (2002) *The Brontë Myth*, London: Vintage.

Piesse, Jude (2016) *British Settler Emigration in Print, 1832–1877*, Oxford: Oxford University Press.

Plasa, Carl (2004) *Critical Issues: Charlotte Brontë*, Basingstoke: Palgrave Macmillan.

Shuttleworth, Sally (1996) 'The dynamics of cross-culturalism in Charlotte Brontë's fiction', in Eleanor McNees (ed.), *The Brontë Sisters: Critical Assessments*, 4 vols., Mountfield: Helm Information, vol. IV, pp. 340–52.

Stevens, Joan (ed.) (1972) *Mary Taylor: Friend of Charlotte Brontë – Letters from New Zealand and Elsewhere*, Auckland: Auckland University Press.

Taylor, Mary (1870) *The First Duty of Women: A Series of Articles Reprinted from the Victoria Magazine, 1865–1870*, London: Victoria Press.

—— (1990) *Miss Miles*, ed. Janet Horowitz Murray, Oxford: Oxford University Press.

—— (2003) *Swiss Notes by Five Ladies: An Account of Touring and Climbing in 1874*, ed. Peter A. Marshall and Jean K. Brown, Lancaster: Peter A. Marshall.

3

Brontë countries: nation, gender and place in the literary landscapes of Haworth and Brussels

Charlotte Mathieson

The legacy of Charlotte Brontë is inextricably bound up with place: even before the author's death in 1855, intrigued readers had begun to visit Haworth parsonage, and the publication of Elizabeth Gaskell's *Life of Charlotte Brontë* in 1857 further encouraged a steady stream of visitors in the following years. With the establishment of a Brontë museum in 1895 and the acquisition of the parsonage by the Brontë Society in 1928, the Brontë literary tourist industry at Haworth has continued to grow throughout the twentieth century to present numbers of around 75,000 visitors a year.[1] The landscape of 'Brontë country' also resonates in print, with numerous guides to literary tourism in the region and a growing field of literary and critical discussion of touristic practices in Haworth emerging in recent years (see Gardiner, 1992; Watson, 2006; Alexander, 2008; Tetley and Bramwell, 2011; Barnard, 2011).

The focus of critical attention on Haworth, while important in its own right, has obscured the legacy of Charlotte Brontë at another site that was prominent in both her life and works: the Pensionnat Heger and surrounding locale of the Quartier Isabelle in Brussels, Belgium. It was here that Charlotte, along with her sister Emily, travelled in February 1842 to improve their proficiency in foreign languages, staying until October of that year when the death of their Aunt Branwell necessitated their return home; following this, Charlotte returned to Brussels alone at the start of 1843 and stayed for a further year. Brussels was a signifi-cant and shaping force in Charlotte Brontë's novels *The Professor* (1857) and *Villette* (1853) and as such there is no shortage of criticism on the city's presence in her novels. So too has Charlotte's time in Brussels attracted much biographical interest focused on her relationship with Monsieur Heger, husband of the Pensionnat Heger's owner and French teacher to Charlotte and Emily, and on whom the character of Monsieur Paul in *Villette* is based.[2]

Less readily discussed, however, is Charlotte Brontë's afterlife in Brussels itself, where generations of readers have gone in search of a 'Brontë country' to be traced in the city's streets. While the culture of literary tourism in Brussels is nowhere near the scale of the industry that has developed at Haworth, it nonetheless bears consideration for the alternative narratives of Charlotte Brontë that are plotted into the cityscape: Brontë's Brussels journeys resist straightforward interpretation as narratives of female independence and autonomy, full as they are of ambivalence and struggle. But nonetheless, here in the Belgian capital Charlotte developed a sense of independence away from home and her sisters, and in a new national context. Reading this identity as it is crafted through and into the Brussels cityscape offers new approaches to and perspectives on the cultural locating of Brontë and her works.

This chapter seeks to reassert the presence of Brontë in Brussels through analyses of literary tourists' accounts of their journeys to and around the Pensionnat Heger. Reading these narratives within a critical framework of literary tourism theory, I aim to demonstrate how Brussels literary tourism is situated within and contributes to the Brontë legacy more broadly, particularly with regard to the parallel mythologisation of the Brontë sisters at Haworth parsonage. I focus on two themes that have emerged as the dominant issues at stake in the legacy of Brontë tourism at Haworth to date: gender and nation. While Haworth serves to reiterate Charlotte Brontë's place as an English, female writer, I suggest that Brussels offers a space where an alternative narrative unfolds, one that offers possibilities for reading the crafting of female independence through cosmopolitan interactions, and in doing so provides a crucial counterpart to the Haworth myth in both the historical assessment and future trajectory of Charlotte Brontë's legacies and afterlives.

Brontë myths

By way of situating Brussels within Charlotte Brontë's legacy, it is useful to start by considering how the place of the Brontë parsonage at Haworth has been put to cultural work in accounts of the author's afterlife. Lucasta

Miller identifies that Charlotte Brontë's legacy can be defined by two 'distinct and conflicting myths': 'the positive myth of female self-creation embodied by her autobiographical heroines, Jane Eyre and Lucy Snowe' in contrast with the idea of Charlotte as 'a quiet and trembling creature, reared in total seclusion, a martyr to duty and a model of Victorian femininity'. 'The second', Miller adds, was 'designed to deflect attention from the first' (2002: 2). Place has been central to sustaining the latter myth: Charlotte's representation of the sisters in the 1850 Preface to *Wuthering Heights* as naive, reclusive women 'relied on an exaggeratedly romantic view of Haworth as a place of complete isolation inhabited only by mythic "unlettered moorland hinds and rugged moorland squires"' (Miller, 2002: 24). If this image was perpetuated by Gaskell's *Life of Charlotte Brontë*, whose opening pages depict Haworth as an isolated, remote place where female domesticity reigns, then it has been further extrapolated through the development of the Brontë parsonage into a tourist site. In the space of the parsonage a distinctly gendered narrative of feminine domesticity is plotted which is intently focused on the sisters' biography and which collapses the three individual authors into a single, domestic unit of 'the Brontë sisters': the effect, as Nicola Watson notes, is that Haworth 'dramatizes female authorship as unsuccessful to the point of invisibility' (2006: 92). This construct of the sisters is, as Watson further notes, a retrospective formation that has been 'made into the likeness of the Brontës subsequently, and so betrays more explicitly what the culture wished to make of the sisters' (2006: 92). The cultural weight that this image carries is clearly evident in the strength of association attributed to 'the mythic status of Haworth as a pilgrimage site', held in 'almost religious awe' by 'a fully-fledged cult [...] complete with pilgrims and relics' (Miller, 2002: 36, 98).

Haworth enshrines the myth of secluded domesticity and ideal femininity, and so too does it work to locate the myth of the Brontës within the nation, inscribing their place as specifically English authors. The growth of literary tourism in the nineteenth century was coterminous with the rise of cultural nationalism, and Haworth is an apt example of how a literary site has been inscribed within the national cultural landscape.[3] While the novels themselves connote strong associations with the surrounding locale through evocative descriptions of the Yorkshire moors, this has been further capitalised upon in the marketing of 'Brontë country' and in the work of the local tourist board to 'aggressively and successfully' embed the parsonage 'within a generalised "heritage" landscape' (Watson, 2006: 92).[4] In this way, the Brontë legacy's location within the nation-place is not just a neutral by-product of its geographical situation but specifically produced to emphasise the place of the authors as embedded within the historical national map.

If Haworth locates the myth of ideal Victorian femininity within a national setting, so too has this emphasis on the parsonage as prime Brontë location served to deflect attention away from the site where the 'positive myth of female self-creation' came into being. While the act of female self-creation was tempered by feelings of loneliness and displacement in a foreign city, the Belgian capital nonetheless provides a site where Charlotte could develop as an autonomous individual away from her sisters, the domestic space of home, and in a distinctly cosmopolitan setting. In Brontë's fiction these features are central in the creation of characters such as Jane Eyre and Lucy Snowe, as well as informing the use of Belgium as a site where new models of national identity are encountered and negotiated. In what follows, we will see that Brussels has similarly provided a space where alternative approaches to gender and nation have shaped the legacy and afterlife of Charlotte Brontë, in ways that provide an important counterpart to the mythologisation of Charlotte's legacy at the Haworth parsonage.

Literary tourists in Brussels

As a foreign location, Brussels has a much more complex relationship with the Brontë legacy than Haworth does: Charlotte's works are less than generous on the subject of the Belgian people, and her writing of the *pensionnat* owner, Madame Heger, into the formidable character of Madame Beck of *Villette* was such that the family were not forthcoming about remembering or memorialising her time there. The Brontë legacy was further compromised by the demolishing of the Pensionnat Heger as part of an extensive regeneration of the Quartier Isabelle in 1909, and, as such, there has until recently been no obvious focal point for literary tourists in search of Brontë's Brussels. Yet it is this openness of the space, free from master narratives that seek to construct and market the Brontë mythology, which has allowed for alternative discursive formations of Charlotte Brontë's legacy to come into play. Away from the domestic space of the parsonage, detached from narratives of the three sisters, and determined by the particular spaces of the city streets, Brussels serves to evoke a legacy of female authorship that figures as significant in histories of Charlotte's legacy, and which it is necessary to revive in the ongoing production of her afterlife in the future.

In the late nineteenth and early twentieth centuries, following Charlotte's death and up until the *pensionnat*'s demolition in 1909, there was a small but sustained interest in the Brussels locations of Charlotte Brontë's life and works. The accounts that follow include articles by a young American girl, Adeline Trafton; the American writer, Theodore Wolfe; the British writer, Gerald Cumberland, whose visit hinges upon the anticipated demolition of the *pensionnat*; and an anonymous visitor to the site, as well as reflections from two women, Frederika Macdonald and Janet Harper, who were schoolgirls at the *pensionnat* in the years after Charlotte Brontë's visit. There are also accounts drawn from the more substantial research of Marion Harland, whose piece 'In "Villette"' forms part of the book *Where Ghosts Walk: The Haunts of Familiar Characters in History and Literature* (1898), and Marion Spielmann, whose centenary piece in the *Times Literary Supplement* appeared in the wake of the publication of Brontë's letters to M. Heger in *The Times* in 1913 and marked an important moment in preserving the vanishing history of the rue d'Isabelle.[5] After 1916, it appears from extant sources that there was a subsequent decline in literary tourism publications until recent years in which there has been a rediscovery of Brontë in Brussels, as recorded in Helen MacEwan's *Down the Belliard Steps: Discovering the Brontës in Brussels* (2012).

The earliest known account of literary tourism in Brussels is that of the American Adeline Trafton, published in *Scribner's Magazine* in 1871. Trafton describes how her party of American girls find themselves on an impromptu search for Brontë's locations on one day of their holiday in the city. It is a hopeful, speculative excursion which begins only with their recalling 'was not the scene of *Villette* laid in Brussels? Is not Charlotte Brontë's boarding-school here? I am sure it is. Suppose we seek it out – we four girls alone' (Trafton, 1871: 186). They have no guide but their memory of the novel and how 'Lucy Snow [*sic*] reached the city alone and at night? […] This must be the park'; as they walk, they gradually uncover the route across the park, arriving at the statue of 'some military hero' and then descending the flight of steps 'which [Lucy] descended, and found instead of the inn, the pensionnat of Madame Beck' (Trafton, 1871: 187). Immediately noticeable in this account is that their impulse for tourism is self-inspired by personal desire to locate the text rather than following a prescribed narrative as suggested by a guidebook. This is evident in Theodore Wolfe's later account of how, on holiday in Brussels, his party sets out on 'the accomplishment of one of the cherished projects of our lives, the searching out of the localities associated with Charlotte

Brontë's unhappy school-life' (1885: 542). While this might be a long-cherished project, the journey occurs only after they 'had "done" Brussels after the approved fashion' (Wolfe, 1885: 542), thus clearly locating the Brontë tour as off the beaten track of typical tourist destinations. Marion Harland's later account, however, suggests that 'it is doubtful if we should have come to the miniature Paris' if it were not for the Brontë connection: 'we are here because Brussels is Villette, and an impulse we are ready, in the end, to respect as inspiration, moved us to see, with bodily vision, a locality familiar to the mind's eye' (2000: 79). Again, though, they have no guide and must seek out the route by way of guesswork, accompanied by a sense of trepidation: Harland's party heard rumours that the *pensionnat* is soon to be demolished, and, as they approach the top of the Belliard steps, she notes that '*Fin-de-siècle* scepticism halts us even here' (Harland, 2000: 80).

Tourists in the late nineteenth century, however, were met by the sight of the Pensionnat Heger at the bottom of the Belliard steps: 'a handsome house, large, square, white, with a plentiful complement of windows, a very model of monumental and prosperous respectability' as Harland writes (2000: 79). The *pensionnat* was still a fully functioning school until the end of the nineteenth century; nevertheless, the tourists – most of them visiting in the quiet summer months – each succeed in gaining entrance at the mention of the Brontë connection and are given tours, sometimes reluctantly, by the remaining Heger inhabitants. In the accounts that unfold at the site of the *pensionnat*, there is much that is highly resonant both with experiences at Haworth, and with the broader framework of literary tourism.

Especially prevalent for these tourists is the impression that the house, and in particular the garden, is haunted by a ghostly presence that lends an indefinable yet significant atmosphere to the place. Trafton's account is indicative in finding that, despite a number of changes to the garden, 'the whole place was strangely familiar and pleasant to our eyes' (1871: 188). Recalling scenes from *Villette* in which Lucy wanders in the *pensionnat* garden beneath 'old and huge fruit trees', most notably 'a Methuselah of a pear-tree, dead, all but a few boughs' (Brontë, 2004: 117), Trafton writes of her sense of familiarity at finding the 'row of giant pear trees – huge, misshapen, gnarled – that bore no fruit to us but associations vivid as memories' (1871: 188). While the place itself is empty – 'the pupils were off for the long vacation' – it is noted, in contrast, 'how full the place was to us' as a result of the resonant memories it holds (Trafton, 1871: 188). Trafton's feeling that every part of the place is heavy with association is typical of the emotional investment often afforded to heritage sites, imbued with feelings of nostalgia that remain undefinably vague and yet of central importance. As Juliet John writes, heritage tourism depends on 'an emotional attitude to the past' and involves an 'almost spiritual investment' in the value of places which offer 'a sense of organic and emotional connection to our ancestors, a sense of roots and of belonging' (2011: 253). Such impressions are discernible in Wolfe's account, where 'the sense of familiarity with the vicinage grew as we observed our surroundings', and in the garden he notes how 'the coolness and quiet and, more than all, the throng of vivid associations which fill the place tempted us to linger' (1885: 543, 546). For Wolfe, nostalgia comes from the feeling of return to a place once known: 'the garden is not a spacious, nor even a pretty one, and yet it seemed to us singularly pleasing and familiar, – as if we were revisiting it after an absence' (1885: 546).

In Gerald Cumberland's account, this impression goes a step further in that the spirit of the place seems to come alive as a realisable presence: 'one can still wander through the house with Villette [*sic*] in one's hand, and live again those vivid and memorable scenes that have been painted for all time' (1911: 606). Noticeable here is that the feeling is not just of familiarity but of the place being haunted by past spirits that appear as 'vivid' and 'memorable' scenes: this is expressed more fully by Trafton who finds that 'the very leaves overhead, the stones in the walls around us whispered a story as we walked to and fro where little feet, that tired even then of life's rough way, had gone long years before' (1871: 188). The sense of ghostly haunting is, as Watson notes, a key source of the appeal of literary tourism, in which tourists 'actively seek out the anti-realist experience of being haunted, of forcefully realizing the presence of an absence […] a form of tourist gothic powerfully characteristic of literary pilgrimage' (2006: 7). Indeed, writers like Cumberland appear in active pursuit of this ghostly feeling, writing of how 'it is impossible to give the reader any idea of the vivid sense of reality, of living actually in the past, that I experienced in walking through this house and in treading the floors […] that Charlotte Brontë herself trod hundreds of times' (1911: 608). In his repeated retracing of the floors of the *pensionnat*, Cumberland is intent on experiencing Brontë's ghost lingering in his path.

For Cumberland, the sense of haunting takes on the familiar theme of 'invoking the author's "footsteps"' (Watson, 2006: 174), while for others this haunting comes from moments of stillness that allow the imagination to bring to life vivid impressions of Charlotte, Emily and the fictional Lucy Snowe inhabiting the place. Demonstrating a blurring of life and literature that is common among literary tourists, Charlotte and her fictional character Lucy Snowe become indistinct and interchangeable in these images. Sitting in the garden, Theodore Wolfe reflects on how 'we could well believe that Charlotte and her heroine found here restful seclusion', going on to imagine:

> how often in the summer twilight poor Charlotte had lingered here in restful solitude after the day's burdens and trials with 'stupid and impertinent' pupils! How often, with weary feet and a dreary heart, she had paced this secluded walk and thought, with longing almost insupportable, of the dear ones in far-away Haworth parsonage! In this sheltered corner her other self – Lucy Snowe – sat and listened to the distant chimes and thought forbidden thoughts and cherished impossible hopes.
>
> (Wolfe, 1885: 546)

Wolfe's imagination not only conjures up the haunting, ghostly presence of Charlotte but also attempts to actively bring the past into the present, to collapse time through the shared space of the garden. Cumberland similarly attempts this when he writes of how:

> I tried to annihilate time, for my presence here had vanquished the space that hitherto had separated me from the novelist who had kindled my imagination more than any other I have ever read. My mind reached backward, longing to get into direct communication with her who had brought me hither.
>
> (Cumberland, 1911: 609)

The literary tourist's seeking of 'direct communication' here approaches spiritual proportions, attempting to achieve a connection of mind and spirit that transcends the everyday: Cumberland concludes that it was a moment 'in which something miraculous might happen' (1911: 609). For others, though, such an attempt is disappointed, as schoolgirl Janet Harper found when she writes of how 'sometimes at twilight on a summer evening in the pear tree *allée* I tried to realise that Charlotte and Emily had walked there just as we simple people were doing'; but her attempt is futile, 'I cannot truthfully say that I did realise it. One cannot force these things' (1912: 469).

Throughout these recollections of bringing ghosts of the past into the present, Charlotte, Emily and Lucy Snowe appear to merge into one another. Of the three, it is the fictional Lucy Snowe whose presence lingers most strongly: when Cumberland reflects on his sense of treading in the authors' footsteps, he conjectures that these ghostly floorboards are important '*not only* [because] Charlotte Brontë herself trod hundreds of times' but because here 'the feet of Lucy Snowe and Paul Emanuel walked so often'; he continues, 'the interest of this place is twofold. Here Charlotte and Emily Brontë, real people of history, lived a part of their lives, and here Lucy Snowe, no less real a figure to thousands of readers, passed through suffering to happiness' (Cumberland, 1911: 608). Harland's party goes further in finding only the presence of Lucy Snowe, writing that 'we lost Charlotte and Emily as soon as we struck upon Dr Bretton's track and felt the presence of the pale mute shadow' (2000: 80). The fluidity of movement between life and literature is common within literary tourist accounts, in which authors' landscapes are often a conflation of text and author, but the negotiation of life and literature in Brussels forms an interesting contrast with the Brontë parsonage: if there it is the impulse towards biography which predominates, here the reverse seems true and literary works resonate most strongly.[6]

On their departure from the *pensionnat*, the accounts are each marked by the desire for a souvenir of their visit: Trafton's party of girls ask to take a leaf from the pear tree and they are invited to take 'as many as you please'; 'we plucked them with our own hands, tenderly, almost reverently' she writes (1871: 188). By the time of Theodore Wolfe's visit it seems that this has become common practice, and 'leaves from the overhanging boughs were plucked for us as souvenirs of the place' (Wolfe, 1885: 546). The leaves from the garden are described as 'souvenirs', but the role they play fits less within the tradition of the tourist souvenir and instead accords more strongly with that of the tourist relic. While the souvenir is a manufactured commodity that may bear little or no relation to the tourist site, the relic is a non-commodified product that has a physical connection with the place and therefore appears to be imbued with an essence or spirit, forming part of the desire of tourists to 'construct a more intimate and exclusive relationship with the writer' (Watson, 2006: 34).[7] This is evident in Trafton's account, whereupon returning to the rest of their holiday group the girls offer up 'our glistening trophies' as proof of their journey, exclaiming '"Do you not know? Can you not see? Oh, do you not feel?" we cried' (1871: 188).

These encounters at Brussels thus evoke familiar themes of literary tourism, finding an experience of nostalgic connection and emotional resonance within the *pensionnat*, yet they locate this as an individual process of self-discovery rather than through the directions of a guidebook within a heavily commercialised destination-point. Further to this, while the *pensionnat* is the prime site of this experience, the surrounding city landscape is crucial to the way in which the touristic encounter at the *pensionnat* is contextualised and, in turn, interpreted. The beginnings of each tourist's account starts not at the *pensionnat* but with a journey through the city, with each writer signifying the importance of tracing the route of Charlotte's (and Lucy Snowe's) arrival into the city through the park, across to the Belliard statue, down the steps, and then arriving at the *pensionnat*. Resonant across these accounts is the desire to follow in the author's and character's footsteps, but this is crafted as a methodical process of uncovering the route in preparation for arrival at the *pensionnat*, as if the building can only make sense as the end-point to the prior journey.

Apparent in this process is that the route is not mapped in advance but instead unfolds through the textual associations that the space offers up: Wolfe notes that 'for our purpose no guide was available, or needful, for the topography and local colouring of "Villette" and "The Professor" are as vivid and unmistakable as in the best work of Dickens himself' (1885: 542). Read through the text of Brontë's works the space itself becomes the guide, the landscape imbued with textual associations that map out and navigate the tourists through the space. In this, the accounts make evident, as Watson writes, that 'the text itself invents and solicits tourism' (2006: 12). Watson suggests that there is something particular in the way in which certain authors write about place that invites the searching out of locations and locales by literary tourists. In these Brussels accounts, a further point becomes clear: the landscape becomes written through the text. As the tourists make their way across the park they construct a landscape which is implicitly crafted through and by the literary work, such that their journeys appear to emerge as a naturalised production of this space, each route leading with predictable inevitability to the site of the *pensionnat*.

In doing so, the tourists construct and solidify an idea, or mythologisation, of the place which strongly iterates a seemingly naturalised relationship between author, text and landscape. A further effect of this is to centralise the tourist as the producer of meaning in this landscape: without the signs of a museum or the descriptions of a guidebook to direct them, the way in which these tourists read, interpret and move through this space is dependent upon their own knowledge, memories and associations that work to produce the literary landscape. As Tetley and Bramwell caution, in discussing literary tourism it is too often assumed that 'people are not in active negotiation with their material and symbolic environment, but are passively shaped by it', and they counter that 'when people visit a literary destination they make their own sense and value, their own knowledge, albeit negotiated within a myriad of influences' (Tetley and Bramwell, 2011: 157). This is starkly apparent in the open city landscape of Brussels, where the only signs for the tourists to negotiate are those that the texts and their memories produce: Trafton's account, for example, is marked by the repetition of 'Do you remember [....] Don't you remember?' as they reach each stage of the route, thus centralising the individual memory of the text as guide (1871: 187). Literary tourism here becomes a performative act, an interaction of self and landscape in which tourists 'actively participate in the production of meaning, [and] create an account of the places they visit depending on the cultural concepts and markers available to them' (Kilian, 2002: 267). Ultimately the meanings that they create might, after all, be remarkably similar; but it is nonetheless evident that these meanings have been forged through the self as active producer, rather than consumer, of knowledge.

Mobility through and around a landscape of locations thus becomes central to the tourist experience in Brussels, and arrival at the *pensionnat* is prefigured by an unfolding process of location in which the tourist creates and curates their own experience of the landscape. The mobile mapping of a trail through the urban landscape in turn figures as important in the relationship between literary legacy and gendered discourses that is forged in the city streets. In the movement of literary tourists following the journeys of Charlotte/Lucy in the open spaces of the city, their mobility makes visible, and indeed performs, the 'myth of female self-creation' in which an active, independent woman negotiates her way within the public, masculine space of the street. Brontë's accounts of this and other journeys around the city in *Villette* are not straightforwardly celebratory of female mobility, describing Lucy's trepidation at her situation and finding herself facing censure from those she encounters: her first walk through the town when she arrives at night, for example, describes how 'two moustachioed men' follow Lucy through the streets, speaking 'with insolence' towards her, such that she is 'driven beyond my reckoning' (Brontë, 2004: 70). Nonetheless, this and other episodes describe experiences which foreground and examine gendered discourses of space and their impact upon female identity; Lucy's walk above, for example, also sees her strengthen her resolve – 'not the least fear had I', she says (Brontë, 2004: 70). The literary tourists' traversals of this route works to similar effect in drawing attention to gendered discourses of public space, as their accounts of this journey necessitate the rewriting and re-performing of these passages from *Villette*, and thus centralise the issues raised by these passages through their own accounts.

If at Haworth the image of domesticated femininity predominates, then here the city provides a space in which alternative narratives of gendered interaction become visible. At the same time however, the writers serve to undercut Charlotte's own involvement in such spaces: the tourists almost exclusively find themselves unable to evoke an image of Charlotte walking through the streets, instead reverting to the passage from *Villette* by way of safely fictionalising the moment.[8] In doing so, they serve to reiterate a deflection of attention away from Brontë's potential independence as a woman in the public sphere, obscuring her participation in social discourse through a conflation of author and fictional character. Such collapsing of life into literature is not altogether uncommon in literary tourist accounts, as seen already at the *pensionnat*, but here it becomes clear that this serves a particular discursive process that accords with the broader Brontë myth of self-effacing femininity. Yet it is a mythologisation that nonetheless draws attention to its own process of negation while simultaneously reviving the act that it seeks to supress through the tourists' own performances of the journey. Furthermore, while earlier accounts seek to conflate author-text, this mobile re-recreation opens up a space of potential for contemporary readers and critics to redress and reassert these gender negotiations as pertaining to Charlotte Brontë in the ongoing projections of her legacy.

The tourist map created around Brussels thus serves an important point in terms of the gender positioning of Charlotte Brontë in contrast to Haworth and, as a space detached from England, it also offers a location where Charlotte Brontë's national positioning can come into view through new perspectives. An emphasis is placed on nationality in late nineteenth-century accounts, with an especial focus on an American/English divide: Trafton's article tells of how 'Americans often come to visit the school and the garden' (1871: 188), and Wolfe is similarly told that 'some American tourists had before called to look at the garden' (1885: 545); Harland goes further to say that 'so many English and Americans, many more Americans than English, come here every year, and talk, oh, so much!' (2000: 80). Another writer contextualises this within the Belgian tourist landscape, writing that the Pensionnat Heger:

> has become the Mecca of American travellers. The average Britisher is content with worshipping at the shrine of the Waterloo ballroom, but the

literary Yankee finds out Charlotte Brontë's school, searches in vain for the Allée Défendue, and carries away a leaf from one of the giant pear trees.
(Anon., 1890: 68)[9]

While it is difficult to judge the veracity of these reports, given that there are no records of visitor numbers to the *pensionnat* at this time, the frequency with which this is repeated suggests that a great number of Americans did visit the site and, perhaps, felt that they could claim greater ownership of it than the Yorkshire parsonage: while Haworth represents the holy shrine of English literary pilgrims, the *pensionnat* at Brussels can become 'the Mecca of American travellers'.

While these early accounts gesture towards a sense of national rivalry in their discussions, the potential of internationalism is more positively reframed in the subsequent history of the Brontë connection to Brussels, and in its revival in the present day. Since the demolishing of the Pensionnat Heger the history of the Brontës in Brussels diminished somewhat, with the site of the school and the Brontës' visit there commemorated only by a bronze plaque on the side of a new building. While the Brontë Society's efforts throughout the twentieth century focused intently on Haworth as the site of its commercial and legacy interests, Brussels received little attention from any formal endeavours of the society, and thus remained off the Brontë literary map.

Yet in recent years this has begun to change: Helen MacEwan's journey to the *pensionnat* site marked the start of her discovering other Brontë enthusiasts residing in and around the city, and in turn, the establishment of an official involvement within Brussels. MacEwan's account suggests that while official records of visitors died out, there was an ongoing presence of Brontë literary pilgrims who have found their way to Brussels over the years and, quietly but surely, sought to maintain the memory of the sisters in the city: this is evident, for example, in the discovery of an unofficial plaque to the Brontë sisters in the rue Terarken (Fig. 6) designed to resemble the official blue plaque scheme and created and placed as a personal tribute by a Brontë devotee (MacEwan, 2012: 40–1).

While such 'underground' movements may have lingered throughout the twentieth century, in recent years the presence of the Brontës in Brussels has become increasingly formalised with the establishing of a Brussels Brontë Group as a branch of the Brontë Society; not only does the group hold regular talks and events for Brontë enthusiasts within the city, but it also seeks to keep alive the physical traces of the sisters in the city through guided literary tours of Brontë locations. The group

6 Blue plaque on rue Terarken, Brussels, Belgium

is distinctive for its cosmopolitan membership that encompasses British expats, a diverse range of international inhabitants in Brussels and even members who travel from surrounding countries to participate in events. In doing so, the group provides a uniquely cosmopolitan space in which to position Brontë as open to interpretation within multiple national contexts that provide new perspectives on and approaches to the works.

In Charlotte Brontë's works, Belgium provides a space away from Britain in which to explore the creation of new models of identity formation and from which to reflect back upon ideologies shaped within the nation; for critics of Brontë's legacy today, Brussels similarly provides a space both for discovering alternative afterlives and for reflecting back on the myths of identity forged within England. In the history of Brussels literary tourism there emerge modes of touristic performance that privilege alternative discursive formations of Brontë as female writer, and that allow for her legacy to be considered from a multiplicity of national perspectives. In the legacies of Brontë at Brussels today, the 'myth of female self-creation' is reasserted as an active presence in the city, created through a convergence of cosmopolitan interests in the writer. At the moment of her bicentenary, such narratives provide an important complement and counter to the mythologisation of Charlotte Brontë's legacy at Haworth and a point of departure for the ongoing production of her afterlives in the future.

Notes

1 Annual visitor numbers are not publicly recorded at present. Figures for 2012 were reported in the local press: www.thetelegraphandargus.co.uk/news/local/district/district_bradford/10155157.Fall_in_visitors_at_Bronte_Parsonage_Museum_in_Haworth (accessed 13 August 2016).

2 Belgium appears also in *Shirley* (1849) with the Belgian characters Robert, Louis and Hortense Moore. On the Continental inspiration in Brontë's work, see, for example, Enid Duthie's *The Foreign Vision of Charlotte Brontë* (1975), which details links between people and places in Brontë's life and writing, and Herbert E. Wroot's *The Sources of Charlotte Brontë's Novels* (1935), which provides a detailed plotting of the fictional locations against those of Brontë's real experience in Brussels. Many biographers have sought to uncover the details of Charlotte's feelings for M. Heger, for critical discussion of which see Miller (2002). The focus of more recent criticism has largely shifted away from biography to consider such themes as cosmopolitanism in the Belgium novels; see, for example, Lawson and Shakinovsky (2009) and Longmuir (2009).

3 See Watson (2006) on the relationship between literary tourism and cultural nationalism; on the nineteenth-century rise of cultural nationalism more broadly, see, for example, Trumpener (1997).

4 On the surrounding evocation of 'Brontë country', see, for example, local tourist-board information at www.visitbradford.com/discover/Haworth.aspx and sites dedicated to 'Brontë country', including www.bronte-country.com/ (accessed 13 August 2016).

5 After her return to England, Charlotte wrote regularly to M. Heger. The four letters that have survived, all written in French, are not conventional 'love letters' but display an increasing emotional intensity towards M. Heger: she describes writing to him as 'the only joy I have on earth' and displays a desperate longing at awaiting his reply, writing 'I am in a fever – I lose my appetite and my sleep – I pine away' (Brontë, 2007: 68). Each of the literary tourist pieces cited can be found reprinted in Ruijssenaars (2000) and are available in the original sources cited below.

6 On this theme, see Wynne (Chapter 1 in this volume).

7 On the souvenir, see Stewart (1992), which discusses the souvenir as a manufactured replica that becomes a starting point for narratives of touristic experience rather than having any intrinsic connection to the tourist place itself.

8 Only the anonymous author of 'Charlotte Brontë's School' (1890) writes of Charlotte's journey with her father across the park.

9 On the British relationship with Belgium and travel to Waterloo, see François (2008) and Morgan (2000).

References

Alexander, Christine (2008) 'Myth and memory: reading the Brontë parsonage', in Harald Hendrix (ed.), *Writers' Houses and the Making of Memory*, London and New York: Routledge, pp. 93–110.

Anon. (1890) 'Charlotte Brontë's school', *The World*, 10, 33–4.

Barnard, Robert (2011) 'Tourism comes to Haworth', in Mike Robinson and Hans-Christian Andersen (eds.), *Literature and Tourism: Essays in the Reading and Writing of Tourism*, Andover: Cengage, pp. 143–54.

Brontë, Charlotte (2004) *Villette*, ed. Helen M. Cooper, London: Penguin.

—— (2007) *Selected Letters of Charlotte Brontë*, ed. Margaret Smith, Oxford: Oxford University Press.

Cumberland, Gerald (1911) 'Charlotte Brontë's street in Brussels today', *Cornhill Magazine*, 30.179, 604–9.

Duthie, Enid (1975) *The Foreign Vision of Charlotte Brontë*, London: Macmillan.

François, Pieter (2008) 'Belgium: country of liberals, Protestant and free – British views on Belgium in the mid-19th century', *Historical Research*, 81.214, 663–78.

Freeman, John (1963) *Literature and Locality: The Literary Topography of Britain and Ireland*, London: Cassell.

Gardiner, Juliet (1992) *The World Within: The Brontës at Haworth*, London: Collins & Brown.

Gaskell, Elizabeth (1975) *The Life of Charlotte Brontë*, ed. Alan Shelston, London: Penguin.

Harland, Marion (2000) 'In "Villette"', in Eric Ruijssenaars (ed.), *Charlotte Brontë's Promised Land*, Keighley: The Brontë Society, pp. 79–83.

Harper, Janet (1912) 'Charlotte Brontë's Heger family and their school', *Blackwood's Magazine*, 191.1158, 461–9.

John, Juliet (2011) *Dickens and Mass Culture*, Oxford: Oxford University Press.

Kellett, Jocelyn (1977) *The Haworth Parsonage: The Home of the Brontës*, Keighley: The Brontë Society.

Kilian, Eveline (2002) 'Exploring London: walking the city – (re-)writing the city', in Hartmut Berghoff, Barbara Korte, Ralf Schneider and Christopher Harvie (eds.), *The Making of Modern Tourism: The Cultural History of the British Experience, 1600–2000*, Basingstoke: Palgrave Macmillan, pp. 267–83.

Lawson, Kate and Lynn Shakinovsky (2009) 'Fantasies of national identification in *Villette*', *Studies in English Literature, 1500–1900*, 49.4, 925–44.

Longmuir, Anne (2009) '"Reader, perhaps you were never in Belgium?" Negotiating British identity in Charlotte Brontë's *The Professor* and *Villette*', *Nineteenth-Century Literature*, 64.2, 163–88.

MacEwan, Helen (2012) *Down the Belliard Steps: Discovering the Brontës in Brussels*, Hythe: Brussels Brontë Editions.

Miller, Lucasta (2002) *The Brontë Myth*, London: Vintage.

Morgan, Marjorie (2000) *National Identities and Travel in Victorian Britain*, New York: St Martin's Press.

Ruijssenaars, Eric (2000) *Charlotte Brontë's Promised Land: The Pensionnat Heger and Other Brontë Places in Brussels*, Keighley: The Brontë Society.

Stewart, Susan (1992) *On Longing: Narratives of the Miniature, the Gigantic, the Souvenir, the Collection*, Durham, NC: Duke University Press.

Tetley, Sara, and Bill Bramwell (2011) 'Tourists and the cultural construction of Haworth's literary landscape', in Mike Robinson and Hans-Christian Andersen (eds), *Literature and Tourism: Essays in the Reading and Writing of Tourism*, Andover: Cengage, pp. 155–70.

Thomas, Edward (1928) *A Literary Pilgrim in England*, London: Jonathan Cape.

Trafton, Adeline (1871) 'A visit to Charlotte Brontë's school at Brussels', *Scribner's Monthly*, 3.2, 186–9.

Trumpener, Katie (1997) *Bardic Nationalism: The Romantic Novel and the British Empire*, Princeton, NJ: Princeton University Press.

Watson, Nicola (2006) *The Literary Tourist*, Baskingstoke: Palgrave Macmillan.

Wolfe, Theodore (1885) 'Scenes of Charlotte Brontë's life in Brussels', *Lippincott's Magazine*, 36, 542–8.

Wroot, Herbert E. (1935) *The Sources of Charlotte Brontë's Novels*, Shipley: Caxton Press.

4

Reading the revenant in Charlotte Brontë's literary afterlives: charting the path from the 'silent country' to the seance

Amber Pouliot

The Brontës have long been associated with the ghostly, an association that continues to this day. Haworth guides offer ghost walks. Although principally an educational centre, the Brontë Parsonage Museum has held seances for those eager for a more immediate, extra-textual encounter with the dead authors. Throughout the early twentieth century, critics, biographers and creative writers often portrayed Emily as a mystic who longed for death and communed with spirits; as Lucasta Miller has observed, under those circumstances, the seance held in her former home in 1940 would have seemed apposite (2005: 259). But as recently as 2006, Turner Prize nominee Cornelia Parker, accompanied by novelist Justine Picardie, participated in and recorded a seance at the parsonage as part of her exhibition, *Brontëan Abstracts*. Commissioned by the Parsonage Museum to produce new work responding to its collections, Parker explained the reason for this foray into spiritualism: 'I have these burning questions building up in my mind, and I couldn't use science to find all the answers, so to ask a psychic seems to be an interesting experiment' (Picardie, 2006). Sylvia Plath might have understood this impulse. After a visit in 1956, she suggestively described the museum, with its collection of relics that seemed to conjure up their dead owners, as 'a house redolent with ghosts' (1998: 148). Recent works of fiction have similarly connected the Brontës with the supernatural. In Jane Urquhart's *Changing Heaven* (1990), Emily's spirit discusses *Wuthering Heights* (1847) with

96

a dead balloonist. Denise Giardina's *Emily's Ghost* (2009) presents the author as a medium who gleans her stories from chatty spirits. Aviva Orr's *The Mist on Brontë Moor* (2012) supernaturalises the family for the young adult reader with the story of a girl who travels through time to meet the teenaged Brontës.

The connection between seances held in the former family home and recent works of fiction exploring their lives and afterlives might not seem immediately apparent, but both are underpinned by a similar motivation. Spiritualists who attempt to contact the dead Brontës, summoning them from the past into the present, seek new communications that will shed light on the dim places in the Brontë story. When Parker and Picardie took part in their seance, they asked whether Branwell had a daughter and whether he wrote any of *Wuthering Heights*, questions that have occupied Brontë enthusiasts since the nineteenth century. Similarly, Brontë fictional biographies reanimate and creatively reconstruct the lives of the family, integrating what may be termed the known facts of their existence with imaginative speculation, approaching the absences, or perceived absences, in the historical record as opportunities to write into the void and fill the silence. In both cases, the Brontës are conjured and ventriloquised; the medium claims to deliver communications from the dead, speaking on their behalf, while fictional biographers supply their subjects with words that the historical Brontës never uttered. From their first appearance in the inter-war period, Brontë fictional biographies featured the family as ghosts (as well as living characters) and figured their home as a site of Gothic suffering. Yet, prior to the twentieth century's resurrection of the dead Brontës on the stage and printed page, they were subjected to still less corporeal forms of fictionalisation in nineteenth-century commemorative poetry. In contrast to inter-war and later works of fictional biography, these poems focused on the family's existence in the afterlife, presenting them as both bodiless and voiceless.

This chapter traces the process by which the Brontës came to be peculiarly associated with the ghostly, beginning in the nineteenth century, and views it as inextricably connected with their transformation from historical figures to fictional characters. It focuses, in particular, on the history of Charlotte's representation as revenant. Although all four adult siblings were imagined as ghosts in nineteenth-century commemorative poetry, Charlotte's death provided the occasion for the writing of the first of these poems. Most importantly, it was Charlotte's first authorised biographer, Elizabeth Gaskell, who consolidated and popularised existing understandings of the Brontës as haunted and haunting in *The Life of*

Charlotte Brontë (1857). By doing so, she catalysed the process of their fictionalisation. This chapter considers how tropes of haunting are deployed across three distinct phases in Charlotte's fictionalisation: Gaskell's biography, nineteenth-century commemorative poetry, and inter-war fictional biographies. These poems and biographies were influenced by Gaskell, working along similar lines of fictionalisation, but they engaged differently with the Brontës and the supernatural. This chapter sustains a particular focus on the poetry of the late nineteenth century as a bridge between Gaskell's biography and inter-war fictional biography. It traces a gradual approach to fictional biography as the nineteenth century progressed, a transition from speechlessness and passivity to an imagined vocalisation and acquisition of agency. In order to begin to understand this cultural fascination with the family's spiritual afterlives, it is necessary to trace its development from the mid-nineteenth century, when Charlotte was widely considered to be the most fascinating member of the family, and to map her journey from 'the silent country' of Matthew Arnold's elegy (1890b: l. 69) to the loquacity of Rachel Ferguson's inter-war seance.

'Unquiet souls!' The Brontës in poetic proto-fiction

The first writer to explore the Brontës' afterlives through the medium of commemorative poetry was Matthew Arnold in 'Haworth Churchyard', published in May 1855. However, the majority of these poems were written or published towards the end of the nineteenth century. Even Arnold's elegy underwent substantial revision, reappearing in 1890 with an 'Epilogue' answering his original injunction to 'Sleep, O cluster of friends' with an acknowledgement of the spirits' unabated activity (1890b: l. 178):

> Unquiet souls!
> – In the dark fermentation of earth,
> In the never idle workshop of nature,
> In the eternal movement,
> Ye shall find yourselves again!
>
> (Arnold 1890a: ll. 10–14)

Arnold's revision reflects a tendency in commemorative poetry to depict the spirits of the Brontës as increasingly active and 'unquiet' and to move further from elegiac commemoration of the dead and closer to ghost narrative and fictional biography as the century progressed.

'Haworth Churchyard' was followed by Emily Dickinson's 'Charlotte Brontë's Grave', published in 1896 but written around 1860; George Barlow's 'In Memory of Patrick Branwell Brontë, Genius', dated 1870; Francis William Lauderdale Adams' 'To Emily Brontë', published in 1887; Lionel Pigot Johnson's 'Brontë', dated 1890; and Harriet Prescott Spofford's 'Brontë', published in 1897. While these poems were ostensibly written to lament the deaths and celebrate the achievements of the deceased authors, their engagement with the Brontës is more complex and fraught than this implies.

The poems in question are meditations on the family's spiritual existence in the afterlife. They imaginatively engage with the Brontë family but do not fictionalise lived experience or once-living bodies; they focus instead on the figure of the ghost. As such, they construct proto-fictional biographies that precede, but also differ markedly from, biographical fictions of the inter-war period. Inter-war writers sometimes reduced the Brontës to stock characters, portraying Branwell as a drunkard, Patrick as a grim Victorian patriarch and Charlotte as a love-sick spinster – but these individuated characters conformed, in many respects, to standard biographical descriptions. In the poems, however, the ghostly Brontës are mostly shorn of the attributes they were said to possess in life. Not only are they unnamed in the bodies of the above-mentioned poems, with the exception of Dickinson's, the siblings are also sometimes treated as an indistinguishable conglomerate. They are described by Arnold as 'a sisterly band' and 'cluster of friends' (1890b: ll. 81, 112); referred to by Johnson as 'royal sisters of the North' (l. 64) and transformed into an interchangeable 'three ghosts upon the stair!' by the end of Spofford's poem (l. 99). In contrast to fictional biography, these poems are unconcerned with biographical verisimilitude or with the imaginative exploration of lacunae in the Brontë story. Rather, they offer a subjective depiction of the Brontës in the afterlife, using the trope of haunting as a metaphor to describe their continued cultural and personal significance after death.

These poems also enact an imagined literary pilgrimage. They do not actually engage with Charlotte's final resting place near the altar of St Michael and All Angels Church in Haworth; instead, they imagine the spirits of the Brontë siblings haunting their former home, the moors surrounding Haworth, or an unspecified natural landscape. Still, they are analogous to the large body of commemorative poetry composed by literary tourists, often referred to as pilgrims, at the sites of poets' graves throughout the nineteenth century. Samantha Matthews explains that while the expected attitude of the pilgrim poet is awe and veneration in the presence of the deceased writer, this poetry actually registers a contest between the commemorator and the commemorated:

> The pilgrim's typical self-presentation is humbled, grieving, overwhelmed and silenced in the presence of the remains of immortal, transcendent "genius". However, he or she is generally "literary" also […], and the pose of humility is often qualified or undermined by gestures that assert the visitor's own agency, and inscribe his or her subjectivity onto the grave of "genius".
>
> (Matthews, 2009: 25)

Pilgrim poets palimpsestuously inscribe themselves and their impressions of a writer – of the life and literature – over the graves of their subjects, asserting their living creative agency in contrast to the dead poet's silence. This fraught relationship is not only evident in the silence of the ghostly Brontës, but, in some cases, in the way the commemorating poet positions himself in relation to the siblings. For example, Matthew Arnold was critical of Charlotte as a writer and woman, complaining that *Villette* (1853), with its frank exploration of its heroine's turbulent interiority, was 'hideous, undelightful, convulsed' and betrayed the author's 'hunger, rebellion, and rage' (quoted in Miller, 2005: 52, 53). It does not take much imagination to read condescension and relief in his assurance of her silence in death. And although George Barlow proclaims Branwell's genius in the title of his poem, he uses the Brontë brother as a warning to other men to practice self-control:

> A poor pale finger-post he seems to stand,
> Saying to men that follow in his wake,
> […]
> "One of two courses, brothers, you must take,
> Either for Emptiness yourself forsake,
> Or hold your Whole self in tenacious hand."
>
> (ll. 9–10, 12–14)

Barlow's poem is didactic. Branwell's behaviour supplies the moral lesson and Barlow positions himself as superior in judgement. Unlike his ghostly subject, he recognises the importance of moderation. It is also important to note that Barlow uses the word 'seems' when describing how Branwell's experience should be read. Branwell does not supply the message in this poem; it is Barlow who verbalises the moral he extracts from Branwell's behaviour. Therefore, even though there is some ambiguity, this poem similarly persists in denying Branwell a voice.

The most significant difference between nineteenth-century ghost poetry and later fictional biographies is the speechlessness pervading the poetry. In inter-war fiction the Brontës are ventriloquised, with lines taken from their novels, poems, letters and diary papers, or with newly invented dialogue – they are speaking, writing, communicant presences. This is true even when they appear as ghosts. In the prologue to M. B. Linton's play, *The Tragic Race* (c.1926), the ghosts of Charlotte and Emily initially function as a kind of silent chorus, preparing the audience for the ghostly Charlotte's revelation at the close of the play. However, in the final scene, the angelic spirit of Charlotte returns to proclaim the existence of the afterlife and to reassure the audience that marriage and wifely duty were her most significant accomplishments: '"Not fame, but love; not an end, but a beginning; not death, but victory"' (Linton, c.1926: 31). In Rachel Ferguson's *Charlotte Brontë: A Play in Three Acts* (1933), Emily encounters the ghost of her sister Elizabeth offstage. While Emily does not relay any straightforward oral message from Elizabeth, the ghostly child communicates by leading Emily to the experiences that provide the material for her novel. Elizabeth's revelation of her spirit's confinement in the natural world means that, within the framework of the text, Emily is the medium through which Elizabeth communicates her experiences with readers of *Wuthering Heights*.

Rachel Ferguson's *The Brontës Went to Woolworths* (1931) is not a straightforward work of biographical fiction, although it too fictionalises the Brontë family. Throughout the text, it remains unclear whether the Brontës are ghosts or have actually travelled through time to invade the domestic and imaginative space of the modern Carne family. In this novel about three sisters (Deirdre, Katrine and Sheil), who, like the Brontës, cultivate a shared imaginative world, the ghosts are vocal, disruptive and vaguely sinister. Even before they materialise, the ghostly sisters communicate in a variety of ways with the Carnes and their governess, Miss Martin. Charlotte inscribes harsh annotations on aspiring novelist Deirdre's rejected manuscript. Several Brontës speak through a seance, during which they demand their auditors '*Remember Maria. Remember Elizabeth*', '*And remember Anne*' (Ferguson, 2009: 52). Finally, Charlotte and Emily pay a visit to Miss Martin, and Charlotte convinces the governess to abandon her degrading teaching position to pursue work with the clergyman she loves. On one level, the Brontës are the disruptive, mischievous poltergeists of more conventional ghost narratives. Yet they also return in order to control their posthumous reputations: they demand remembrance for the three sisters who are most frequently marginalised in inter-war biography and literary criticism, and they revise the idea that Charlotte was a prudish slave to duty.

There are a number of possible explanations for inter-war biographers' insistence upon the Brontës' relationship with the supernatural. It was not a simple appropriation of nineteenth-century ghost motifs or a mimicked interest in the Brontës' spiritual survival. Throughout the inter-war period, in England and the United States, spiritualist beliefs in the ability of the dead to communicate with the living were pervasive, just as they had been in both countries throughout the second half of the nineteenth century. Georgina Byrne describes the permeation of spiritualist beliefs and rhetoric in England into what she terms the 'common culture' shared by people from a variety of socio-economic, educational and political backgrounds (2010: 9). Similarly, Jenny Hazelgrove argues that spiritualism accommodated mainstream religion and traditional, rural, folkloric belief in the supernatural, '[matching] expectations in heterodox pockets of Christianity where continuity between matter and spirit, earth-life, and afterlife was already assumed' (1999: 413). Charlotte's and Emily's novels in particular are suffused with traditional stories of the supernatural. In *Shirley* (1849), the elderly servant, Martha, reminisces about encounters with fairies before the factories drove them away; Jane mistakes Rochester's dog for the legendary Gytrash; and both *Jane Eyre* (1847) and *Wuthering Heights* mention spirits returning from the dead to protect vulnerable children, with Jane fearing Mr Reed's return while in the red room and Bessie lulling Hareton to sleep with the song, 'It was far in the night, and the bairnies grat, / The mither beneath the mools heard that' (E. Brontë, 2008: 67). Under these circumstances, it is hardly surprising that the Brontës were popular subjects for those interested in spiritualism and the ghostly during the inter-war period.

Inter-war fictional biographies of the Brontës should be considered early examples of neo-Victorian fiction. And yet, Ann Heilmann and Mark Llewellyn's belief that neo-Victorian novelists often incorporate the supernatural as 'a re-articulation of the Victorians' […] fascination with seances, spectres and other spookish things' is not sufficient on its own to explain this persistent engagement with a spectral Brontë family (Heilmann and Llewellyn, 2010: 147). After all, it is no more remarkable that inter-war writers imagined encounters with the spirits of the dead Brontës than that their nineteenth-century predecessors did so. The identification of tropes of haunting and mediumship, metaphors for the continued presence of the Victorian past and attempts to conjure and recreate it in works of neo-Victorian fiction, is an established feature of the critical field.[1] In both nineteenth-century proto-fictionalisations and inter-war fictional biographies, the Brontës' haunting presence certainly functions in this way. Their ghosts invite readers to confront the presence of the past and to question the reasons behind their enduring cultural and personal appeal. But this is not enough to explain the Brontës' singular association with the supernatural; rather, it is the particular legacy of Elizabeth Gaskell's biography and how it encouraged readers to imagine the family's lives.

The commemorative ghost poem provided the space to creatively explore and critique the Brontës' lives and legacies without the need to adhere to facts. Authors who wished to engage with the family's experiences through the medium of fiction may have chosen to depict them as spectral presences in order to avoid offending their survivors. Patrick Brontë lived until 1861. Arthur Bell Nicholls, who doggedly protected his wife's privacy, lived until 1906, and Charlotte's lifelong friends, Mary Taylor and Ellen Nussey, lived until 1893 and 1897 respectively. They could and often did object to what they felt were unfair or inaccurate portrayals of their dead friends. Fictionalising the siblings' experiences (by inventing speeches they did not make and events they did not experience) so soon after their deaths, and while their family and friends were still living, would likely have been viewed as a falsification of their experiences and a violation of their privacy. The author might also be accused of libel and threatened with legal action, just as Gaskell discovered following the publication of her controversial biography. Due to the necessarily subjective nature of what was being imagined (the afterlives rather than the lives of the Brontë family), these poems were provided with a measure of safety. They liberated authors from the biographical record, allowing them to consider counterfactual possibilities. Yet this does not explain the continued portrayal of the Brontës as revenants into the twentieth and twenty-first centuries, long after there was any need to spare the feelings of survivors.

Matthew Arnold composed the first Brontë ghost poem as an act of commemoration prior to the publication of Gaskell's *Life*. Writing commemorative poetry about dead authors, their final resting places and afterlives, was an established practice in nineteenth-century literary culture. However, as Samantha Matthews observes, the reading public's appetite for poetical remains (which included both the unpublished fragments of the poet's corpus and the biographies and poems written to commemorate him or her) hinged on a sense of personal connection, 'of participating, even in a diminished form, in a common emotional culture with the poet' (2004: 10). Gaskell's biography made this kind of identification possible for a greater number of writers and readers: she allowed a curious public unprecedented access to information about the lives of the reclusive Brontë family, and, by providing detailed and emotionally charged accounts of their tragic deaths, made it possible for readers to participate in processes of mourning. As Lucasta Miller has observed, Gaskell's cultivation of an 'aura of homely intimacy' around her subject inspired such sympathy and affection that readers sought out relics of the dead author in the same way that Victorians collected mementos of dead friends and relatives (2005: 111). Gaskell's portrayal of the family became the urtext for subsequent versions of the Brontë story. In Barlow's poem, we can see the influence of a biography that described Branwell's fall and its effects on his family in near biblical terms: 'he shocked and distressed those loving sisters inexpressibly; the blind father sat stunned, sorely tempted to curse the profligate woman, who had tempted his boy – his only son – into the deep disgrace of deadly crime' (Gaskell, 1997: 211).[2] In the same way, in *The Brontës Went to Woolworths*, we can read Ferguson's decision to make Charlotte an advocate for the unhappy governess, whose wages help support her family, as a reaction against Gaskell's insistence on Charlotte's self-abnegation, evident in her description of Charlotte's and her sisters' determination to continue teaching even though they hated it, '[feeling] that it was a duty to relieve their father of the burden of their support' (Gaskell, 1997: 110).

Suffused with the supernatural: Elizabeth Gaskell's *Life of Charlotte Brontë*

Elizabeth Gaskell's *Life of Charlotte Brontë* was essential to the development of Brontë fictional biography. It was the source from which most early fictional biographers derived their material as well as their model for explaining the sisters' literary production in autobiographical terms. Gaskell's highly wrought appeal to readerly sympathy, her dramatic account of the development of her heroine's genius against the backdrop of inexorable family suffering, and even her minutely described domestic setting, lent a distinctly novelistic quality to the biography (acknowledged by contemporary critics, including Jenny Uglow, Juliet Barker, Lucasta Miller, Angus Easson and Enid Duthie). The *Life's* semi-fictional quality and the role it played in enshrining the Brontës as characters in the cultural consciousness were not lost on nineteenth-century readers either. In a letter dated 15 April 1857, G. H. Lewes congratulated Gaskell on creating a preeminent narrative with the emotional force to rival a work of fiction: 'fiction', he enthused, 'has nothing more wild, touching and heart-strengthening to place above it' (quoted in Uglow, 1999: 429).

One of the ways Gaskell effected the semi-fictionalisation of Charlotte and her family was by infusing her biography with the supernatural, and this feature of the *Life* is largely responsible for the Brontës' gradual and persistent association with the ghostly. There were, of course, aspects of the family's writing and experience that encouraged this connection. Charlotte wrote vividly about the feeling of being haunted in *Jane Eyre* and *Villette*. While imprisoned in the red room, Jane not only fears the spirit of her uncle, she also fearfully experiences her reflection in the mirror as an encounter with the uncanny. By allowing Jane to mistake herself for one of the 'tiny phantoms' of Bessie's stories, beings suspended between life and death, Charlotte conveys Jane's liminal and self-alienating position at Gateshead (Brontë, 2008: 14). Similarly, the sham ghostly nun of *Villette*, which initially terrifies Lucy Snowe, also functions as her double and evokes the destructiveness of her self-repression. The ghosts of Cathy and Heathcliff, while never verified as the returned spirits of the dead, are not easily discounted as figments of the imagination. Charlotte's and Emily's writing provides a model for connecting the figure of the spectre with the exploration of identity and psychological states, but the supernatural tales Gaskell includes in the biography centre upon Charlotte in particular. That Charlotte's home overlooked a graveyard, that she outlived all five of her siblings, that Gaskell met her when she was still in a state of mourning, all this contributed to the biographer's sense that, apart from literary production, the defining features of Charlotte's life were death and bereavement.

However, Gaskell's inclusion of ghost stories in the *Life* is as much a reflection of her enduring interest in the genre, and her readiness to imagine her subject in the light of a Gothic heroine, as anything in Charlotte's actual circumstances. Gaskell wrote ghost stories, some of which were likely inspired by the Brontës and their fiction. Miriam Allott argues that the ghost child in 'The Old Nurse's Story', published in the 1852 Christmas number of *Household Words*, was inspired by the ghostly Catherine of Lockwood's dream (1961: 101–2). While collecting material for the *Life*, Gaskell also began 'The Poor Clare', a supernatural story which, Uglow suggests, 'seized on something hidden in the life Elizabeth was planning to write. It is the story of a gentle and pious girl, Lucy, haunted by a sexual double' (1999: 399). By associating Charlotte with tragic ghost stories, Gaskell fostered the sense that her heroine existed in an eerie, semi-wild and otherworldly space dislocated from more civilised parts of England – where the supernatural existed side by side with the more prosaic occurrences of life and where she could not help witnessing the brutality and coarseness that some readers believed had marred her writing.

In the early chapters delineating the environment and customs of Haworth and the West Riding, Gaskell relates several supernatural tales. One is the story of a young girl who died after being seduced by her brother-in-law and forced, by her cruel father, into a miserable marriage:

> The tale went, that passers along the high-road at night time saw the mother and young daughter walking in the garden, weeping, long after the household were gone to bed. Nay, more; it was whispered that they walked and wept there still, when Miss Brontë told me the tale – though both had long mouldered in their graves.
>
> (Gaskell, 1997: 45)

Although she initially discounts it as 'a specimen of the wild stories afloat in an isolated village', Gaskell concludes her tale with a statement that seems to affirm its truthfulness: 'The strong feeling of the country-side still holds the descendants of this family as accursed. They fail in business, or they fail in health' (1997: 44, 45). Similarly, Gaskell embeds her supernatural tales of Hammond Roberson's communion with 'black demons' after tracking down the Luddites, and of Captain Batt's post-mortem appearance at Oakwell Hall, in a series of facts about boarding schools and woollen mills (1997: 86).

In one remarkable passage, however, Gaskell supernaturalises the Brontës themselves. She creates a ghost narrative about the family that emphasises their suffering and, at the same time, explains and excuses one particularly sexually charged scene in *Jane Eyre*. Describing Charlotte's agonising loneliness and longing for her dead sisters, Gaskell explains that:

> All the grim superstitions of the North had been implanted in her during her childhood by the servants, who believed in them. They recurred to her now, – with no shrinking from the spirits of the Dead, but with such an intense longing once more to stand face to face with the souls of her sisters, as no one but she could have felt. It seemed as if the very strength of her yearning should have compelled them to appear. On windy nights, cries, and sobs, and wailings seemed to go round the house, as of the dearly-beloved striving to force their way to her. Some one conversing with her once objected, in my presence, to that part of "Jane Eyre" in which she hears

Rochester's voice crying out to her in a great crisis of her life, he being many, many miles distant at the time. I do not know what incident was in Miss Brontë's recollection when she replied, in a low voice, drawing in her breath, "But it is a true thing; it really happened."

(Gaskell, 1997: 318–19)

Jane Eyre was, of course, written and published prior to the deaths of Emily and Anne, but, by prefacing her reference to that text with a tragic description of Charlotte's bereavement, Gaskell anachronistically locates the origins of Charlotte's fiction in the events of her life. Jane hears Rochester's disembodied voice at a moment of crisis when she is on the brink of accepting St John Rivers' offer of a loveless marriage and life of Christian servitude in India. The voice elicits an almost orgasmic response: Jane describes how 'the flesh quivered on my bones', and she responds with the cry, 'I am coming! [...] Wait for me! Oh, I will come!' (Brontë, 2008: 419, 420). The emotional and sexual bond between Jane and the man who tried to trick her into a bigamous marriage is thus sanitised. It becomes, instead, a fictional representation of Charlotte's communication with the spirits of her beloved sisters. The gloom and ghostliness that Gaskell cultivates throughout the biography has the dual effect of inscribing Charlotte's experiences within her fictional worlds and of making the supernatural and macabre a part of the topography of her life – as much a fact of her existence as the mills and moors.

The influence of Gaskell's biography on the emergence of ghostly proto-fictionalisations cannot be overestimated. In the years following the publication of the *Life*, five of the six Brontë ghost poems previously discussed were written or published, with Arnold's elegy also undergoing a significant revision that intensified the activity and asserted the noisiness of its previously silent and passive ghosts. Towards the end of the nineteenth century, when Arnold and others were invoking the dead siblings in their poetry, at least two spiritualists claimed to have actually made contact. In 1872, Harriet Beecher Stowe told George Eliot that she 'managed a two-hour conversation with Charlotte in a gossipy seance, a "weird and Brontëish" chat' (quoted in Showalter, 1977: 106). In 1893, an alleged spirit photograph of Charlotte was printed in Thomas Slaney Wilmot's *Gleams of Light and Glimpses Thro' the Rift*. Wilmot claimed that 'the touched-up negative, from which this plate was taken, revealed a glorified angel from earth, with messenger Spirits in her train; she gave her name as Charlotte Bronté [*sic*]' (1893: 285). His construction of the author as angelic messenger is clearly derived from the popularity of Gaskell's portrayal of Charlotte as a Christian heroine who, despite the terrible losses she suffered, still strove 'for strength to say, "It is the Lord! let Him do what seemeth to Him good"' (Gaskell, 1997: 282). In turn, this photograph's legacy can be seen in Linton's *The Tragic Race*, in which Charlotte returns as a shining spirit, proclaiming a message of hope and love.

From silent sleepers to speaking spectres

Although nineteenth-century Brontë spectres were largely inarticulate, depictions of the family evolved as the century progressed; they were transformed from mute and inaccessible spirits to listening, noisy poltergeists striving to communicate with the living. Both Matthew Arnold in 'Haworth Churchyard' and Lionel Pigot Johnson in 'Brontë' exhort the dead Brontës to rest, implying the poetic construction of an afterlife in which the dead are not merely active but can also be reached by the words of the living. But this appears to be a matter of convention, a call for peace and rest to succeed lives that were perceived as overshadowed by tragedy and trauma, and in each poem the Brontës are described as both silent and deaf to human communication. In Johnson's poem, any noise associated with the Brontës refers to past communications: he describes Emily as one 'Whose soul conversed with vehement nights' (l. 10); and although he employs the present tense to announce 'Your [Charlotte's and Emily's] mighty music storms our heart' (l. 2), this music was 'blown forth' long ago (l. 1). It is the reverberation of the music that sounded with the publication of their poetry. In their present state, the sisters are 'Silent and sleeping' and ultimately unreachable (l. 60).

Arnold similarly emphasises the impassable barrier between living and dead in terms that evoke an aural obstruction. Charlotte's ear is 'earth deafen'd' (1890b: l. 36), an expression he repeats in order to more fully convey his inability to reach her:

> Console we cannot, her ear
> Is deaf. Far northward from here,
> In a churchyard high 'mid the moors
> Of Yorkshire, a little earth
> Stops it for ever to praise.

(1890b: ll. 50–4)

Arnold provides yet another proof of the total separation between the living and the dead when he imagines the sisters' reunion in the afterlife, where Emily and Anne will for the first time 'Hear with delight of thy [Charlotte's] fame!' (1890b: l. 87). Despite his repeated direct address to the family, the siblings have traversed 'the path / To the silent country' (1890b: ll. 68–9), where the sounds of earth and life cannot penetrate. Still, the later 'Epilogue' demonstrates that, even if he did not revise his notion of the impossibility of communication between the dead Brontës and their living readers, he did change his conception of their silence and restfulness, pronouncing them 'Unquiet souls!' (l. 10).

In Emily Dickinson's posthumously published 'Charlotte Brontë's Grave' there is a similar emphasis on the muteness attendant on death. However, in this instance, it functions as a comment on Charlotte's posthumous cultural transformation from a self-determined, communicant author to the silent, passive subject of the communications of others. Dickinson conveys this transformation by employing and reversing the myth of Philomela. Variations of the myth exist, but the basic outline, according to Ovid, is as follows. Philomela was raped by her brother-in-law, Tereus, who cut out her tongue. In revenge, Philomela and her sister, Procne, killed Tereus' son and fed him to his father. Philomela and Procne fled, pursued by Tereus, and the gods transformed Procne into the swallow and Philomela into the nightingale.

Philomela's voice was stolen in life and only restored through the shedding of her human body and her transformation into a new being: a songbird. This transformation, involving the loss of humanity and the restoration of what was taken in life, has obvious parallels to popular, compensatory ideas about the afterlife. However, Dickinson subverts both the Philomela myth and the notion of the restorative Brontëan afterlife that features in Arnold's and Johnson's poetry. Instead, she describes the loss of the 'nightingale['s]' voice upon her death, when her subject is transformed from Currer Bell, the author known through and for her song, to the silent, lamented and sung-for corpse of the woman, Charlotte Brontë (l. 12). Dickinson's first stanza imagines her subject's resting place:

> All overgrown by cunning moss,
> All interspersed with weed,
> The little cage of "Currer Bell,"
> In quiet Haworth laid.

> (ll. 1–4)

The description of an outdoor grave does not appear to be simply a mistake, as was the case in Arnold's poem. Dickinson read *The Life of Charlotte Brontë* in late 1857 and was aware of Charlotte's interment in the family vault at St Michael and All Angels (Powers, 2007). Rather, it appears to be a symbolic rendering of Charlotte's post-mortem place in the nineteenth-century transatlantic cultural consciousness. The word 'cunning' has several definitions, including the more common 'able, skilful, expert, dexterous, clever', but cunning can also refer to the steering of a ship (*OED*). The overgrowth of moss and weed suggests the covering and choking of the ground that surrounds Currer Bell in death. If cunning is taken to imply both ingenuity and purposed steering, then, taken together with the smothering growths surrounding the dead writer, we can read this stanza as a comment upon the way in which ideological constructions of Charlotte's life supplant the voice of the writer. The use of the word 'quiet' in the final line of the stanza supports this interpretation, and one wonders if Dickinson had Gaskell's biography in mind. By the time Charlotte enters Heaven, she is transformed from the singing nightingale to the silent listener upon whose 'puzzled ear' (l. 18) 'Soft fall the sounds of Eden' (l. 17).

In her poem, 'Brontë', Harriet Prescott Spofford describes the materialisation of the ghostly sisters, neatly encapsulating the progression from inaccessibility and mutism to communication that is apparent in this body of poetry. With each succeeding stanza, the ghosts of Anne and Emily assert their presence more forcefully, gaining in strength to communicate with and manipulate Charlotte until the barrier between the dead and the living is eroded. Anne and Emily begin as 'Two hovering wavering shapes and pale' (l. 25), before gaining in distinctness and visibility. Spofford describes the process of their sinister encroachment on Charlotte, increasing her despair and desire for death as they make their presence more palpably known. They progress from exciting her general sense of their presence – 'She feels them stealing nigh and nigher' (l. 60) – to emitting inarticulate sound: 'Far off soft voices seem to fall, / Soft footsteps falter through the room' (ll. 68–9). Next they take control of Charlotte's body, staying and moving her hand:

> The gentle cunning fails her hand,
> [...]
> The needle poised, the pencil prone, –
> Pale fingers moving with her own.
>
> (ll. 73, 76–7)

Spofford's description evokes the popular spiritualist practice of automatic writing, whereby a medium temporarily relinquishes control to spirits who guide their hand to reveal messages. Yet while this suggests the possibility of collaboration between the living and dead sisters, the ghosts impede Charlotte's writing. Their 'cunning', as before, is a purposed steering: it 'fails her hand', forcing her to lay aside her 'prone' pencil. These ghosts prevent Charlotte from continuing to produce literature and silence her authorial voice, making her the passive medium for their communications. This scriptural haunting is similar to an episode in *The Brontës Went to Woolworths*, when Deirdre finds Charlotte's critical comments inscribed on her manuscript. Like Spofford's Charlotte, who lays down her pencil, the haunted and discouraged Deirdre destroys her manuscript. Still, in contrast to the fictional biographies of the inter-war period and after, the reader is given no indication of the message conveyed by the soft voices or guided writing.

Finally, Anne and Emily take full possession of Charlotte, haunting her from 'within her heart!' (l. 90) as well as from without. After this conquest, Anne and Emily essentially function as sirens. Their soft voices increase in strength and clarity, and they lure Charlotte to her death, calling her away from what Spofford views as a life of love and happiness with Arthur Bell Nicholls:

Oh, love was sweet, and life was dear, –
But, hark! those voices, strong and clear,
They wail, they call, she must not stay –
[…]
Oh, love past death and death's despair,
There are three ghosts upon the stair!

(ll. 94–6, 98–9)

Although the sisters' message remains unclear, mediated by the speaker rather than given directly to the reader, their voices are potent and dangerous. Spofford's sisters, unlike the aloof, sleepy ghosts of Arnold's and Johnson's poetry, relentlessly pursue the sister they have left behind. More importantly, they are no longer mute.

Spofford's 'Brontë' must be viewed as part of the prehistory of a work like Ferguson's *The Brontës Went to Woolworths*. Nicola Humble argues that during the inter-war period, when Brontë fictional biography became an established form, the family were often portrayed as 'gruesome relics': 'although they are depicted in middlebrow women's fiction with a gossipy familiarity and intimacy, their fascination lies as much in their *distance* – in the gap between their world of damp, graveyards, and repression, and the bright modernity of the years after world war one' (Humble, 2001: 183). Spofford's poem reveals that the Brontës were viewed in this way almost twenty years before the First World War's perceived severing of the Victorian past from the inter-war period's 'bright modernity', and nearly thirty years before the appearance of Brontë fictional biography. Importantly, Spofford's poem also appears to appropriate and rewrite that passage in Gaskell's *Life* in which she transforms Rochester's sexually potent call into Charlotte's encounter with the ghosts of her sisters. Yet while Gaskell stresses sisterly love, Spofford recasts the bonds between Charlotte and her family as destructive and fatal. Nineteenth-century ghost poetry must be viewed as both the precursor to inter-war fictional biography and the progeny of Gaskell's *Life*. These works indicate a trajectory along which imaginative writing about the Brontë family developed, from elegiac commemorations of subjects figured as passive, silent ghosts, to supernatural narratives that imagine the activities of spirits on the brink of eloquence.

The pervasiveness of the Brontës' association with the ghostly in the nineteenth century is a testament to the influence of Gaskell's novelistic and supernaturalising account of family tragedy. By the time Clement Shorter published *Charlotte Brontë and Her Circle* (1896), a collection of letters interspersed with a remarkably neutral commentary that sought to avoid the sentimental and supernatural touches imparted by Gaskell, her view of the family was so entrenched that an anonymous reviewer mused:

> The battle is so fierce, the agony and the despair of it are so terrible and so real, that we find it difficult to persuade ourselves that it is all ended, and can readily understand why the spirits of the unhappy dead are believed to return to the scenes of their sorrows and to re-enact the tragedies in which there they bore a part. No imaginative reader of Mr. Shorter's book could visit the Haworth Parsonage […] without fancying that his entrance had been the signal for the sudden dispersion of startled ghosts.
>
> (Anon., 1897: 34)

The reviewer's sense that the Brontës' experience of death and suffering is what fascinated readers, prompting them to imagine the family as still-suffering ghosts, is perceptive. It mirrors the trajectory of Gaskell's own journey from experiencing imaginative sympathy for Charlotte's sufferings to creating a semi-fictional narrative about a life overshadowed by death, mourning, and encounters with the supernatural. More importantly, it reveals that Gaskell's emphasis on suffering transformed the family into characters capable of haunting the cultural imagination.

Notes

1 See Kontou (2009), Arias and Pulham (2010) and Heilmann and Llewellyn (2010).

2 Gaskell presents Branwell's affair with Lydia Robinson as a fall from grace, evoking Adam's fall in the Garden of Eden (Genesis 3). Robinson is portrayed as an unrepentant, Eve-like temptress who seduces the once promising young man. Just as Eve's sin brings death to man, Gaskell goes so far as to blame Robinson for the deaths of all four siblings: she is not just responsible for 'the suffering of her guilty accomplice [Branwell]' but for 'the misery she caused to innocent victims [his three sisters], whose premature deaths may, in part, be laid at her door' (Gaskell, 1997: 212). Patrick's lament for his son's lost promise and early death might be compared to David's lament for the death of his rebellious son, Absalom (2 Samuel 18); and Branwell's deathbed repentance is like the return of the prodigal son (Luke 15), with Charlotte reporting that his 'mind had undergone the peculiar change which frequently precedes death, [...] the calm of better feelings filled it; [and] a return of natural affection marked his last moments' (Gaskell, 1997: 275).

References

Adams, Francis William Lauderdale (1887) 'To Emily Brontë', *Poetical Works of Francis W. L. Adams*, London: Farran & Co.

Allot, Miriam (1961) 'Mrs. Gaskell's "The Old Nurse's Story": a link between "Wuthering Heights" and "The Turn of the Screw"', *Notes and Queries*, 8.3, 101–2.

Anon. (1897) 'Art III: The Brontë Letters', *London Quarterly Review*, 28.1, 27–34.

Arias, Rosario, and Patricia Pulham (ed.) (2010) *Haunting and Spectrality in Neo-Victorian Fiction: Possessing the Past*, Basingstoke: Palgrave Macmillan.

Arnold, Matthew (1855) 'Haworth Churchyard', *Fraser's Magazine*, 51.305, 527–30.

—— (1890a) 'Epilogue', *Poetical Works of Matthew Arnold*, London: Macmillan, pp. 303–4.

—— (1890b) 'Haworth Churchyard', *Poetical Works of Matthew Arnold*, London: Macmillan, pp. 299–303.

Barker, Juliet (1999) *The Brontës*, London: Phoenix.

Barlow, George (1902–14) 'In Memory of Patrick Branwell Brontë, Genius', *Poetical Works of George Barlow*, 11 vols., London: Henry J. Glaisher.

Brontë, Charlotte (2000) *Villette*, ed. Margaret Smith and Herbert Rosengarten, Oxford: Oxford University Press.

—— (2008a) *Jane Eyre*, ed. Margaret Smith, Oxford: Oxford University Press.

—— (2008b) *Shirley*, ed. Herbert Rosengarten and Margaret Smith, Oxford: Oxford University Press.

Brontë, Emily (2008) *Wuthering Heights*, ed. Ian Jack, Oxford: Oxford University Press.

Byrne, Georgina (2010) *Modern Spiritualism and the Church of England, 1850– 1939*, Woodbridge: Boydell.

Dickinson, Emily (1896) 'Charlotte Brontë's Grave', *Poems by Emily Dickinson*, ed. Mabell Loomis Todd, Boston, Mass.: Roberts Brothers.

Duthie, Enid L. (1980) *The Themes of Elizabeth Gaskell*, London: Macmillan.

Easson, Angus (1979) *Elizabeth Gaskell*, London and New York: Routledge.

Ferguson, Rachel (1933) *Charlotte Brontë: A Play in Three Acts*, London: Ernest Benn.

—— (2009) *The Brontës Went to Woolworths*, London: Bloomsbury.

Gaskell, Elizabeth (1997) *The Life of Charlotte Brontë*, ed. Elisabeth Jay, London: Penguin.

Giardina, Denise (2009) *Emily's Ghost: A Novel of the Brontë Sisters*, New York: W. W. Norton.

Hazelgrove, Jenny (1999) 'Spiritualism after the Great War', *Twentieth Century British History*, 10.4, 404–30.

Heilmann, Ann and Mark Llewellyn (2010) *Neo-Victorianism: The Victorians in the Twenty-First Century, 1999–2009*, Basingstoke: Palgrave Macmillan.

Humble, Nicola (2001) *The Feminine Middlebrow Novel, 1920s to 1950s: Class, Domesticity, and Bohemianism*, Oxford: Oxford University Press.

Johnson, Lionel Pigot (1915) 'Brontë', *Poetical Works of Lionel Johnson*, London: Elkin Mathews.

Kontou, Tatiana (2009) *Spiritualism and Women's Writing: From the Fin de Siècle to the Neo-Victorian*, Basingstoke: Palgrave Macmillan.

Linton, M.B. (c.1926) *The Tragic Race: A Play about the Brontës*, Aberdeen: W. and W. Lindsay.

Matthews, Samantha (2004) *Poetical Remains: Poets' Graves, Bodies, and Books in the Nineteenth Century*, Oxford: Oxford University Press.

—— (2009) 'Making their mark: writing the poet's grave', *Literary Tourism and Nineteenth-Century Culture*, ed. Nicola Watson, Basingstoke: Palgrave Macmillan, pp. 25–36.

Miller, Lucasta (2005) *The Brontë Myth*, New York: Anchor.

Picardie, Justine (2006) 'A brush with the Brontës', *The Age*, www.theage.com.au/news/books/a-brush-with-the-brontes/2006/12/28/1166895419958.html (accessed 10 May 2016).

Plath, Sylvia (1998) *The Journals of Sylvia Plath*, ed. Frances McCullough, New York: Anchor.

Powers, Wendy Anne (2007) 'Emily Brontë and Emily Dickinson: parallel lives on opposing shores', *Brontë Studies*, 32.2, 145–50.

Orr, Aviva (2012) *The Mist on Brontë Moor*, Salt Lake City, UT: WiDo Publishing.

Shorter, Clement (1896) *Charlotte Brontë and Her Circle*, London: Hodder & Stoughton.

Showalter, Elaine (1977) *A Literature of Their Own: British Women Novelists from Brontë to Lessing*, Princeton, NJ: Princeton University Press.

Spofford, Harriet Prescott (1897) 'Brontë', *In Titian's Garden and Other Poems*, Boston, Mass.: Copeland & Day, pp. 39–42.

Uglow, Jenny (1999) *Elizabeth Gaskell: A Habit of Stories*, London: Faber & Faber.

Urquhart, Jane (1990) *Changing Heaven*, Toronto: McClelland & Stewart.

Wilmot, Thomas Slaney (1893) *Gleams of Light and Glimpses Thro' the Rift*, London: E. Allen.

5

Charlotte Brontë on stage: 1930s biodrama and the archive/museum performed

Amber K. Regis

The Brontës were big business upon the 1930s stage. Adaptations of the sisters' novels, particularly Charlotte's *Jane Eyre* (1847), had always been popular at the box office; but from the late 1920s there was an unprecedented biodrama boom (see Appendix). 'There have been at least a dozen plays written about the Brontës recently', remarked C. Mabel Edgerley in 1934, reporting to the Brontë Society as corresponding secretary (Edgerley, 1934: 152). A year previously she reserved special praise for the work of Clemence Dane, novelist and playwright, who had presented a copy of her biodrama *Wild Decembers* (1932) to the Parsonage Museum. This was grist to the society's mill, serving as 'evidence of ever-increasing interest in the Brontës' (Edgerley, 1933: 102). The boom reached its peaked in 1932–33. Theatre-going and play-reading audiences were treated to a litany of works taking Haworth parsonage as their scene: Oscar Firkins' *Empurpled Moors* (1932), Elizabeth Goudge's *The Brontës of Haworth* (first performed 1932; published 1939), John Davison's *The Brontës of Haworth Parsonage* (first performed 1933; published 1934) and Ella Moorhouse's *Stone Walls* (first performed 1933; published 1936), to name but a few (see Rauth, 1974). But the spectacle of the Brontës on stage was not universally welcomed, and by March 1936 fatigue was beginning to set in. Writing for the *New York Post*, tongue very firmly in cheek, Willela Waldorf called for the formation of a 'National Society for the Suppression of Plays about the Brontës'. The NSSPB would resist this theatrical plague, for Waldorf contended that Haworth parsonage had never been staged 'with the faintest degree of success', and much would

116

be gained for playwrights and audiences alike if the Brontës were 'permitted to rest in peace in the library' (Waldorf, 1936: 17).

But these spaces were home to the Brontë muse: parsonage and library, as physical and imagined repositories for Brontë relics and remains, provided the spur for much 1930s biodrama.[1] Playwrights were responding to developments in Brontë scholarship and literary tourism, setting their scene in the family home and drawing upon an ever-expanding corpus of Brontë writings. The opening of the Parsonage Museum in 1928 was a landmark event, and in the ten years that followed the Shakespeare Head Brontë (1931–38) issued new editions of the novels, poetry and unpublished works, including four volumes of letters and life-writing. Museum and scholarly edition were differing manifestations of a shared impulse: to collect the Brontës' textual and material remains, curating them within a single, concentrated site. The purchase of Haworth parsonage had been an objective of the Brontë Society since its establishment in 1893, while the Shakespeare Head Brontë was the latest in a series of biographical and editorial interventions, inaugurated by Elizabeth Gaskell's *Life of Charlotte Brontë* (1857), which sought to reconstitute the Brontë corpus by making private texts such as juvenilia and personal letters publicly available. Playwrights taking the Brontës as their subjects in the 1930s enjoyed access to more primary material than ever before: printed texts, commemorative spaces and museum objects.

Brontë biodrama draws upon these sources to construct and authenticate a particular account of the family's interconnecting lives: actors speak lines extracted from the Brontë corpus as they perform on stages filled with reproduction copies of their former possessions, prop relics that find their counterpart in the objects on display at the Parsonage Museum. But theatre is a paradoxical medium for life narratives. Appropriating and assembling materials from accessible texts and museum collections, these collage-like theatricals work to fashion a seemingly coherent biographical portrait: the assemblage appears whole for the duration of its performance. The stage, however, inevitably foregrounds artifice. Biodramatic texts draw attention to the archival and curatorial contingencies from which their narratives emerge: those ineluctable gaps, elisions and errors that permeate the historical record, textual and material, rendering provisional any attempt to write or perform a life. This chapter explores Brontë biodrama as a critically reflexive art: a notable example of popular culture in dialogue with scholarship, heritage and tourism. Following a brief survey of the public interest afforded to Brontë relics and remains during the 1920s and 1930s, two case studies are developed: Alfred Sangster's popular stage success, *The Brontës* (1932) and Rachel Ferguson's satirical failure, *Charlotte Brontë* (1933). Both examples take Charlotte as their main subject, for hers was the life that left behind the greatest number of textual and material traces. This chapter examines biodrama's creative engagement with archival and curatorial evidence, exploring how their contingencies construct competing life narratives and serve to (re-)produce myth – traditions that supply a lack within, or counter the historical record. Thus biodrama is critical in its praxis. These plays authorise particular versions of Charlotte's life, selecting and replicating textual and material evidence on stage; and yet, in doing so, they emphasise (and on occasion, dramatise) the problems of performing the museum and archive. For Charlotte, as for her sisters, the result has been a vital and varied theatrical afterlife.

Relics and remains: museum, biography and edition

The Brontë Society was established in 1893 at a meeting in Bradford. The minutes record:

> THAT a Brontë Society be and is hereby formed and that the objects of such Society be, amongst other things, to establish a Museum to contain not only drawings, manuscripts, paintings and other personal relics of the Brontë Family, but all editions of their works, the writings of others upon those works or upon any member of the family, together with photographs of places or premises with which the family was associated.
>
> (quoted in Lemon, 1993: 3)

Collection was at the heart of society business. The committee sought to prevent the further dispersal of Brontë relics and textual remains scattered across the globe in private salesrooms and auctions, expediting their return by founding a museum. The first society museum opened above the Yorkshire Penny Bank in Haworth in 1895. The following year, F. C. Galloway compiled a private catalogue, enumerating the collection and subdividing material into loans, gifts and purchases. Galloway's descriptive practice reinforced the imaginative connection between Brontë relics and life narratives, interspersing biographical anecdotes to justify an object's place in the museum. A pair of scissors, for example, 'formerly belonging to Charlotte Brontë', is listed with the following commentary: 'The Scissors have been blunted at the ends. Mr. Brontë would not allow pointed scissors in the house' (Galloway, 1896: 11). The first public catalogue appeared in 1908 as an issue of the society's *Transactions*, its official journal. Incorporating the text of Galloway's earlier account, this new catalogue supplemented his biographical descriptions and documented the steady growth of the museum collection during its early years.

The society was largely dependent upon gifts and loans; it did not possess the purchasing power to acquire expensive relics, their price increasing with haptic proximity – such as those personal possessions, worn and used, which seemed to promise a surrogate encounter, touching the objects touched by the Brontës. *Transactions* listed these new acquisitions and acknowledged the generosity of members and benefactors. A turning point came in 1926: Henry Houston Bonnell, an American collector, died and requested in his will that much of his Brontëana collection be transferred to the society at the discretion of his widow. Museum premises above the Penny Bank were no longer adequate, so efforts were renewed to acquire Haworth parsonage from the Church of England, in whose possession it remained, inhabited by a series of incumbents following the death of Patrick Brontë in 1861. Sir James Roberts purchased the property and donated it to the society. While refurbishment work was carried out at the parsonage, a new museum catalogue was commissioned and prepared by J. A. Symington. Published in 1927, it surveyed the society's history and activities and undertook a census of the current collection before the arrival of the Bonnell bequest. But these new acquisitions and the opening of the museum were keenly anticipated: Bonnell was praised for his 'gathering together' of exiled Brontëana in America, while the parsonage was heralded as 'the natural home for such an institution' (Symington, 1927: 15). The Brontë Parsonage Museum opened to the public on 4 August 1928. Following a ceremony and speeches, visitors were admitted to view the rooms and displays of 'books, manuscripts and other relics of the Brontës' (*Official Opening of the Old Parsonage*, 1928).

Before 1928, visitors to Haworth rarely gained access to the parsonage itself, though patient incumbents had sometimes opened the door. Marion Harland was one of the lucky few to cross the threshold, but in *Charlotte Brontë at Home* (1899) she acknowledged the present curate's just reluctance, calling for John Wade (incumbent at Haworth parsonage, 1861–98) to be 'less bitterly censured for declining to grant the run of his premises to the curious and the sentimental public' (Harland, 1899: 297). Denied access, visitors were more likely to remain outside, testing the limits of trespass. In 1914, Esther Chadwick recorded the impact of a burgeoning tourist industry upon Haworth: the parsonage was 'always an object of interest', and it was common to see 'Brontë pilgrims […] in the churchyard, looking over the low wall which separates it from the vicarage garden' (Chadwick, 1914: 482). Before the Parsonage Museum, access to the family home was largely narratival: an imagined act enabled by a plethora of Brontë biographies and editions. By the close of the 1920s, physical access was granted to all who could make the journey and afford the price of entry (3d, with the opportunity of spending further money on souvenir postcards from a kiosk in the kitchen). But the parsonage did not cease to be an imagined, narratival space. Symington's report on the museum's first year reveals the continuing importance of biographical storytelling as an integral part of its function:

> The rooms at the Parsonage lend themselves particularly well for the arrangement of the relics. In the original house there is the Rev. Patrick Brontë's study; the old parlour, which has now been converted into a strong room for the preservation and exhibition of the collection bequeathed by the late Mr. Henry H. Bonnell, of Philadelphia; Mr Nicholl's study; Charlotte's bedroom, which makes an admirable setting for Charlotte's personal relics and drawings; the nursery, containing toys and other juvenile relics, on the walls of which were discovered several drawings by the Brontë children, embedded in the whitewash; the room used by Branwell and the Rev. Patrick Brontë, now almost entirely devoted to the display of Branwell's pictures and manuscripts; and Tabitha's room (formerly the servants' bedroom), which contains many interesting miscellaneous relics.
>
> (Symington, 1929: 210–11)

The Bonnell bequest arrived in January 1929, and Symington supervised its installation. His hands were tied in the matter of its display: a condition of the executed bequest was safe storage in a fire-proofed strong room. But elsewhere he was free to match relics to rooms and biographical accounts of their use. Visiting the old Penny Bank site in 1904, Virginia Woolf had complained of the museum's deathly, funereal effect: it was a 'mausoleum' filled with a 'pallid and inanimate collection of objects' (1979: 196). Her response anticipates Theodor Adorno, whose work would explore the connections between museum and mausoleum. He considered '*museal*' objects to be 'in the process of dying', where preservation depends upon 'market value' and the privileging of 'historical respect' over and above 'the needs of the present' (Adorno, 1990: 175, italics in the original). Symington's report seeks to elide this museal quality: he provides a virtual narrative tour, animating the museum and its collection through an evocative combination of space, relic and biographical storytelling. His report also reveals how physical access to the parsonage could prompt and sustain creative engagements, in evidence here through curatorial and narratival representation.

The society's commitment to collecting Brontë relics has never wavered. This principle underpins its founding statement, recurs in catalogues and official publications and continues to inform acquisition policies to this day. And yet, desires to accumulate invoke the utopia of completion: comprehensive acquisition and display, an impossible dream that must continually fail. The Parsonage Museum and Bonnell bequest raised the society's profile, attracting a steady (and increasing) flow of visitors, loans and donations. But every new acquisition raised the spectre of missing relics, potential purchases, longed-for loans and donations – not to mention the irrevocably lost. There was also the persistent threat of error and deception, of forgeries, fakes and competing claims to authenticity. In 1951, the society president, Donald Hopewell, reflected upon a new era of professionalism inaugurated by the opening of the Parsonage Museum. In response to 'one of the severest charges levelled against the Society, – that it had admitted to its Museum too much that was of doubtful genuineness', a 'strict policy of examination and selection' was introduced. The collection was 'carefully and tactfully sifted', with items of questionable provenance removed (Hopewell, 1951: 21). Thus acquisition and display in the Parsonage Museum seemed to guarantee authenticity. But the society's authority and competence as an 'official' custodian of Brontë material did not go unchallenged at this period. Symington resigned his position as librarian curator in January 1930, having recently taken on two new roles: editor of the Shakespeare Head Brontë and private librarian to Lord Brotherton at Leeds. His successor, Rosse Butterfield, reported in May 1930 that Symington failed to hand over a full complement of society 'objects and papers' (quoted in Lemon, 1997: 115).[2] The museum as storage site – safe, secure and static – is thus an authorising fiction: accessions and de-accessions, entrances and exits (whether licit or illicit), reveal the space and institution to be penetrable, mutable and fallible.[3]

Brontë biography and edition are similarly contested – an inevitable feature of works that depend upon obsolescence and supersession. As the first Brontë biographer after Charlotte, who wrote a brief account of her sisters' lives, Elizabeth Gaskell was also the first Brontë editor: *The Life of Charlotte Brontë* made public selected material from private writings, curated and interpreted for its readership. Editing is thus a form of archiving: it orders and preserves (in print) the subject's textual remains.

Writing to George Smith as she prepared the biography, Gaskell reflected upon the problems posed by her use of personal letters:

> I do not wish the letters to assume a prominent form in the title or printing; as Mr Nicholls has a strong objection to letters being printed at all; and wished to have all her letters (to Miss Nussey and every one else) burned. Now I am very careful what extracts I make; but still her language, where it can be used, is so powerful and living, that it would be a shame not to express everything that can be, in her own words. And yet I don't want to alarm Mr Nicholls' prejudices.

(Gaskell, 1966: 405)

Eschewing the title 'Life and Letters', requesting that extracts not be foregrounded in the typographical arrangement, Gaskell sought to disguise the biography's archiving function from Charlotte's widower, Arthur Bell Nicholls. It was thus a partial archive, where that word signifies doubly: the published work was necessarily incomplete and necessarily biased. Reading biography and edition in these terms is to invoke Michel Foucault's conception of the archive not as an institution or physical site but as a process that permits and orders public discourse. For Foucault, the archive is 'the law of what can be said, the system that governs the appearance of statements as unique events'; it 'defines […] *the system of its enunciability*' (Foucault, 2002: 145, 146, italics in the original). Ouroboros-like, Gaskell's biography-as-archive perpetuates the ideologies that shape its construction. Only certain utterances can be authorised at certain moments in time, and Gaskell's selection privileges Charlotte's domestic concerns – befitting her commitment to 'honour her as a woman, separate from her character of authoress' (Gaskell, 1966: 347), a motivation confided to George Smith before she was commissioned to write the biography.

The enuciability of Foucault's archive is socially and historically contingent. Successive Brontë biographers and editors, responding to different demands and pressures, authorise different utterances through their work. One common drive is the desire to expand the accessible corpus: to discover and publish new texts and piece together the previously bowdlerised. Clement Shorter, for example, purchased the copyright in Charlotte's 'letters manuscripts literary remains' from Nicholls in 1895, paying the sum of £150 (quoted in Lemon, 1997: 124). He worked tirelessly to accumulate these texts, publishing *The Brontës: Life and Letters* in 1908: a two-volume compilation that incorporated material from existing biographies alongside previously unpublished letters and life-writing.

Shorter made no effort to disguise his wish to surpass his predecessors, aiming for completion: his title page bore the legend, 'Being an Attempt to Present a Full and Final Record of the Lives of the Three Sisters'. But the attempt was doomed to fail.

The provisional nature of biography and edition is highlighted by Shorter's position on Charlotte's time in Brussels and her relationship with Constantin Heger. In *Charlotte Brontë and Her Circle* (1896) he had dismissed what he considered to be idle speculation:

> It is well to face the point bluntly, for it has been more than once implied that Charlotte Brontë was in love with M. Heger, as her prototype Lucy Snowe was in love with Paul Emanuel. *The assumption, which is absolutely groundless, has had certain plausible points in its favour, not the least obvious, of course, being the inclination to read autobiography into every line of Charlotte Brontë's writings.*
>
> (Shorter, 1896: 108, emphasis mine)

Shorter's biography offers 'an emphatic contradiction' of these rumours, born of a tendency and temptation to consider Charlotte a purely confessional writer (1896: 109). His account leans heavily upon the testimony of Laetitia Wheelwright, Charlotte's friend in Brussels; and in *The Brontës: Life and Letters* he maintained this position. The edition raises the same objections and mounts the same defence; it also cites Paul Heger (Constantin's son) to guarantee the absent archival record: 'I have the assurance of Dr. Heger of Brussels that Miss Brontë's correspondence with his father no longer exists' (Shorter, 1908: I, 20). But five years later, on 29 July 1913, four letters from Charlotte to Heger were published in *The Times*. These letters told of an impassioned Charlotte, one who longed for contact with Heger, for communication and commendation. The case was altered and Shorter was forced to change his position.

Soon after the Brontë–Heger letters were published, Shorter revised and retitled his 1896 biography. *The Brontës and Their Circle* (1914) reproduced the text (and translations) of these letters, and Shorter's commentary was no longer couched in terms of contradiction – significantly, the italicised passage in the above quotation was removed. He was forced to acknowledge the recent reconstitution of the Brontë corpus, the enunciability of the archive having shifted irrevocably, permitting (indeed, requiring) new utterances. Shorter adjusted his portrait of Charlotte as biographical subject, but his narrative remained determinedly sexless:

> There are various ways of falling in love and many kinds of love. That M. Heger was the only man that Charlotte had met who possessed brains

gave her a very natural hero-worship for him which was reflected in certain letters which have lately seen the light.

(Shorter, 1914: 88)

Shorter accommodates the Brontë–Heger letters by presenting them as evidence of a Carlylean hero-worship: he permits 'love' but plays with semantics, requiring Charlotte to love in the absence of the body, desiring the intellect. Thus the Brontë–Heger letters not only reveal the provisional nature of biography and edition, they also reveal the contingent nature of biographical storytelling: those multiple, conflicting narratives that emerge from an always shifting archive.

Brontë biography and edition enjoyed a landmark year in 1932: the Shakespeare Head Brontë, edited by T. J. Wise and J. A. Symington, issued *The Brontës: Their Lives, Friendships and Correspondence*. This work included copies of portraits and other likenesses, facsimiles of letters, diaries and sketches to illustrate transcriptions of letters and life-writing. Wise and Symington's 'Life and Letters' (as these four volumes were labelled on their spines) was the print equivalent of the Brontë Society's aspirations at Haworth:

In the present work an attempt has been made to amalgamate all the information contained in the various biographies, from Mrs Gaskell's *Life* and Mr Shorter's compilations down to the present day, together with many hitherto unpublished letters and records which have come to light, into one complete history of the Brontë family, with the letters of Charlotte, arranged in chronological order, making the main structure of the work.

(Wise and Symington, 1932: I, viii)

In their preface, Wise and Symington acknowledged the work of their predecessors, but the Shakespeare Head 'Life and Letters' sought to combine, complete and, so doing, supersede these previous editorial labours. Their practice shared the impossible dream of completion underpinning the Brontë Parsonage Museum, and, to all intents and purposes, the volumes were marketed as a complete archive – albeit a print reproduction. But the fragility of this claim was signposted within the work itself. Reproduced in an appendix, out of sequence and out of place, is a letter from Charlotte (as Currer Bell) to the publisher Henry Colburn. The original was discovered while the edition was in press and sold at auction on 4 July 1932. Tucked away at the back of the fourth volume, this appendix is an aperture or breach within the body of the work, contesting its claims to completeness.

In just four years, from the opening of the Parsonage Museum in 1928 to the publication of the Shakespeare Head 'Life and Letters' in 1932, the Brontës' textual and material remains had been thoroughly reconstituted. There was increased access to transcriptions of letters and life-writing, collected together and authorised through scholarly edition; to private, familial spaces previously inhabited by the family; and to personal possessions turned relics, curated and displayed in a house museum. This encouraged new interpretations and representations of the Brontës' lives and work – evident in curatorial work undertaken at Haworth parsonage and recorded in society reports and catalogues; and evident in those revised biographical narratives employed to accommodate new archival utterances. These materials, these narratives, were the stuff of 1930s biodrama. Beyond scholarship, heritage and tourism, theatre proved a fertile medium for the testing of relics, remains and their storytelling function, dramatising the archive and museum to rethink the Brontës.

Archival contingencies: Alfred Sangster's *The Brontës* (1932)

Alfred Sangster's *The Brontës* premiered at the Sheffield Repertory Theatre in May 1932. This play soon became one of the era's most popular Brontë biodramas: it was restaged at Croydon in February 1933 and debuted upon the London stage soon after, enjoying a run of more than six months at the Royalty Theatre. Sangster was an actor as well as a playwright, and he took on the role of Patrick Brontë in the Croydon and London productions. Lucasta Miller estimates that *The Brontës* was staged twenty times between 1933 and 1988 (Miller, 2002: 143), later making the leap from stage to screen in an adaptation filmed for the BBC and broadcast in November 1947. Popular success established the play as an archetype for Brontë biodrama, staging iconic scenes that would recur in later plays and productions: the sisters pacing around the parsonage dining table, discussing their ideas and works in progress; Emily beating the dog, Keeper; and Charlotte's experiences in London. These scenes are borrowed from biographical tradition, particularly Gaskell's *Life of Charlotte Brontë* and A. Mary F. Robinson's *Emily Brontë* (1883), and in his 'Author's Note' Sangster acknowledged 'his indebtedness to the many compilers of Brontë literature, to whom he has gone for inspiration' (1932: vii). In some cases this influence is direct, with Sangster embedding the family's writing in their spoken dialogue. Branwell, for example, recites a verse from 'the published poems of the Rev. P. Brontë', while Charlotte, following the discovery of her sister's notebook, delivers lines taken from 'the published poems of Emily Brontë' (Sangster 1932: 1). Elsewhere this influence is indirect, less a matter of recitation than of appropriation. Sangster's portrayal of Brussels and the Pensionnat Heger is an important case in point, throwing into relief the play's creative engagement with the accessible Brontë corpus.

Act II Scenes 1 and 2 are concerned with Charlotte's relationship with Constantin Heger. The first scene takes place within the '*Salon of the Pensionnat Heger*, 1842' (Sangster 1932: 29, italics in the original) and portrays the moment when Charlotte and Emily are recalled to Haworth on account of their dying aunt, Elizabeth Branwell. The second scene returns to the parsonage and imagines Charlotte's disappointment on account of unanswered letters sent to Heger. Sangster takes liberties with the chronology of events and collapses Charlotte's two sojourns in Brussels – the first accompanied by Emily in 1842, the second alone in 1843 – into a single event. But otherwise there is an attempt to ground these scenes in the surviving evidence, drawing upon letters and biographies to reconstruct this otherwise inaccessible space (the Pensionnat Heger was demolished in 1909) and much-obfuscated period in Charlotte's life.

First, extant textual remains provide some limited dialogue. In Act II Scene 1, for example, Heger speaks a version of his written response to Charlotte's *devoir* upon the 'Vision and Death of Moses on Mount Nebo'. These words were first made public in 1857 in Gaskell's biography, and a comparison between source text and dramatisation is telling:

> When you are writing, place your argument first in a cool, prosaic language; but when you have thrown the reins on the neck of your imagination, do not pull her up to reason.
>
> (Gaskell, 1997: 173)

> You write, you have something to say. Bon! You go quietly. You walk. But when the imagination arrives, you throw the reins on the horse's neck and…houpla! You jump the fence…and you do not pull up to reason…Do you hear?
>
> (Sangster, 1932: 35)

Sangster's appropriation reveals the fallacious authenticity conferred by archival quotation and recitation. His biodrama reproduces the source text near verbatim, but its dramatisation shifts the inference from subjunctive to imperative: Heger encourages uninhibited flights of imagination, rather than warning against abrupt disruptions to imaginative prose. His words signify differently, and his advice becomes ambiguous, resonating outwards from the original pedagogical context to bear upon the play's exploration of personal relationships. Imagination stands as cipher, as substitute, for the (as yet) unspoken desires experienced by teacher and pupil.

Second, replica textual remains appear on stage as props. In Act II, Scene 2, Patrick Brontë hands a letter to Charlotte – its author is Heger, and he writes to offer his condolences. The original letter, dated 5 November 1842, was first made public, in French, in Gaskell's biography, while the Shakespeare Head 'Life and Letters' reproduced the text alongside an English translation. The original, however, was not sent by post to the parsonage, as Sangster has it; rather, it was carried by Charlotte and Emily as they journeyed home from Brussels (Gérin, 1971: 214; Brontë, 1995–2004: I, 301). On stage, the actress playing Charlotte does not read aloud from the letter, but Sangster's directions make clear that she is moved by her silent act of reading: it is *'easy to see the writing causes her an intense emotion'* (1932: 41, italics in the original). An observant Anne questions her sister, prompting Charlotte's confession that several of her own letters to Heger have gone unanswered. In performance, audience members familiar with Brontë biography and edition would be free to imagine the words causing Charlotte pain; for those unfamiliar, the importance of Heger's letter as source text would go unrecognised, unacknowledged. But all audience members, wittingly or not, witness the performance of several key details:

> We must not conceal from you that in losing our two dear pupils we feel both regretful grief and anxiety; we are grieved because this sudden separation breaks up the almost fatherly affection which we have devoted to them […]. In a year's time each of your daughters would have been fully prepared for all future contingencies; each was both improving her knowledge and learning how to teach. Miss Emily was about to learn the piano – to receive lessons from the best teacher we have in Belgium, and she herself already had little pupils; consequently she was losing both the remaining traces of ignorance and a more embarrassing residue of timidity; Miss Charlotte was beginning to give lessons in French, and to gain the assurance and aplomb so essential in teaching; in another year at the most the work would have been completed and well completed. Then we would have been able, if you were agreeable, to offer your daughters or at least one of the two a position which would have suited her […]. This is not, please believe me sir, this is not a question of our personal advantage, but a question of affection.
> (Brontë, 1995–2004: I, 300)

Heger's letter provides Sangster with limited but significant evidence upon which to build his portrayal of the *pensionnat* salon. Act II, Scene 1 opens with Emily at the piano, her lessening timidity evident in a confrontation with Claire Zoe Heger, Constantin's wife; Charlotte is made an offer of employment as an 'English governess' (Sangster, 1932: 35) at the *pensionnat*; and Heger's 'affection' prompts the declaration: 'I have for you the greatest regard' (38). But Sangster's dramatisation elides the 'we' employed in his letter. Heger alone is agent and instigator, importuning Charlotte to remain at the *pensionnat*: 'I have made up my mind…and it must be so' (Sangster, 1932: 35); 'You will do this because I wish it' (36). This runs counter to the source text and the evidence of Charlotte's letters. Gaskell's *Life of Charlotte Brontë* included extracts from a letter to Ellen Nussey in which Charlotte revealed that 'Madame Heger has made a proposal for both me and Emily to stay another half year, offering to dismiss her English master, and take me as English teacher' (Gaskell, 1997: 174). And, contrary to the dramatisation, this offer was accepted. But it suits Sangster's melodrama for Claire Zoe Heger to be robbed of agency: she merely assents to her husband's proposal despite an evident aversion to the sisters. Just like Charlotte, she is in thrall to this man.

The warmth of Heger's written praise prompts a dramatic investigation of his feelings and behaviour. Sangster turns teacher into tyrant: Heger chastises and dominates; he is a potential seducer who tempts Charlotte with the prospect of a strange *ménage à trois* when familial duty calls her home. She is awed: her '*manner is reverential … it is easy to see that he has completely overwhelmed her*' (Sangster, 1932: 34, italics in the original); and she is almost unrecognisable from the self-determined daughter in Act I who leaves her father's home to work for independence. Heger's bullish behaviour in *The Brontës* owes much to the historical record of Charlotte's second sojourn in Brussels – in particular, her second departure. Sangster's source text appears to be a letter in which Charlotte tells Nussey of an aborted resignation:

> One day lately I felt as if I could bear it no longer – and I went to Mde Heger and gave her notice – If it had depended on her I should certainly have soon been at liberty but Monsieur Heger – having heard of what was in agitation – sent for me the day after – and pronounced with vehemence his decision, that I should not leave – I could not at that time have persevered in my intention without *exciting him to passion* – so I promised to stay a little while longer.
>
> (Brontë, 1995–2004: I, 334, emphasis mine)

Gaskell reproduced a version of this letter in her biography (1997: 194–5), but she made several editorial interventions: material is cut, and the text is combined with that of a second letter, also written to Nussey but sent much earlier in June 1843 (in which Charlotte complains of her increasing estrangement from Claire Zoe Heger).[4] Gaskell also changed Charlotte's words, substituting 'anger' for 'passion' (cf. Gaskell, 1997: 194). Whether Gaskell, Nussey or a member of Charlotte's surviving family, someone was discomfited by the broader connotations of Charlotte's original expression: passion is elided and Heger's feelings couched in pedagogical terms of praise and reproach.

Constantin and Claire Zoe Heger were still living when Gaskell's biography was published, the former assisting with her research. There could be no incentive to subject the Brontë–Heger relationship to close scrutiny so soon after Charlotte's death, and thus some textual remains were suppressed: Charlotte's letters were censored, her utterances not yet permitted to take their place in the public Brontë corpus.[5] But no comparable modesty or debt of gratitude set a limit to Sangster's dramatisaton of the same events. By 1932, the original wording of Charlotte's letter to Nussey had been restored and Heger's 'passion' resurrected – in, for example, Clement Shorter's 1908 compilation, and in Wise and Symington's Shakespeare Head 'Life and Letters'. More broadly, the sentiments expressed in the Brontë–Heger letters had been known since 1913. Charlotte's impassioned waiting for letters that rarely came, her evident distress at Heger's silence and her manifest inability to endure agreed intervals before writing again – these things had been barely conceivable, barely performable until after 1913. But they were undoubted hallmarks of 1930s biodrama. Playwrights delighted in confronting these letters; and, once published, Charlotte's words could not be unheard or unread. But many 1930s playwrights, Sangster included, demurred when it came to the prospect of speaking these words on stage; it is the waiting and silence that looms large. Sangster's portrayal in Act II, Scene 2 is typical:

> CHARLOTTE: Anne! He's written to Papa ... not to me ... not one word ...
> and I've waited, wanted ... (*A pause.*) I've written to him ... twice.
> ANNE: Oh, Charlotte! He's married.
> CHARLOTTE: I couldn't help it. I felt I couldn't live. It was burning me. Oh, how wicked I am! What must he think of me.
>
> (Sangster, 1932: 42, italics in the original)

Sangster's play offers a restricted précis of the Brontë–Heger letters: their existence is acknowledged, and his dialogue hints at their revelation of impatient and conflicted desires. But the letters and the words they contain remain absent: we do not see, or hear, Charlotte's act of composition on stage. Attention turns instead to her pangs of conscience: she confesses; she feels incredulous shame at her persistent act of writing; she condemns herself. Thus Sangster appeases a potentially censorious audience, for he is concerned with Charlotte's internal struggle in the face of temptation – it is no accident that she spends most of Act II, Scene 1 resisting Heger (contrary to the historical record and her return to the *pensionnat* in 1843 without Emily as chaperone). Sangster's melodrama insists upon the essential moral rectitude of its heroine while Heger is made to occupy the stock character role of villain.

Gaskell, Shorter, Wise, Symington and Sangster: the genre and medium differ, but all work as editors, whether biographical or theatrical. Sangster appropriates material from an accessible corpus, and his play constitutes another edition, however partial, of the Brontës' textual remains. Arguing thus, I take my cue from Frances Babbage, whose work explores affinities between theatrical adaptation and edition: both practices fashion a relational text that responds multiply to source materials and other adaptations alike, intervening in 'an ongoing process […] that itself influences the meaning and shape a text assumes over time' (Babbage, 2014: 5). Sangster's activities as playwright contribute to broader processes of selection that constitute the Brontë corpus (where his source materials are drawn from biographies and editions, prior selections and representations). These acts of edition and adaptation produce differing interpretations, differing narratives. Sangster's account differs from Gaskell and Shorter in particular, but all these editions serve a similar end: Charlotte's pain is translated into a conflict between familial duty and desire – for education, opportunity and experience in the case of Gaskell and Shorter; for love, in the case of Sangster.

Curatorial contingencies: Rachel Ferguson's *Charlotte Brontë* (1933)

In the early 1930s, Rachel Ferguson visited Haworth. A novelist and journalist, she was best known for the satirical 'Rachel' column in *Punch* and for her recent novel, *The Brontës Went to Woolworths* (1931) – a fantastical tale in which the Carne sisters and their governess, Miss Martin, commune with the Brontës' ghosts and receive visits from Charlotte and Emily. Riding high upon the novel's success, Ferguson embarked upon a pilgrimage to the Brontë shrine: she hired a car, motored to Haworth and paid her admission to the Parsonage Museum. She was underwhelmed.

In her memoirs, *We Were Amused* (1958), Ferguson remarks upon the thriving local tourist industry – she took refreshment 'at one of the many places which call themselves The Brontë Tea-room and The Charlotte Café' (Ferguson, 1958: 192) – and expresses her disappointment at finding the parsonage a homely, comfortable space: 'I received no psychic glooms or depressions' (Ferguson, 1958: 193). But nor is her behaviour in the museum spared mockery: 'Here is that domed Ark of the Covenant in which Charlotte and Emily packed their clothes when off to Brussels as pupils of Heger, in the rue d'Isabelle. I lifted its lid, florally paper-lined' (Ferguson, 1958: 193). She is irreverent, but a pilgrim nonetheless. Ferguson's hyperbole ridicules the significance invested in the travelling trunk as museum object; and yet, her bathetic touch – her pilgrim's hands that reveal not treasure or divine truth but the banal presence of floral lining paper – suggests a satirical complicity. She, too, fetishises material remains, albeit knowingly: they endure as the ineluctable sign, symbol and 'Covenant' of the Brontës' mythologised lives. Soon after this visit. Ferguson turned her attention to the stage, writing her first play: *Charlotte Brontë* (1933). It was not a success. Overlooked by an industry surfeited with Brontë biodrama, Ferguson failed to find a professional company willing to produce her work:

> By that time there were two other plays in circulation: one by Clemence Dane, whose published script was reviewed with mine, and another by Alfred Sangster […]. The sole production I achieved was in Australia, where *Charlotte Brontë* was put on for a week by a large girls' school.
>
> (Ferguson, 1958: 189–90)

If the popularity of Sangster proved the archetype, Ferguson's play proved the aberration. Yet at first glance there is little to distinguish *Charlotte Brontë* from the roll-call of 1930s biodrama: the action is largely confined to the parsonage, several now-iconic scenes recur, and, like Sangster and others before her, Ferguson draws upon the authority of Brontë biography and edition. Her 'Author's Note' bemoans the scarcity of 'recorded *speech*' uttered by the Brontës, excepting 'stray remarks' in letters (Ferguson, 1933: 6, italics in the original). She acknowledges the canonisation of these verbal traces – they are 'unanimously agreed upon and quoted by their many biographers' – and she follows suit by having her characters repeat these words in dialogue: 'wherever possible, the known sentences spoken by the Brontës have been used, verbatim' (Ferguson, 1933: 6). But this apparent care for the Brontës' words finds no counterpart in Ferguson's treatment of their material remains. Her play demonstrates a keen scepticism in relation to the storytelling of Brontë relics and the supposed authority of the parsonage as museum.

The play begins with a prologue temporally distinct from the main action. The scene is set during '*The Present*' and takes place in '*A Corner of the Brontë Museum, Haworth*' (Ferguson, 1933: 11, italics in the original). This is later revealed to be the children's study, Emily's bedroom, and, from 1928, a commemorative space complete with museum objects in display cases. Two English tourists, mother and daughter, encounter two American tourists: the Emersons, husband and wife. There is a clash of cultures and the pairings disagree over Brontë biography, the merits of the sisters' works and the pleasures (or not) of literary tourism. Soon they are joined by two further enthusiasts: a tour guide and a clergyman, the latter a repeat visitor to the parsonage. The guide recites a professional patter while the clergyman expresses doubts concerning biographical myth-making and 'the Brontë cult' (Ferguson, 1933: 21). As the scene concludes, the play proper begins: Acts I and II are set in the 1840s, while Act III is set in the 1850s (concluding with Charlotte's death in 1855). Without the prologue, Ferguson's play would be largely indistinguishable from the mass of 1930s Brontë biodrama. But this additional scene casts a long satirical shadow, enacting a form of dramatic prolepsis: the main action portrays the parsonage as a family home, but the prologue bears witness to its later transformation into a museum; and, while the objects referred to in dialogue and stage directions are, by necessity, props – the simulacra of stagecraft – they perform a double role as personal possessions (in Acts I–III) and museum objects on public display (in the prologue).

Ferguson presents no party, neither tourist nor guide, as a model response to the museum and its treasures: all are satirised, ridiculed. The guide signifies authority, variously understood and exercised. He disciplines the space ('Kindly refrain from leaning on the case, Madam', Ferguson, 1933: 19) and refuses permission to touch the relics; he also articulates an official discourse as the representative, if not the employee, of the Brontë Society. He speaks the language of museum catalogues, labels and interpretation cards, animating the collection through biographical storytelling. Thus he reveals the underlying process of museum myth-making, of metonym and synecdoche, whereby an object stands as substitute for its former owner. This tendency is dramatised and lampooned in the various readings and responses offered by the tourists on stage.

Ferguson's American tourists, Edna and Elliott Emerson, are collectors of sites, sights and souvenirs. But collection is their goal and motivation, nothing more: they do not seek knowledge for its own reward, nor do they seek to understand the Brontës' work. Though Elliott's 'heart swelled' (Ferguson, 1933: 16) while standing in the parlour, reflecting 'that those great works were composed just there' (15), his response is unthinking, uncritical. And though he has, presumably, read the sisters' published works, his boast of seeing a manuscript is full of errors: 'I've seen the original manuscript've *The Professor*. We've got that in Philadelphia. Mr Rockefeller acquired it' (Ferguson, 1933: 16). In fact, Pierpont Morgan purchased the manuscript in 1909, and it has since formed part of the collection at the Pierpont Morgan Library in New York. Ferguson's portrayal draws upon class and national prejudices alike, emphasising the vulgarity of the Emersons' interests, their conspicuous consumption and speculation. They seek after profit and possession, purchasing copies of every postcard on sale at the kiosk and taking photographs – or 'snap[s]' (Ferguson, 1933: 20) – to evidence their visit and confirm their presence in the Brontës' former home (adding to an implied though absent album of similar literary-touristical images). But the Emersons are frustrated in their efforts to collect Brontëana: 'Now with us, it isn't so much the notion of these Brontës havin' sat all over the Parsonage takes our fancy as the ability to check up on rock-bottom souvenirs!' (Ferguson, 1933: 17). Where the Brontë Society speaks of relics, the Emersons speak of souvenirs bought and sold. Edna suggests they should ask the price of Emily's writing desk ('It's good an' rubbed. Kind of chipped. Do you think they'd consider an offer? They've so many other souvenirs in the Museum', Ferguson, 1933: 14), while Elliott cherishes the hope of discovering a supposed 'missin' likeness' gifted to a servant: 'if I had another three days [...] I'd find that likeness if it cost me my last cent. And it would be "the Emerson Brontë." That'd be great' (15). Ferguson intends a satire upon the trade in relics, a marketplace that frustrates and undermines (to this day) society efforts to recollect and reassemble material at the Parsonage Museum. But, for the Emersons at least, collecting is a means to accrue cultural capital, where the ambiguity of that phrase underscores the play's humour: 'My slogan is: When we Americans cease to own the capacity for wholesome enthusiasm for objects of history an' high-class culture, we shall cease to be an up-an'-coming people' (Ferguson, 1933: 16). Their collecting is attributed to a New World lack – of history, culture – supplied through purchase, filled with stuff, in stark contrast to the 'wholesome' curiosity that Elliott hopes to demonstrate. Having collected the parsonage and its postcards, the Emersons cannot conceive of a reason to return: 'Now, we've seen the Museum an' we're pushin' right on to something else. We see more objects, that way' (Ferguson, 1933: 18).

Ferguson's English tourists are equally absurd. Sylvia and her mother are 'trippers' (Ferguson, 1933: 22): their interest is fleeting, and their thoughts return, time and again, to the availability (or otherwise) of appropriate places to have lunch. They are no more concerned with the Brontës' work than are the Emersons; in fact, they take great delight in frustrating their American acquaintances by proudly declaring their ignorance and dislike: 'I can't even begin most of the Brontë novels. I tried to get through *Shirley*, but I got stodged' (Ferguson, 1933: 16). They have journeyed to Haworth on account of the Brontës' celebrity but suffer headaches and irritation on account of their exertions. To exorcise their annoyance, they complain about the parsonage's former inhabitants: 'I think Charlotte would have spoilt [Christmas] with some matter-of-fact remark, or Emily by some brainstorm. Oh! what a relief it is […] to admit that Charlotte was sometimes enraging!' (Ferguson, 1933: 21). Here the Brontë myth is turned against itself: Charlotte's sense and Emily's sensibility – reified personality traits that emerge from biographical tradition – are used to censure not sanctify. But the trippers' show of resistance is undermined by context: mother and daughter raise dissenting voices, but they speak within the primary site of Brontë tourism having willingly paid their entrance fee.

The clergyman too is critical yet complicit. Like Ferguson lifting the lid of the Brontës' trunk, that 'Ark of the Covenant', he comes to the parsonage as a doubting pilgrim. To the Emersons' surprise he has returned to the museum having visited once before, soon after its opening in 1928. Despite this apparent loyalty to the Brontë Society's endeavours at Haworth, he questions the provenance of items within the collection:

> GUIDE: The case over there contains a pair of Mr. Brontë's spectacles.
> CLERGY. (*smiling*): I wish I were as sure of that as you are!
> GUIDE: Eh?
> CLERGY.: You know, of course, that when Brontë relics became in demand, no less than – I think it was fifteen pairs of spectacles were sent in by contributors as having belonged to Mr. Brontë!
> GUIDE (*grinning*): Eh, well, sir, they do say he was a champion short-sighted gentlemen.
> CLERGY.: As for the upright piano in the parlour, at least three pianos were submitted as having belonged to Charlotte. But dear me!

I mustn't spoil the market, and the piano and spectacles are the only disputed items.

(Ferguson, 1933: 18–19, italics in the original)

Speaking its official discourse, the guide is an integral part of the museum's myth-making. But his interaction with the clergyman suggests an ironic self-awareness. He silently concedes to the clergyman's complaint – a grin offering non-verbal assent in reply to the clergyman's smile – but he chooses his words carefully: though playful, he draws upon biography to confirm the objects' provenance and offers no direct challenge to the society's authority. His jocular misdirection sidesteps the clergyman's doubt, leaving it to stand.

Visitors to Haworth have regularly expressed doubts over the accuracy (and desirability) of the museum's storytelling, and Ferguson's clergyman provides an opportunity to dramatise this sceptical vein in Brontë tourism. In 1932, Godfrey Fox Bradby, a Rugby schoolmaster and literary critic, published an essay entitled 'Brontë Legends'. He set out to debunk biographical myths, taking Emily's life as a case study:

Under a glass case at Haworth Parsonage, in the little narrow room over the hall, which was once Emily Brontë's bedroom, there is[1] a comb with charred teeth. To the untrained eye it has all the appearance of being a dog-comb; but a label informs the curious that this was Emily Brontë's comb, and that there is a story attached to it. Rumour has it that five other combs with charred teeth were aspirants for the honour of admission to the glass case. If this be true (I cannot vouch for its truth) and if any one of the five was less suggestive of the kennel, it seems a pity that the story could not have been attached to *it*; for the Brontë sisters were fastidious people and liked pretty things.

[…]

[1] Or was in April 1930. The small rooms of the Parsonage are now so filled with glass cases that they have ceased to look like living rooms, and it is difficult to realize that anything ever happened in them.

(Bradby, 1932: 37, italics in the original)

It is almost certain that Ferguson drew upon Bradby's essay when writing her prologue. Similarities are legion: both locate their opening scene in Emily's bedroom; both subject the burnt comb to particular scrutiny; and both lampoon the provenance of relics (Bradby's five combs become Ferguson's fifteen spectacles and three pianos). But Ferguson's clergyman is a cipher: he is both a cynical Bradby and a curious tourist. In the former guise, he ventriloquises Bradby's complaint and draws attention to the parsonage's funereal effect. For Bradby, this commemorative space fails (paradoxically) to preserve the lives of its former inhabitants: the parsonage is reconstituted as a deathly space, not a series of 'living rooms'. The clergyman repeats this accusation, noting the onset of *rigor mortis*: 'The exhibits have made for a certain stiffness of effect, of course' (Ferguson, 1933: 22). Bradby and the clergyman join Virginia Woolf in anticipating Adorno's concept of museal objects and display, but their criticism goes to the elision of history in the museum space, not its being privileged. History is threatened by counterfeits and contraband, but the clergyman remains an idolater:

> CLERGY.: Do you know what appeals to me the most, in this room? (*Pointing.*) That. Not an attractive object, is it? Charred, worn. Emily's comb. The last thing she was known to handle before it fell from her fingers into the ashes of that "treat" fire she was allowed in her bedroom. What that comb could tell us!
>
> (Ferguson, 1933: 22, italics in the original)

It is, significantly, Emily's comb that he accepts as a true relic – the very thing Bradby sought to deconsecrate. As tourist, the clergyman persists in his faith in museum objects, looking to the comb as a teller of tales, a loquacious (though silent) repository for biographical narratives. Ferguson roundly caricatures these inconsistencies, but the full force of her satire is not felt until later in the performance when the scene is changed.

During the main action several prop relics recur as prop possessions, and biographical speculations in the prologue are reinvoked, contested and lampooned. Though Elliott Emerson defends the Brontë family against charges of surviving on a diet of potatoes, it is potatoes nonetheless that we see Anne prepare as the curtain is raised upon Act I. And relics doubted by the clergyman are shown in use: Charlotte plays the piano, and Patrick appears wearing '*smoked glasses*' (Ferguson, 1933: 53, italics in the original). But the sanctified comb does not recur. Just before her death, which occurs off stage, Emily '*pulls the ribbon from her hair and lets it fall down her shoulders*' (Ferguson, 1933: 65, italics in the original). But she does not comb it, nor is she depicted enjoying a 'treat' fire. Potential audience members with good memories will laugh at these subtle, reflexive allusions: official and unofficial authorities, museum and tourist, are both proved partially right, partially wrong by the play's main action (which, in turn, is an acknowledged fiction). The truth lies somewhere significantly obscure, inaccessible: relics and remains appear to promise facts and certainties, but their use in storytelling is not to be trusted.

These suspicions reach their climax in Act III, Scene 2 with Charlotte's death. The Charlotte who now appears on stage is subject to delusions: her mind wavers, and she confuses husband with publisher, father with William Thackeray. She regains her senses only after touching Emily's possessions, now relics following their owner's death but not yet museum objects. She recognises her husband, Arthur Bell Nicholls, after he places Emily's work basket into her hands; and, shortly before her death, she calls for Emily's writing desk, later declaring: 'I love it. It's full of her' (Ferguson, 1933: 87). The desk is filled with Emily's things: buttons, a Brussels medallion and clothing bill – the contents previously listed by Elliott Emerson in the prologue. Charlotte's words substitute these objects for her sister ('It's full of her'); she too, it seems, is an idolater. But she also discovers a manuscript poem: Emily's 'No Coward Soul'. And this unhistorical, incongruous discovery warrants closer examination.

Emily's writing desk had been the prize relic acquired by the Brontë Society as part of the Bonnell bequest. It was put on display in 1929 and was the first listed item in the accompanying catalogue. The desk's contents were more extensive than Ferguson's play allows, and they also included material belonging to Charlotte. But among the possessions belonging to Emily was a letter from her publisher, Thomas Newby, addressed to Ellis Bell, in which he expressed 'his willingness to arrange for the publication of another novel' (*Catalogue of the Bonnell Collection in the Brontë Parsonage Museum*, 1932: 13). This letter has prompted speculation as to whether Charlotte destroyed some of her sister's papers, including a potential second novel. And this may explain why Ferguson has Charlotte exclaim to Nicholls, on first touching the desk: 'You won't destroy my manuscripts, will you?' (1933: 86). 'No Coward Soul' thus stands as substitute for archival caesurae, for those missing and suppressed materials that we persistently desire but whose existence we doubt.

As Charlotte '*picks out the paper*' (Ferguson, 1933: 87, italics in the original), Ferguson's play rushes towards its conclusion. Here the intended stagecraft focuses intently and reflexively upon biodrama's raw materials: we see a replicated textual remain (the poem manuscript) contained within a replicated relic (the writing desk). But these authorities prove doubly false as Ferguson manipulates the historical record: there was no deathbed discovery, for Charlotte edited and published the poem as part of her 'Selections from Poems by Ellis and Acton Bell', a short piece accompanying her 1850 edition of *Wuthering Heights* and *Agnes Grey*. Yet

Ferguson's appropriation takes its cue from Charlotte. As editor, she had appended an explanatory note to the poem – 'The following are the last lines my sister Emily ever wrote' (see Brontë, 1995: 270) – framing the text as a final utterance (despite its being written more than two years before Emily's death).[6] Thus, Ferguson enacts one further substitution: sister for sister. Charlotte reads aloud the opening and closing stanzas, and Emily's lines become her final words: they are presented as a message from beyond the grave, reassuring Charlotte of immortality (in the next life, but also in terms of enduring fame): 'Thou – Thou art Being and Breath, / And what Thou art may never be destroyed' (Ferguson, 1933: 88). And yet, by incorporating this extract from 'No Coward Soul', Ferguson's final scene is more eloquent on the subject of uncertain and false provenance than she perhaps realised – for the words spoken on stage do not match Emily's manuscript. As editor, Charlotte had manipulated Emily's poems. In the case of 'No Coward Soul', she introduced punctuation, substituted words and mistranscribed the penultimate line. Ferguson's script makes use of Charlotte's edited text, thus Emily's words – 'Since Thou art Being and Breath' (Brontë, 1995: 184) – remain unspoken. It is unlikely that Ferguson was aware of the difference. Charlotte's editorial interventions were not widely known until the Shakespeare Head Brontë published *The Poems of Emily Jane Brontë and Anne Brontë* in 1934. In their preface, Wise and Symington noted Charlotte's 'various alterations and corrections' (1934: x), and the edition restored Emily's words and reproduced a facsimile of the manuscript – all too late for Ferguson.

This final revelation reinforces Ferguson's broader scepticism towards the treatment of Brontë relics and remains: the play is suspicious of curatorial storytelling (and editorial storytelling, as the case turns out) and suspicious of touristical (mis-)reading. She brings the artifice of theatre to bear upon the official spaces, collections and narratives of the house museum. Satire and metatheatricality introduce an important bathetic element that gently mocks these authorities. As tourist, Ferguson lifts the lid of a travelling trunk, an 'Ark of the Covenant', to reveal its incongruous floral lining paper; as playwright, she lifts the lid of a false reliquary.

'They and I belong to the immortals.'

Works by Sangster and Ferguson represent two very different examples of 1930s Brontë biodrama: one popular, one failed; one played straight (or as straight as melodrama permits), and one played for laughs. Both, however, make use of textual and material remains to anchor their stagecraft in the surviving and accessible record of the Brontës' lives: their words, possessions and inhabited spaces are replicated on stage. Sangster exploits the contingent archival record: his play is the product of recovery and reconstitution, adaptation and edition, creative processes that permit new narratives and performances. His Charlotte is a fiction drawn from half-caught whispers: those partial, public utterances that form the accessible Brontë corpus. Ferguson, by contrast, is sceptical: her play questions our desire to read biographical narratives into material relics and museum objects. In the museum, just as on stage, objects are made to perform and speak variously, sometimes falsely. Her Charlotte is a cause for contention, the infuriating subject of myth. Differing concerns and responses aside, both Sangster and Ferguson shed light (and cast doubt) upon relics and remains as guarantees of authoritative biographical storytelling. Like dreams of archival and curatorial completion, authenticity proves necessarily illusive. Playwrights working in the early 1930s enjoyed unprecedented access to the Brontës' letters and life-writing, the family home (turned museum) and personal possessions on display. Transforming this raw material into the stuff of theatre, biodrama proves a reflexive craft: it performs Brontë myth-making while dramatising the very processes that accommodate and reify these textual and material remains.

Acknowledgements

I am grateful to Sarah Laycock for her assistance and hospitality during a research visit to the Brontë Parsonage Museum. Material from printed catalogues is reproduced with the kind permission of the Brontë Society. Frances Babbage has been unfailing with her advice and encouragement.

Notes

1 I employ the term 'biodrama' to denote a performance or play text that reconstructs and retells the life narrative of a historical person (or persons), living or dead. This inclusive definition differs from more specialist usage that requires meta-narration on the part of the auto/biographical subject (cf. Poore, 2012).

2 The whereabouts of a rare edition of Charlotte's letters to Ellen Nussey, privately printed by J. Horsfall Turner in 1886–87, caused particular concern as a missing item from the Bonnell bequest (Lemon, 1997: 115).

3 Doubts concerning provenance persist to this day. See, for example, Deborah Lutz's account of Society safeguards and a pair of jet ovals first acquired by the novelist, Stella Gibbons (Lutz, 2015: 250–4).

4 The Shakespeare Head Brontë followed Clement Shorter in dating this letter to November 1843 (Wise and Symington, 1932: I, 308–9). Margaret Smith revised the dating in her Clarendon Press edition (C. Brontë, 1995–2004: I, 324–6).

5 It is almost certain that Gaskell read or heard the contents of Charlotte's letters when visiting Brussels in May 1856. To George Smith, she remarked, 'I can not tell you how I should deprecate anything leading to the publication of those letters of M Hégers [*sic*]' (Gaskell, 1966: 400–1). She included several short extracts in her biography, taken from a selection transcribed and sent to her by Heger (Gaskell, 1997: 207–8, 210–11).

6 By 1934, Charlotte's chronology was contested: two versions of Emily's Gondal poem, 'Why ask to know what date, what clime?', were then known to post-date 'No Coward Soul', while the Shakespeare Head Brontë erroneously dated 'The Wanderer in the Fold' (Charlotte's title for 'E.W. to A.G.A.') to 1848 (Wise and Symington, 1934: 135, 160–1, 180–1).

References

Adorno, Theodor (1990) 'Valéry Proust Museum', *Prisms*, trans. Samuel Weber and Shierry Weber, Cambridge, Mass.: MIT Press, pp. 175–85.

Babbage, Frances (2014) 'Practices of edition: adapting *The Anatomy of Melancholy* for performance', Unpublished research paper, University of Sheffield.

Bradby, G. F. (1932) *The Brontës and Other Essays*, London: Oxford University Press and Humphrey Milford.

Brontë, Charlotte (1995–2004) *The Letters of Charlotte Brontë*, ed. Margaret Smith, 3 vols., Oxford: Clarendon Press.

Brontë, Emily (1995) *The Poems of Emily Brontë*, ed. Derek Roper and Edward Chitham, Oxford: Clarendon Press.

Catalogue of the Bonnell Collection in the Brontë Parsonage Museum (1932). Haworth: The Brontë Society.

Chadwick, Esther (1914) *In The Footsteps of the Brontës*, London: Isaac Pitman.

Edgerley, C. Mabel (1933) 'Report of the honorary corresponding secretary for the year 1932', *Brontë Society Transactions*, 8.2, 101–3.

—— (1934) 'Report of the honorary corresponding secretary for the year 1933', *Brontë Society Transactions*, 8.3, 151–3.

Ferguson, Rachel (1933) *Charlotte Brontë: A Play in Three Acts*, London: Ernest Benn.

—— (1958) *We Were Amused*, London: Jonathan Cape.

Foucault, Michel (2002) *The Archaeology of Knowledge*, trans. A. M. Sheridan Smith, London and New York: Routledge.

Galloway, F. C. (1896) *A Descriptive Catalogue of Objects in the Museum of the Brontë Society at Haworth*, Bradford: Privately Printed.

Gaskell, Elizabeth (1966) *The Letters of Elizabeth Gaskell*, ed. J. A. V. Chapple and Arthur Pollard, Manchester: Manchester University Press.

—— (1997) *The Life of Charlotte Brontë*, ed. Elisabeth Jay, London: Penguin.

Gérin, Winifred (1971) *Charlotte Brontë: The Evolution of Genius*, Oxford: Oxford University Press.

Harland, Marion (1899) *Charlotte Brontë at Home*, London and New York: Knickerbocker Press.

Hopewell, Donald (1951) 'New treasures at Haworth', *Brontë Society Transactions*, 12.1, 18–26.

Lemon, Charles (1993) *A Centenary History of the Brontë Society, 1893–1993*, Haworth: The Brontë Society.

—— (1997) 'John Alexander Symington (1887–1961) and the Brontë Society', *Brontë Society Transactions*, 22.1, 113–26.

Lutz, Deborah (2015) *The Brontë Cabinet: Three Lives in Nine Objects*, New York: Norton.

Miller, Lucasta (2002) *The Brontë Myth*, London: Vintage.

Official Opening of the Old Parsonage, Haworth, as a Museum and Library, the Gift of Sir James Roberts, Bart., LL. D., J.P. (1928). Haworth: The Brontë Society.

Poore, Benjamin (2012) *Heritage, Nostalgia and Modern British Theatre: Staging the Victorians*, Basingstoke: Palgrave Macmillan.

Rauth, Heidemarie (1974) 'A survey of Brontë plays', *Brontë Society Transactions*, 16.4, 288–90.

Sangster, Alfred (1932) *The Brontës*, London: Constable.

Shorter, Clement K. (1896) *Charlotte Brontë and Her Circle*, London: Hodder & Stoughton.

—— (ed.) (1908) *The Brontës: Life and Letters*, 2 vols., London: Hodder & Stoughton.

—— (1914) *The Brontës and Their Circle*, London: J. M. Dent.

Symington, J. A. (1927) *Catalogue of the Museum and Library*, Haworth: The Brontë Society.

—— (1929) 'Report of the curator and librarian of the Brontë Museum', *Brontë Society Transactions*, 7.4, 210–12.

Waldorf, Willela (1936) 'Society for the suppression of plays about the Brontës', *New York Post*, 27 March, p. 17.

Wise, T. J. and J. A. Symington (ed.) (1932) *The Brontës: Their Lives, Friendships and Correspondence*, 4 vols., Oxford: Shakespeare Head and Basil Blackwell.

—— (ed.) (1934) *The Poems of Emily Jane Brontë and Anne Brontë*, Oxford: Shakespeare Head and Basil Blackwell.

Woolf, Virginia (1979) 'Haworth, November 1904', *Books and Portraits*, ed. Mary Lyon, London: The Hogarth Press, pp. 194–7.

Part II

Textual legacies: influences and adaptations

6

'Poetry, as I comprehend the word': Charlotte Brontë's lyric afterlife

Anna Barton

Yet if I tell the dream – but let me pause.
What dream? Erewhile the characters were clear,
Graved on my brain – at once some unknown cause
Has dimmed and rased the thoughts, which now appear,
Like a vague remnant of some by-past scene; –
Not what will be, but what, long since, has been.

Charlotte Brontë, 'Pilate's Wife's Dream' (ll. 97–102)

'Pilate's Wife's Dream', the first poem in the Brontës' first published work, *Poems by Currer Ellis and Acton Bell* (1846), meditates on the relationship between past and future, life and afterlife. Taking as its starting point Matthew 27:19, which briefly describes the futile intervention of Mrs Pilate into her husband's condemnation of Christ, the poem imagines the night before the crucifixion, constructing and inhabiting it as a spatial, temporal and (therefore) narrative void that might, if we recognise the metaphorical significance of the lamp that is accidentally snuffed out in the poem's opening lines ('I've quenched my lamp, I struck it in that start / Which every limb convulsed', ll. 1–2), be taken for a kind of death-in-life that allows past experience to mingle with prophesies about the future. The dream that Pilate's wife describes sets in train a sequence of bitter reflections about her life with Pilate that, in the lines quoted above, cause her to lose sight of the dream itself, which is reduced in her mind's eye to 'a vague remnant of some by-past scene; / Not what will be, but what, long since, has been' (ll. 101–2). This moment of erasure, which might have something to say about the limited capacity of human interpretation and articulation in the face of divine revelation, is also itself

145

a moment of revelation in that it recognises the crucifixion as an event that, from a Christian perspective, has always already happened, immune as it is to the contingencies of will and agency that constitute human history. Brontë's poem therefore creates a hiatus in the gospel story that challenges our assumptions about and faith in the linear constructions of narrative and in doing so deliberately fails to distinguish the afterlife as a separate or even consequent condition.

'Pilate's Wife's Dream' is therefore an apt introduction to *Poems* and to Charlotte's whole poetic oeuvre, which inhabits a kind of bibliographical after-world right from the start, confounding biographical and autobiographical accounts of her artistic development. In one sense, to write an essay about the legacy of Charlotte Brontë's poetry might be taken to be an exercise in futility. Of all her works, Charlotte's poetry is the least enduring. Scarcely making a mark during its lifetime, it fell swiftly into oblivion, helped on its way by Brontë herself and by her first biographer, Elizabeth Gaskell. The facts of this brief publication history are by now well known, having been detailed in the careful scholarship of, among others, Christine Alexander (1983) and Tom Winnifrith (1984). In brief, *Poems* was first published by Aylott & Jones in 1846. Despite receiving a clutch of mildly encouraging reviews, the collection is said to have sold only two of its 1,000 copies. Following the publication of *Jane Eyre* (1847), *The Tenant of Wildfell Hall* (1848) and *Wuthering Heights* (1848), Smith, Elder bought up the remaining stock and rebound and reissued them under their name, successfully selling a further 279 copies.

The poetry has enjoyed a slightly more visible posthumous existence. The Aylott & Jones selection was reprinted as part of at least two complete works (1872 and 1893). In the first decades of the twentieth century a handful of selections of previously unpublished poems were privately printed, but the next major editions of Charlotte's poetry were not published until the third decade of the twentieth century. In 1923, *The Complete Poems of Charlotte Brontë*, which aimed to include both the published and previously unpublished poetry and which was the product of the vexed editorial partnership of C. W. Hatfield and Clement Shorter, was brought out by Hodder & Stoughton. This was followed by *The Poems of Charlotte Brontë and Patrick Branwell Brontë*, which was included as part of the Shakespeare Head edition of the Brontës' collected works in 1934. A gap of fifty years then followed before Tom Winnifrith produced what remains the authoritative edition, *Poems of Charlotte Brontë*, which was published by Blackwell in 1984. Nevertheless, compared to the rich legacy left by her four novels, the little life of Charlotte's poetry was proceeded by an afterlife of relative obscurity.

In another sense, however, Charlotte's poetry achieves a condition of afterlife-in-life that demands a different critical approach, one that pays closer attention to the imbrications of poetry and prose that characterise Charlotte's compositional method throughout her career. As my reading of 'Pilate's Wife's Dream' aims to suggest, this approach involves a more flexible understanding of textual legacy, which, rather than viewing life and afterlife as mutually exclusive states, might allow them to coexist within a published work as part of an ongoing and revisionary internal exchange. Robert Douglas-Fairhurst's important study of the different manifestations of influence in the nineteenth century, *Victorian Afterlives: The Shaping Influence of Victorian Poetry*, provides a useful touchstone for the development of this kind of reading. Seeking a version of influence that charts a course between the Scylla of Bloomian anxiety and the Charybdis of what he sees as the cultural relativism of new historicism, Douglas-Fairhurst looks to the Romantics and Victorians themselves for models of influence that might inform their, and our, understanding of literary legacy, defining 'the afterlife of writing' as 'a developing social encounter between a work and its successive readers' (Douglas-Fairhurst, 2004: 59). This social, sociable encounter includes the encounter between a work and the author herself, who, perhaps more than anyone else, is a reader sensitive to the influence of their own writing.

To take such an approach is to break away from a critical paradigm set in place by Charlotte herself. Sending a copy of *Poems* to Elizabeth Gaskell in 1850, she wrote, 'I do not like my own share of the work nor care that it should be read. [...] Mine are chiefly juvenile productions, the restless effervescence of a mind that would not be still. In those days the mind too often "wrought and was tempestuous," and weed, sand, shingle – all turned up in the tumult' (Brontë, 1995–2004: II, 475). It is perhaps worth noting that even this brief description betrays an ambivalence that might complicate an understanding of the elder sister's attitude towards her early poetic productions. The biblical allusion that Charlotte includes in her letter to Gaskell implies that if Charlotte is Pilate's wife, she is also a second recipient of divine revelation, Jonah, her composing mind the storm-tossed sea that threatens to overwhelm Jonah's boat as he flees his calling in doubt and disobedience. The allusion may be casual, but it still grants her poetry a kind of trace or remnant divinity that brings Charlotte closer to her own sense of Emily as poet-visionary than is conventionally allowed. Nevertheless, Charlotte's account of her early work, faithfully reproduced by Gaskell, is usually taken as permission to disregard Charlotte's contribution to the Aylott & Jones collection and to focus instead on Emily's poetry.

Even Winnifrith, the most assiduous and dedicated editor of Charlotte's poetry, seems to bring her compositions to light only to dismiss them. 'Charlotte was', he writes in his introduction to *Poems*, 'probably the worst poet in her family after her father'. He continues: 'With the success of *Jane Eyre*, Charlotte's career as a poet was virtually over. [...] [S]he had turned her prosaic poetry into poetic prose' (Brontë, 1984: xii, xviii). Remaining faithful to Charlotte's estimation of her poetic output and insisting on a distinct division between Brontë the poet and Brontë the novelist, Winnifrith's introduction frames Charlotte's poetry in a way that forces criticism onto a defensive footing. If the poetry stands alone and comes before the fiction then it would seem appropriate to assess it according to the critical lexicon of early nineteenth-century poetics in order to assert its value. And there is a clutch of readings of the poetry that takes this approach, seeking to rehabilitate Charlotte's reputation as a poet on the basis of, for example, her engagement with a Miltonic poetics of inspiration (Pfeiffer, 2003), her relationship to the late Romantic poetess, Laetitia Elizabeth Landon (Miller, 2011), or her 'revisionary views of Romanticism, transitional position in the female poetic canon and feminist protest' (Sadiq, 2012: 834). While this work frequently includes illuminating local insights into particular poems and has been especially successful in its assertion of Charlotte's poetic literacy, it remains the case that Charlotte is not a recognised member of the canon of either nineteenth-century poets or nineteenth-century women poets.

This in spite of the fact that Charlotte's compositional practice militates against an understanding of the poems and novels as distinct and separate kinds of writing. Heather Glenn's pioneering critique of Brontë's career is fruitfully sceptical about accounts of a 'definitive break' separating Charlotte's juvenile and mature productions, characterising it as one that creates a false division between fantasy and romance on the one hand and realism on the other. Glenn's concern is by and large with the intellectual and ideological content of Charlotte's work, but by comparing the afterlife of the juvenilia to a 'signature tune' that echoes through the novels, Glenn points towards their formal hybridity (2002: 2). Charlotte's early work is a mixture of verse, prose and drama, its formal variety contributing to her sophisticated experiments with voice and character. Rather than falling away as Brontë grew older, her mixed modes approach to literary production continued even as she began to turn towards realism. Alexander records that in 1830 Brontë wrote three times as many poems as she had done the previous year and that her Angrian stories increasingly integrate poems into their narratives. The nine 'novelettes' that Charlotte wrote before embarking on *The Professor* (published posthumously, 1857) also include verse compositions, which are usually the first extant versions of poems that Charlotte later extracted and reproduced in 'copy books', a practice that foregrounds her editorial approach to the production of *Poems by Currer, Ellis and Acton Bell* (Alexander, 1983: 66, 170). And, as I will discuss, the first two full-length novels she wrote, *The Professor* and *Jane Eyre*, both also include original poems or songs that are inserted into the narrative. At the same time, Charlotte Brontë's published output is shaped by the kind of self-encounter understood by Douglas-Fairhurst as a species of afterlife. Winnifrith's edition demonstrates that Charlotte's contributions to the 1846 collection are drawn from a range of manuscript sources. Some are untraced but others are lifted from earlier prose manuscripts and reframed as stand-alone works. 'Mementos' is taken from an 1836 manuscript, a prose account describing the return home of Zamorna, one of Brontë's most enduring heroes; 'Life' comes from the manuscript of *Henry Hastings*, one of the early novelettes, and also appears on the last page of a manuscript edition of *Caroline Vernon*, a second novelette, and 'Regret' is taken from a third prose manuscript, dated 1837. From this perspective it becomes difficult to make a meaningful separation between either Charlotte's prose and her poetry or between the life and the afterlife of the poetry, which, in its first published manifestation, is already a ghost or fragment of its original, multi-form Angrian existence.

These self-hauntings, I argue, interrogate and respond to the shifting set of relationships between poetry, print and the novel that characterise those decades of the nineteenth century spanned by Brontë's career. Living on into print in a variety of forms, Brontë's manuscript lyrics enact what Matthew Rowlinson describes as the Victorian lyric's transformation into 'a genre newly totalized in print' (2002: 60). Rowlinson traces a development from the published collections of traditional songs and ballads by Percy, Scott and Ritson in the last decades of the eighteenth century, to the Romantic adoption of traditionally oral forms in original compositions that took print as their native medium, to the Victorian lyric in which the oral and manuscript forms survive only as 'a mute presence whose non-response structures the very utterance it records' (2002: 60). Within this context, the lyric voice, private, expressive and therefore conventionally gendered feminine, confronts a kind of colonisation that it must negotiate if it desires to be heard. Mary Ann Favret's exploration of the use of original lyric compositions in eighteenth-century novels by writers such as Ann Radcliffe demonstrates that this negotiation is also the work of the novel (Favret, 1994). Favret's sense of Radcliffe's lyrics as forms that demonstrate the reification and commodification of female utterance provides a model for reading Brontë's later experiments in lyric afterlife that are also informed by a Romantic inheritance that theorises poetry in ways that enable it to adapt and survive even as it participates in its erasure into print.

Charlotte's correspondence contains evidence of a direct engagement with Romantic and post-Romantic poetics that is motivated by an interest in the implications of these radical revisionings of poetry for the novel. Crucially, it is clear from these letters that Brontë considers 'poetry' to refer to a quality not bound by the material concerns of form. In 1848, Brontë took part in a brief exchange of letters with G. H. Lewes, following his review of *Jane Eyre* published in the *Westminster Review* in January of the same year. The letters, which concern their different opinions of Jane Austen, touch on the question of poetry and the novel. Brontë's second letter quotes Lewes back to himself, writing:

> You say I must familiarize my mind with the fact that "Miss Austen is not a poetess, has no 'sentiment' (you scornfully enclosed the word in inverted commas), no eloquence, none of the ravishing enthusiasm of poetry," and then you add, I <u>must</u> "learn to acknowledge her as one of the greatest artists, <u>one of the greatest painters of human character</u>, and one of the nicest senses of means to an end that ever lived."
>
> The last point only will I ever acknowledge. Can there be a great artist without poetry? What I call – what I will bend to, as a great artist, then – cannot be destitute of the divine gift. But by <u>poetry</u> I am sure you understand something different to what I do, as you do by 'sentiment'. It is <u>poetry</u>, as I comprehend the word, which elevates the masculine George Sand, and makes out of something coarse, something godlike. It is 'sentiment', in my sense of the term, sentiment jealously hidden, but genuine, which extracts the venom from that formidable Thackeray, and converts what might be only corrosive poison into purifying elixir. If Thackeray did not cherish in his large heart deep feeling for his kind, he would delight to exterminate; as it is, I believe, he wishes only to reform.
>
> Miss Austen being, as you say, without 'sentiment', without <u>poetry</u>, may be – <u>is</u> sensible, real (more <u>real</u> than <u>true</u>), but she cannot be great.
>
> (Brontë, 1995–2004: II, 14)

Brontë's assertion that poetry is the defining characteristic of artistic greatness, and that it is closely related to sentiment, identifies her as the pupil of Wordsworthian Romanticism, which lays claim to literary traditions of sentiment (traditions that, in fact, find their most modern origin in eighteenth-century prose fiction) in order to make a new bid for poetry's relevance, philosophical power and moral authority. A reading of Charlotte's influences along these lines risks the accusation of 'special pleading' that Stephen Gill levels at critics who make universal claims for Wordsworth's influence among the Victorians. Making direct reference to Brontë, Gill writes that she 'allude[s] to Wordsworth, use[s] the figure of Wordsworth for local purposes, even acknowledges largely his significance, but Wordsworth does not fundamentally shape [her] art' (1998: 116). *Pace* Gill, I argue that Brontë's epistolary allusions to Wordsworth signal a much closer relationship between the works of the two writers than Gill allows. The aesthetic categories described in the letter to Lewes resemble those set out in the Preface to *Lyrical Ballads* in which Wordsworth insists that 'there neither is, nor can be, any essential difference between the language of prose and metrical composition'; and that therefore poetry and prose ought not to be understood as opposites of one another but that both together exemplify a mode of understanding and a creative impulse that stands in opposition to 'Matter of Fact or Science' (Wordsworth, 1991: 254). Likewise, her scepticism regarding Lewes' account of poetry as 'ravishing enthusiasm' expresses a similarly Wordsworthian concern with the cultivation of a poetics of restraint that might cure rather than cause the 'degrading thirst after outrageous stimulation' (Wordsworth, 1991: 249) that characterises the literary taste of the late eighteenth century. Of these two ideas about poetry, it is this second that is Brontë's explicit concern: the first, that poetry might be a property of the novels of Austen or Thackeray (or, by implication, of Brontë herself), is something that can be taken for granted.

If Brontë is a daughter of Romanticism, she is also self-consciously Victorian in her sense of poetry's declining voice in the modern world. A letter to, W. S. Williams, the literary adviser to Smith, Elder, written in 1850, provides a picture of the author's reading habits:

> You say I keep no books: pardon me – I am ashamed of my own rapaciousness: I have kept Macaulays History and Wordsworth's "Prelude" and Taylor's "Philip Van Arlevelde", I soothe my conscience by saying that the two last – being poetry – do not count – This is a convenient doctrine for me; I meditate acting upon it with reference to the "Roman", so I trust nobody in Cornhill will dispute its validity or affirm that "poetry" has a value – except for the trunkmakers.
>
> (Brontë, 1995–2004: II, 488)

This letter deals with a more conventional definition of poetry as metrical language, but Charlotte encloses the word in inverted commas in order to imply her Wordsworthian scepticism regarding this kind of, as she sees it, limited understanding of poetry's true identity. Her ironic assertion of the view that the 'Prelude' and 'Philip Van Arlvedale' 'do not count' and that 'poetry' is only worth the paper it is printed on engages with the economics of the print industry, demonstrating Charlotte's shrewd understanding of the shrinking market for poetic publications even as it identifies her as a reader unmoved by prevailing trends. A Romantic reader in a Victorian marketplace, Charlotte is equipped to incorporate both poetry and 'poetry' into her own literary productions in a way that might both grant it a marketable posthumousness and secure the survival of the (feminine) lyric voice for the printed page.

Lyrics and old ballads in *The Professor* and *Jane Eyre*

This work of incorporation often carries on the debates that begin in the private forums of Brontë's letters about the kind of poetry that the novel might be willing and able to accommodate. The author's preface to *The Professor* acts as paratextual gatekeeper to the novel, attributing its struggle into print to a public appetite for poetry:

> I [...] had come to prefer what was plain and homely. [...] In the sequel, however, I found that Publishers in general scarcely approved this system, but would have liked something more imaginative and poetical – something more consonant with highly wrought fancy, with a native taste for pathos – with sentiments more tender – elevated – unworldly – indeed until an author has tried to dispose of an M.S. of this kind he can never know what stores of romance and sensibility lie hidden in breasts he would not have suspected of casketing such treasures.
>
> (Brontë, 1987: 3)[1]

Preparing *The Professor* for what would, in the end, be its posthumous publication, Brontë reflects on her earlier unsuccessful attempts to find a home for the manuscript. Her account, like Wordsworth's 'Essay Supplementary to the Preface' (1815), which appeared in later editions of *Lyrical Ballads*, makes a claim for the originality of her debut novel by suggesting that when she first sought publication her work had yet to create the taste by which it could be enjoyed; and its ironic sketch of the elevated sentiments of the publishing industry imply a market driven instead by the hackneyed tastes of the book-buying public. Brontë's own stated preference for the 'plain and homely' comes close to Wordsworth's search for poetic authenticity in the 'plainer and more emphatic language' of 'rustic life' (Wordsworth, 1991: 245). And so her apparent refusal to satisfy the poetical expectations of her readership are not a rejection of poetry per se but can be understood as part of an attempt to create a new poetry within her fiction, risking, as Wordsworth does, the possibility that her readers will 'look round for poetry, and will be induced to inquire by what species of courtesy these attempts can be permitted to assume that title' (Wordsworth 1991: 7). However, Charlotte's preface is marked by an awareness of gender that distinguishes it from its Wordsworthian model. Using the masculine pronoun 'he' to refer to herself, Charlotte/ Currer mocks her/his publishers for their implicitly womanish appetite for poetry, a sly joke that tacitly acknowledges that any discussion of literary tradition and form is underpinned by assumptions about the relationship between gender and genre.

Charlotte's 'attempts' at achieving an afterlife for her poetry in her early novels explore this relationship via a set of intertextual exchanges that perform the failure of the Romantic lyric within the Victorian novel. *The Professor* and *Jane Eyre* house the ghost of an original verse composition, the inclusion of which allows both novels to participate together in a conversation about the novel's capacity to embody and sustain a lyric afterlife. The original verse survives as an undated manuscript of nineteen stanzas of common metre, describing the development of a romantic relationship from the first-person perspective of a female speaker (see Winnifrith, 1983). This text, which might be described as a lyrical ballad, is rewritten, first as a poem composed by Frances Henri about her tutor, William Crimsworth, and then as Rochester's love song to Jane. As well as this shift in the speaker's gender, the circumstances in which the poem is seen and heard changes from one novel to the next. In *The Professor* the poem is overheard, and then translated from French to English by William as he stands behind a closed door to a room wherein Frances recites the poem to herself. In *Jane Eyre* the song is performed by Rochester at the behest of Jane. Whereas in *The Professor* Frances is identified as the author of the poem, in *Jane Eyre* it is not clear who composed the song. This succession of different versions of the poem: from original manuscript, to fictional private manuscript, to fictional performance tests the possibility of a universal lyric utterance and suggests Brontë's early novels as a proving ground for the manifold materialisations/colonisations of a single 'lyric' experience. This is not simply to say, as Tom Winnifreth suggests (1983: 13), that Charlotte's poem leads us back to her own complex relationship with M. Heger, which her novels play out again and again; rather that, taken together, her fiction constitutes an experiment in the relationship between lyric and narrative that seeks, as Charlotte does in her letter to G. H. Lewes, to understand poetry as a fundamental aspect of the novel's textuality and, in turn, to propose the novel as a solution to the gendered assumptions that both constitute and compromise lyric idealism in a Victorian print cultural context.

In both novels this proposal is made via the juxtaposition of Charlotte's original composition alongside a borrowed lyric in a way that gives the lie to the lyric's claim to unmediated utterance. In *The Professor*, the first thing William hears through the door is the voice of his pupil reciting 'an old Scotch ballad':

> "And ne'er but once, my son," he said,
> 　　　Was yon dark cavern trod;
> In persecution's iron days,
> 　　　When the land was left by God

(Lockhart, 1845: 85)

The ballad is not, in fact 'an old Scotch ballad', but a new Scott ballad, 'The Shepherd's Tale' by Walter Scott, an unfinished poem, published in Lockhart's memoir of Scott (1837–8), in which the shepherd, the ballad's ancient-mariner-like narrator, tells his son a supernatural story of a fatal encounter between a wanderer and a Brownie in a cave in Scotland. Its first three stanzas are recorded by William, who then resumes his narrative:

> The old Scotch ballad was partly recited, then dropt; a pause ensued; then another strain followed, in French, of which the purport, translated, ran as follows:

> I gave, at first, attention close;
> 　　　Then interest warm ensued;
> From interest, as improvement rose,
> 　　　Succeeded gratitude.

> Obedience was no effort soon,
> 　　　And labour was no pain;
> If tired, a word, a glance alone
> 　　　Would give me strength again.

> From others of the studious band,
> 　　　Ere long he singled me;
> But only by more close demand,
> 　　　And sterner urgency.

> The task he from another took,
> 　　　From me he did reject;

He would no slight omission brook,
    And suffer no defect.

If my companions went astray,
    He scarce their wanderings blam'd;
If I but falter'd in the way,
    His anger fiercely flam'd.

(Brontë, 1987: 214)

Scott's ballad appears to supply the form for William's translation, establishing an unlikely continuity between the supernatural ballad and the domestic lyric that recalls Wordsworth's juxtaposition of the natural and the supernatural in *Lyrical Ballads*. However, in the context of Brontë's novel, the relationship between the two kinds of poetry is complicated by the fact that it is achieved as part of an act of translation and that it is taken out of the hands of the (female) poet. Like the old Scotch ballad that Scott's own modern composition imitates and usurps, Frances's verse, translated and incorporated into the printed text of the novel by her tutor-lover, is erased into print.

Likewise, in *Jane Eyre*, Rochester's song is preceded by a flirtatious exchange between the newly affianced couple that concludes with Rochester insisting that, 'it is your time now, little tyrant, but it will be mine presently; and when once I have fairly seized you, to have and to hold, I'll just – figuratively speaking – attach you to a chain like this (touching his watch-guard). Yes, bonny wee thing, I'll wear you in my bosom, lest my jewel I should tyne' (Brontë, 1848: 220). Rochester's last word on the matter of his forthcoming marriage is borrowed from a second Romantic balladeer, Robert Burns, which includes the refrain:

Bonie wee thing, cannie wee thing,
    Lovely wee thing, was thou mine,
I wad wear thee in my bosom,
    Lest my Jewel it should tine.

(Burns, 1968: II, 618)

Rochester is perhaps put in mind of this poem by the day's events, which begin with Rochester penning a letter to his bank in London, requesting that he be sent 'certain jewels [...] heir-looms for the ladies of Thornfield' that he intends to 'pour into [Jane's] lap' (Brontë, 1848: 220), but which Jane refuses to accept. Rochester's reference to Burns implies that, if Jane will not wear the jewels that will identify her as Rochester's possession, then she herself must be figured as a jewel and possessed in song. In this second novel it is not the form but the spirit of the ballad that survives into Rochester's own song, which insists, as Burns' refrain does, that he and his love will be inseparably bound together in marriage:

> My love has placed her little hand
>   With noble faith in mine,
> And vowed that wedlock's sacred band
>   Our nature's shall entwine.

(Brontë, 1848: 247)

Once again Brontë's love poem becomes part of an interrogation of the gender politics that inhere within the recollection of lyric utterance. Sung by Rochester, Charlotte's manuscript poem, far from bodying forth the authenticity and expressive sincerity of the lyric, becomes part of the mechanics of a courtship that, at this point in the novel, seeks to evade the truth of Rochester's bigamous intentions. In Brontë's first two novels, then, the published afterlife of Brontë's poetry is self-consciously compromised, giving rise to a measure of scepticism regarding the possibilities of conventional poetic form for a female-authored novel.

The quiet poet in *Shirley*

About half way through *Shirley* (1849), in a scene that establishes the animosity between Mrs Yorke and Caroline Helstone that becomes a key obstacle to the betrothal of Caroline and Robert Moore, Mrs Yorke and her children visit the Moore household where they meet Robert's sister, Hortense, and, to Mrs Yorke's disgruntlement, Caroline. In spite of Mrs Yorke's rudeness, Caroline takes an interest in the Yorke children and in Rose especially, who she 'felt […] was a peculiar child, – one of the unique: she knew how to treat her. Approaching quietly, she knelt on the carpet at her side, and looked over her little shoulder at her book. It was a romance of Mrs Radcliffe's, – "The Italian"' (Brontë, 1979: 450). The two read together in silence and then fall into a conversation that reveals Rose's hankering for travel and liberation and Caroline's fear of risking everything in the pursuit of what she desires. The interest of this incident largely has to do with what it reveals about Caroline's character. However, it is also important for a consideration of the novel's engagement with questions of genre. *The Italian* is the only novel named in *Shirley*, and, as such, we are invited to consider its intertextual significance. The conversation between Caroline and Rose suggests Brontë's interest in accommodating the expansiveness of Gothic romance within her domestic fiction. This expansiveness involves not only geographical reach and extraordinary incident but also a formal heterogeneity that includes Radcliffe's own verse compositions and that draws the reader's attention to the heteroglossic nature of Brontë's novel, its inclusion of poems by writers from Chenier to Cowper to Hemans, hymns and journal entries. Unlike *The Italian*, and unlike *The Professor* and *Jane Eyre*, *Shirley* does not contain any original verse and yet, of all of Charlotte's works, it is perhaps the novel most concerned with establishing an afterlife for poetry within the realist novel. If the novel seeks to negotiate room for what Caroline describes as, Radcliffe's 'other sort of sky' (Brontë, 1979: 450) within its own domestic compass, it also asks whether the lyric interludes that characterise Radcliffe's style might survive as an aspect of narrative prose.

The opening paragraphs of *Shirley* closely resemble her Wordsworthian preface to *The Professor*:

> If you think, from this prelude, that anything like a romance is preparing for you, reader, you never were more mistaken. Do you anticipate sentiment, and poetry, and reverie? Do you expect passion, and stimulus and melodrama? Calm your expectations, reduce them to a lowly standard. Something real, cool and solid lies before you; something unromantic as Monday morning, when all who have work wake with the consciousness that they must rise and betake themselves thereto.
>
> (Brontë, 1979: 1)

To a certain extent this earlier rejection of poetry from the novel is a rhetorical move that, as well as rehearsing a distinctly Romantic understanding of aesthetic category and value, has something in common with the acts of authorial repression that have become central to critical, particularly feminist, understandings of both *Jane Eyre* and *Villette*. But Brontë's narrator expunges poetry and takes up 'the real' in plain sight, carrying out a self-conscious, self-reflexive performance of repression that therefore achieves the reverse of its stated intention so that questions of genre, form and tradition are not so much answered as raised for the reader, and the novel proposes itself as a meta-fictional, meta-poetic experiment. From the outset, Brontë's poetry is given such a shallow burial that its forms continue to shape *Shirley*'s generic and narrative landscape.

The question of poetry is brought up repeatedly in the descriptions of and interactions between *Shirley*'s central characters and becomes key to the way the novel seeks to understand the relationship between individual subjectivity and the kinds of 'social problem' that motivate its plot. The description of Mr Yorke, to which Brontë devotes two chapters, includes a lengthy aside, motivated by the observation that he 'did not possess poetic imagination himself' and that 'he considered it a most superfluous quality in others' (Brontë, 1979: 56). The narrator distinguishes Yorke's attitude towards poetry from his opinion of other art forms, writing that he 'could tolerate, and even encourage' painters and musicians 'because he could relish the results of their art; he could see the charm of a fine picture, and feel the pleasure of good music' (Brontë, 1979: 56); by comparison 'a quiet poet – whatever force struggled, whatever fire glowed, in his breast […] might have lived despised, and died scorned, under the eyes of Hiram Yorke' (56–7). The narrator continues:

> And as there are many Hiram Yorkes in the world, it is well that the true poet, quiet externally though he may be, has often a truculent spirit under his placidity and is full of shrewdness in his meekness, and can measure the whole stature of those who look down on him and correctly ascertain the weight and value of the pursuits they disdain him for not having followed. […] The true poet is not one whit to be pitied; and he is apt to laugh in his sleeve, when any misguided sympathiser whines over his wrongs. Even when utilitarians sit in judgement on him and pronounce him and his art useless, he hears the sentence with such a hard derision, such a broad, deep, comprehensive and merciless contempt of the unhappy Pharisees who pronounce it, that he is rather to be chidden than condoled with.
>
> (Brontë, 1979: 57)

This lengthy defence of poetry is the first of a series of present absences whereby poetry asserts its significance for the 'cool, solid' form of Brontë's novel. Prompted by a character trait that is only remarkable for its deficiency in a character who is himself peripheral to the main action of the novel, the digression sits awkwardly in the middle of the chapter and is at first difficult to account for. However, Brontë's repeated reference to the 'quiet' poet allows an understanding of poetry as something that is separate from, or that precedes expression, and that therefore might lie beneath or behind a literary work, regardless of its genre. Her descriptions of the 'misguided sympathiser' who whines over the wrongs suffered by the poet and of the utilitarians that judge him are borrowed from a review of *Poems* that Charlotte used in the preface to a later edition of the collection:

> They in whose hearts are chords strung by nature to sympathise with the beautiful and true in the world without, and their embodiments by the gifted among their fellow men, will recognize in the compositions of

Currer, Ellis and Acton Bell, the presence of more genius than it was supposed this utilitarian age had devoted to the loftier exercises of the intellect.

(Anon., 1974: 60)

Brontë's narrative aside offers a response to this reviewer that declines the
reader's sympathy and derides the utilitarian temper of the age, achieving
an intertextual echo that suggests Brontë herself as the true poet whose
genius is not recognised by Yorke. *Shirley's* interest in poetry might therefore be read as self-interest: it is a text that continues to think through
what it might mean for Brontë's poetry to survive into the novel.

Throughout *Shirley*, Charlotte's essay on poetry is sustained in a
sequence of character descriptions. 'Poetry' is employed as a kind of
shorthand for certain aspects of selfhood and provides a clue to the sympathetic reader about where the narrator's own sympathies lie. Caroline
Helstone memorises French poetry and, when questioned on the subject by Robert Moore, states: 'When I meet with *real* poetry, I cannot
rest till I have learned it by heart, and so made it partly mine' (Brontë,
1979: 107). The young heroine's emphatic use of the qualifying adjective
'*real*' recalls the narrator's description of the 'true' poet; her impulse to
possess and incorporate this kind of poetry carries it beyond the page and
into the real world, blurring the boundary between two kinds of reality.
Shirley, the novel's second heroine, whose character is drawn in contrast
to Caroline, nevertheless shares this experience of poetry. A late episode
in the novel sees Shirley engrossed in a book, which she then puts to one
side, 'and walks through the room. […] The still parlour, the clean hearth
the window opening on the twilight sky, and showing its "sweet regent,"
new throned and glorious, suffice to make earth an Eden, life a poem,
for Shirley' (Brontë, 1979: 436–7). The narrator goes on to describe this
moment of inspiration as a 'trance' that renders Shirley 'quite mute' and
sends her 'quietly' from the room. Significantly this 'quiet poet' is quiet in
two senses of the word in that she both does not speak and never puts pen
to paper. The narrator tells us that 'If Shirley were not an indolent, a reck-
less, an ignorant being, she would take up the pen at such moments; or at
least while the recollection of such moments was yet fresh on her spirit'
(Brontë, 1979: 436–7). This markedly Wordsworthian account of poetic
inspiration as the recollection of spontaneous feeling is written in the
conditional mood and the narrator tells us that 'indolent as she is, […]
she […] will die without knowing, the full value of that spring whose
bright fresh bubbling in her heart keeps it green' (Brontë, 1979: 438). For
Shirley, as for Caroline, poetry is a matter of the heart, and the reader

159

does not quite believe either the admonishments that the narrator levels at her heroine, or her expression of regret that she does not give voice to her inspiration.

The poetry embodied by Caroline and Shirley also figures briefly in descriptions of the novel's more minor characters. Continuing in Wordsworthian vein, the text frequently understands poetry as the preserve of madmen and children. Michael Harley, the 'mad Calvinist and Jacobin weaver', one of the workers who protest against the mechanisation of Moore's mill, is recognised by Moore as someone who 'would be half a poet, if he were not wholly a maniac; and perhaps a prophet, if he were not a profligate' (Brontë, 1979: 267). Likewise, Martin Yorke, Mr Yorke's younger son and the child who is instrumental in bringing Caroline Helstone and Robert Moore together, is a boy who 'professedly [...] tramples on the name of poetry', but is viewed 'wandering alone, waiting duteously on Nature, while she unfolds a page of stern, of silent, of solemn poetry, beneath his attentive gaze' (Brontë, 1979: 645–6). Martin is drawn in contrast to his brother, Mark, for whom, poetry 'will not exist [...], either in literature or in life; its best effusions will sound to him mere rant and jargon: enthusiasm will be his aversion and contempt' (Brontë, 1979: 169). The narrator continues, 'Mark will have no youth: while he looks juvenile and blooming, he will be already middle-aged in mind' (Brontë, 1979: 169), suggesting Mark's lack of poetry as symptomatic of this larger deficiency in his character. Likewise, the poetry that Shirley never voices finds contrast in her would-be suitor, Sir Philip Nunnely who, has 'a literary turn: he wrote poetry, sonnets, stanzas, ballads':

> Miss Keeldar thought him a little too fond of reading and reciting these compositions; perhaps she wished the rhyme had possessed more accuracy – the measure more music – the tropes more freshness – the inspiration more fire: at any rate, she always winced when he recurred to the subject of his poems, and usually did her best to divert the conversation into another channel. [...] He did not seem to know, that though they might be rhyme, they were not poetry.
>
> (Brontë, 1979: 535–6)

Nunnely's poetic pretensions may only be a 'slight drawback' (Brontë, 1979: 535) in his friendship with Shirley, but, as with Mark Yorke, they signify something greater. That this fault manifests itself in the only character in the novel who actually composes poetry in the conventional sense, a character who also represents the old order of landed wealth in a plot driven by the forces of modernity, is a further indication of Brontë's interest in establishing a novel poetics that might do away with the conventions of the sonnet, stanza and ballad.

Brontë's interest in poetry as something that enjoys a life beyond or after the bounds of formal verse finds its fullest expression in the culmination of the love plot between Shirley and Louis Moore. This plot is a third iteration of the teacher–pupil romance first described in *The Professor* and then transposed into the relationship between master and governess in *Jane Eyre*. Whereas in these earlier novels lyric verse, discovered or proffered as gift, is the means to and signifier of emotional intimacy, in *Shirley* this kind of lyric intimacy is recollected into the prose narrative. Shirley and Louis are united after a separation of some years and so the spontaneous power of romantic revelation that secures the union of hero and heroine in the earlier novels is replaced by the longer work of reflection and memory that is still (and perhaps more authentically) the work of poetry. The reader views the relationship between Shirley and Louis from Louis's perspective, revealed to us by the omniscient narrator and, more directly, through extracts from Louis's journal (Shirley's interiority, like that of Lucy Snowe in *Villette*, remains hidden from the reader throughout). In contrast to Shirley's other suitor, Louis insists that he is 'neither nervous, nor poetic, nor inexperienced' (Brontë, 1979: 570), but he also confesses to being moved by poetry in a way that mirrors Shirley's quiet experience of inspiration. Having spent the morning with Shirley, he reports that he,

> passed from her sunny presence into the chill drawing room. Taking up a little gilt volume, I found it to contain a selection of lyrics. I read a poem or two: whether the spell was in me or in the verse, I know not, but my heart filled genially – my pulse rose: I glowed, notwithstanding the frost-air.
>
> (Brontë, 1979: 695–6)

Poetry is once again understood as an embodied experience that occupies the boundary between material and ideal/subjective reality. The contents of the gilt volume remain undisclosed, perhaps because it is incidental to what might nevertheless be understood as a moment of lyric experience. Fittingly, whereas Rochester's love song renders Jane as jewel, *Shirley*'s silent songs puncture a plot in which the jewels belong to the novel's heroine. Trespassing on the private ground of Shirley's unlocked desk, Louis Moore finds 'the keys of all her repositories, of her very jewel-casket. […] Let me lock up the desk and pocket the keys: she will be seeking them to-morrow: she will have to come to me' (Brontë, 1979: 594, 598). This reversal of fortune is characteristic of this later novel's more confident assertion of feminine authority, an assertion matched and enabled by Brontë's confidence in the poetry of her fiction: poetry the form of which is buried, though not suppressed, within the more frankly material exchanges that are the stuff of realism.

Conclusion: lyrics and old ballads in *Jane Eyre* II

In 2014, a production of *Jane Eyre*, directed by Sally Cookson, was staged at the Old Vic in Bristol. The four-hour adaptation featured live music from musicians who were situated centre-stage throughout the performance, in among the bare scaffolding that made up the minimal set of the production. The music, devised by Benji Bower, included a range of styles, from classical to acoustic to pop, but was perhaps most strongly influenced by the folk tradition and featured a number of snatches from traditional folk songs, which punctuated the progress of the narrative. The Old Vic production, which adapted the printed form of the novel into the oral and visual form of theatrical performance, thereby carried out a second act of recovery, unearthing the poetry that lives within the heterogeneric structure of Brontë's most popular novel. Bower's and Cookson's incorporation of the folk tradition into the soundscape of their play provides an apt coda to this essay, which has proposed Charlotte Brontë's fiction as a sequence of experiments in the poetics of the Victorian novel, experiments that retrieve and reform the colonised voice of the lyric as part of a quiet poetry that, in its silence, evades the material determination of print.

Note

1 This casket and its sentimental treasures, of course, reappear in *Villette* (1853). In Chapter 12, 'The Casket', Lucy is the unintended recipient of a small ivory box containing an overwrought, sentimental love letter which is expressed using a conventional courtly rhetoric that contrasts sharply with Lucy's own complex, inarticulate passion.

References

Anon. (1974) 'Review of *Poems by Currer, Ellis and Acton Bell*', in Miriam Allott (ed.), *The Brontës: A Critical Heritage*, London and New York: Routledge, p. 60.

Alexander, Christine (ed.) (1983) *The Early Writings of Charlotte Brontë*, Oxford. Blackwell.

Brontë, Charlotte (1848) *Jane Eyre: An Autobiography*, London: Smith, Elder.

—— (1979) *Shirley*, ed. Herbert Rosengarten and Margaret Smith, Oxford: Clarendon.

—— (1984) *The Poems of Charlotte Brontë*, ed. Tom Winnifrith, Oxford: Blackwell.

—— (1987) *The Professor*, ed. Margaret Smith and Herbert Rosengarten, Oxford: Clarendon.

—— (1995–2004) *The Letters of Charlotte Brontë*, ed. Margaret Smith, 3 vols., Oxford: Clarendon.

Burns, Robert (1968) *The Poems and Songs of Robert Burns*, ed. James Kinsley, 3 vols., Oxford: Clarendon.

Douglas-Fairhurst, Robert (2004) *Victorian Afterlives: The Shaping of Influence in Victorian Poetry*, Oxford: Oxford University Press.

Favret, Mary A. (1994) 'Poetry in the romantic novel', *Studies in the Novel*, 26.3, 281–300.

Gill, Stephen (1998) *Wordsworth and the Victorians*, Oxford: Oxford University Press.

Glenn, Heather (2002) *Charlotte Brontë: The Imagination in History*, Oxford: Oxford University Press.

Lockhart, J. G. (1845) *Memoirs of the Life of Walter Scott*, Edinburgh: Cadell.

Pfeiffer, Julie (2003) 'John Milton's influence on the inspired poetry of Charlotte Brontë', *Brontë Studies*, 28.1, 37–45.

Miller, Lucasta (2011) 'Sex and the woman writer: Charlotte Brontë and the cautionary tale of L.E.L.', *Brontë Studies*, 36.1, 38–43.

Rowlinson, Matthew (2002) 'Lyric', in Richard Cronin, Alison Chapman and Anthony H. Harrison (eds), *A Companion to Victorian Poetry*, Oxford: Blackwell, pp. 59–79.

Sadiq, Ebtisam (2012) 'Negation, selection, substitution: Charlotte Brontë's feminist poetics', *English Studies*, 93.7, 833–57.

Winnifrith, Tom (1983) 'Charlotte Brontë and Mr Rochester', in Edward Chitham and Tom Winnifrith (eds), *Brontë Facts and Brontë Problems*, London: Macmillan, pp. 1–13.

Wordsworth, William and S. T. Coleridge (1991) *Lyrical Ballads*, ed. R. L. Brett and A. R. Jones, 2nd edn, London and New York: Routledge.

7

The legacy of Lucy Snowe: reconfiguring spinsterhood and the Victorian family in inter-war women's writing

Emma Liggins

Commenting on the 'absurdity' of finding something new to say about the Brontë sisters in 1912, May Sinclair added: 'it was impossible to write of Charlotte after Mrs. Gaskell' (1912: 2). Gaskell's glorification of her friend in the biography as dutiful Victorian daughter and tragic genius continues to haunt Brontë Studies, and our understandings of what it means to be 'Victorian'. Gaskell's *Life of Charlotte Brontë* (1857) presents the 'motherless' girls trapped in their 'wild Yorkshire village' (Gaskell, 2009: 172) with a controlling, widowed father, confirming readers' expectations of Victorian paternal tyranny. Committed to telling the 'truth' of Charlotte's womanliness (Gaskell, 2009: 419), Gaskell's extensive use of letters and the gaps in the text tell other stories about spinsterhood, sisterhood, desire and female friendship. As Drew Lamonica contends, 'for the generations that followed her, Charlotte Brontë was clearly recognized and promoted as a public voice – a feminist voice – condemning the plight of unmarried women, their aimless existence, their economic and emotional dependency' (2003: 32). The subtext of protest about the precarious economic conditions of the Victorian spinster in Brontë's writing became an important aspect of her legacy to women writers of the early twentieth century, who were equally concerned with reinventing singleness for new kinds of heroines (Lamonica, 2003: 30). The 'coarseness' of the Brontës' work which offended mid-Victorian reviewers, and the 'violations of propriety' Gaskell famously protested against in a conversation with Charlotte about women writers (2009: 426), were revalued as daring and revolutionary by subsequent generations. We need to consider the ways in which modernist writers, anticipating the neo-Victorian writers explored in other chapters in this volume, were '*self-consciously engaged with the act of (re)interpretation (re)discovery and (re)vision concerning the Victorians*' (Heilmann and Llewellyn, 2010: 4, italics in the original).

This chapter traces women writers' reinterpretations and reworkings of Brontë's 'feminist voice' between 1910 and 1940, considering political and auto/biographical writing by Virginia Woolf, May Sinclair and Vera Brittain, before focusing on the new spinster heroines of modernist novels such as Sinclair's *The Three Sisters* (1914) and Winifred Holtby's *The Crowded Street* (1926). While Woolf's feminist polemic *A Room of One's Own* (1929) and Brittain's autobiography about her experiences as a nurse in the First World War, *Testament of Youth* (1933), are still well known, the novels of Sinclair and Holtby may be less familiar to modern readers. These prolific writers, who moved in the same literary circles as Woolf, are being re-evaluated for their contributions to debates about psychology, education and women's suffrage; indeed, the 2011 BBC One adaptation of Holtby's *South Riding*, starring Anna Maxwell Martin, has helped to raise her profile. Prominent figures in the inter-war literary landscape, Sinclair and Holtby are worth (re)exploring for the ways in which they challenged and reconfigured assumptions about the Victorian family, often through invoking the 'myth' of Charlotte Brontë. Indeed, since the end of the Victorian period, this mythologising of Charlotte as both dutiful daughter and champion of female singleness was important to feminists, as they traced the genealogies of the woman writer and of women's political achievements. As Patsy Stoneman argues, 'readers' construction of the Brontës *as authors* has [...] been an important part of the Brontë myth', although in her book she foregrounds the adoption of Emily Brontë as muse and *Wuthering Heights* as inspiration for the New Woman writers of the 1890s (1996: 216, 57–67). For women writers from the 1910s to the 1940s, Charlotte Brontë was revered as a pioneering woman writer who, despite being emblematic of the Victorian daughter's entrapment within the patriarchal household, created modern, rebellious heroines. Looking back to representations of solitude, independence and singleness in Charlotte's letters and in her last novel *Villette* (1853), a text whose influence on later writers has often been overshadowed by a fixation with the romance plot of *Jane Eyre* (Stoneman, 1996: 107), modernist authors used their spinster heroines to reject purely domestic identities in order to embrace the world of paid work.

The Brontë myth and mid-Victorian reticence

Stoneman has noted how many Victorian and modernist female novelists followed Gaskell in writing critical or biographical commentaries on the Brontës as part of the process of coming to terms with the authors, their texts and the 'combined prominence and ambiguity of the Brontë inheritance' (1996: 78). In an assessment of Victorian women novelists in 1897, Margaret Oliphant's admiration for the innovative depictions of 'the longing, the discontent [...] involved in that condition of unfulfilment to which so many grey and undeveloped lives are condemned', and her reinforcing of the unspoken assumption that for the middle classes 'everything depended upon whether the woman married or did not marry', allows for the possibility that those who did not marry also had a story to be told (1897: 49). In Virginia Woolf's radical discussion of women and fiction *A Room of One's Own* (1929), Charlotte Brontë's experiences in London and Belgium are ignored in order to emphasise the isolated woman writer's anger about her confinement and her exclusion. Woolf's influential commentary on Jane Eyre's proto-feminist speech about women suffering from 'too rigid a restraint, too absolute a stagnation' (Brontë, 2008: 109) leads into her protest against the author's circumstances: 'She had been made to stagnate in a parsonage mending stockings when she wanted to wander free over the world' (Woolf, 1993: 66). According to May Sinclair, the cry of frustration released in *Villette* inspired a new tradition of women's writing, intent on revealing 'all that proud decorous mid-Victorian reticence most sedulously sought to hide' (1912: 152). Brontë's final novel was re-evaluated as revolutionary in its championing of not only female passion but also the unmarried middle-class woman's right to secure a professional position.

   In her discussion of our contemporary need to reinvent the Victorians, Cora Kaplan has pointed out that modernist and popular writing in the first half of the twentieth century 'defined itself through an explicit or tacit rejection of the cultural preferences and social mores of the Victorian world' (2007: 6). Woolf's eager embracing of the dismantling of 'all barriers of reserve and reticence' associated with the nineteenth century in her essay on 'Old Bloomsbury' (1922) is an example of the modernist rejection of the Victorian, where words like 'reticence' and 'restraint' became a kind of shorthand to signal what was considered to be old-fashioned and prudish (2002: 56). What was seen as sinful and unnatural in the 'dark' nineteenth century would be redefined in the new century, according to Woolf and her Bloomsbury circle. Lucasta Miller's examination of inter-war 'psychobiography' of the Brontë family suggests that the 1930s was the 'era of Emily's ascendancy', by which time her elder sister had 'come to epitomise the current negative stereotype of the Victorian age: prim, priggish, and a prude' (2002: 135). This twentieth-century rejection of Victorian models of sexuality and restraint was partly fuelled by a post-Freudian reaction against repression. However, the moderns were also fascinated by what novelist Elizabeth Bowen identified in 1950 as the 'particular spell' of the nineteenth century: 'while we may think ourselves lucky in being clear of the tabus [*sic*] and restrictions of Victorianism, we hanker after its solidity, its faith, its energetic self-confidence, its domestic glow' (1986: 57). Women writers of Woolf's generation deliberately distanced themselves from the familial model of mid-Victorian reticence which had shaped their own childhoods, even as they obsessively chronicled and reinterpreted the troubled transition from domestic stagnation to an uncertain liberation in their own fiction.[1] The modernist rejection of the Victorian world was, then, contradictory and incomplete.

Victorian spinsterhood and changing perceptions of women's work

In the 1850s, agitation for middle-class women's employment beyond the badly paid and limiting positions of governesses and teachers was hotly debated in the press alongside the social problem of the surplus or redundant woman. Charlotte Brontë engaged with debates about female singleness by reconfiguring the redundancy of so-called 'old maids' and depicting middle-class women entering the labour market, particularly in *Villette*. Margaret Oliphant identified the surplus woman debates as key to interpreting Brontë's depictions of 'that solitude and longing of women', explicitly linking heroines such as Lucy Snowe to 'the extra half-million of women' in Victorian society (1897: 45, 22). Oliphant's rather reductive labelling of Brontë as an 'undesired and undesirable spinster' and her short marriage as a 'catastrophe', a sinking into 'the humdrum house between the old father and the sober husband', also signals the limited choices afforded to Victorian women (1897: 53–4).

The solitary heroine of *Villette* is propelled by the fortuitous deaths of her family into teaching abroad, thus avoiding the experience of live burial in the kinds of work open to 'ladies' in the 1850s. The Miss Marchmont episode in Chapter 4 lulls the reader into an acceptance of

Lucy Snowe's passive, docile commitment to service, isolation and womanly work, caring for a crotchety invalid in 'two hot, close rooms' (Brontë, 1979: 97). However, Miss Marchmont's death (following closely on from the unnarrated deaths of Lucy's family) precipitates the homeless heroine into travel abroad, teaching, the learning of another language and, eventually, the occupation of an alternative domestic space, a 'pretty, pretty place' (Brontë, 1979: 585) adjoining her own school. While the disabled elderly spinster had survived for thirty years on the memory of a grand passion, the reader imagines that the legacy of singleness she also bequeaths to Lucy, whose 'house is ready' (Brontë, 1979: 595) in anticipation of a man's return, will be more enabling. The heroine's transition from a position of being 'anomalous; desolate, almost blank of hope' (Brontë, 1979: 107), typical attributes of the mid-Victorian 'surplus' woman, to a satisfying, if limited, independence abroad can be read as a validation of the need to shake off family ties and the docility they perpetuate. Not only does Lucy benefit from the financial legacy left by Miss Marchmont (which enables her to expand her premises), but she also benefits from an emotional legacy: the women of the next generation must learn from the mistakes of their foremothers. In Ella Hepworth Dixon's New Woman novel, *The Story of a Modern Woman* (1894), the spinster journalist Mary Erle is less interested in 'the lurid emotion of *Wuthering Heights*' than a 'well-thumbed', 'cherished' copy of *Villette*. Mary commiserates with 'poor drab, patient, self-contained Miss Snow [*sic*]!' and her final 'pessimistic, despairing' fate and questions whether all women are destined to be unhappy (Dixon, 1990: 23). By the 1890s and beyond, the spinster heroine resists this pessimism, proving that singleness does not automatically signal confinement and redundancy.

In the mid nineteenth century, however, women were less confident about asserting the value of their work, as Gaskell's *Life* indicated, with its mixed messages about women's labour and singleness. The sensitivity to the plight of the spinster in Charlotte's letters often conflicts with the operations of patriarchal power left unchallenged by Gaskell. Critics frequently quote Brontë's comment from a letter of 1846, 'I speculate much on the existence of unmarried and never-to-be-married women nowadays; and [...] there is no more respectable character on this earth than an unmarried woman, who makes her own way through life quietly, perseveringly, without support of husband or brother' (Gaskell, 2009: 233). Her friend Mary Taylor's courageous struggle to make a living running a shop in New Zealand elicits from Brontë the response, 'Mary T. finds herself free' (Gaskell, 2009: 222). Yet Charlotte's advocacy of the 'lone woman' and her freedom took second place to her own duty to support her father: 'all her care was to discharge her household and familial duties, so as to obtain leisure to sit down and write' (Gaskell, 2009: 245), where writing becomes 'leisure', a woman's accomplishment, rather than a form of paid work. One way to think about the Victorian family is as the site where 'restrictions were set, transgressions punished, restraints internalized, conscience developed, and the principles of subordination implanted according to a hierarchy of power relations' (Lamonica, 2003: 16). Yet Gaskell's contradictory reading of Patrick's regard for his daughter makes her both subservient and superior:

> He never seemed quite to have lost the feeling that Charlotte was a child to be guided and ruled, when she was present; and she herself submitted to this with a quiet docility that half amused, half astonished me. But when she had to leave the room, then all his pride in her genius and fame came out.
> (Gaskell, 2009: 440)

A few pages later, this subservience becomes admirable rather than amusing, 'I could not but deeply admire the patient docility which she displayed in her conduct towards her father' (Gaskell, 2009: 443). The obsession with her father's health, ensuring that 'of course, I could not leave *him*' (Gaskell, 2009: 455, italics in the original), testifies to the strength of the father–daughter bond, though perhaps an aspiring female author also preferred a quiet life. There are recurring complaints in the 1840s letters about the monotony of being 'buried' at Haworth, but Charlotte's lament 'I long to travel; to work; to live a life of action' (Gaskell, 2009: 221), significantly precedes her acknowledgement that such a life is possible for women. The reiterated docility of the daughter at home (perhaps overemphasised in the biography in order to appease the mourning husband and father) is then in tension with the letters' admiration for the unmarried women who escape dependency.

In their critiques of the Victorian family, inter-war feminist writers often took their cue from the progressive views on the freedoms of female singleness expressed in Brontë's letters, while questioning Gaskell's apparent endorsement of a daughter's duty. Writing on the differences between boys' and girls' education in the 1920s, Vera Brittain seized upon the laments in Brontë's letters about being buried alive to further her argument about the need for professional women to leave home and weaken family ties:

> In the days of Charlotte Brontë not resolution but submission was the whole duty of woman. We are living still under the shadow of an age which

made a woman the first servant of her parents, with the usual alternative of standing in the same relation to her husband, and later to her children. Should unpropitious fortune withhold from her these objects of solicitude, she drifted into attachment to a relative, or possibly (the terms were frequently synonymous) to an invalid.

(Brittain, 1923: 123)

Recasting Victorian filial duty as 'weary martyrdom' becomes a feminist strategy to expose the damaging ideology that makes daughters behave like servants. Charlotte's letters about degenerate daughters trapped in domestic idleness were also quoted in *Conflicting Ideals: Two Sides of the Woman's Question* (1913) by the Fabian socialist B. L. Hutchins, which called for 'the abolition of the economic dependence of woman on the family' (1913: 21–2, 16).[2] This leads into Hutchins' argument that the position of single women is slowly changing for the better: 'If she does not marry [the young woman] has a far better position, and is of much greater social value and significance than the "old maid" of previous generations' (1913: 59). From a self-consciously post-Victorian vantage point, daughterly duty and attachment to invalids are exposed as anachronistic. A reminder of Brontë's 'submission' was necessary to jolt twentieth-century women into fulfilling their potential after the Sex Disqualification (Removal) Act of 1919, celebrated by Woolf as a crucial element of women's independence, opened more doors into the professions (Woolf, 1993: 141).

The vexed question of the significance of Charlotte's spinsterhood to her reputation as feminist pioneer was taken up by May Sinclair in *The Three Brontës* (1912), which insisted that Gaskell's 'too tragic' *Life* was 'incomplete' (1912: 47–8). Sinclair's obsession with the Brontës has been analysed by her biographer Suzanne Raitt in terms of her identification with their domestic confinement and forward-looking outlook: Sinclair admired 'the ways in which the Brontës had anticipated the values of an age they would not live to see' (Raitt, 2000: 117). Sinclair positions Charlotte on the threshold between the Victorian and the modern, 'writing in the mid-Victorian age, about mid-Victorian women, the women whom she saw around her […] in the days before emancipation, when marriage was the only chance of independence that a woman had' (1912: 65). In her interpretation of Charlotte becoming 'the head of her father's household' after her aunt's death in 1842, Sinclair observes, 'in that dark mid-Victorian age it was sin in any woman to leave her home if her home required her', going on to reinforce the 'homesickness' for Haworth which haunted her stay in Brussels (1912: 74). By the 1910s biographers had begun to speculate about Charlotte's potentially adulterous desires for her tutor M. Heger during her time at the Belgian *pensionnat*, a possibility Gaskell had chosen to edit out of her biography. In 1913, *The Times* printed four letters Charlotte had written to Heger in 1844–5, which seemed to indicate her feelings of unrequited love, a father fixation, or an excessive gratitude for a great teacher (Miller, 2002: 109). This questioned the public image of Charlotte as a restrained spinster, a questioning continued in Michèle Roberts' neo-Victorian novel *The Mistressclass* (2004), which imagines additional letters Charlotte might have written to Heger, which echo, evoke and rewrite scenes and lines from the Brontë archive. Sinclair preferred to deny Charlotte's passion, in order to anchor her creativity in her decision to remain single. This dismissal of the value of the Heger letters, which appeared between the first and second editions of Sinclair's study, shows the unmarried female modernist's investment in the ideal of Charlotte as 'heroine of other-worldliness' and prototype for the 'single woman artist' (Miller, 2002: 119–20). Disproving that her idol was a 'foredoomed spinster' by listing her four suitors, Sinclair tries to show female independence as a choice which women, particularly artists, can make, borrowing from suffrage arguments about women's capacity to resist domestic entrapment by entering the public sphere (1912: 70).

Written twenty years after the publicity around the Heger letters, Margaret Lawrence's chapter on the sisters in *We Write as Women* (1937) validates their position within 'the history of the feminist movement' (1937: 82). Gaskell's fashioning of Charlotte into a 'great heroine', a 'literary pioneer', is linked to her canny investment in the Brontës' 'tragic' origins: 'She knew it would make a gorgeous biography' (1937: 83). Lawrence also explains the editing of the Brussels episodes in the interests of 'fix[ing] the attention of all future historians of the Brontës' on Haworth's 'household of terrible emotion', rather than on Charlotte's possible adultery, which was 'enough to disturb a lady-like biographer' (1937: 65–6). In accordance with inter-war leanings towards sexual liberation, Charlotte's validation of her heroines' right to work becomes inextricable from their sex lives: 'What she was really saying, though it is not clear that she knew it consciously, was that women needed a wider intellectual arena in order to find a more satisfying erotic life' (Lawrence, 1937: 85). The problem in Gaskell's careful canonisation of her friend was not only the presence of sin, as Lawrence sensationally proclaimed, but also the way in which it offered a limited view of female singleness. Future historians who seized on the *Life*'s exposure of paternal tyranny and daughterly submission as the only way to read the Victorian spinster were in danger of passing on a misleading and simplified version of Charlotte Brontë as a victim of patriarchy.[3]

But this was not the only way in which Brontë was interpreted in the early twentieth century. For Woolf, Charlotte Brontë is representative of those 'unnatural daughters' who rebelled against Victorian fathers in their desire to gain independence through paid work. In her anti-war protest, *Three Guineas* (1938), influenced by the modernist interest in Victorian psychology, paternal disapproval of the marriages of Victorian daughters is attributed to infantile fixation. Patrick Brontë, in Woolf's account, has the same fixation as Sophia Jex-Blake's father who forbade her to work for money, preferring 'to keep his daughter in his own power' (Woolf, 1993: 260), before reluctantly allowing her into the medical profession. Attesting, 'it was the woman, the human being whose sex made it her sacred duty to sacrifice herself to her father, whom Charlotte Brontë and Elizabeth Barrett had to kill', Woolf demonstrates how killing the 'lady', as well as the 'Angel in the House', was necessary for the woman worker:

> Infantile fixation was protected by society. Nature, law and property were all ready to excuse and conceal it. It was easy for Mr Barrett, Mr Jex-Blake and the Rev. Patrick Brontë to hide the real nature of their emotions from themselves. If they wished that their daughter should stay at home, society agreed that they were right. If the daughter protested, then nature came to their help. A daughter who left her father was an unnatural daughter; her womanhood was suspect. Should she persist further, then law came to his help. A daughter who left her father had no means of supporting herself. The lawful professions were shut to her.
>
> (Woolf, 1993: 262, 263)

This indictment of Victorian paternal control spells out the operations of disciplinary power as well as the need for 'unnatural' daughters to shake off the shackles of 'nature, law and property'.

Post-Freudian accounts of Victorian women also speculated about the potential lesbianism of the supposedly sexless spinster, as I have argued elsewhere.[4] Margaret Lawrence suggested that, like other inter-war women writers, Charlotte 'had gone almost homosexual in her devotion to Ellen Nussey', writing her letters that were 'nearly amorous' and expressing the desire to live with her (1937: 73). In a more recent discussion of Victorian life-writing, Sharon Marcus talks about female friendship as a 'fundamental component of middle-class femininity and women's life stories', using evidence from Sarah Ellis's conduct books published in the 1840s (Marcus, 2007: 39). In Gaskell's account, Charlotte's visits to friends are recorded very briefly and Ellen is not named. She also edits out Arthur Nicholls' intervention in the 'dangerous' letters sent between his new wife and Ellen Nussey in 1854, which he stipulated should be burnt after reading. The husband's threat to 'read every line [Charlotte] write[s] and elect himself censor of our correspondence' is suggestive of the silencing and censorship of female friendship/desire, '[men] always seem to think us incautious' (Brontë, 2007: 238–9). Sinclair argues that Charlotte's 'tremendous power of self-repression' would not have permitted a tragic passion but that her 'large and luminous ideas of friendship' informed her relationship with Heger; she also interprets the strength of her feelings for Mary Taylor and Ellen as evidence of a 'genius for friendship' (1912: 81–2, 86). Sinclair does, however, acknowledge that some of the letters display 'a lover's ardour and impatience', sure evidence of 'her passionate affection', even if they also enclose a troubling 'secrecy' (1912: 91). In a letter of 1850, which alludes to the 'sincere' attachments between female friends, Charlotte writes, 'single women often like each other much and derive great solace from their mutual regard' (Brontë, 2007: 154). Certainly, her 'genius for friendship', whether we read it as 'almost homosexual' or not, can be seen to anticipate the strengths of the bonds between middle-class women, which inter-war women writers increasingly celebrated in their fictional and auto/biographical work.

Vera Brittain's affectionate prologue to *Testament of Friendship* (1940), her biography of Holtby, pays homage to Gaskell's friendship for Brontë and protection of her womanliness and reputation. Endorsing the 'genius for friendship' of the woman writer, it implies that Brittain's reverence for her friend is partly modelled on the bonding between the two Victorian writers. Brittain and Holtby co-habited while working as journalists in London after the war, also sharing child care while Vera's husband worked abroad; the women's mutually supportive relationship only ended with Winifred's premature death. The first chapter, 'Pilgrimage to Rudston', indirectly evokes Haworth by imagining the future phenomenon of literary tourism to Yorkshire, 'hallowed by association with celebrated writers of this generation' (Brittain, 1980: 5), including Holtby, J. B. Priestley, Phyllis Bentley and Storm Jameson. Describing the country churchyard where her friend is buried, a direct comparison with Charlotte Brontë is made in terms of both authors dying in their late thirties, and the book ends with references to Holtby's 'unwritten books' and the 'problem of the twentieth-century woman artist', 'a typical product of her age' (Brittain, 1980: 440, 441). 'The likeness between the two Yorkshire women' and their stories is reinforced by quoting a significant passage from Sinclair's introduction to the reissue of Gaskell's *Life*, about the effects of family life on 'great women':

> Their lives are inseparable from them, their works in many cases inexplicable without them. [...] A woman cannot get away from her family even in its absence. She may abandon it; it may abandon her; but she is bound to it by infrangible, indestructible bonds. [...] Imagine then what its influence must have been on Charlotte Brontë, who never abandoned or ignored it.
>
> (Brittain, 1980: 10)

The lives of great women, unlike those of great men, cannot be either lived or narrated outside the family, despite the modern precedent of leaving home (attested in Holtby's own life of Woolf, which shows the woman writer fixated on her dead mother). To frame Holtby's life in relation to Sinclair's version of Gaskell's Brontë is not only to reinforce the significance of family to the female genius but also to suggest that the success of the twentieth-century woman artist, more so than her Victorian counterparts, depended upon her bonds with other women writers. By the modernist period Brontë had become an icon of spinsterhood, an inspirational figure in a newly formed tradition of women's writing and a crucial reference point for feminist interventions into debates around women's work and the family.

Rebelling against the Victorian family: the spinster heroines of May Sinclair and Winifred Holtby

Rewritings of what Woolf referred to as Charlotte Brontë's 'stagnation' enabled a modern readership to understand what had already become 'old-fashioned' about the spinster's capitulation to domestic imprisonment. Modernist spinster narratives, which are often set partly in the second half of the nineteenth century, heighten the difficulties of the 'unnatural', rebellious daughter by trapping the spinster heroine in an already outdated Victorianism (Liggins, 2014: 142). They anticipate neo-Victorian novels in setting out to reinvent and reimagine the nineteenth century, while showing that the hard-won freedoms of modernity did not always guarantee the disappearance of hampering social conventions. The clergyman's daughter, often stoically caring for a widowed father, is a recurring character, as in F. M. Mayor's novel *The Rector's Daughter* (1924) and E. H. Young's *The Vicar's Daughter* (1928). In their confrontations with the legacy of the old maid, such texts sometimes pathologise singleness, denying educated daughters opportunities for travel, fulfilling work and independent living. However, they also reformulate notions of Victorian reticence by giving the usually silent spinster a voice, moving her from the margins of the narrative to the centre.

The Three Sisters (1914), inspired by the Brontës' lives, is the first of a series of spinster novels written by May Sinclair during and immediately after the First World War, when the surplus woman question became more topical with the huge loss of British men in the trenches. Self-consciously evoking Haworth by its haunting descriptions of the remote, desolate Northern village of Garth, the novel opens with the three Cartaret sisters in the vicarage, 'doing nothing […] waiting for something to happen' (Sinclair, 1982: 3). The refrain 'Nothing happened' (Sinclair, 1982: 339), borrowed from Charlotte's letters, signifies their deadening weekly routine. The novel's title also recalls Anton Chekhov's late play *Three Sisters*, first performed in Moscow in 1901, which may have been a possible inspiration for Sinclair's representations of frustrated sisterhood. Protesting against the stultifying provincialism that confines two unmarried sisters in the family home, the play also anatomises women's boredom, with adultery a possible, if risky, way out. Sinclair's sisters compete for the attention of the new doctor, Stephen Rowcliffe, who treats Alice, the 'unhappy ghost' (Sinclair, 1982: 354), for her neurasthenic illness, goes on secret trysts with the 'wild, strong' Gwenda on her night-time roaming of the moors, before finally marrying the 'sweet and womanly' Mary (1982: 10), whose complacent maternity quickly gives her an increased 'social value' (1982: 310). Sally Shuttleworth has pointed out that, 'as a literary character, the doctor takes on new prominence in the Victorian era, […] usually hovering in the wings, waiting to diagnose the incipient signs of latent insanity or mental disorder' (1996: 10). Charlotte Perkins Gilman's Brontësque *The Yellow Wallpaper* (1892) illustrates this power of the doctor-husband over an unnamed bored Victorian wife confined to her bed in an old nursery, imprisoned in both the domestic space and medical constructions of proper femininity. By the 1890s and beyond the doctor was less an admirable heroic figure whose medical knowledge could be socially useful than a sinister psychiatrist, knowingly acquiescing in the pathologising of his patient/wife/object of desire through the limiting narratives of hysteria.

Sinclair's three sisters rehearse the self-sacrificing roles of the 'outdated' mid-Victorian heroine, denied training for professional work. According to Alison Pease, Sinclair's female characters 'adopt boredom as a passive form of protest against the stultifying, male-privileged families in which they find themselves. Their boredom is a self-evacuation from desire and power' (2006: 174). The vicarage is a carceral space with little privacy, in which the sisters are doomed to wait passively for the visits of men: '[Alice] hated the whole house. It was so built that there wasn't a corner in it where you could get away from Papa […] he was aware of everything you did, of everything you didn't do' (Sinclair, 1982: 12). Alice's 'defiance of the house and her revenge' is her passionate piano-playing with 'its vindictive quality' (Sinclair, 1982: 15), which comes to signal hysteria. While Gwenda, the second sister, initially evokes Emily's mysticism, love of nature and disregard for convention, she comes to embody the dreams and docility attributed to Charlotte, briefly escaping her home duties for paid work as secretary to her stepmother's friend, before being drawn back to the vicarage to care for her ailing father. By the end of the narrative she is trapped in her father's clutches, 'We're all tied up together in it, tight. We can't get away from each other. It isn't as if I could leave. I'm stuck here with Papa' (Sinclair, 1982: 384). Her capacity to jest about 'funny fathers', an observation made by the doctor, appears to prove Gwenda's strength and sanity, but 'Rowcliffe had seen women made bitter, made morbid, driven into lunatic asylums by fathers who were as funny as Mr Cartaret' (Sinclair, 1982: 100). The doctor's belief that Alice's hysteria is 'absolutely curable' (Sinclair, 1982: 182) by marriage is another ominous echo of the frightening inertia of Charlotte Perkins Gilman's newly married heroine struggling with the 'rest cure' for her (post-natal) depression.

The spinster's passive performance of duty is contrasted with the contentment of the unmarried servant-girl, Essy, who is thrown out of the vicarage for her pregnancy but ultimately welcomed back, despite her having an illegitimate son. Mary's embracing of her passivity prompts Gwenda's resolution that 'we've only got to sit tight and play the game' (Sinclair, 1982: 192). Despite her refusal of her father's bullying in the first half of the novel, and threats to get out of the windows of locked rooms if necessary, Gwenda, like Charlotte, is not strong enough to beat the trump card of paternal illness, under which she becomes 'his to bend or break or utterly destroy' (Sinclair, 1982: 306). Gwenda's 'woman's passion, forced inward', may have 'sustained her with an inward peace, an inward exultation' (Sinclair, 1982: 339), but her denial of her feelings for the doctor could also signal the 'abnormality' of the spinster's frigidity. Sinclair underlines that the costs of adultery would have been less for the respectable doctor than for the isolated unmarried daughter who agrees to become his mistress, leaving the spinster heroine doomed to a life of passion unfulfilled. For Stoneman, this flawed novel 'reads like a demonstration of Freud's comments on the difficulty, for women, of negotiating the Oedipus complex [...] all [the sisters] are condemned to less than full humanity by their repressive father' (1996: 70). Such an investment in passivity may be at odds with Sinclair's position on women's needs to participate more fully in public life, but it is a characteristic of her fiction that her heroines cannot always transcend the repressive powers of Victorian parents.

Holtby's fiction more radically develops the *Villette* plot in its championing of the spinster heroine's escape from provincial domesticity into a more satisfying world of paid professional work. Plain, prim Victorian daughter Muriel Hammond in *The Crowded Street* (1924) dashes her mother's hopes of a good marriage by living with a female friend and working for a reform league in post-war London. Transformed from a reluctant wallflower into a spokesperson for the unmarried, the thirty-year-old spinster heroine worries that she is 'only trying to cover the shame of her retreat' (Holtby, 1981: 243) yet ultimately acquires the courage to turn down the stuffy suitor Godfrey she had initially admired. Ostensibly rejecting mid-Victorian narratives, Muriel throws down Brontë's social-problem novel *Shirley* 'unheeded', as she 'was not interested in curates' (Holtby, 1981: 156). However, this intertextual link acts as a reminder of Brontë's analysis of female singleness as both problematic and desirable in the conversations between Shirley and Caroline. There are similar tensions in Holtby's novel between the heroine's desire to be married and her recoiling from the boredom of the social round this would entail. Rather than accepting the role of society wife and hostess, Muriel prefers to return to London alone, inspired by 'an idea of service'; this leaves Godfrey musing, 'how queer women were!' (Holtby, 1981: 270, 271). Like her mentor, Delia, who has lost her fiancé in the war, like Lucy Snowe with her memories of her romance with M. Paul, the 'queer' spinster heroine can then go forward, bolstered by the knowledge that she has been desired. Holtby's novel significantly ends in 1920, after women over thirty had been granted the vote, reflecting the optimism felt by women writers about future possibilities for female autonomy.

In her last novel, Holtby depicts in greater detail the admirable life of Sarah Burton, the headmistress heroine of *South Riding* (1936). An inspiring role model for her female pupils, Sarah is a new kind of spinster, devoted to her work and her friends but also interested in male attention. In her feminist pamphlet *Women and a Changing Civilisation* (1934) Holtby had already highlighted the damage done by the 'legend of the Frustrated Spinster' (Holtby, 1978: 125); here she showed her professional heroine to be sexually confident. In an argument defending teachers wearing lipstick, Sarah seeks to restore lost femininity and sexual allure, 'my trouble is to persuade my girls that membership of my profession need not imply complete indifference to all other sides of life' (Holtby, 1988: 146). Her offer to be the mistress, rather than the wife, of an MP consolidates her position as one of the 'desirable and desired' (Holtby, 1988: 49), a spinster whose feminism does not cancel out her erotic drives and flirtatiousness. The new headmistress's position is favourably compared to those of other less fortunate and stereotypical spinster-teachers, like the inefficient retiring Miss Holmes who goes off to share a villa with a widowed sister. Sarah's romance with the brooding Robert Carne, and the revelation that he has an insane wife in an asylum, has echoes of the *Jane Eyre* plot, which was also influential on other inter-war novels such as Daphne du Maurier's *Rebecca* (1938). Du Maurier's celebrated Gothic romance set in Manderley, a country house haunted by the ghost of Maxim de Winter's glamorous, flirtatious first wife, Rebecca, reveals its debt to Brontë's plots in the transformation of its self-effacing, nameless heroine from a nervous paid companion to mistress of Manderley and second wife of the Byronic de Winter. The second wife can only shake off her diffidence and 'timidity of strangers' when the husband, like Rochester, suffers from his home being set on fire and feels shorn of his power: 'it is his dependence which has made me bold at last' (du Maurier, 1992: 13). Avril Horner and Sue Zlosnik have noted the disruptive presence of the 'dark double', the sexually confident first wife, at the end of du Maurier's novel, but in narrative terms she must be killed off or consigned to the past to enable the heroine's survival and a satisfying plot closure (1998: 125).

Ultimately though, Holtby's headmistress heroine is a descendant of Lucy Snowe, refusing either to be 'caught, trapped in emotion' (Holtby, 1988: 257) or to tame a Byronic hero like Jane Eyre or the second Mrs de Winter. Sarah's aim to 'live safely in impersonal action, forgetful of herself, concerned only with the children and their future' (Holtby, 1988: 257), becomes possible only because she does not have family dependents or a husband to hold her back. The indomitable Sarah grows to positively relish her singleness as a form of citizenship, shaping the values of the next generation of women. The strategies of diminishing the importance of the family, and killing off her suitor rather than his wife, leave the spinster heroine free to inspire her female pupils, and shape their futures. She is inspired and supported in turn by her mentor, the alderman Emma Beddowes, and 'that valour of the spirit' (Holtby, 1988: 492) which is passed down to women through the generations. If citizenship can only be achieved at the cost of romance, that is a small price to pay for autonomy, more readily achieved in Holtby's work through female bonding rather than heterosexual ties. Abandonment of both family and convention, to a greater or lesser degree, is increasingly seen as necessary for the educated, post-war spinster to gain access to the public sphere.

The mythologising of Charlotte Brontë as both 'the embodiment of all old-fashioned restrictions' (Oliphant, 1897: 49) and as revolutionary thinker impacts on many modernist accounts of repression, family, singleness and women's work. Woolf's generation of feminist writers filled in the gaps in Gaskell's 'gorgeous' biography and were inspired by Brontë's championing of female independence, professional work and the possibilities of 'a life of action' for women. May Sinclair and Winifred Holtby developed the *Villette* plot in their spinster fiction in order to explore possible ways out of the Victorian daughter's isolation. While Sinclair's critique of the paternal tyranny of Victorianism ultimately leaves the spinster heroine trapped in the domestic space, with her unsatisfied adulterous desire, Holtby's novels go further in demonstrating how spinsters can be rescued from rural stagnation by embracing the world of paid work, with bonds between women replacing heterosexual and family ties. Holtby's Sarah Burton inherits and fiercely articulates Lucy Snowe's spirit of protest. Looking back with anger to Charlotte Brontë's stagnation in the 'patriarchal' parsonage and taking up this protest against passivity became a key response to her legacy for twentieth-century women writers.

Notes

1 See Wynne, Chapter 1 in this volume, addressing Woolf's troubled response to the 'cult' of Charlotte on visiting Haworth.
2 Charlotte's letter, written to W. S. Williams at Smith, Elder, in 1849, advises about the viability of teaching for his daughter. It includes the comment, 'teachers may be hard worked, ill-paid and despised, but the girl who stays at home doing nothing is worse off than the hardest wrought and worst paid drudge of a school. Whenever I have seen, not merely in humble, but in affluent houses, families of daughters sitting waiting to be married I have pitied them from my heart' (Hutchins, 1913: 21–2).
3 Later feminists have read her life as more complicated. See, for example, Hattaway (2014).
4 See Liggins (2014: 5–8, 163–70) for an examination of representations of relationships between women in both Victorian and modernist women's

writing, which looks in particular at the figure of the lesbian heroine in modernist fiction.

References

Bowen, Elizabeth (1986) 'The bend back', in *The Mulberry Tree: Selected Writings of Elizabeth Bowen*, ed. Hermione Lee, London: Virago, pp. 54–60.

Brittain, Vera (1923) 'The whole duty of woman', *Time and Tide*, 23 February, pp. 120–3.

—— (1980) *Testament of Friendship*, London: Virago.

Brontë, Charlotte (1979) *Villette*, ed. Mark Lilly, Harmondsworth: Penguin.

—— (2007) *Charlotte Brontë: Selected Letters*, ed. Margaret Smith, Oxford: Oxford University Press.

—— (2008) *Jane Eyre*, ed. Margaret Smith, Oxford: Oxford University Press.

Dixon, Ella Hepworth (1990) *The Story of a Modern Woman*, ed. Kate Flint, London: Merlin Press.

Du Maurier, Daphne (1992) *Rebecca*, London: Arrow.

Gaskell, Elizabeth (2009) *The Life of Charlotte Brontë*, ed. Angus Easson, Oxford: Oxford University Press.

Hattaway, Meghan Burke (2014) '"Such a strong wish for wings": *The Life of Charlotte Brontë* and Elizabeth Gaskell's fallen angels', *Victorian Literature and Culture*, 42.4, 671–90.

Heilmann, Ann and Mark Llewellyn (2010) *Neo-Victorianism: The Victorians in the Twenty-First Century*, Basingstoke: Palgrave Macmillan.

Holtby, Winifred (1978) *Women and a Changing Civilization*, Chicago, Ill.: Academy Press.

—— (1981) *The Crowded Street*, ed. Claire Hardisty, London: Virago.

—— (1988) *South Riding*, ed. Lettice Cooper, London: Virago.

Horner, Avril and Sue Zlosnik (eds.) (1998) *Daphne du Maurier: Writing, Identity and the Gothic Imagination*, Basingstoke: Palgrave Macmillan.

Hutchins, B.L. (1913) *Conflicting Ideals: Two Sides of the Woman's Question*, London: Thomas Murby.

Kaplan, Cora (2007) *Victoriana: Histories, Fiction, Criticism*, Edinburgh: Edinburgh University Press.

Lamonica, Drew (2003) *'We are Three Sisters': Self and Family in the Writing of the Brontës*, Columbia, Miss.: University of Missouri Press.

Lawrence, Margaret (1937) *We Write as Women*, London: Heinemann.

Liggins, Emma (2014) *Odd Women? Spinsters, Lesbians and Widows in British Women's Fiction, 1850s–1930s*, Manchester: Manchester University Press.

Marcus, Sharon (2007) *Between Women: Friendship, Desire and Marriage in Victorian England*, Princeton, NJ: Princeton University Press.

Miller, Lucasta (2002) *The Brontë Myth*, London: Vintage.

Oliphant, Margaret (1897) 'The Sisters Brontë', *Women Novelists of Queen Victoria's Reign*, London: Hurst & Blackett, pp. 1–59.

Pease, Alison (2006) 'May Sinclair, feminism and boredom: "a dying to live"', *English Literature in Transition*, 49.2, 168–93.

Raitt, Suzanne (2000) *May Sinclair: A Modern Victorian*, Oxford: Oxford University Press.

Roberts, Michèle (2004) *The Mistressclass*, London: Virago.

Shuttleworth, Sally (1996) *Charlotte Brontë and Victorian Psychology*, Cambridge: Cambridge University Press.

Sinclair, May (1912) *The Three Brontës*, London: Hutchinson.

—— (1982) *The Three Sisters*, ed. Jean Radford, London: Virago.

Stoneman, Patsy (1996) *Brontë Transformations: The Cultural Dissemination of Jane Eyre and Wuthering Heights*, Hemel Hempstead: Prentice Hall/Harvester Wheatsheaf.

—— (2002) 'The Brontë myth', in Kate Flint (ed.), *The Cambridge Companion to the Brontës*, Cambridge: Cambridge University Press, pp. 214–41.

Woolf, Virginia (1993) *A Room of One's Own, and Three Guineas*, ed. Michèle Barrett, Harmondsworth: Penguin.

—— (2002) 'Old Bloomsbury', *Moments of Being: Autobiographical Writings*, ed. Jeanne Schulkind, London: Pimlico, pp. 43–61.

8

Hunger, rebellion and rage: adapting *Villette*

Benjamin Poore

In the past thirty years the critical status of Charlotte Brontë's final novel, *Villette* (1853), has grown considerably. Lucasta Miller surely expressed a growing consensus when she declared the novel to be a 'stunning achievement' and Brontë's 'masterpiece' (2002: 52, 30). Yet there have been no film adaptations of *Villette*, and the only television adaptations of the novel, one in 1957 and one screened on BBC2 in 1970, are missing, presumed lost, rather like the novel's unconventional hero, Paul Emanuel, in the final chapter. Does this matter? Well, it could be argued that the critical reappraisal of *Villette* came rather too late in the twentieth century for the novel to become canonised in Hollywood film adaptations in the manner of *Jane Eyre* (1847) and *Wuthering Heights* (1847), with direct consequences for the status of *Villette* today and the likelihood of it being adapted to film in the future. As Thomas Leitch has noted, the recent growth in adaptation studies in universities, often within or adjacent to English departments, has produced 'a new canon [of literature of the long nineteenth century] shaped by adaptation' (2011: 14). While this is in many ways an exciting turn in literary and intermedial studies, it may have the effect of replacing one canonical hierarchy (literary 'quality') with others (historical popularity, or a text's being 'famous for being famous', or the availability of film and television adaptations), which can be just as rigid.

At the same time, the innumerable plays and films about the Brontë sisters' lives, from the 1930s to the present day, have limited the opportunities for adaptations of the Brontës' other works (see Miller, 2002: 143–6; Poore, 2012: 138–40).[1] The notion of 'three brilliant novelists under one roof' seems to surpass the dramatic potential of the tribulations of a lonely Brussels schoolteacher depicted in *Villette*. Nevertheless, the novel has become a popular text to adapt for radio and theatre, having been broadcast in different adaptations on BBC Radio 4 in 1989, 1999 and 2009, and having inspired four stage adaptations since the 1990s, by Judith Adams, Julia Pascal, Patsy Rodenburg and Lisa Evans. A new modernised reimagining of *Villette* by Linda Marshall-Griffiths, staged at West Yorkshire Playhouse in Leeds in 2016, was announced as this chapter went to press. So, rather than lamenting *Villette*'s lack of exposure, we might instead investigate some of the reasons for it being a difficult novel to adapt for the screen while also considering why, conversely, it has been adapted more frequently for stage and radio. As Leitch goes on to remark, there 'would be little point in expanding the Victorian canon' through studies of adaptations, 'if the new entries did not yield new insights' (2011: 10). Adaptation, from Leitch's perspective, allows us to look at the source text with fresh eyes, achieving a critical re-viewing or defamiliarisation that comes as a result of analysing the processes of adaptation that have been considered necessary in turning a novel into a play or radio drama. Similarly, Robert Stam argues for an '[i]ntertextual dialogism' that 'helps us transcend the aporias of "fidelity"' (2005: 4).

This chapter will begin with a survey of the critical fortunes of *Villette*: what might be characterised as its struggle to obtain autonomy as a novel, rather than as Charlotte Brontë's thinly disguised autobiography. It then moves on to consider the problem of transmedial adaptation for a novel that has such a distinctive vision, and that can be interpreted as, in some ways, always already an adaptation of other texts. The second part of the chapter identifies in more detail a series of perceived or potential problems in adapting *Villette*'s themes of surveillance and education, along with its characterisation of Lucy and Paul, and its ambiguous ending, arguing that the solutions that radio and theatre adapters have found can force us into a reassessment of *Villette*'s power and distinctiveness.

'Hunger, rebellion, and rage'

From its first publication, *Villette* has been the subject of what Miller aptly calls *ad feminam* attacks, especially since Charlotte Brontë by this point was no longer able to conceal her gender and identity behind the pseudonym of Currer Bell (2002: 53, 47). What is still surprising today, on reading the contemporary critical responses, is how unapologetically personal they are, and how directly and uncomplicatedly Brontë is assumed to 'be' Lucy Snowe, *Villette*'s protagonist. In a grimly comic echo of the surveillance and espionage that characterise the *pensionnat* in the town of Villette where Lucy lives, Brontë seems in these reviews to be constantly scrutinised, her character examined. Anne Mozley's review of *Villette* in the *Christian Remembrancer* remarks that the author 'has gained both in amiability and propriety since she first presented herself to the world, – soured, coarse, and grumbling', as though Brontë had written a series of autobiographies, rather than novels (reprinted in O'Neill, 1968: 18). Matthew Arnold lays bare the *ad feminam* tendency of such criticism when he writes in a letter of April 1853 that *Villette* is 'disagreeable' because the 'writer's mind contains nothing but hunger, rebellion and rage, and therefore that is all she can, in fact put into her book […] it will be fatal to her in the long run' (reprinted in Allott, 1974: 201). What is striking about this condemnation is, first, the assumed authority with which Arnold claims to be able to see the entire contents of Brontë's mind; secondly, the complete contrast to Mozley's assessment of Brontë's character through her work, quoted above; and, third, the pseudo-medical prognosis that such defects 'will be fatal to her' (though whether in literary or medical terms it is not quite clear). The confidence of his judgement perhaps calls to mind Paul Emanuel's initial examination of Lucy's physiognomy in *Villette*, where Madame Beck asks him to 'Read that countenance' and pronounce on the character there contained (Brontë, 2000: 66–7). In the letter, Arnold follows his condemnation of Brontë's mind with a more indulgent response to Edward Bulwer-Lytton's *My Novel* (1853), suggesting that the work of a male author with personal defects can still afford 'great pleasure' where a female novelist's assumed personality is inseparable from her work (reprinted in Allot, 1974: 201).

This desire to discipline and punish Brontë for the thoughts and behaviour of the fictional character of Lucy Snowe, and for the fictional events of Labassecour (Brontë's name for Belgium), might be dismissed as the peculiar mid-Victorian response to female authorship, if it had not continued well into the twentieth century. David Cecil's 1934 reading of *Villette*, for example, is full of confident assertions of how Charlotte Brontë 'felt', how her hand could 'falter', to what she was 'indifferent', and the 'restraint' that her imagination did not know (reprinted in O'Neill, 1968: 24–5). Robert A. Colby, writing in 1960, suggests that '*Villette* is most fruitfully approached as Charlotte Brontë's literary, not her literal, autobiography', a formulation that nevertheless seems to minimise *Villette*'s power as a novel (reprinted in O'Neill, 1968: 39). It harks back to reviewers' strange attempts to reclassify *Villette* in the 1850s when they insisted it was not 'a novel in the ordinary sense of the word' (quoted in O'Neill, 1968: 19). They argued that the book's strength did not lie 'in the story' (reprinted in Allott, 1974: 179) and asserted that 'it is the plot alone that is defective', noting the 'poverty and scantiness of the material' (reprinted in Allott, 1974: 196). Brontë's uncontrolled – and monstrously female – channelling of 'hunger, rebellion and rage' was considered far too instinctive, even for some of her sympathetic critics, to conform to logical, 'masculine' novelistic structural proprieties.

   This denial of authorial agency to Brontë is, of course, the flip side to the success of the 'Brontë myth', partly set in motion, as Miller documents, by Elizabeth Gaskell's 1857 publication of *The Life of Charlotte Brontë* (Miller, 2002: 57–9). The circumstances of Charlotte Brontë's life's work take over from the life's work itself, like a Derridean supplement. As I have argued elsewhere, this can make it very difficult to read the novels as novels, since they come to us already saturated in cultural investment in the Brontës' life stories (Poore, 2012: 128–9). As Catherine Malone has noted, the publisher Smith, Elder's decision to publish Gaskell's *Life of Charlotte Brontë* and the previously unpublished *The Professor* (1857) in rapid succession helped to ensure a positive critical reception for the recently deceased author's first novel (Malone, 1996: 175). However, arguably it also helped to cement the public perception that Brontë's 'masterpiece' was her own life, as related by Gaskell, and that therefore *The Professor* and *Villette* were simply coy fictionalisations of the 'real thing', that is, Brontë's time as a student and teacher in Belgium in 1842–3, and her unrequited feelings for her tutor, Constantin Heger.[2]

'Old and new acquaintance': *Villette* as always already adapted

Looked at another way, *Villette* can be read as an adaptation of *The Professor*, which seeks a different perspective through its use of a male narrator, William Crimsworth, to relate events based on Brontë's experiences in Belgium and at the Pensionnat Heger. While the plots of the two novels differ considerably, they both feature a similar school building with an *allée défendue* (a secluded walkway in the schools' gardens, out of bounds to pupils); each of their girls' schools is run by a woman (Mlle Reuter in *The Professor* and Mme Beck in *Villette*) skilled in surveillance and espionage; both novels include a male teacher who spies on his female pupils; and both teacher protagonists, Crimsworth in *The Professor* and Lucy Snowe in *Villette*, assert their authority over an unruly class by ripping a girl's work in two. Crimsworth, like Lucy, is also prone to 'hypochondria' (now understood as depression). Hence, although *Villette* is not a direct adaptation of *The Professor* with regard to plot, the setting and characters often overlap. In addition, as numerous critics have pointed out, *Villette* is in many ways a revisioning of *Jane Eyre*.[3] Given *Jane Eyre*'s success, comparisons with the earlier novel had been inevitable from *Villette*'s first publication. *Puttnam's Monthly Magazine* made an extended comparison, concluding that *Villette* is 'quite as bold, original, and interesting, allowing always for the fact that we have had the type in the earlier book' (reprinted in Allott, 1974: 215). As Alison Milbank notes, it is not only the point of view of the narration, or the vivid interior world, that is similar (2009: 91–2). Heather Glen sees *Villette* as in some ways a comic retelling of *Jane Eyre* (2002: 197–8).

Hence, a screen adaptation of *Villette* would inevitably be compared with the long list of film and TV adaptations of *Jane Eyre*. This would be an unfair comparison, given *Jane Eyre*'s place in popular and literary culture (which is, it can be argued, itself partly a result of twentieth-century film adaptations). A single adaptation of *Villette* would be burdened with the task of representing everyone's idea of what the novel is about, where, by contrast, we are used to the notion that different adaptations of *Jane Eyre* will emphasise – or expand upon – different aspects of the novel. Mark Bostridge, commenting at the time of the 1999 radio adaptation, further illuminates when he suggests that it is 'Lucy's evasiveness, and the reader's nagging suspicion that she can't be trusted, that has most discouraged dramatists from adapting *Villette* for other media' (1999).

Spying and surveillance in *Villette*

There are several elements of *Villette* that forcibly remind us of how different the nineteenth century was from today. Especially, perhaps, in turning from the familiarity of the culture-text that is *Jane Eyre* to the lesser known and less adapted *Villette*, we are required to rethink the nineteenth century. This is an issue for adaptation, since the rhetoric of transmedial adaptation itself seems to imply that its source text is a 'story for today', a work with contemporary relevance.[4] For instance, a would-be adapter of *Villette* to the screen is forced to consider how far to replicate the claustrophobic, scopophilic and oppressive atmosphere of the rue de Fossette. As Clarke suggests, Catholic culture and surveillance seem to be tied together by the novel's narrative, in the figures of Madame Beck and Paul Emanuel, who knows the secret door to the garden of the girls' school (Clarke, 2011: 977), and 'constantly spies on his pupils' (Cohn, 2012: 848). As Margaret L. Shaw notes, both de Hamal and M. Paul spy 'into the secret interior of women' by watching them from windows, Paul even employing a spyglass for such a purpose, and defending his practice in terms of being their 'guardian angel' (1994: 816). For Boone, however, modern readers (and, I would add, viewers) are likely to interpret the talk of 'spy glasses, master keys, magic lattices [and] bottom doors' as Freudian metaphors of penetration (1992: 22). In representing this shadowy world of spies and voyeurs, any screen adaptation of *Villette* would risk reproducing a scopophilic 'male gaze' that has become politicised by twentieth-century film theory (Mulvey, 1975). To reproduce this 'male gaze' would be an especially unwelcome irony, given the centrality of the female gaze to the novel's narrative action.

In the theatre, where point of view is not directed by camerawork, there is a paradoxical sense of being able to observe everything, but only in a limited sense as an individual audience member. There is collective, not individuated, surveillance. Lisa Evans' adaptation of *Villette* was staged at the Stephen Joseph Theatre in Scarborough in 2005, a particularly appropriate venue since it is a permanent theatre-in-the-round. The stage entrances were covered by imposing Gothic doors, enhancing the feeling of claustrophobia and espionage (the doors could also be interpreted as confession grilles, or Paul Emanuel's observational lattice). In Judith Adams' 1997 adaptation for the Sheffield Crucible (revived at RADA's Jerwood Vanbrugh Theatre in 2008), the adaptational concept is metatheatrical, with painted flats, '[a]s with a Pollock's theatre played with by a child' and clothes 'draped everywhere – masks, puppets, dummies, icons' (Adams, 1997: 2). The audience is taken into the performance space by Lucy 'DRESSED LIKE A GREY SHADOW' with a key around her neck (Adams, 1997: 5). The audience steps inside to find a corridor of distorting mirrors and three men looking at the statue of Cleopatra; all the actors introduce themselves as Lucy Snowe. Here, not only surveillance and espionage are suggested but also the fractured, intersecting subjectivities that make the novel's narration compellingly inconsistent. The metatheatricality also corresponds, of course, to the novel's repeated scenes of performance (such as the fête in the park and 'Vashti', the actress, on stage at the Villette theatre), as well as Lucy's own self-aware performance as a 'grey shadow' (see Litvak, 1988: 478–9).

The Pensionnat Beck and education

Education, a key theme in *Villette*, is one of the most politicised issues in twenty-first-century anglophone cultures. But it is clear that attitudes towards education have changed enormously since the 1840s, the decade in which Brontë sets the novel. At the rue de Fossette, the unspoken understanding between the pupils' parents and Madame Beck is that their daughters should be kept under lock and key in a Spartan finishing school until they are in a position to be married off. For modern audiences, weaned on film narratives of one idealistic teacher making a difference, the expectation might well be that Lucy does the honourable thing and immediately resigns her untenable position as a teacher in such a corrupt establishment.[5] Rather, Lucy stays and saves her money. Lucy, Mme Beck and Paul Emanuel have little interest in education as we would understand it today. Lucy makes no secret of choosing favourite pupils with whom to walk out and recommends the crushing of students' self-respect – and the deployment of sarcasm – as the best ways to establish order and respect (Brontë, 2000: 83–4). Furthermore, Lucy makes it clear that she (and by extension, the school) has low intellectual expectations of the pupils; for Lucy, this is tied to her chauvinism regarding the superiority of English learners compared to the 'swinish multitude' of Labassecourienne girls (Brontë, 2000: 83).

This populous school setting poses a potential problem for adaptations of the novel. Limited by the prohibitive costs of large companies in the case of theatre, and the limits of the listener being able to track large numbers of voices in radio drama, adaptations of *Villette* typically feature the school as a backdrop rather than a setting. In common with most workplace dramas, the actual hours of repetitive labour are edited in order to focus on the intrigues of the staff. The common practice of theatrical multi-rolling means that actors are not identified with the roles of pupils for more than a few moments, with the exception of Ginevra Fanshawe, who is hardly a victim of the rue de Fossette, and, in her elopement with the Count de Hamal, could be said to have played Madame Beck at her own game and won. In Adams' play, the out-of-focus quality of the schoolgirls' presence is explained by the note that the theatrical space represents the interior of Lucy's head (Adams, 1997: 2). In Evans' adaptation, although only three pupils are named (Ginevre [*sic*], Virginie and Blanche), their appearances are deftly orchestrated to illustrate Lucy's assumption of a role of authority, Paul's effect on the classroom and Lucy's passionate nature (there is a scene where Lucy climbs onto the window sill during a thunderstorm and announces, to the girls' con-sternation, 'I should knock a nail through the temples of this longing') (Evans, 2005: 18–20, 57–9, 29).

In fact, Evans' adaptation, with its brief classroom scenes – all but four of which have well under 100 lines – throws new light on the atmosphere of the school. The girls, and Mme Beck, refer to the paren-tal pressure that can be brought to bear on stern or wayward teach-ers, reminding us that the pupils place the staff under surveillance as much as the other way around (Evans, 2005: 20, 29). And, in its rapid switches between lamentation and mirth, the timing brings out the absurdities not only of the girls' histrionic mood swings but also how that behaviour is echoed in Lucy's and Paul's comic courtship (Evans, 2005: 74–8).

Paul Emanuel

While M. Paul's biographical model, Constantin Heger, may have been a bold and innovative educationalist in his time, we only catch glimpses of these methods in the teaching philosophy of Crimsworth in *The Professor* (see Lonoff, 2001: 463–5). In *Villette*, Paul Emanuel's pedagogi-cal approach is hardly touched on, and instead we hear successive reports of his bullying, intimidation and harassment of pupils and colleagues. He frequently makes his pupils cry and seems to have hardly any self-control, on one occasion 'raving from the estrade almost livid' and losing his tem-per with the iron door of a stove (Brontë, 2000: 240). Brontë sets Paul up as the novel's comic villain in the first 300 pages, having Lucy exclaim of him: 'Really that man was dreadful: a mere sprite of caprice and ubiquity' (Brontë, 2000: 242). This is rapidly reversed in the last 200 pages, creating an overall impression that is so contradictory as to be hard to assimilate into conventional notions of character. Indeed, critics have often simply assumed that such unconventional characterisation is incompetence on Brontë's part; G. H. Lewes highlights her perceived failures of charac-terisation in his review in the *Westminster Review* (reprinted in O'Neill, 1968: 19), while Cecil found Brontë incapable of drawing any character but her own (reprinted in O'Neill, 1968: 23–4).

Hence, radio adaptations consistently soften Paul's behaviour, excis-ing those lines from exchanges which are too suggestive of what Joseph A. Boone calls the 'beady-eyed despot' that Paul frequently is in the novel (Boone, 1992: 33). The 1989 adaptation by Valerie Windsor provides an additional backstory for Paul – that he nearly married Zélie St Pierre, one of the teachers at Mme Beck's school, until he 'observed the flaws in her character', implying both a motivation for his constant inquisitorial obstruction of Lucy, and also, strangely, that the memory of his dead fiancée, Justine Marie, had not exclusively occupied his affections these past twenty years (Windsor, 1989: Ep. 5). Where stage adaptations can play with tone in the moment of performance in front of a live audience, radio adaptations have no such flexibility. In the 2009 radio adaptation by Rachel Joyce, Paul is made rather less hypocritical in the encounter before the painting of Cleopatra in the art gallery; rather less ridiculous in his ill-temper at the concert; and his speech at the Hotel Crécy inspires only pleasant feelings in Lucy: 'You should have seen him smile! His very complexion lightened' (Joyce, 2009: Ep. 6). Again there is the difficulty of adapting both for audiences familiar with *Villette* and those who have not read the novel and who may, perhaps, not be able to follow a ten-part serial unless there is a more straightforward, teleological romantic development between Lucy and Paul. As Boone points out, 'Lucy's experiencing and narrating selves blur indiscriminately' so that it is never clear whether Lucy is describing what actually happened or, instead, how things felt at that moment (1992: 31, n. 21). Thus, the narrative's treatment of Paul Emanuel (and Dr John, Ginevra and Madame Beck, to name a few others), varies unpredictably rather than develops in a linear fashion.

Voicing Lucy Snowe

A further daunting challenge in adapting *Villette* is Lucy Snowe's narrative voice, for Lucy is the very definition of the unreliable narrator. Although she details precisely, and often disapprovingly, the spying activities of others, she represents her own surveillance and eavesdropping as innocent (see Shaw, 1994: 823). Lucy hides important information from the reader; as Boone, Shaw and Litvak note, this is most markedly the case when Lucy reveals that she had been keeping her knowledge that Dr John was her childhood acquaintance John Graham Bretton from the reader for several chapters (Boone, 1992: 30; Shaw, 1994: 818; Litvak, 1988: 474). By such an action, she 'double-crosses those policing readers' (Boone, 1992: 31), engaging in 'rhetorical one-upmanship' (Litvak, 1988: 474), but crucially severs the bond of trust between reader and narrator, which the confessional subjectivity of the narrative mode (and, perhaps, the earlier experience of reading *Jane Eyre*) had led us to take for granted.

All four of the adaptations for theatre discussed in this chapter diffuse the problem of the unreliable narrator through some form of metatheatricality, where the single vision of Lucy Snowe is replaced by the presence of a shape-shifting ensemble. In Evans' *Villette* at Scarborough – a co-production with Frantic Assembly – the characters' inner impulses were rendered through an energetic physical performance style that was the counterpart to their careful self-monitoring in speech. As noted earlier, Adams' *Villette* is set in Lucy's mind, which itself resembles a toy theatre. Patsy Rodenburg's collaboration with Graeae, *Not Much to Ask*, weaves together testimony from Lucy, from Charlotte Brontë, and from a disabled visitor to the Brontë Parsonage Museum at Haworth.[6] Julia Pascal's *Charlotte Brontë Goes to Europe* gives Lucy Snowe a distinctive Yorkshire accent and moves back and forth between the novel's action and a modern-day visitor to Brussels on the Eurostar, who may or not be Lucy, or who may or not have dreamed Lucy's adventure. Lucy's accent is used to comic effect when the actress playing her pronounces 'Cleopatra' as 'Cle-o-pattera', and in the earthy tone of her response to Dr John, 'Cultivate Happiness? Happiness is not a potato!' On the British Library's recording of the performance, both these lines elicit audience laughter (Pascal, 2000).

Radio adaptations tend to rely on the predominance of Lucy's solo, narrating voice (indeed, the novel also exists in at least three audiobooks, in the Talking Classics, Naxos and Penguin series, where there is one reader throughout).[7] The 1989 BBC serial uses music sparsely, suggesting location through sound effects (horses' hooves, a church organ, footsteps), as if to give a Puritan quality of simplicity and transparency to the testimony of Lucy (played by Joanna Mackie). The 2009 adaptation cast Anna Maxwell Martin as Lucy Snowe; at that time the actress was best known for her much admired performance as Esther Summerson in Andrew Davies' BBC television adaptation of *Bleak House* (2005). This casting perhaps implies a similarity between Esther's self-effacing narration and that of Lucy, and could be taken as an attempt to make Lucy more likeable or trustworthy. Certainly, Maxwell Martin is able to convey an amused, intriguing tone to her voice, as for instance when she detects Madame Beck in a lie (Joyce, 2009: Ep. 3) which invites a wry confidence with the listener, rather than 'double-crossing' or 'one-upmanship'. Indeed, Joyce's adaptation even includes Lucy's confession that she had misled the listener concerning her knowledge of John Graham Bretton. The script selects passages from Lucy's narrative that seem calculated to inspire pathos rather than suspicion or betrayal; Lucy says, 'But I had kept this to myself. Hidden as if by a cloud, I had freely watched him shine' (Joyce, 2009: Ep. 5). Maxwell Martin's Lucy weeps a great deal in this adaptation, often accompanied by a Chopin piano theme, which seems like a calculated attempt to assimilate Lucy into the ranks of deserving Victorian heroines.

The most distinctive radio version is the 1999 recording, an adaptation by James Friel, directed by Catherine Bailey. Like the stage adaptations discussed, the serial is set in the claustrophobic, tormented mind of Lucy (played by Catherine McCormack). The opening words are a whispered 'What are you? Who are you? Are you anything at all?', and the adaptation consistently, and daringly, reproduces Lucy's inner dialogues and self-reprimands, with complex soundscapes of overlapping voices and melancholy music, including a repeated guitar figure that punctuates shifts of thought or feeling. Of all the adaptations discussed here, Friel and Bailey's is the most Gothic rendering of a novel that has been interpreted as switching with bewildering unpredictability between Gothic and realist modes.[8] In comparison, the BBC radio adaptation that followed in 2009 seems like a reaction to this aural intensity of feeling. Paradoxically, however, Friel considered his adaptation to have been more straightforward because it dispenses with the 'wicked authorial game' whereby Lucy is in full control of the narrative yet repeatedly misdirects the reader (quoted in Bostridge, 1999).

'There is enough said': the ending of *Villette*

The last adaptation challenge I want to consider is *Villette*'s highly ambiguous ending: a 'notoriously inconclusive ending' (Litvak, 1988: 488–9); an ending of 'radical uncertainty', that offers 'no teleological finality' to the narrative (Boone, 1992: 38, 30); an ending that 'provides no validating closure to the attention [the novel] has lavished on Lucy Snowe for nearly six hundred pages' (Braun, 2011: 189). For Lucie Armitt, the final two sentences provide an 'almost satirically false anti-climax' to the story (Armitt, 2002: 227). To attempt to translate it into another medium immediately raises problems. How to weight those rhythmic sentences, so significant and yet so terse, and on the surface so neutral? But the surprising evasiveness of the ending also draws the potential adapter's attention to other points in the novel where – unlike *Jane Eyre*, unlike *The Professor* – it is simply not clear where Lucy has come from and what has happened to her. Armitt and Braun both argue that the loss of Lucy's family is a trauma that shapes the novel by its absences and evasions (Armitt, 2002: 225; Braun, 2011: 190).

Only Evans' adaptation, of the four theatre texts, ends with (some of) the words of *Villette*'s closing passage, delivered in direct audience address, albeit without the final remarks on the fate of the 'secret junta' (Brontë, 2000: 460). Pascal's and Rodenburg's adaptations end with a return from the novel's imaginative landscape, providing a metatheatrical jolt. The former's final moments bring us back to the Eurostar, and Rodenburg's script presents us with much of the text of 'Finis' (the novel's final chapter) but follows on with biographical details of Charlotte Brontë and, seemingly, a return to the 'institution' for disabled people in which the adaptation is set: a man says: 'You put the book away. Then the dream can end' (Rodenburg, n.d.: 39). For me, the most interesting fusion of theatrical and literary languages is Judith Adams' end sequence, where Mme Walravens puts a paper boat in the basin of water, which Lucy wrecks as the howl of a banshee is heard (Adams, 1997: 142). One of the actors (representing Paul) dies, but suddenly sits up and demands of Lucy, 'Go on with your story', placing his frock coat on her. He adds: 'Play you must, play you shall. I am planted there'; as he attempts to dictate what she should be writing, she 'holds up her hand to silence him, they smile at each other, she goes on writing' (Adams, 1997: 142). Torn letters fall onto the stage, as voices softly repeat, 'Lucy Snowe' (Adams, 1997: 143). This ending seems to me to find a theatrical translation for the novel's closing sequence and one which also acknowledges Lucy Snowe in the act of composing her history (and hers alone). It is an ending that does not seek out the wider validation of Charlotte Brontë's life but instead, unlike so many critics, responds to *Villette* on its own terms.

Conclusion

It is fascinating to note the almost perfectly balanced forces of opposition at play in the seven adaptations considered here. Of the four play texts, two decide that it is impossible to detach the figure of Charlotte Brontë from a rendering of *Villette*, and two decide that *Villette* must be considered on its own. Of the three radio adaptations, spaced at regular ten-year intervals, it is hard to imagine that the adapters did not consider the previous BBC radio versions. Consequently, we have a stripped-down and straightforward soundscape in 1989, a complex, claustrophobic Gothic mix in 1999 and a return to aural simplicity in 2009. The pendulum swings back and forth between the realist and Gothic modes. And while there is perhaps something very satisfying for scholars of *Villette* about the idea of historical redress in Adams' and Evans' versions – finally allowing Lucy, and the novel, the textual autonomy that they have been consistently denied since 1853 – inevitably such an act involves a conscious renunciation of knowledge about Charlotte Brontë that we already possess. So these adaptations, taken together, remain, like Lucy, evenly poised between 'Reason and Feeling' (Brontë, 2000: 253), between knowledge and forgetting. Long may we lack a 'definitive' adaptation of *Villette*.

Notes

1 See also Regis, Chapter 5 in this volume, addressing 1930s stage plays that explore the Brontës' life stories.
2 Even in a 2004 biography for children, *Charlotte Brontë: The Girl Who Turned Her Life into a Book* by Kate Hubbard, Brontë's ability to spin her life into literary gold with *Jane Eyre* is the main theme. *Villette* is mentioned only once ('Battling against depression and bad health, she managed to write her fourth novel') and does not even feature on her timeline at the end of the book (Hubbard, 2004: 78, 88).
3 To complicate the picture further, both *Villette* and *Jane Eyre* can be read as adaptations of the Bluebeard story (Kim, 2011: 410).
4 For instance, Judith Adams is quoted, on a flyer for the Sheffield Crucible production of her adaptation, as saying that '*Villette* is an astonishingly modern novel [...] a book long overdue for theatrical investigation' (1997: 2).
5 Films and television series focusing on influential teachers include *Dead Poets' Society* (1989), *Dangerous Minds* (1995), *Goodbye Mr Chips* (2002), *School of Rock* (2003) and *Glee* (2011–15).
6 'When I visited Haworth and the museum / They allowed me to be carried through the ground floor rooms [...] I saw the room where Charlotte wrote. / I couldn't go upstairs' (Rodenburg, n.d.: 2).
7 The readers are Juliet Stevenson (Penguin), Carole Boyd (Talking Classics) and Mandy Weston (Naxos).
8 See, for example, Robert B. Heilman's distinction between Brontë's 'old Gothic', 'anti-Gothic' and 'new Gothic' modes (quoted in O'Neill, 1968: 32–6) and Colby (quoted in O'Neill, 1968: 46).

References

Adams, Judith (1997) *Villette*. Unpublished play script, Manuscript no. 7543, British Library, London.
Allott, Miriam (ed.) (1974) *The Brontës: The Critical Heritage*, London: Routledge & Kegan Paul.

Armitt, Lucie (2002) 'Haunted childhood in Charlotte Brontë's *Villette*', *The Yearbook of English Studies*, 32.1, 217–28.

Boone, Joseph A. (1992) 'Depolicing *Villette*: surveillance, invisibility, and the female erotics of heretic narrative', *Novel*, 26.1, 20–42.

Bostridge, Mark (1999) 'Sister of the more famous Jane', *The Independent*, 1 April, www.independent.co.uk/arts-entertainment/arts-sister-of-the-more-famous-jane-1084393.html (accessed 20 December 2014).

Braun, Gretchen (2011) 'Great break in the common course of confession: narrating loss in Charlotte Brontë's *Villette*', *ELH*, 78.1, 189–212.

Brontë, Charlotte (2000) *Villette*, ed. Margaret Smith and Herbert Rosengarten, Oxford: Oxford University Press.

Clarke, Micael M. (2011) 'Charlotte Brontë's *Villette*, mid-Victorian anti-Catholicism, and the turn to secularism', *ELH*, 78.4, 967–89.

Cohn, Elisha (2012) 'Still life: suspended animation in Charlotte Brontë's *Villette*', *SEL: Studies in English Literature, 1500–1900*, 52.4, 843–60.

Evans, Lisa and Charlotte Brontë (2005) *Villette: Adapted from the Novel by Charlotte Brontë*, London: Oberon Books.

Friel, James and Charlotte Brontë (1999) *Villette*, BBC Radio 4, 4–18 April.

Glen, Heather (2002) *Charlotte Brontë: The Imagination in History*, Oxford: Oxford University Press.

Gregor, Ian (ed.) (1970) *The Brontës: A Collection of Critical Essays*, Eaglewood Cliffs, NJ: Prentice Hall.

Hubbard, Kate (2004) *Charlotte Brontë: The Girl Who Turned Her Life into a Book*, London: Short.

Joyce, Rachel and Charlotte Brontë (2009) *Villette*, BBC Radio 4, 3–14 August.

Kim, Katherine J. (2011) 'Corpse hoarding: control and the female body in "Bluebeard", "Schalken the Painter", and *Villette*', *Studies in the Novel*, 43.4, 406–27.

Leitch, Thomas (2011) 'Introduction: reframing the Victorians', in Abigail Burnham Bloom and Mary Sanders Pollock (eds), *Victorian Literature and Film Adaptation*, Amherst, NY: Cambria Press, pp. 1–24.

Litvak, Joseph (1988) 'Charlotte Brontë and the scene of instruction: authority and subversion in *Villette*', *Nineteenth-Century Literature*, 42.4, 467–89.

Lonoff De Cuevas, Sue (2001) 'The education of Charlotte Brontë: a pedagogical case study', *Pedagogy*, 1.3, 457–77.

Malone, Catherine (1996) '"We have learnt to love her more than her books": the critical reception of Brontë's *Professor*', *The Review of English Studies*, 47.186, 175–87.

Milbank, Alison (2009) 'Bleeding nuns: a genealogy of the female Gothic grotesque', in Diana Wallace and Andrew Smith (eds), *The Female Gothic: New Directions*, Basingstoke: Palgrave Macmillan, pp. 76–97.

Miller, Lucasta (2002) *The Brontë Myth*, London: Vintage.

Mulvey, Laura (1975) 'Visual pleasure and narrative cinema', *Screen*, 16.3, 6–18.

O'Neill, Judith (ed.) (1968) *Critics on Charlotte and Emily Brontë*, London: George Allen & Unwin.

Pascal, Julia (2000) *Charlotte Brontë Goes to Europe*, British Library, London. Events collection, recorded 10 January, recording no. 1CDR0004534.

Poore, Benjamin (2012) *Heritage, Nostalgia and Modern British Theatre: Staging the Victorians*, Basingstoke: Palgrave Macmillan.

Rodenburg, Patsy (n.d.) *Not Much to Ask*, unpublished play script, manuscript no. 2141, British Library, London.

Shaw, Margaret L. (1994) 'Narrative surveillance and social control in *Villette*', *Studies in English Literature, 1500–1900*, 34.4, 813–33.

Stam, Robert (2005) *Literature through Film: Realism, Magic, and the Art of Adaptation*, Oxford: Blackwell.

Windsor, Valerie and Charlotte Brontë (1989) *Villette*, BBC Radio 4, 19 May–23 June, British Library reference no. 75782.

9

The ethics of appropriation; or, the 'mere spectre' of Jane Eyre: Emma Tennant's *Thornfield Hall*, Jasper Fforde's *The Eyre Affair* and Gail Jones's *Sixty Lights*

Alexandra Lewis

'We are, of course, not Victorian', proclaim Ann Heilmann and Mark Llewellyn in their recent chapter 'On the Neo-Victorian, Now and Then' (2014: 493). 'We are the Victorians. We should love them. We should thank them. We should love them', concludes Matthew Sweet in his *Inventing the Victorians* (2001: 232). But what does it mean to 'be' (or not to be), to embody, or even to remember the Victorians? If the Victorians 'made us – good and bad – what we are today' (Sweet, 2001: 232), what does it mean for our contemporary identities when we continue to reinvent (and potentially recover, or further obscure) that inherited past in historical fiction? In this chapter I explore the ethics of neo-Victorian appropriation through close analysis of three very different Brontëan afterlives: novels by Emma Tennant, Jasper Fforde and Gail Jones. I am interested in the impact that the writing of Charlotte Brontë has had on the developing field of neo-Victorian fiction – and vice versa. How has Brontë's *Jane Eyre* (1847) been reflected upon and invoked in twentieth- and twenty-first-century novels about the Victorians, and with what range of textual and wider cultural effects?

Recent decades have seen a proliferation of Charlotte Brontë's novelistic afterlives: from direct rewritings, prequels and sequels to more oblique resonances and reworkings.[1] From novels that invoke Charlotte

Brontë as a character (such as Lin Haire-Sargeant's *Heathcliff: The Return to Wuthering Heights*, 1992); seek to connect with her afterlives in a modern setting (D. M. Thomas's *Charlotte*, 2001); fill perceived gaps in the original narrative (Tennant's *Thornfield Hall*, 2002); collapse the boundaries between fiction and biography (Sheila Kohler's *Becoming Jane Eyre*, 2009); self-reflexively engage with issues of literary influence and value (Fforde's *The Eyre Affair*, 2001); or draw more generally upon Brontëan tropes that will import meaning into a neo-Victorian narrative (Maggie Power's *Lily*, 1994, and Jones's *Sixty Lights*, 2004), it is clear that Brontë's legacies for contemporary fiction are manifold. Numerous of these works – some more transparently than others – allow biography, or what Lucasta Miller has called the Brontë 'myth' (2002), and fiction to intertwine and create a new version of 'Charlotte Brontë's *Jane Eyre*' for the twenty-first century. This exploration of some of the different types of legacies, with close analysis of novels by Tennant, Fforde and Jones, is attuned to shifting approaches to the life and consciousness of the individual as reflected in the novel genre at the mid-nineteenth century and today; depictions (and historically oriented understandings) of violence and suffering; and the issue of alienation, or the self alone. I contend that the varying recent engagements with Brontë's life and fiction by creative writers have much to reveal to us about nostalgia and about our own cultural moment. Neo-Victorian novels often draw upon the Brontëan legacy to invite particular readings of their central female characters as well as issues of gender, race and class. How has the trajectory of the 'poor, obscure, plain, and little' heroine (Brontë, 2003: 284) – she of the famous feminist plea for equality for men and women, and the infamous fairytale-love-plot ending – been revisited, reinterpreted, or even revisioned, in a number of neo-Victorian novels?

At the conclusion of my chapter for *The Brontës in Context*, concerned with current trends in Brontë scholarship, I posed some questions about the link between academic scholarship and creative imagination and about the ethical implications of neo-Victorian fiction:

> Creative revisionings illuminate the problems and pleasures of all historical fictions: while they offer opportunities for insightful recuperation, they are attended by the risk of perpetuating inaccurate impressions which might in turn delimit the range of readings of the Brontës' own works. Will a blurring of the line between archive and imagination in twenty-first-century popular fiction contribute to new Brontëan myth-making of disturbing proportions? Or do the more compelling among these works register a wider turn

away from modernist scepticism regarding the redemptive power of fiction towards a new vision (born of twenty-first-century optimism, desperation and uncertainty) which encompasses enduring Victorian cultural and literary models of empathy and transformation?

(Lewis, 2012: 204)

The afterlives fashioned by Emma Tennant, Jasper Fforde and Gail Jones each offer distinct perspectives on why and how Charlotte Brontë the author, Jane Eyre the character and *Jane Eyre* the novel have proven such evocative neo-Victorian muses. Tennant's, Fforde's and Jones's works, moving respectively further away from a straightforward relation to or dependence on the original, each engage to different extents in self-conscious examination of the ethics of appropriation of Brontë's novel. These narratives grapple with issues of intertextuality and originality; fidelity and creativity; the prospects and limitations of revisiting nineteenth-century concerns, characters and textual fabrics from a twenty-first-century authorial standpoint; and the way the allusive power (or broad communal meaning) of an archetypal text can be contingent upon the oversimplification of literary and cultural complexities.

Students taking my 'Neo-Victorian Transformations' Honours English course are often astounded by the sheer number of works inspired by *Jane Eyre* – and the diversity of genres and styles of appropriation including (in the collective sentiment of this year's seminar group) 'really bad fan fiction' (see Appendix).[2] Whilst we are attuned to complex issues of literary and aesthetic 'value', tradition and canonicity, most students question the purpose and likely longevity of novels such as *Jane Slayre: The Literary Classic with a Bloodsucking Twist* (2010, billed as written by 'Charlotte Brontë and Sherri Browning Erwin', with the tagline 'Reader, I buried him'). April Lindner's *Jane* (2010) raises the pressing question you hadn't realised needed asking – 'What if Jane Eyre fell in love with a rock star?' – and L. K. Rigel's *My Mr Rochester* (2014) purports on the cover (citing a review by 'KindleObsessed') to be 'the version all classic lovers know was buried behind an era's expectations', pointing towards the wider trend in erotic rewritings. While Laura Joh Rowland has transposed Brontë the author into the role of detective (*Bedlam: The Further Secret Adventures of Charlotte Brontë*, 2010), James Tully's lurid *The Crimes of Charlotte Brontë: A Novel* (1999) goes further, claiming to reveal 'a cold-blooded and calculating murderer at the heart of the Brontë household'. The back cover explains the choice of bio-fiction genre thus: 'so dark and unexpected were the results of [the criminologist Tully's] researches he decided to tell the story in the form of a novel'. These rewritings and bio-fictions raise serious questions about the handling of textual inheritance and the ramifications of intertexual re-membering: questions which are taken up more directly by Tennant (whose novel indulges the traditional neo-Victorian fascination with 'excluded' stories), Fforde (whose concern is with textual stability, or stories under threat) and Jones (who creatively yet critically examines the ways stories are retold, and potentially altered with each retelling).

Respect or retaliation, nostalgia or theft: accessibility, unresolved tensions and the contours of the past

The concentration on particular aspects of a novel at the expense or even complete erasure of others is nothing new, and certainly not where Brontë's novel is concerned. Even a quick look at a range of theatrical adaptations from throughout the nineteenth century shows us that the way *Jane Eyre* is interpreted and the emphases it is given (be it by stage directors or by critics) can reveal as much about the context of inter-pretation as it can about the original work. In John Courtney's version of 1848 – the year of *The Communist Manifesto*, the final Chartist peti-tion, and revolutions in Europe – prominence is given to newly invented servant characters, even though the play 'is not revolutionary in its out-come' (Stoneman, 2007: 8). As Patsy Stoneman has shown, across each of eight versions first performed between 1848 and 1898, Rochester's moral status fluctuates as different aspects of the financial, political and sexual situation of women come under the spotlight. In some scripts, the madwoman is not Rochester's wife; by 1882, W. G. Wills was using his adaptation as a vehicle to raise 'uncomfortable questions' about sexually transmitted disease (Stoneman, 2007: 16). Public debate surrounding the second Married Women's Property Act, finally passed in 1882, can be seen to motivate the fact that Jane's inheritance is revealed at a much earlier point in the plot in some of the plays, changing the resonances of the central character's vulnerability. Female solidarity is pointed up when, in an 1879 production, Blanche Ingram is rendered as a fallen woman, with whom Jane offers to share her eventual fortune, calling her 'sister' (Stoneman, 2007: 330).[3]

When acknowledging *Jane Eyre* as a springboard for numerous twenty-first-century neo-Victorian ventures, we are prompted to consider (and hopefully to reconsider) not only the layers of accreted baggage sur-rounding the text – the attachments of popular culture both to the novel itself and to the lives of the Brontë family – but also the problem of the apparent universality of the original. As Heather Glen has observed, 'the Brontë sisters are not obviously difficult writers. Indeed, they may seem all too easily accessible' (2002b: 1). For Virginia Woolf the 'exhilaration' of the emotions in *Jane Eyre* 'rushes us through the entire volume, without giving us time to think, without letting us lift our eyes from the page' (1925: 196–7). But reading without thinking can be dangerous, and the point is that the apparently universal experiences – from desire to distress – that cause us to race through *Jane Eyre* are inflected, sometimes subtly, sometimes sharply, with a sense of difference. So that, for Glen, the 'naïve impulse of identification' should always be complicated by 'the recurrent sense' that Charlotte Brontë's novels 'are abrasive, embarrassing, enigmatic […] curiously unsettling to read' (2002a: 2). We should keep in mind the ways in which Brontë's inherited preoccupations and discourses 'are tantalisingly different from ours' (Glen, 2002b: 1). There are specifically early to mid-nineteenth-century discourses of class, gender and race; of imperialism and slavery; of childhood, religion, duty and evangelicalism at work, shaping the contours of *Jane Eyre* and emerging reconfigured by the author's unique perspective. As Dana Shiller has observed, our 'unflagging desire for knowledge of the past' may not 'be extinguished by doubts as to how accessible it really is', but our continued attempts at access are doubly complicated by the extent to which we know the past through the lens of fiction: our 'sense of "Victorianism" comes to us already emplotted by the nineteenth-century novel' (Shiller, 1997: 557, 547).

Furthermore, although the heightened affective experiences in Brontë's novel risk seeming simplistically 'universal' (which reduces their potent historical significance), it is yet the case that interpretation of these experiences – and of their ideological framework – has proven no simple matter. In *Victoriana*, Cora Kaplan aptly queries whether Brontë's fiction has a 'highly problematic, complicit relationship with the construction of racial thinking', or instead demonstrates a 'partial but emphatic resistance to it'? (2007, 29). We might ask – as do several neo-Victorian reworkings – a similar question about the text's overarching perspective on the limited rights and role of, and opportunities for, women, as focalised through Jane's trajectory; and also about Brontë's representation of gender and madness. Recognising the nuances and perhaps unresolved tensions of the Victorian original will be crucial in fostering a fully rounded debate on the ethics of appropriation, and particularly the question of whether certain neo-Victorian novels may best be seen as acts of respect or retaliation, nostalgia or theft, or something in between.

201

Complicated layers of re-vision: the presence of *Wide Sargasso Sea*

It is important to note, at this juncture, the ways in which reworkings of *Jane Eyre* often also speak directly to the accreted meanings of prior neo-Victorian revisions, as well as their critical contexts. As Peter Widdowson has noted, 're-visionary novels almost invariably have a clear cultural-political thrust' and are concerned with revising culture's 'master-narratives' by 'restoring a voice, a history and an identity to those hitherto exploited, marginalized and silenced by dominant interests and ideologies' (2006: 505–6). In this complicated layering, afterlives of Brontë's text are often, to a greater or lesser extent, also after-echoes of Jean Rhys's influential post-colonial critique *Wide Sargasso Sea* (1966).

It was not just the state of insanity but indeed the dangers of false imprisonment that preoccupied a number of nineteenth-century authors. Both Charles Dickens and Wilkie Collins had visited asylums, and Collins's novel *The Woman in White* (1859–60) reveals the way madness could be induced and manipulated for personal or financial gain. There were fears throughout the nineteenth century that diagnosis often echoed prejudices of the male medical establishment about social and sexual norms, and that medical collusion and corruption could ensure confinement of the female patient 'well beyond need' (Appignanesi, 2008: 96). Though the narrative is sympathetic to Rochester's despair at what he bitterly calls his 'sole conjugal embrace', Charlotte Brontë is alive to the dangers of incarceration. Mrs Rochester growls and grovels 'like some strange wild animal', yet we note that she has been restrained in 'a room without a window' for almost fifteen years (Brontë, 2003: 327–8). Novelist Jean Rhys famously follows these implications through, using the fictional vehicle of a prequel to show how Bertha's psychological breakdown might not have been the result of a 'savage' or inherently corrupt nature. This is an act of re-vision in Adrienne Rich's terms: where 'seeing with fresh eyes' and 'entering an old text from a new critical direction' becomes, for women, 'an act of survival' (1972: 18).

Telling the story of the first Mrs Rochester, Rhys provides a history where in Brontë's text there has been silence or a muffled scream. Renaming Bertha 'Antoinette', Rhys recounts the character's troubled girlhood in Jamaica, her arranged marriage to Edward Rochester (who is not named in the text but who along with Antoinette narrates it in part), and the collapse of their union in a maze of cultural misunderstandings and sexual betrayal. Some neo-Victorian novels demand knowledge of the Victorian novel and period only in general terms. Is it the case, as Anne Humpherys has claimed, that we need to have read *Jane Eyre* in order to understand *Wide Sargasso Sea*? For Humpherys, 'a reader would not be able to make even rudimentary meaning of the narrative strategies […] without knowledge' of the 'pretext' (2002: 445). Certainly a great deal is lost without the intertextual point of comparison – in particular the expectation of fire and destruction at the end of the novel which is referenced but not repeated – but the very awareness that this text could be enjoyed without knowledge of Brontë's sense of a specific, fitting ending opens up the realm of possibility for different interpretations – and gestures towards the shifting sands on which rest many neo-Victorian points of reference and allusion. Emma Tennant, who 'occupies a sadly Pluto-like position' in Nick Turner's 'canonical solar system' (Turner, 2010: 113) of post-war British women writers, has made a career out of literary legacies. Though, like Rhys, Tennant seeks to create greater imaginative space for competing female voices or perspectives, her work is far more dependent on the reader's knowledge of (and investment in tracing) specific details of Brontë's original, bordering on what Georges Letissier has called, in relation to neo-Dickensian fiction, 'an enterprise of downright *Victorianophagy!*', or 'textual cannibalism' (2004: 126, italics in the original). Sharing the obsession of neo-Victorian theory with spectres, Tennant's oeuvre is 'haunted by the influential ghosts of other stories' (Wesley, 2000: 176). *Thornfield Hall* is no exception, summoning not only both 'pretexts' but also the reader's awareness of the interplay between Brontë's and Rhys's novels.

'Worn to nothing'? Depletion, originality and the 'mere spectre' of Jane Eyre

In Brontë's novel, when Jane Eyre arrives on St John's doorstep, his sisters (and, we later learn, her cousins) exclaim that she is 'worn to nothing. How very thin, and how very bloodless!' The Jane they see – who has taken flight after Rochester's attempted bigamy – is 'a mere spectre!' (Brontë, 2003: 377) She is too depleted, mentally and physically, to give an 'account' of herself: the firm first-person voice of fictional autobiography falters. It is notable that, in the three reworkings I will now explore in detail, Brontë's narrator remains on some level a 'mere spectre'. This spectrality could capture, on one hand, the loss inherent in cruder Brontë imitations (often striving towards some kind of modern double, but raising a fainter or weaker version than the original) but also simultaneously maps onto the sense I share with Miller (who makes the observation in relation to bio-fiction) that 'the most interesting recent Brontë fictions are those which approach the topic tangentially' (Miller, 2002: 152). The further these Brontëan-inspired afterlives stray from their Victorian original (seeking not to rewrite or replace but otherwise to engage with Jane Eyre/*Jane Eyre*), the more compelling they, and their comments upon fiction's enduring place and power within our culture, become. In Jasper Fforde's *The Eyre Affair*, set in a version of the world where, in 1985, London's criminal gangs kidnap characters from works of fiction, the centrality of Jane's autobiographical self and its inevitable exclusion of other perspectives is parodied by the white pages left in fans' copies when the heroine goes missing. As one special operative puts it, with the protagonist gone, 'there isn't much to read […] it's anyone's guess as to what happens next' (Fforde, 2001: 298). In Gail Jones's *Sixty Lights*, Jane is present as remembered literary experience only (or, if in human form, through a set of likenesses and divergences that influence characters' modes of reading their own world). Though Emma Tennant's *Thornfield Hall* is a direct rewriting, there is a great deal to read that does not involve Jane, who is first mentioned on page 45 and does not appear until page 59. Cleverly, Jane is figured by Tennant as so peripheral to the principal narrator Adèle's early consciousness that the moment of her arrival as governess goes unannounced.

Doing a similar plot in different voices: secrets, marginalisation and multiplicity

Tennant's novel remains true to the basic elements of plot as told by Brontë's Jane – there is no denying Jane's increasing importance to Rochester and at Thornfield, and this is reflected in Adèle's growth from narcissism to gratitude. But this version of life at Thornfield Hall delights in pointing up intersections and inventing new twists that enable the revelation of either 'secrets' or alternatives. There is a whole subplot concerning Adèle's friendship with Antoinette (for Tennant's imagery hearkens back to *Wide Sargasso Sea*), and a thrilling if somewhat melodramatic suggestion of criminality among the loyal servants. Not only does Tennant provide a startling alternative as to the cause of the infamous fire, or fires, at Thornfield Hall, she also fills in Rochester's history in Paris and transforms this into an ongoing future through the (imaginative and actual) travels of Adèle.

Many resonances with Brontë's depiction of Jane abound in this expansion of Adèle's story, and the exploration of a child's view is used to good effect by Tennant. Importantly, though, *Thornfield Hall: Jane Eyre's Hidden Story* (2002) was first published under the title *Adèle* (2002), its renaming for paperback perhaps gesturing to the importance of place and context, of community and the dialogic imagination, over individual voice – in Tennant's vision for the work and, arguably, in the neo-Victorian enterprise more broadly. (We might also note the likely economic imperative to this renaming: an ethics of marketability, with the Brontëan source text more immediately recognisable in the title.) Chapters in *Thornfield Hall* are told in the first person by Adèle, Edward Rochester, Grace Poole and Mrs Fairfax (but intriguingly not Bertha/Antoinette), and this multiplicity of voices opens up perspectives on a host of other characters from Brontë's text and beyond, including Adèle's mother Céline and a colourful Parisian cast. Tennant's enjoyment of layered textual puzzles is apparent, as several recognisable historical figures are included – from the photographer Nadar to the poet Monsieur de Nerval (who scuttles his lobster through the text as he was said to do through the parks of nineteenth-century Paris).[4]

Betrayal, strength, duty and violence are all important in this reworking, sometimes appearing with great subtlety. If Tennant inherits Rhys's legacy and provides a more rounded portrait of Bertha Mason than Brontë's Jane was capable of assimilating – in this text, the injustice of her incarceration and indeed the fact that imprisonment is responsible for her madness are boldly stated on more than one occasion – it is yet the case that Adèle is able to lose her sensitive connection with Antoinette when other needs intervene. Antoinette is returned to the descriptive realm of 'the mad Creole wife' (Tennant, 2007: 163) with as much callous indifference as Rochester (in all three versions) has confined her to the upper (and untold) stor(e)y of the ancestral dwelling. The confusion in Tennant's text over when Bertha has died does make way for a working through, to some extent, of guilt over her death, with Adèle in her moment of crisis admitting to seeing herself as 'a girl who was born with a stone in place of her heart' (Tennant, 2007: 176).

For all the possibilities opened up along the way, the sense of an ending is much the same, though Adèle's prominence overwrites the slightly unsettling focus on St John Rivers in the closing section of Brontë's novel. The family are noted to live 'happily ever after' (Tennant, 2007: 224), in true fairy-tale form, though not without an opportunity for grim humour in this text that has insistently referenced the French literary folktale of the murderous Bluebeard. Mr Rochester had 'taken care to install a steel door between the third story and the rest of the house', and so it survives despite the terrible arson: 'Though whether', Tennant continues, 'as some wags said, this door had been erected as a safeguard in the event of Mr. Rochester's second wife's going mad, it was never known' (2007: 223–4). Keeping in mind Tennant's text's heightened sense of the unfairness of Rochester's dissatisfaction with his first wife and, more strongly, the damage caused by his incarceration of her, this has ominous tones; overall though it serves to reassure, as the need for such a door in Jane's case will, it is implied, remain untested.

Tennant uses Adèle's awareness of the life of the performer – tightrope walker, circus clown and tragic actress – as well as the presence of other artists obliquely to comment, I suggest, on the act of writing and the ethics of the neo-Victorian enterprise. At one point, where Adèle muses painfully on history, memory and duration, she 'can feel [her] own face become a part of the artist's close scrutiny' (Tennant, 2007: 166). It is the photographer's gaze to which Adèle refers, but these are terms in which Tennant might envisage her own practice: subjecting the spaces and questions left by the surface of the original text to a creative analysis – dissection, even – that probes beyond the superficial, the physiognomical. It is almost possible to discern, in Adèle's growing awareness of the construction of identity and her search for information on her true heritage, Tennant's ironic viewpoints on multiplicity, plot and the constraints of realism. Adèle wonders at her place within the whole (text, as crowd), marvelling that 'everything was as usual on the day when all had changed for me' (Tennant, 2007: 174), and feels herself to be the 'helpless recipient of yet another terrible possibility' (2007: 185) in an unfolding familial mystery. In moments of urgency and terror, she says, 'scenes that had little meaning at the time race forward to prove they are the missing parts of the puzzle you have carried within you all your life' (Tennant, 2007: 173), and yet in her wanderings as *flâneur* she suggests a more leisurely mode of engagement that might be taken as a productive way of reading, and gleaning: 'walking' through the neo-Victorian text 'in that special way, disengaged yet enchanted, a spectator rather than a buyer' (Tennant, 2007: 165). But of course it is hardly possible to wander through an entire text without investing – or ceasing the stroll – and there must, of necessity, be any number of roads not taken. It was Brontë's Jane who described herself as 'obscure, plain, and little', though the rich detail of her fictional autobiography discounts such a claim. Tennant winkingly has Adèle make the observation that, without the biographical and emotional textures of her existence unfurled, 'my life will be as meaningless as if I had never been born […] I might as well live in obscurity' (2007:171). This, to an extent, she does in Brontë's novel, lovingly but summarily disposed of in the final chapter (where Jane Eyre has cause to clarify: 'You have not quite forgotten little Adèle, have you, reader? I had not' [Brontë, 2003: 499; Tennant, 2007: x]).

Tennant's novel positions itself as an ethical intervention into the past, or past fiction, and our understanding of it. Seeking to tell a 'hidden' story – giving voice to a minor or marginalised character in Brontë's narrative – it yet stays relatively close to the original. Often, direct retellings of Victorian novels (including, also, those works that purport to present a very similar story in a fresh time, setting or genre) exclude as much as they claim to recover. Ironically, the closer these rewritings adhere to the major plot points of the original, the more they (perhaps unwittingly) risk obscuring key aspects and complexities, the range of potential meanings, and, fundamentally, the aesthetic pleasures of the original. An ethics of inclusion/recovery (of what the original purportedly 'missed'), or even homage through direct retelling-with-variation, can certainly have its casualties. Tennant's novel (though less overtly inventive than Jean Rhys's prequel) is sufficiently self-reflexive to avoid falling into this reductive trap, but it does raise interesting questions about, first, the kinds of judgements twenty-first-century reading audiences make about the silences in nineteenth-century texts and, second, whether a focus on one (narrative) voice will always necessarily obscure another.

Metafiction or literary heresy? Preservation-through-appropriation as ethical act in *The Eyre Affair*

Like Tennant, Jasper Fforde has made a career from engaging with (and, playfully, drastically altering) literary history, but to quite different ends, and with an overt metafictive commentary on the ethics of appropriation. Fforde's first novel, *The Eyre Affair*, offers two worlds: a 1980s Britain, where the Crimean War has continued for over 130 years and dodos are bred as pets, and – via a child's imaginative engagement and then a futuristic Prose Portal – the world of Brontë's novel as a space available for textual (ex)change and literary tourism. Alterations made to the text of *Jane Eyre* (and perhaps, the implication is, the ways we read it, and importantly the ways we adapt and rewrite this and other iconic narratives at different points in history) have direct effects in the future realm, so the accuracy of both text and interpretation could prove vital in determining the direction and even survival of humanity. As Jack Schitt of the Goliath Advanced Weapons Division confirms, 'over the last hundred years there has been an inexplicable cross-fertilisation between works of fiction and reality' (Fforde, 2001: 211). Victor Analogy, the head of Swindon LiteraTec, has been 'investigating the phenomenon for some time' (Fforde, 2001: 211). But who owns a narrative, or its likely meaning? Is popular necessarily best? How do we define literary value? And how much can we 'stretch the boundaries of a story' (Fforde, 2001: 67) before it becomes another story, or point of reference, entirely?

Fforde's novel is alive, at times painstakingly, to the problems of neo-Victorian reference and exchange. The very audacity of the terms of its intervention (imagining a situation where texts, if mishandled, can vanish – and history can be literally rewritten) means that it by and large preserves elements of Brontë's original that other reworkings either silently or self-reflexively change. This preservation-through-appropriation is, in Fforde's text, an ethical act. Ironically, Fforde achieves a sense of homage in part by proposing that Brontë intended a different ending from that which (outside of *The Eyre Affair*) we know to be real. It will be Thursday Next's visits to the endlessly repeating pages of the novel that insert the changes making possible a resolution where Jane marries Rochester rather than journeying to India as St John's assistant, and this allows Fforde some laughter as he explains or 'solves' the supernatural elements of Brontë's plot. It is not Rochester's voice Jane hears calling her back to Thornfield but Thursday Next crouched outside the Rivers' house and emulating Rochester's 'hoarse whisper': 'it wasn't a good impersonation but it did the trick. I saw Jane start to fluster and pack almost immediately' (Fforde, 2001: 346). As 'a small, usually unexcitable man' named Plink, 'the Brontë Federation expert' of Fforde's imagining, exclaims of this plot development: 'It's pure Charlotte Brontë but it *definitely* wasn't there before!' (Fforde, 2001: 345, italics in the original). SpecOps agent Next has donned a bonnet and intervened to save the text from ruination or erasure by Acheron Hades – for in Fforde's fictionalised late-twentieth-century Britain, beloved novels are of central political and cultural significance and are valuable tools within a landscape of corruption (thus open to manipulation and abuse): as Hades threatens, 'I have the *Chuzzlewit* manuscript and I'm not afraid to disrupt it' (Fforde, 2001: 220). Next is credited by a Toad News Network Reporter with 'saving *Jane Eyre*', and congratulated on her 'successful reconstruction of the novel' (Fforde, 2001: 360); Walter Branwell, chairman of the 'federation splinter group "Brontë for the People"', shares the public's delight with the 'new [i.e. Brontë's actual] ending' (2001: 361).

The exchange is two-way. Rochester intervenes in Thursday's modern existence, returning the favour by fixing her ailing love plot with Landen Parke-Laine. Fforde's Rochester acknowledges how 'unsuitable' Blanche Ingram is for him (2001: 333), drawing a parallel with Landen's then fiancée. In an unexpected and rather brilliant ironic twist, Mrs Jane Rochester sends Mrs Nakajima (one of the Japanese tourists-from-the-future-into-fiction from whom Rochester makes a tidy profit) and Mr Briggs to disrupt Landen's wedding to Daisy Mutlar with news of her existing marriage to Murray Posh ('Bigamy is hardly nonsense, I think, sir' [Fforde, 2001: 353]). Briggs reports that Jane and Rochester have by now not one but two children, the second named after important women in both Brontë's and Fforde's textual worlds: Helen Thursday Rochester (Fforde, 2001: 354). In another echo, Thursday avoids the advances of her colleague Bowden, who appears as something of a modern-day secular St John (she would not be joining him in Ohio 'as either wife or assistant' [Fforde, 2001: 369]). As Juliette Wells has noted, the 'reciprocal series of rewarding acts' between Fforde's Rochester and Thursday 'significantly revises the power imbalance between Brontë's heroine and hero' (where only with Jane's inherited fortune and Rochester's blindness – not to mention the death of Bertha Mason – does union seem possible at the conclusion of Brontë's novel): in *The Eyre Affair*, 'neither Thursday nor Rochester maintains the upper hand' (Wells, 2007: 205).

Fforde's Jane does not appreciate being displaced or removed from her original plot by the villainous Hades. In Brontë's novel, Jane longs for a 'power of vision that might overpass' the 'limit' of her view from Thornfield – a comment on the horizon of possibility for women constrained by 'custom' to a life sentence of domestic boredom (Brontë, 2003: 125–6). In *The Eyre Affair*, the kidnapped Jane says that the view from her window onto the world of 1985 'pales when compared to my window at Thornfield [...] dependable and unchanging' (Fforde, 2001: 306). Her 'tone' is 'restrained' at first but she then speaks 'angrily' (Fforde, 2001: 306) – echoing the language both of Brontë's novel (in Jane's rebellious protest, women 'suffer from too rigid a restraint' [Brontë, 2003: 125]) and of Virginia Woolf's subsequent criticism (in Woolf's opinion, Charlotte Brontë's anger infects characterisation and textual integrity; see Lewis, 2016). On his website, Fforde describes the feeling of putting 'words into Jane's mouth' as akin to committing 'literary heresy' (Fforde, n.d.), and this (in conjunction with the more practical reasons outlined as part of the plot) may be why Jane remains a 'mere spectre' in this rewriting that revolves around preserving her fictional autobiography.

Less clear is why Bertha Mason remains voiceless – and attacks Hades with a pair of scissors, thus acting to save the very text in which she has been so unfairly imprisoned not only by Rochester but also (as many critics have argued) by Charlotte Brontë. However, Fforde's novel should not necessarily be viewed as emerging from, as Andrea Kirchknopf suggests, 'a postfeminist or even antifeminist theoretical framework', where there may be 'a connection between the comic mode and the inattention to, or rejection of, the feminist agenda' (Kirchknopf, 2013: 169). As Jürgen Wehrmann concludes (in a chapter that acknowledges the 'phenomenon of post-feminism' to be somewhat 'ambiguous'), Fforde's novel 'validates the original ending' of *Jane Eyre* by emphasising 'the continuous importance of love, marriage, and family even for a strong, independent woman', thus showing 'how difficult it still is to imagine the reconciliation of a woman's private and professional lives – even in the fantastic world of science fiction' (Wehrmann, 2007: 163). Thursday's closing statement that her career is 'only just beginning' (Fforde, 2001: 373) may function primarily to pave Fforde's way for the inevitable and highly marketable sequels, including *The Well of Lost Plots* (2003), but it also obliquely reminds us of the inspiration Thursday has drawn from the steadfastness of Brontë's Jane:

> When she turned I could see that her face was plain and outwardly unremarkable, yet possessed of a bearing that showed inner strength and resolve. I stared at her intently with a mixture of feelings. […] I felt myself stand more upright and clench my jaw in subconscious mimicry of her pose.
> (Fforde, 2001: 66)

As is the case in Gail Jones's *Sixty Lights*, there are glancing and layered references to other Victorian novels and the cultural meanings they continue to import into current understandings of selfhood, safety and sexuality, such as Fforde's allusion to Thomas Hardy's *Tess of the d'Urbervilles* (1891) through Thursday Next's passing remark that 'all of a sudden I had that out-of-the-frying-pan-and-into-the-fire feeling' (Fforde, 2001: 360). The constant threat to fictional heroines of various power imbalances between men and women, ventriloquised in this way by recourse to observations drawn from nineteenth-century fiction, may provide comic relief in Fforde's text but also points towards the continued relevance of past dangers and injustices – and their inheritance in the lived present moment.

Fforde's Rochester assures Thursday that 'Your intervention *improved* the narrative' (2001: 190, italics in the original). As a young girl falling into the text by mistake during an imaginative reverie at the 'Brontë museum', Thursday has, Fforde asserts, caused Rochester's horse to slip, making the meeting between Jane and Rochester 'more dramatic' (2001: 190) than in Fforde's alternative fictive-original. But, of course, as Fforde's reader is bound to know, or to realise, this dramatic meeting was in Brontë's novel all along. Rochester tells Thursday knowingly that 'you weren't the first visitor we have had. And you won't be the last, if I'm correct' (Fforde, 2001: 190). Fforde's Rochester means Hades (whose intended imprint on the novel is entirely destructive and self-serving), but this observation resonates beyond the internal logic of Fforde's text. Brontë's original will continue to be (if not quite so literally) revisited, reshaped and appropriated – whether for good or for ill – both by academic criticism and by creative interventions.

Travelling *Jane Eyre*/migrations of meaning: shining *Sixty Lights* on intertextual memory

Jane Eyre has become, as Patsy Stoneman noted in 1996, what Umberto Eco calls an 'intertextual archetype' (quoted in Stoneman, 1996: 127) – and often, as Lloyd Jones acknowledges in the epigraph (also from Eco) to his neo-Dickensian *Mister Pip* (2006), archetypes or 'characters migrate'. Chris Baldick observed, in the context of Mary Shelley's *Frankenstein* (1818), that texts which acquire the status of iterable myths are reduced 'to the simplest memorable patterns' (Baldick, 1987: 3) – and it is true that, while 'artists inspired by *Jane Eyre* have responded to the diverse aspects of the novel quite differently' (focusing on childhood, or rebellion, or dealing critically with perceived blind spots), 'many famous re-writings' of Brontë's novel 'focus on a heterosexual love relationship' either to deconstruct its myth or reinforce its ubiquity (Rubik and Mettinger-Schartmann, 2007: 12). Gail Jones's *Sixty Lights*, a complex refiguration of narrative inheritance and exploration of what is obscured behind 'memorable patterns', not only focuses on the nature of love, and embodied emotion, but also deals directly with the modes of intergenerational and global migrations of meaning that have affected cultural (and personal) understandings of *Jane Eyre* since 1847.

Writing of cultural portability within the nineteenth century, John Plotz observes that 'studying how art objects are nationally marked in their global peregrinations perpetually reminds us that divisions between places, times, or cultures constantly change, and the identity of any one person, any one text (to whom it belongs, where it belongs), is mutable' (2008: 171). As with belonging, so too might meaning or significance be unstable, shifting, open to mutation. While Jones's Lucy Strange observes that it is 'Strange […] how fiction predicts' (Jones, 2005b: 102), implying that there are common understandings about texts that can be used retrospectively to read patterns within lived experience, *Sixty Lights* plays with the ways that stories as common cultural capital are at once central to identity (retold and shared at key moments of the text and used by Lucy and her brother to recapture familial memory and process traumatic loss) and yet retold, as is the story of the flying Dutchman, with varying degrees of accuracy, modification and even variant endings. Will *Jane Eyre*, then, along with other texts (and Lucy's own prose-photographs), be capable of providing a solid basis for forms of self-interpretation that can transcend the sense of alienation amid the bewildering global storehouse of images and experiences that appear as if refracted by the shattered mirror that opens the novel, holding the world 'in bits and pieces' (Jones, 2005b: 4)?

Jones has written elsewhere of 'an ethics of consubstantiating difference', pointing out the importance, in Australian scholarship and fiction, of imagining 'the subjective and inter-subjective worlds of hybrid communities' (2006: 21), and in a sense *Sixty Lights* is concerned with uniting past and present in one common substance, or 'memory text' (Jones, 2005a), the fabric of which speaks of an emphasis on connection. This echoes wider movements in neo-Victorian fiction. As Jay Clayton observes, while 'the twentieth-century response' obsessed over difference, the twenty-first century 'outpouring' of creative reimaginings has brought a 'new' focus on 'relation', even 'within the context of great, sometimes overwhelming historical change': 'the pleasure is in seeing parallels' (2012: 726).

Lucy Strange is a neo-Victorian heroine with 'entirely modern' sensibilities, 'a woman of the future' (Jones, 2005b: 141) not only in terms of the impressive powers of prediction (regarding not-yet-invented photographic technologies) bestowed upon her by her twenty-first-century author.[5] Unlike Brontë's Jane, Lucy is unperturbed that her first lover, William, has a wife (and four children), and – perhaps freed by the third-person narration of Jones's text as well as her commitment to maculate visuality (that which is 'spotted, stained, blemished' [2005b: 146]) – is concerned accurately to consider and to depict the sensual and bodily aspects of life. Sex, childbirth and death are all recorded. As with Jasper Fforde's Thursday Next, equivalences and counterpoints with Brontë's

Jane are etched into characterisation: Lucy is 'not well educated enough to apply for work as a governess' but does long 'in a way she could not even identify – for a small community of sympathetic women' (Jones, 2005b: 99). As a child, she feels that alignment with those who have existed in the fiction of her own century will 'guard and protect her': 'If she were asked she would say: "Yes, I am an orphan, like a girl in a book"' (Jones, 2005b: 76). As a young adult she tends to view the present moment through the lens of fiction, though depending on her mood this results in equivalences more or less flattering to the literary history she summons: 'it was like a scene in a novel. Lucy saw how melodramatically they confronted each other. How stale their words were. [...] Yet another tale of a sacrificial woman' (Jones, 2005b: 132). Words from pages past are not always stale: at times they become the flashbulb moments of shared illumination that, like a photograph, can 'crack [...] open time' (Jones, 2005b: 233), providing a bank of images that can – ideally – be exchanged in deep interpersonal shorthand ('"Like Lowood School? Like the School in *Jane Eyre*?" Violet confessed she had never read the novel' [Jones, 2005b: 181]). Lucy discovers the ship's library on her passage to India:

> She thought for the first time about what it meant to read a novel. What process was this? What seance of other lives into her own imagination? Reading was this metaphysical meeting space – peculiar, specific, ardent, unusual – in which black words neatly spaced on a rectangular page persuaded her that hypothetical people were as real as she, that not diversion, but knowing, was the gift story gave her. She learnt how other people entered the adventure of being alive [...]; and in this moment, composed of alphabets, Lucy knew the shape of her own yearning.
>
> (Jones, 2005b: 114)

The uses she makes of fiction are also more modern, or at least self-aware, than those of her mother and Violet: for those 'unaccustomed to fiction' can sink into 'enchantment' (Jones, 2005b: 242), whereas Lucy – more like a neo-Victorian novelist – will allow her thoughts about narratives such as Collins's *The Woman in White* to become 'unplaited and reversed', serving new purposes (Jones, 2005b: 243). Lucy may be caught in the framework of Jones's plot – her death laid out before the reader on page 4 – but her modes of observation, of '*Special Things Seen* and *Photographs Not Taken*' (Jones, 2005b: 220), allow her a creative agency, it is suggested, never attained by the mother who Lucy in part reclaims through her love of story: the cryptic underlinings in a copy of the novel left behind, along with other objects (2005b: 45), and a remembered 'inordinate fondness' (2005b: 227) for *Jane Eyre*.

There is the suggestion that Lucy's mother, Honoria, invests too much of herself (and her great expectations) in existing plot lines and is not able to seek ways of enjoying the world when life becomes (ironically, in marriage and motherhood – the culmination of Brontë's original) 'rather literal and prosaic' (Jones, 2005b: 61). Initially:

> She travelled *Jane Eyre*. She was sped on by its melancholy and motivating desire.
> *I am Jane Eyre*, she secretly told herself. *I am honourable but unnoticed. I am passionate and strong. I need a lover who will carry my future in the palm of his hand.*

(Jones, 2005b: 12, italics in the original)

On their first night together, Honoria tells Arthur 'the entire plot of Charlotte Brontë's famous novel, *Jane Eyre*. Her triangle-shaped face lit up as she spoke. She was impassioned, fixated; she knew whole paragraphs by heart' (Jones, 2005b: 16). It may be that the act of travelling *Jane Eyre* gives Honoria 'the aura of erotic intensity' that captures Arthur's attention after their literal 'happy collision': it was 'as though she had travelled with special knowledge from a foreign country', that of 'romance' (Jones, 2005b: 14, 12). Like Fforde, Jones makes reference to the supernatural element in Brontë's novel: Honoria and Arthur refer to this explicitly and choose also to interpret 'prophesying icons' as confirmation of 'the progress of their romance': 'I know it's preposterous […] But isn't it also wonderful?' (Jones, 2005b: 47). Sad then that their marriage becomes for Honoria an immobilisation of passion, and she thinks, 'with ridiculous intensity, of the locked-away madwoman', assailed by 'an indistinct sense' of her own 'imprisonment' and remembering 'almost daily the character who chose immolation' (Jones, 2005b: 62).

Gail Jones has commented in an interview that 'I'm interested in using the Victorian novel as a kind of paradigm to unpick' and that part of her project in *Sixty Lights* – which is structured as a series of photographic images – was to bring post-Victorian ideas about time and rupture to bear on the traditional *Bildungsroman*: 'there's a lot of prefiguring, replication and playing around with how images return to us redoubled' (2005a). I argue that, in doing so, Jones draws upon ideas already being explored by Brontë regarding the nature of the visual imagination and the links between representation and reality. Not only is Jane Eyre aware of the supply of certain recollections either 'very dim' or 'indelibly' fixed, such as the 'iteration of one idea – this strange recurrence of one image' that can come to the mind in sleep as presentiment (Brontë, 2003: 379, 248–9), but she is also attentive to the shaping power of reading and painting in ways that pre-empt Lucy Strange's photographic endeavours. Brontë's novel is itself in a sense what Jones calls a 'memory text', and Jane's evocations of character and psychology depend (though less forcefully than Lucy's) upon the flash of images within conscious awareness: Rochester's face 'was like a new picture introduced to the gallery of memory; and it was dissimilar to all the others hanging there […]. I had it still before me […]; I saw it as I walked fast down hill all the way home' (Brontë, 2003: 132). Jane Eyre has her own proto-photographic mental gallery of special things seen: or, as she calls them, 'striking' scenes observed 'with the spiritual eye'. The 'copies' come out of the furniture of 'my head' (Brontë, 2003: 142); Jane's watercolours are, like Lucy's 'chamber of [mental] images' (Jones, 2005b: 220), fragmentary and symbolic. At nineteen, Jane holds much of Lucy's adventurous determination: 'I am ready to go to India, if I may go free' (Brontë, 2003: 451). The harsh attempted realism of Jane's self-portrait in crayons and the counterpoint 'ivory miniature' of an 'imaginary Blanche Ingram' diverges, however, from Lucy's photographic practice, intended by Jane not as a way of knowing the world but of curtailing it: a 'wholesome discipline' to stifle desire (Brontë, 2003: 184).

Jane Eyre desired 'a power of vision which might overpass that limit' of 'practical experience […], of acquaintance with variety of character, than was here within my reach' (Brontë, 2003: 125). In *Sixty Lights* it is Jacob who envies Lucy her Strange position as 'seer' (Jones, 2005b: 230): 'liberated' (2005b: 216), in part by her positioning in London and later in the century than Brontë's Jane, to wander the city streets at night, which she relishes as 'nothing less than a gallery of spectacles' – indeed, free (in some senses of the word) to wander the world, gathering 'a whole fugitive empire of images to which she felt affinity and loyalty' (Jones, 2005b: 178). Lucy realises that her 'salutary estrangement' has made her life 'a tripod. Australia, England and India all held her – upheld her – on a platform of vision, seeking her own focus' (Jones, 2005b: 212). This symbolic tripod provides a higher vantage point than does the attic trapdoor of Thornfield Hall. As Elaine Freedgood and others have argued, the violence of empire is marginalised in Brontë's novel: Jane's 'purchase and placement of mahogany furniture symbolizes, naturalizes, domesticates and internalizes' histories of deforestation, exploitation and slavery (Freedgood, 2009: 35). But Jones's Lucy is well placed to be loudly 'disgusted […] by National Spirit' (Jones, 2005b: 185): much as a portrait can capture either something genuine, or merely a staged 'world of props and false objects' (2005b: 139), there is a sense that escape from the 'impeding knowledge' of one's own culture (2005b: 135) requires an open immersion in the unfamiliar, an attempt to avoid the affirming gaze of one's own 'ignorance' or assumed superiority in the bustling marketplace of the imagination. Ultimately, Lucy's realisations remind us that there will always be stories in the margins – secret narratives either overlooked, or withheld. Seeing her servant Bashanti and her mother in silent communication, Lucy suddenly perceives 'why Bashanti, who knew English, refused to speak it: to keep her own world intact. To keep it safe' (Jones, 2005b: 221).

As the genetic and adopted clans of *Sixty Lights* reveal, 'families contain peculiar routes of similitude and dissimilitude' (Jones, 2005b: 147): so too do textual families, such as the (ever-proliferating) group of novels each responding in very different ways to *Jane Eyre*. For Lucy Strange, the world 'returned to itself' is an act, 'surely […] of devotion' (Jones, 2005b: 154), but while this is perhaps true of the photograph, it is not necessarily so in the realm of neo-Victorian literature. Envisaging the photograph as a kind of kiss, Lucy writes to Isaac that 'it is another form of love, is it not, the studied representation? It is devotional. Physical. A kind of honouring attention' (Jones, 2005b: 208); she also realises, however, that a blurry or filtered composition may bring interesting effects, or transformations. Familiar subjects viewed in Strange ways may make possible new understandings, enabling the viewer or reader to grasp towards that which lies 'just beyond human recognition' (Jones, 2005b: 208).

There is a sort of current, a connection, established between Jones's and Brontë's texts: a 'prickling charge' in the way *Sixty Lights* and *Jane Eyre* lie together, as do Lucy and Jacob, so that Jones's reader is 'aware of the proximity' and 'side-by-side permission': 'Seduction, she thought, is never face to face' (Jones, 2005b: 210). Lucy, contemplating mortality, is acutely aware of 'all these selves brought into being in such small unspeakable moments' (Jones, 2005b: 210), and perhaps it is the case that the original novel, *Jane Eyre*, has within it multiple 'selves' too, each illuminated or refracted by subsequent textual responses. Jane Eyre's own reading of texts varies according to mood and purpose: *Gulliver's Travels*, beloved as a child, fails to comfort once Jane has felt herself to be 'a most desolate wanderer', or captive, in the 'dread' red room (Brontë, 2003: 29). Perhaps every act of reading (let alone rewriting or literary response) is an appropriation: a taking possession of and making to do the work of one's own desired meaning and interpretive framework.

The novels by Tennant, Fforde and Jones at once participate in and comment on this appropriative process, providing insights into the revisionary impulses and strategies that adhere to the Victorian period and Brontë's *Jane Eyre* in particular. They pose serious questions about textual inheritance and forms of intertextual remembering: ranging from stories (perceived to be) excluded, and recovered (Tennant); under threat from deliberate misreading or alteration (Fforde); or retold in new contexts, inevitably with emphasis on certain elements and tensions, and thus the accretion of new meanings (Jones). There are many different versions of and afterlives for Brontë's Jane Eyre, and *Jane Eyre*, some of which might horrify or amuse the twenty-first-century reader, others which, as acts of insightful homage, might be imagined as perspectives which would likely have delighted Brontë and her heroine, bringing at the very least 'action' and debate, rather than stultifying 'tranquillity' (Brontë, 2003: 125) to the scene of Brontë studies today. Fforde's novel, with its emphasis on manuscripts, reminds us of the centrality of the original, that 'first act of creation' (Fforde, 2001: 208), and warns that 'maximum disruption' to a text and its reception history can be akin to a change in 'the genetic code of the first mammal': one false move and 'every one of us' – or at least our detailed interpretations and overarching sense of Brontë's *Jane Eyre* – 'would be completely different' (2001: 208). On the other hand, invention has always been key: as Fforde's Rochester reminds us with a 'forced, gruff smile', 'I was never real to begin with' (Fforde, 2001: 189). Well might we hope that *Jane Eyre* will survive the ongoing afterlives trend – and perhaps even thrive as a result of the additional attention – to be appreciated afresh by subsequent generations not only as 'mere spectre' haunting the margins of twenty-first-century reworkings of the literary past but also on its own terms: as vibrant 1847 original, ensnared by no neo-Victorian net and proudly brandishing its 'independent will' (Brontë, 2003: 284) long into the future.

Notes

1 For a comprehensive study of reproductions and reworkings of *Jane Eyre* up to 1996, including discussion of what Patsy Stoneman calls the 'sequels syndrome', see Stoneman (1996).

2 'Neo-Victorian Transformations', Honours English course designed and delivered by Dr Alexandra Lewis, University of Aberdeen, 2011 to present.

My thanks to the excellent students who have taken part so enthusiastically in debate and discussion during the course.

3 See, further, Lewis (2010).

4 Another example of Tennant's layered textual puzzles: the French actress Rachel Félix is referenced as the idol of Adèle's mother, and Tennant's novel closes with an unnamed voice (taking over, silently, from Mrs Fairfax's narrative) recounting Adèle's sixteenth-birthday visit with 'her stepmother Jane' to the Apollo Theatre, London, to see Rachel in *Phèdre*. Adèle introduces herself backstage as 'the daughter of the famous *danseuse de corde*, Céline Varens' (Tennant, 2007: 244), and it is decided that Adèle will train with Rachel in Paris for a year. There is a link here with Charlotte Brontë's novel *Villette*: the character Vashti in *Villette* is said to have been based on Rachel, whom Brontë had seen perform in London.

5 Lucy Strange's prescience regarding future technology may seem unrealistic, but note Jones's clever authorial manoeuvre, giving Lucy one major faulty prevision that aligns her temporally with that atmospheric feature prominent in so many neo-Victorian novels, the gas lamp: 'When she peered into the future she knew that London would for ever be illuminated by gas; no other technology would exceed or supplant it' (Jones, 2005b: 217).

References

Appignanesi, Lisa (2008) *Mad, Bad and Sad: A History of Women and the Mind Doctors from 1800 to the Present*, London: Virago.

Baldick, Chris (1987) *In Frankenstein's Shadow: Myth, Monstrosity and Nineteenth-Century Writing*, Oxford: Clarendon Press.

Brontë, Charlotte (2003) *Jane Eyre*, ed. Michael Mason, London: Penguin.

Clayton, Jay (2012) 'The future of Victorian Literature', in Kate Flint (ed.), *The Cambridge History of Victorian Literature*, Cambridge: Cambridge University Press, pp. 712–29.

Freedgood, Elaine (2009) *The Ideas in Things: Fugitive Meaning in the Victorian Novel*, Chicago, Ill.: University of Chicago Press.

Fforde, Jasper (2001) *The Eyre Affair*, London: Hodder & Stoughton.

—— (n.d.) 'Writing *The Eyre Affair*', www.jasperfforde.com/beginnings.html (accessed 19 August 2016).

Glen, Heather (2002a) *Charlotte Brontë: The Imagination in History*, Oxford: Oxford University Press.

—— (2002b) 'Introduction', in Heather Glen (ed.), *The Cambridge Companion to the Brontës*, Cambridge: Cambridge University Press, pp. 1–12.

Heilmann, Ann and Mark Llewellyn (2014) 'On the neo-Victorian, now and then', in Herbert F. Tucker (ed.), *A New Companion to Victorian Literature and Culture*, Malden, MA: John Wiley & Sons, pp. 493–506.

Humpherys, Anne (2002) 'Afterlife of the Victorian novel: novels about novels', in Patrick Brantlinger and William B. Thesing (eds.), *A Companion to the Victorian Novel*, Oxford: Blackwell.

Jones, Gail (2005a) Interview by Lyn Gallacher, *Books and Writing*, Radio National, 27 March, www.abc.net.au/radionational/programs/booksandwriting/gail-jones/3630050 (accessed 19 August 2016).

—— (2005b) *Sixty Lights*, London: Vintage.

—— (2006) 'A dreaming, a sauntering: re-imagining critical paradigms', *Journal of the Association for the Study of Australian Literature*, 5, 11–24.

Kaplan, Cora (2007) *Victoriana: Histories, Fictions, Criticism*, Edinburgh: Edinburgh University Press.

Kirchknopf, Andrea (2013) *Rewriting the Victorians: Modes of Literary Engagement with the 19th Century*, Jefferson, NC: McFarland.

Letissier, Georges (2004) 'Dickens and post-Victorian fiction', in Susana Onega and Christian Gutleben (eds.), *Refracting the Canon in Contemporary British Literature and Film*, Amsterdam: Rodopi, pp. 111–28.

Lewis, Alexandra (2010) 'Page to stage: the Brontës in the world of the Arts', *Women: A Cultural Review*, 21:3, 338–42.

—— (2012) 'Current trends in Brontë criticism and scholarship', in Marianne Thormählen (ed.), *The Brontës in Context*, Cambridge: Cambridge University Press, pp. 198–206.

—— (2016) '"Supposed to be very calm generally": anger, narrative and unaccountable sounds in Charlotte Brontë's *Jane Eyre*', in Susan Bruce and Katherine Smits (eds.), *Feminist Moments: Reading Feminist Texts*, London: Bloomsbury, pp. 67–74.

Miller, Lucasta (2002) *The Brontë Myth*, London: Vintage.

Plotz, John (2008) *Portable Property: Victorian Culture on the Move*, Princeton, NJ: Princeton University Press.

Rich, Adrienne (1972) 'When we dead awaken: writing as re-vision', *College English*, 34:1, 18–30.

Rubik, Margarete and Elke Mettinger-Schartmann (2007) 'Introduction', in Margarete Rubik and Elke Mettinger-Schartmann (eds.), *A Breath of Fresh Eyre: Intertextual and Intermedial Reworkings of Jane Eyre*, Amsterdam: Rodopi, pp. 9–21.

Shiller, Dana (1997) 'The redemptive past in the neo-Victorian novel', *Studies in the Novel*, 29:4, 538–60.

Stoneman, Patsy (1996) *Brontë Transformations: The Cultural Dissemination of Jane Eyre and Wuthering Heights*, Hemel Hempstead: Prentice Hall/Harvester Wheatsheaf.

—— (2007) *Jane Eyre on Stage, 1848–1898: An Illustrated Edition of Eight Plays with Contextual Notes*, Aldershot: Ashgate.

Sweet, Matthew (2001) *Inventing the Victorians*, London: Faber and Faber.

Tennant, Emma (2007) *Thornfield Hall: Jane Eyre's Hidden Story*, New York: Harper.

Turner, Nick (2010) *Post-War British Women Novelists and the Canon*, London: Continuum.

Wehrmann, Jürgen (2007) 'Jane Eyre in outer space: Victorian motifs in post-feminist science fiction', in Margarete Rubik and Elke Mettinger-Schartmann (eds.), *A Breath of Fresh Eyre: Intertextual and Intermedial Reworkings of Jane Eyre*, Amsterdam: Rodopi, pp. 149–66.

Wells, Juliette (2007) 'An Eyre-less affair? Jasper Fforde's seeming elision of Jane', in Margarete Rubik and Elke Mettinger-Schartmann (eds.), *A Breath of Fresh Eyre: Intertextual and Intermedial Reworkings of Jane Eyre*, Amsterdam: Rodopi, pp. 197–208.

Wesley, Marilyn C. (2000) 'Emma Tennant: the secret lives of girls', in Abby H. P. Werlock (ed.), *British Women Writing Fiction*, Tuscaloosa, Ala.: University of Alabama Press, pp 175–90.

Widdowson, Peter (2006) '"Writing back": contemporary re-visionary fiction', *Textual Practice*, 20:3, 491–507.

Woolf, Virginia (1925) '*Jane Eyre* and *Wuthering Heights*', *The Common Reader: First Series*, London: The Hogarth Press, pp. 196–204.

10

'The insane Creole': the afterlife of Bertha Mason

Jessica Cox

'[S]uch a poor ghost'
> (Jean Rhys on Charlotte Brontë's Bertha Mason; 1969: 5)

Charlotte Brontë's *Jane Eyre* (1847) is haunted by the ghostly figure of Rochester's mad wife, Bertha Mason: her eerie laugh and uncanny presence pervade the narrative, as they do Thornfield; they haunt the reader's imagination, as they do Jane's. It seems apt, therefore, that the cultural afterlives of the novel should also be haunted by this strange and troubling figure. In contrast to her spectral presence, Bertha Mason figures heavily in critical and creative reiterations of Brontë's novel. She has become, as Laurence Lerner observes, 'one of the major characters of English fiction [...] central not only to the plot of *Jane Eyre* but also to its emotional economy and its construction of woman' (1989: 273). This chapter explores the legacy of *Jane Eyre* through a consideration of reimaginings of Bertha Mason – a character presented in unequivocally negative terms in Brontë's narrative but variously reinvented in subsequent adaptations as object of pity, femme fatale, proto-feminist figure and Gothic monster.[1]

Brontë's Bertha is dehumanised, silenced, ostracised: not only as a consequence of her mental state and her physical position at Thornfield but also through her limited narrative presence. She represents a crude caricature of the figure of the madwoman, functioning primarily as a plot device – a preventative to Jane's marriage to Rochester. She disrupts the narrative's love story, undermines Rochester's heroic qualities and problematises feminist readings of the text. Virginia Woolf suggests the novel was written by 'someone resenting the treatment of her sex' (2008: 132), but this resentment is undermined by the narrative's treatment of Bertha. At a time when attitudes towards mental health were shifting, Bertha represents a regressive stance: madness as dangerous, uncontrollable, animalistic, with the emphasis placed on containment rather than treatment. She is, as Rick Rylance observes, a 'grotesque, pot-boiling confirmation of stereotypes of the insane' (2002: 165). Consequently, she stands as a significant obstacle for those adapting the novel: to treat her in the same manner as Brontë replicates her degradation. However, presenting her sympathetically has possible ramifications for the characterisation of Rochester as romantic hero. The discussion that follows examines a variety of creative responses to Brontë's madwoman, in a range of mediums, including various literary genres (young adult, literary fiction, mash-up), film, television, theatre and art. Beginning with a brief survey of Bertha's afterlives, the chapter moves on to consider these representations in relation to three key aspects of her characterisation: her madness, appearance and death. Significant differences are apparent in the multiple revisitations to *Jane Eyre*: screen adaptations tend to adopt a more conservative approach to the figure of the madwoman and frequently elide crucial details from their reinterpretations of the text, while literary reworkings (and some stage versions) often take an interrogative approach to the original narrative, drawing the reader's attention to Brontë's troubling portrayal of the madwoman. Though divergent, taken together these recreations of Bertha's character point to an ongoing desire to recover Bertha from the margins of Brontë's original novel.[2]

Bertha's afterlives: from the Victorian to the contemporary

The process of adapting *Jane Eyre* began soon after its publication: John Courtney's melodrama *Jane Eyre; or, The Secrets of Thornfield Manor* appeared in London in 1848 and was followed by several more stage adaptations over the course of the nineteenth century.[3] Early literary adaptations include M. E. Braddon's *Lady Audley's Secret* (1862), Charlotte Perkins Gilman's *The Yellow Wallpaper* (1892) and Henry James's *The Turn of the Screw* (1898), for all of which *Jane Eyre* serves as an important intertext, even as the narratives do not explicitly acknowledge the debt. The process of adapting the novel continued in the twentieth century, with dozens of literary and stage versions appearing in the first few decades.[4] The 1960s and 1970s witnessed the publication of two seminal responses to the novel, both of which offer important reconsiderations of the character of Bertha: Jean Rhys's novel *Wide Sargasso Sea* (1966) and Sandra M. Gilbert and Susan Gubar's key work of feminist scholarship, *The Madwoman in the Attic* (1979). Rhys's sympathetic portrayal of Rochester's first wife remains the most influential literary adaptation, while Gilbert and Gubar's claim that Bertha represents Jane's 'truest and darkest double' (1984: 360) redefined the figure in the cultural and critical imagination. Polly Teale's stage play *Jane Eyre* (1998) is one of a number of creative responses which draws on the notion of Bertha and Jane as doubles. In this version, part of a trilogy of plays by Teale that engage with the Brontë biography, *Jane Eyre* and *Wide Sargasso Sea*, all of which include Rochester's first wife, Bertha appears on stage with Jane throughout the production.[5] In the accompanying notes, Teale writes, 'Central to the adaptation is the idea that hidden inside the sensible, frozen Jane exists another self who is passionate and sensual. Bertha (trapped in the attic) embodies the fire and longing which Jane must lock away in order to survive in Victorian England' (1998: 3). Other post-Victorian theatrical versions of the novel include ballets, operas and musicals, as well as multiple conventional dramatic adaptations.[6]

Screen adaptations of *Jane Eyre* also proliferate, with in excess of forty film and television adaptations to date. Several silent films appeared in the 1910s and 1920s, with the most recent movie version, directed by Cary Fukanaga, released in 2011, starring Mia Wasikowska as Jane and Michael Fassbender as Rochester. These tend to prioritise the romantic relationship between Rochester and Jane, frequently resulting in alterations to the original narrative to render the characters more appealing as romantic leads, in order to overcome what Martha Stoddard Holmes terms the 'marketing problems' of '"plain" Jane Eyre and "ugly" Edward Rochester' (Stoddard Holmes, 2012: 151). Rochester's deceitful behaviour tends to be downplayed and the injuries sustained in the fire limited,[7] while Jane – in contrast to Brontë's descriptions – often appears as the stereotypically beautiful heroine. In romantic adaptations, the problem of Bertha has the potential to become even more acute, in light of Rochester's role as hero. As Stoddard Holmes notes, 'Any of the dimensions of [Rochester's] disgust for Bertha, which intertwines sexism, racism, ableism, and colonialism, offers a cinematic production of *Jane Eyre* a hefty obstacle' (2012: 153). Film-makers have taken various approaches, including altering the storyline to render Rochester less culpable. In *Woman and Wife* (1918), Bertha is believed to be dead, and, when she materialises, Rochester attempts to have the marriage annulled. Similarly, in Christy Cabanne's 1934 production, Colin Clive's Rochester endeavours to annul his marriage before he marries Jane. In some early stage adaptations, including Charlotte Birch-Pfeiffer's *Jane Eyre; or, The Orphan of Lowood* (1870), the plot is altered to make Bertha the wife of Rochester's brother, again removing his intention to commit bigamy. Such alterations tend to elide key aspects of Rochester's character and are indicative of a trend within visual media in particular to obscure or transform elements of Brontë's plot in order to avoid the potential conflict the reader may experience in being encouraged to sympathise with a problematic hero.

In contrast to screen versions, literary adaptations exhibit a greater tendency to explore the more problematic aspects of the text, suggesting an explicitness that contrasts the trend of filmic and televisual reticence in dealing with these issues. The most famous of these remains Rhys's *Wide Sargasso Sea*, which evokes a highly sympathetic portrait of Bertha (Antoinette), shifting the focus from Jane. Recent years have witnessed a significant increase in fictional adaptations of *Jane Eyre* – partly a consequence of the rise of self-publishing and online fan fiction.[8] Literary reworkings of the novel participate in a wide variety of genres. *Wide Sargasso Sea* represents the best known example of a post-colonial revision; Gothic and sensational returns include Hilary Bailey's *Mrs Rochester* (2012) and Jane Stubbs' *Thornfield Hall* (2014); Jasper Fforde's *The Eyre Affair* (2001) represents the most successful science-fiction adaptation to date; while erotic versions of the story include Karena Rose's *Jane Eyrotica* (2012) and Eve Sinclair's *Jane Eyre Laid Bare* (2012). Both these latter texts belong to the emerging genre of mash-up fiction, which is partly indebted to online fan fiction and introduces new passages into original narratives – here, focusing on characters' sexual experiences.[9] Another contribution to *Jane Eyre* mash-up fictions is Sherri Browning Erwin's *Jane Slayre* (2010), which repositions the novel as horror story: the Reed family are vampires, Lowood is inhabited by zombies, and Bertha is a werewolf, with Jane appointed heroic destroyer of these supernatural creatures. Other innovative literary adaptations include Lin Haire-Sargeant's *Heathcliff: The Return to Wuthering Heights* (1992), which represents Emily Brontë's anti-hero as the son of Bertha and Rochester. Further multi-modal adaptations include radio dramas, parodies, comics, graphic novels and online versions. As well as the extensive body of online fan fiction, the latter includes a modernised web series entitled *The Autobiography of Jane Eyre* (2013–14), in which the Bertha character (here renamed Beth) suffers from post-natal depression and drug addiction.[10] The emergence of the Internet as a site of creativity over the past two decades has thus provided a new space for innovative reworkings of Brontë's narrative. In addition, the novel itself has been repeatedly reissued, and, while new editions of the text obviously retain Brontë's characterisation, a number are of interest for their illustrations of the madwoman.

Among these various trends in the afterlives of *Jane Eyre*, there are a significant number of adaptations and retellings specifically targeted towards younger readers. These include April Linder's *Jane* (2010) – a young-adult revision of Brontë's novel, in which Rochester is transformed into rock star Nico Rathburn. There are several abridged editions for younger readers, and these tend to be heavily truncated, with various events and characters omitted. As with many of the film adaptations, priority is frequently given to the romance plot. Although these retellings do not drastically alter the original plot, subtle changes impact on characterisation. In Maggie Pearson's Classics Retold version, Rochester does not resist Bertha's attack following the interrupted wedding; Jane states, 'I think he would have let her tear him limb from limb if Grace Poole had not dragged her away' (Pearson, 2011: 38). The effect of this is to construct Rochester as utterly despairing and Bertha as capable of wilful murder – an exaggeration of the sentiments of the original novel, and one that creates greater sympathy for the narrative's 'hero' and antipathy for the madwoman. In this respect, many of the texts aimed at a younger audience tend to follow a similar patter to screen versions, eliding some of the more problematic aspects of the text and emphasising the romance. By representing Rochester as less culpable, and emphasising his status as victim, these narratives subtly justify his suitability as a husband for Jane.

'The true daughter of an infamous mother': revisiting Bertha's madness

In Brontë's *Jane Eyre*, Bertha's monstrosity is firmly associated with her mental state, which, in turn, is variously linked to hereditary tendencies, her racial identity and sexuality. Victorian stage adaptations tend to follow Brontë's lead in representing Bertha as a monstrous, inhuman figure: as in the novel, in which her only reported articulation is her threat to 'drain [Mason's] heart' (Brontë, 2001: 181), she rarely speaks and is described in dehumanising and degrading terms. In the first stage production of the text, Courtney's 1848 adaptation, Bertha's brother Mason descends into madness at the end of the play. Although this may indicate a hereditary tendency (suggested by Brontë's Rochester, who declares Mason 'will probably be in the same state' as his sister 'one day' [Brontë, 2001: 181]), when Mason's madness is read in conjunction with Bertha's bite, it appears to suggest the notion of the madwoman as rabid dog, who risks 'infecting' those around her, reinforcing Brontë's construction of an animalistic madwoman. The notion of madness as contagious aligns with Victorian conceptions of mental illness: an article published in 1851 cited 'living with insane persons' as a cause of insanity (Anon., 1851: 273). Following the attack on Mason in T. H. Paul's 1879 production, Rochester declares, 'the chemist will know what is best for the bite of a dog' (Paul, 2007: 361). John Brougham's 1849 play describes Bertha as 'a wild looking ghost-like thing' (2007: 98), endorsing the notion of Rochester's first wife 'haunting' both Thornfield and the narrative. In James Willing and Leonard Rae's 1879 drama, Mason 'bleed[s] from the throat' (2007: 305) following the attack, recalling Jane's description of Bertha as a 'vampyre' (Brontë, 2001: 242). Such portrayals are in part indebted to Victorian stage traditions and effectively endorse Brontë's construction of Bertha as a type of Gothic monster, thus drawing attention to the parallels between Brontë's proto-sensation novel and nineteenth-century melodrama.

By contrast, some nineteenth-century literary reimaginings, including Braddon's *Lady Audley's Secret* and Gilman's *The Yellow Wallpaper*, offer a more sympathetic representation of the figure of the madwoman. In the final lines of *The Yellow Wallpaper*, the unnamed narrator, addressing her husband, declares 'I've got out at last [...] in spite of you and Jane' (Gilman, 1997: 15), a statement that appears to be an acknowledgement of the text's indebtedness to *Jane Eyre*, and that consequently implicates Jane in the suffering of the 'madwoman'. Rhys continues in this tradition in *Wide Sargasso Sea* by presenting Antoinette (Bertha) in a sympathetic light and removing her from the 'ghostly' realm, granting a voice to Brontë's madwoman. Similarly, in Emma Tennant's *The French Dancer's Bastard* (2006), a text that draws on both *Jane Eyre* and *Wide Sargasso Sea*, Bertha is presented more sympathetically, befriended by Adèle, to whom she reveals details of her previous life in the West Indies. Though Bertha lacks a narrative voice, references to her extended speech contrast with Brontë's novel. In Tennant's narrative, references to her nostalgia for her homeland contribute to her humanisation. Significantly, Tennant retains allusions to an association between Bertha's ethnic identity and her madness. Bertha is described as 'the wretched Creole', 'the foolish Creole', 'the mad Creole wife' and 'the lovely, empty-eyed Creole' (Tennant, 2006: 88, 117, 168, 182). However, these descriptions appear in the first-person narratives of Grace Poole and Adèle, so the echoes of this troublesome aspect of Brontë's novel appear as part of the representation of nineteenth-century attitudes. Far more problematic in its echoing of this association is Fforde's science-fiction novel, *The Eyre Affair*, in which Bertha is violent, 'growl[s] like a caged animal', 'cackl[es] maniacally' and is described as 'demonic' (Fforde, 2001: 340, 338). The implied association between Bertha's racial identity and her madness is expressed through references to her as both 'the insane Creole' and 'the madwoman from Jamaica' (Fforde, 2001: 338). Unlike in Tennant's novel, these descriptions are not articulated by any of the novel's original characters but by Fforde's heroine, Thursday Next, a character from an alternative late twentieth century. Consequently, they appear to represent a troubling endorsement of Brontë's original portrayal of Bertha's racial identity as associated in some way with her madness.

Other literary returns to *Jane Eyre* draw on Brontë's construction of Bertha as animalistic. In Erwin's mash-up, *Jane Slayre*, the madwoman is literally a (supernatural) monster, taking the form of a werewolf, a further echo of Brontë's descriptions of Bertha as ghost, 'vampyre' and animal. The scene of Bertha's attack on Mason lends itself to Erwin's tale: she bites him, 'worrie[s] [him] like a tigress', threatening to 'drain [his] heart' (Brontë, 2001: 181). These descriptions pre-empt the scenes of horror introduced by Erwin and accentuate Bertha's role as Gothic 'monster' in both the original novel and this subsequent adaptation. The horror-fantasy mode of Erwin's text enables the literalisation of Brontë's figurative language. Indeed, such is Brontë's animalistic description of Bertha when Rochester takes the wedding party to see her that there is no need for Erwin to embellish:

> What it was, whether beast or human being, one could not, at first sign, tell. It grovelled, seemingly, on all fours. It snatched and growled like some strange wild animal, but it was covered with clothing, and a quantity of dark, grizzled hair, wild as a mane, hid its head and face.
>
> (Brontë, 2001: 250; Erwin, 2010: 270)

The language of the source text and adaptation remains the same here. Brontë's use of the moon as a potent symbol in *Jane Eyre* also serves Erwin's purposes in this adaptation.[11] Associated with femininity and sexuality, here the moon signals Bertha's transformation into werewolf. Further, the origins of her transformation lie in an earlier sexual encounter, thus Erwin, like Brontë, associates the danger Bertha poses with her sexual behaviour: 'One of her lovers had been afflicted with what they called in the West Indies *lob hombre*. In short, he was a werewolf, and

when he bit her in their lovemaking, he infected her with the condition as well' (Erwin, 2010: 278, italics in the original). The fact of the
infection taking place in the West Indies, as with other texts, suggests an
association between Bertha's madness and her Creole identity and points
to a complicity with Brontë's original novel that echoes Fforde's uncomfortable portrayal. Erwin's narrative draws a distinction between Bertha's
madness and her position as werewolf, but, nonetheless, the portrayal of
Bertha as werewolf emphasises Brontë's problematic association between
mental illness and an animalistic state. This, however, does not necessarily
represent an endorsement of the original characterisation: in taking the
animalisation of Bertha to an extreme by portraying her as a werewolf,
Erwin's narrative encourages the reader familiar with Brontë's novel to
recognise the problematic aspects of her characterisation and the extent
of Bertha's dehumanisation. *Jane Eyre*'s madwoman is, according to Jenny
Sharpe, 'a cannibalistic beast who chews her brother's flesh to the bone, a
fiend who spews forth obscenities, and a monster who cannot control her
sexual appetites' (1993: 45). Transforming her into a werewolf requires
only a small imaginative leap.

Bertha is constructed as similarly monstrous in several abridged editions for younger readers. Jane E. Gerver's version, for example, develops the association between Bertha and the figure of the vampire. As in
Brontë's novel, Jane compares her to a vampire, but here the assertion
is repeated in a reference to 'the vampire woman' (Gerver, 1997: 732),
strengthening the notion of Bertha as a supernatural creature. In *Jane
Eyre: Usborne Classics Retold*, Bertha's strange laugh is described as 'hollow and inhuman – almost like a bark' (Claybourne, 2006: 742). Though
drawing on Brontë's descriptions, the terms 'inhuman' and 'bark' are not
in the original novel and serve to further highlight the construction of
Bertha as animalistic. Gill Tavner's retelling retains Brontë's dehumanising descriptions of Bertha, referring to her as 'the creature', 'the lunatic'
and 'a wild beast' (2009: 37, 41). While this abridged version remains
faithful to the original narrative, the details of Bertha's 'madness' – specifically her 'giant propensities' (Brontë, 2001: 261), her intemperance
and lack of chastity – are absent, presumably in an attempt to sanitise the
narrative for a younger audience. Similarly, in Belinda Hollyer's retelling, some of Brontë's original descriptions are evident – the reference to
Bertha's 'savage, terrifying face', for instance, and the image of 'something
grovelling on all fours and growling like an animal' (2002: 38, 41). In
Hollyer's version, however, slight shifts in language affect the characterisation of Bertha. In the scene following the interrupted wedding in which

Rochester 'introduces' his wife, Bertha is described as a 'poor demented creature' and subsequently, following her death, as a 'poor woman' (Hollyer, 2002: 42, 45). This appellation is not attached to Brontë's Bertha, and its effect here is to construct the madwoman as an object of pity – perhaps prompted by a perceived need to direct younger readers' reactions to her character, to ensure that sympathy rather than horror is the emotional response elicited.

Screen adaptations of the novel construct Bertha's 'madness' in various ways. She is presented as the Gothic, dangerous madwoman in some versions, including Robert Stevenson's 1943 film, starring Orson Welles as Rochester, and Robert Fuest's 1983 BBC television mini-series, featuring Timothy Dalton as Rochester and Joolia Cappleman as Bertha. Several echo Brontë's narrative in their representations of Bertha's madness, referring to a hereditary tendency and implying an association between Bertha's mental state and her sexuality. The tendency of film and television adaptations to prioritise the love story means they are often reluctant to represent the figure of the ignoble hero, altering aspects of the text in order to obscure Rochester's flaws and thus going some way towards exonerating him for his treatment of both Bertha and Jane. As part of this process, there is a tendency to develop his attempts to seek treatment for his wife, in contradistinction to Brontë's novel, in which Rochester dismissively informs Jane that 'since the medical men had pronounced her mad, she had, of course, been shut up', though he claims he has done 'all that God and humanity require' in 'see[ing] that she is cared for as her condition demands' (Brontë, 2001: 262, 263). In Cabanne's 1934 film, Colin Clive's Rochester states, 'She's been insane for years. [...] I've done what I could for her but the specialists have pronounced her mania incurable, hereditary. I kept her here in the care of Mrs Poole rather than send her to an institution' (*Jane Eyre*, 1934). In the original narrative, Rochester's primary motivation in keeping Bertha at Thornfield is not compassion but to ensure that 'her identity, her connection with [him], be buried in oblivion' (Brontë, 2001: 263). Similar adjustments are made in director Robert Young's 1997 adaptation. Following the interrupted wedding, Ciarán Hinds' Rochester reveals:

> It was only after the wedding that I realised that she was insane – like her mother and her grandmother before her. I tried everything in my power to make her well. I hired the best doctors. I sought alternative methods and then finally I realised that there was no cure. I could have run away back to England and left her there but instead I brought her home with me. And

not to have her chained up in some lunatic asylum as some would have it but to keep her safe, here, at Thornfield. With a nurse day and night to tend to every need.

(Jane Eyre, 1997)[12]

Indeed, Rochester appears almost affectionate towards Bertha, cradling her in his arms and kissing the top of her head as he reveals the details of his marriage, actions that stand in stark contrast to those of Brontë's Rochester, and that serve to evoke both pity and admiration: his noble sympathy for his ill wife in this scene further suggests an attempt to create a more appealing romantic hero from Brontë's flawed male lead. Read in conjunction with Foucault's claims that asylums function as a means of controlling inmates, primarily through fear (Foucault, 2001: 229–64), Rochester's insistence on keeping Bertha out of an asylum appears a compassionate act. In Brontë's novel, Thornfield functions as an asylum: Bertha is imprisoned, guarded, forced to control her 'different propensities' (Foucault, 2001: 237), and thus is effectively institutionalised.[13] Rochester's compassion for Bertha in Young's 1990s adaptation, in stark contrast to the original narrative, draws attention to the differences between Thornfield and the early nineteenth-century asylum, evoking notions of compassionate care more closely associated with post-nineteenth-century treatments of madness. Thornfield as 'asylum' in this later adaptation, then, evokes the association between the term 'asylum' and a place of safety or solace.

In Brontë's narrative, Bertha is described as 'at once intemperate and unchaste', her 'excesses' having 'prematurely developed the germs of insanity' (Brontë, 2001: 261). Sharpe contends that 'it is not her madness which [Rochester] finds so intolerable as her debauchery' (1993: 45), but, as the narrative makes clear, the two are inexplicably linked, though whether her sexual behaviour represents a cause or an effect of her mental state is less clear. Brontë, then, associates Bertha's madness with her lack of chastity. Young, like Brontë, suggests a link between Bertha's mental state and her sexuality in his late-twentieth-century screen adaptation. When Rochester enters her 'prison', she casts him an alluring glance, and when he responds, 'No, Bertha, no', she attacks him (*Jane Eyre*, 1997). Her violence is thus precipitated by Rochester's rejection. Awareness of her position as Rochester's wife similarly influences Bertha's violent reactions in Cabanne's and White's productions. In the former, Claire Du Brey's Bertha reacts violently when Grace Poole attempts to return her to her room, shouting, 'You can't separate me from my husband again' (*Jane*

Eyre, 1934). In White's version, which also references hereditary madness ('insanity ran through the family like a black river of disease', *Jane Eyre*, 2006: Ep. 3), her violent response to the visit of the wedding party occurs when she sees Jane in the wedding dress. The scene is echoed in Franco Zefferelli's 1996 feature film, in which Bertha attempts to attack Jane with a burning stick, as well as in Fukunaga's recent movie production, in which she appears to embrace Rochester and spits at Jane. These violent outbursts paradoxically suggest an element of rationality in Bertha's madness, provoked as they are by an awareness of her husband's duplicity and Jane's role as Rochester's love interest. As with Young's production, White associates Bertha's sexuality with her madness: as Rochester details his wife's descent into madness, a flashback shows Bertha with another man, laughing when Rochester discovers them – a contrast to her violent reaction when she encounters the wedding party, suggesting hypocrisy in her divergent attitudes towards her and her husband's indiscretions. This parallels Rochester's own attitude in both the original narrative and subsequent adaptations: he is seemingly disgusted by his wife's lack of chastity but shows no remorse for his own affairs, echoing the prevailing sexual double standard of the nineteenth century. In introducing an element of hypocrisy in relation to Bertha's attitude, White confuses the allusion to the sexual double standard by implying that women as well as men perpetuated hypocritical attitudes and behaviours.

In abridged editions for younger readers, references to Bertha's sexuality are generally omitted. While undoubtedly a consequence of the intended younger audience, the effect of this is to distance Bertha's madness from her sexual behaviour. By contrast, sexuality inevitably plays a central role in erotic adaptations of Brontë's novel. In *Jane Eyre Laid Bare*, Bertha is revealed as 'an all-powerful dominatrix' who has instructed Rochester to 'train [Jane], to strip her of her innocence, to make her pliant and then to bring her to me' (Sinclair, 2012: 308). Rochester, having fallen in love with Jane, plans to marry her and escape from Bertha's clutches, but Mason's revelation at the wedding prevents this. In the confrontation with Bertha that follows, Jane witnesses Rochester unmanned by his sexually aggressive first wife: 'All his manliness had gone from him and he stood before the woman like an apologetic schoolboy' (Sinclair, 2012: 308). Rochester begs Jane to stay, informing her that Bertha 'is nothing to me. She stays out of sight because she is a mad woman' (Sinclair, 2012: 313). Jane refuses, and the narrative concludes with the words 'reader, I left him' (Sinclair, 2012: 322).[14] Despite the dramatic alterations to the original novel, the origins of Sinclair's narrative can be found in the association Brontë makes between Bertha's sexual behaviour and her madness. Bertha is also construed as sexually aggressive in a parody skit from *Saturday Night Live* (2004), featuring Jude Law as Rochester. Bertha appears as a beautiful American with an insatiable sexual appetite, again implying a link between sexual behaviour and mental instability. In these narratives, female sexuality is thus construed as something potentially dangerous, in need of containment. As in the original novel, a clear distinction is drawn between Jane and Bertha in *Jane Eyre Laid Bare*: Jane's sexual desire for Rochester represents something 'acceptable'; Bertha's dangerous desires are, in contrast, construed as 'other'. It is significant in this respect that Rochester represents the dominant party in his sexual relationship with Jane, while he is dominated by Bertha. Hence, in these retellings of *Jane Eyre*, attitudes towards sexual roles appear conservative – indeed, even 'Victorian' – in their constructions of female sexuality.

Ghost, beauty, monster: visualising Bertha

Brontë's representation of Bertha's physical appearance is one of the most troubling (and contradictory) aspects of her characterisation. Jane twice describes Bertha, and both descriptions serve to dehumanise her and contribute to the narrative's racial 'othering' of the madwoman. In the first instance, Jane awakes to find Bertha in her room and describes her as 'fearful and ghastly' with 'a discoloured face […] a savage face': she refers to her 'red eyes and the fearful blackened inflation of the lineaments'; she is 'purple' with lips 'swelled and dark' (Brontë, 2001: 242). When she subsequently encounters Bertha in the third storey following the interrupted wedding, she describes the grovelling figure 'on all fours', comparing her to a 'wild animal': Jane alludes again to Bertha's 'purple face' and to her 'bloated features' and notes her height ('almost equal to her husband') and corpulence (Brontë, 2001: 250). In contrast to these descriptions, which reinforce the notion of Bertha as monstrous, Rochester, detailing the time of his first meeting with her, recalls that his father 'told me Miss Mason was the boast of Spanish Town for her beauty: and this was no lie. I found her a fine woman, in the style of Blanche Ingram: tall, dark, and majestic' (Brontë, 2001: 260). From these contradictory descriptions, it seems evident that the narrative endorses common Victorian assumptions about the effect of character on physical appearance and that Bertha's immoral behaviour and descent into madness are reflected in her physical transformation.[15]

Nevertheless, few visual representations of Bertha adhere with any degree of exactitude to the descriptions in Brontë's novel. While many depict Bertha with dark features and 'wild' hair, few portray the 'bloated features', 'red eyes' or corpulence. Although she often appears with dark hair, in screen and stage adaptations, the role is generally played by a white actress: the 2008 London Children's Ballet production is notable for its employment of a black performer to play the role of Bertha. Some visual representations, including White's television serial, contradict Jane's descriptions by showing Bertha as very beautiful, in line with Rochester's account of her earlier life, while others eschew the problem of how to portray visually the madwoman by concealing her face or omitting her entirely, so she remains a ghostly, unseen presence, thus participating in that (ironic) process of elision which appears particularly evident in screen adaptations of the novel, reflecting a counterintuitive tendency to obscure, despite the visual medium. In Stevenson's 1943 film, the problem of Bertha's appearance is conveniently negated by avoiding any shots in which her features are visible. She is shown grappling with Mason, their figures silhouetted in the window of a Gothic-looking Thornfield, and later attempting to attack Rochester, but in both scenes her features are not visible to the viewer. The sounds that emanate from the darkened room where she is kept support the construction of Bertha as a rabid, dangerous animal, while her lack of visibility accentuates her ghostliness.

An examination of illustrated editions of *Jane Eyre* suggests television and film-makers take their cue from these – particularly in terms of their tendency to omit visual depictions of the madwoman. Images of Bertha are absent from several of these, despite, in some cases, the inclusion of a large number of accompanying illustrations.[16] While the scene in which Jane awakes to find Bertha in her room is popular with illustrators of the novel, some only portray Bertha from behind, so her face remains obscured from the reader. These include illustrations by Ethel Gabain (1922) and F. D. Bedford (1932). Stoneman suggests that Gabain's image 'is the only one to suggest a common perspective, showing the veil-tearing scene with a back view of Jane and of a relatively distant Bertha, a focus ending in the mirror which might well reflect them both' (1996: 104), an early example of an interpretation later articulated by Gilbert and Gubar. In this illustration, the positioning of the two women, and their seemingly similar statures, hair, and attire (white nightdresses), strengthens the suggestion of an uncanny doubling.[17] In Bedford's illustration, by contrast, Jane lies prostrate with fear, while Bertha rips the veil in front of the mirror, suggesting movement and energy.[18] This distinction between the two figures anticipates later critical readings that postulate that Jane must repress her passionate emotions in order to survive, while Bertha's fate is linked to her inability or refusal to control her angry passions. Jane's hair appears lighter, and is neatly arranged, suggesting conformity to convention, while Bertha's mass of dark hair flies out behind her, creating a Medusa-like image. This antithetical representation of Jane and Bertha, rather than Gabain's suggestion of doubling, is more typical of illustrations of the novel, and several screen adaptations present a similar contrast: in Cabanne's film, though neatly attired (visually, Cabanne's Bertha appears 'respectable'), Bertha's dark hair contrasts with Jane's fair hair. In Young's film, Bertha's mass of dark hair initially obscures her face from the viewer. White's Bertha also has long, dark hair, contrasting with Jane's which is pulled neatly behind her head for most of the production, and similar images are found in graphic novels and abridged editions, including the Classics Illustrated version from 1996, the cover of which shows Bertha in the background behind Jane and Rochester, with her hair entirely covering her face. As in the novel, the appearance of Bertha's hair in later adaptations is used to indicate her failure to conform to Victorian conventions of femininity, and thus to hint at her mental state.

These visual parallels between illustrated editions of the novel and screen adaptations point to the latter's indebtedness to the former. By contrast, some visual artists trouble this lineage via alternative representations of Bertha's appearance, which, in some respects at least, are more closely aligned to Brontë's original descriptions of Bertha. Allusions to her corpulence indicate her deviation from Victorian standards of femininity, but few later representations of her character adhere to this description. Artworks by Helen Sewell (1938) and Paula Rego (2002) are exceptions, depicting a corpulent figure in line with Jane's description.[19] These images contrast starkly with other illustrations that depict Bertha's 'ghostliness' – particularly Bernice Oehler's portrayal of Jane's night-time encounter with Bertha (1947), in which the figure of Bertha blends into the curtains that surround Jane's bed, rendering all her features indistinct, and Edmund Garrett's late-Victorian illustration of Bertha's fall from Thornfield, in which her ghostly figure, hair streaming behind her, appears almost to float to her death, and bears a certain resemblance to Victorian images of Ophelia, particularly John Everett Millais's 1851–2 painting, which similarly suggests a kind of ethereal femininity.[20] In contrast, the effect of portraying Bertha's corpulence is to remove her from the ghostly realm she inhabits both throughout much of the novel and in the popular imagination: her size emphasises her physical presence, her corporeality, her materiality, rendering her (and her experiences and suffering) more real. Most film-makers eschew the description of Bertha's size, although in Young's adaptation, the sight of Bertha's partially exposed, full breasts, in the scene following the wedding, contrasts with Jane's slight figure and exerts a similar effect in terms of highlighting the madwoman's corporeality.

'[S]mashed on the pavement': the deaths of Bertha

If there was any doubt about Brontë's unsympathetic attitude towards the figure of the madwoman in *Jane Eyre*, the narrative's treatment of her death provides conclusive evidence. Her leap from the burning Thornfield is construed not as a tragic event but as necessary for the romantic union between Jane and Rochester. Further, as Angelia Poon has noted, her death is described in 'gratuitously gory detail' (2008: 45), Jane's informer bearing witness to the image of 'the stones on which her brains and blood were scattered' (Brontë, 2001: 365). The narrative, then, seems to demand not only her death but the complete destruction of her physical body, and this is immediately followed by Jane's joyful reunion with Rochester. This juxtaposing of Bertha's violent death with Jane's romantic fulfilment speaks volumes about the narrative's perceived value of the life of the madwoman and represents a further obstacle for those adapting the novel. The transformation of Bertha into werewolf in *Jane Slayre* enables her death to be construed as an act of mercy, as Jane makes clear: 'I saw the mercy in killing the afflicted. Did Bertha Mason wish to live as a fiend? Did she not deserve to be set free of such unnatural earthly bonds?' (Erwin, 2010: 276). However, Rochester is determined to protect Bertha, and thus her death occurs in the same manner as in the original text. Nonetheless, Jane's words in this adaptation provide an insight into Brontë's treatment of Bertha's demise: it is not construed as tragic because her life is represented as effectively worthless. The disjuncture between Bertha's violent death and the romantic conclusion appears to sit uncomfortably with film-makers, particularly those privileging the romance, and few include the image of Bertha 'smashed on the pavement' – a further example of the process of elision evident in screen adaptations. Despite the obvious dramatic potential of the scene, many do not portray these events directly but relate them via accounts given to Jane, mirroring the novel but omitting the graphic details of Bertha's death provided by Brontë. This omission seems to reflect an unwillingness to preface the romantic conclusion with graphic images of Bertha's death and can be read as a condemnation of the gratuitous language used by Brontë to describe the event – something that reinforces the narrative's lack of sympathy for the madwoman. In Stevenson's 1943 version, Mrs Fairfax relates the circumstances of Bertha's death with no accompanying visuals, describing her 'smashed on the pavement' (*Jane Eyre*, 1943), but making no reference to her 'brains and blood'. Fukunaga also portrays Mrs Fairfax as the witness to Bertha's death and similarly eschews the novel's violent description. In Young's film, Jane is told only that Rochester 'did his best to save Bertha, but she jumped to her death' (*Jane Eyre*, 1997). White's television serial shows Bertha's fall from the roof and includes a shot of her body lying on the stones beneath but is far from the violent description given in the novel. The image of her falling from Thornfield is shown in conjunction with the image of an owl flying from the roof of the building. With her arms raised above her head, Bertha's posture imitates that of the owl, suggesting flight, freedom, and echoing Rhys's *Wide Sargasso Sea*, in which Antoinette is persistently associated with the image of birds. These allusions are reminiscent, perhaps deliberately so, of Jane's famous line in Brontë's novel – 'I am no bird; and no net ensnares me: I am a free human being' (Brontë, 2001: 216) – and thus serve to articulate the stark differences between Jane's and Bertha's experiences. Most screen adaptations remain relatively faithful to the events surrounding Bertha's death in the novel, despite eschewing the text's graphic description, portraying it as suicide, although in Cabanne's film, this remains ambiguous: Bertha is reported to have started the fire, burning the house to the ground 'and herself in it' (*Jane Eyre*, 1934), but whether she intended suicide is unclear. In Stevenson's adaptation, her death occurs in the context of her attempting to flee from Rochester and anticipates some later literary adaptations, including Rhys's *Wide Sargasso Sea*, in which Rochester appears at least partially culpable.

Indeed, a number of literary adaptations, generally less concerned with remaining 'faithful' to the original text, drastically alter the circumstances of Bertha's death. In some abridged editions, including Hollyer's version, Bertha's death is not reported as suicide: it appears she has died in the fire rather than jumped to her death. This serves to remove an element of agency and reinforces the construction of Bertha as victim (although she is responsible for starting the fire). In both Tennant's and Fforde's literary reworkings, Bertha's death is portrayed as murder, thus constructing her as victim: she is thrown from the roof of Thornfield by arch villain Acheron Hades in *The Eyre Affair*, while suspicion falls on both Adèle and Mrs Fairfax in *The French Dancer's Bastard*. In Brontë's novel, her suicide represents a degree of agency – a means of escape, freedom from the confines of her imprisonment at Thornfield. Narratives representing her murder remove this agency, which offered her the only control she was able to take over her life. They also go some way towards removing blame from Rochester: it is not possible to read Rochester as the agent of Bertha's death in Fforde's narrative (indeed, Rochester is closer to the conventional romantic hero here). Bertha is also portrayed as a murder victim in Bailey's *Mrs Rochester*. Initially, suspicion surrounds Rochester's actions on the night of the fire at Thornfield, but it is subsequently revealed that the murderer is Adèle, intent on paving the way for a marriage between Rochester and her mother, Céline, who is still alive. Through this chain of events, the narrative constructs Adèle as a madwoman, a move that seems to echo nineteenth-century assumptions of an association between femininity and insanity and again exonerates Rochester from any responsibility for his first wife's fate (although Bertha's sister remains convinced of Rochester's involvement).

Bertha's violent and bloody death at the end of *Jane Eyre* in many respects signifies the beginning, rather than the end, of her story. From the ghostly spectre of Brontë's novel, she has evolved over the course of generations to occupy a pivotal position in the afterlife of the narrative. She is reconstructed in the multitude of adaptations of *Jane Eyre* as madwoman, monster, victim and femme fatale. But perhaps most significant is that fact that she *is* reconstructed: she emerges from the dark shadows of Brontë's narrative as a three-dimensional character – granted, in the cultural echoes of the novel, identities and stories of her own, through which shifting attitudes towards women, mental health and sexuality are evident. These echoes can be traced back to Brontë's novel and thus suggest new ways of reading the text. The cultural legacy of *Jane Eyre* is broad, but part of that legacy is the release of Bertha Mason from the net that ensnares her.

Notes

1 Adaptations of *Jane Eyre* in their multiple forms number in the hundreds (see Appendix). This discussion is therefore necessarily selective in focus, considering some of the most prominent and innovative examples whilst attempting to provide at least a partial overview.

2 The discussion is in part a continuation of the debate instigated in Patsy Stoneman's *Brontë Transformations* (1996), which considers reimaginings of the novel from its first publication to the mid-1990s.

3 See Appendix and Stoneman (2007). Many of these dramatic adaptations were unauthorised.

4 See also Stoneman (1996).

5 The other plays in Teale's trilogy are *After Mrs Rochester* (2003) and *Brontë* (2005).

6 Doollee.com include thirty-six productions of *Jane Eyre* in their database of plays which have appeared since 1956: www.doollee.com/plays/plays-J_plays_jan-jer.html (accessed 19 August 2016).

7 For a discussion of this, see Stoddard Holmes (2012).

8 Fanfiction.net includes 216 pieces of work based on *Jane Eyre*: www.fanfiction.net/search.php?keywords=jane+eyre&ready=1&type=story (accessed 19 August 2016).

9 See Yates, Chapter 12 in this volume, addressing erotic versions of *Jane Eyre*.

10 See Pietrzak-Franger, Chapter 11 in this volume, addressing multi-modal and transmedia adaptations, including *The Autobiography of Jane Eyre* web series.

11 On the use of the moon in Brontë's fiction, see Heilman (1960).

12 Similar language is employed in John Cannon's 1973 stage play, see Stoneman (1996).

13 Foucault's language here echoes Rochester's references to his wife's 'giant propensities' (Brontë, 2001: 261).

14 This alternative ending, which dramatically alters Jane's story and suggests her unwillingness to forgive Rochester for his betrayal, is seemingly less a feminist re-visioning of the story and more an indication of a planned sequel: https://twitter.com/RealEveSinclair/status/327100758891843584 (accessed 19 August 2016).

15 On the physiognomy of the madwoman in *Jane Eyre*, see Donaldson (2002).

16 These include a 1946 Fine Editions Press edition, which includes twenty-five images, and a 1991 Folio Society edition, which includes twenty-seven illustrations.

17 For Gabain's illustration, see http://janeeyreillustrated.com/Gabain_9.htm (accessed 19 August 2016).

18 For Bedford's illustration, see http://janeeyreillustrated.com/Bedford_6.htm (accessed 19 August 2016).

19 For Sewell's illustration, see http://janeeyreillustrated.com/Sewell_8.htm (accessed 19 August 2016). Rego's lithographs are reproduced in her *Jane Eyre* (2004).

20 For Oehler's illustration, see http://janeeyreillustrated.com/Oehler_8.htm (accessed 19 August 2016). For Garrett's illustration, see http://janeeyreillustrated.com/Garrett_16.htm (accessed 19 August 2016).

References

Anon. (1851) 'Bethlem Hospital', *London Journal of Medicine*, 27:3, 271–5.

Brontë, Charlotte (2001) *Jane Eyre*, New York: Norton.

Brougham, John (2007) '*Jane Eyre*', in Patsy Stoneman (ed.), *Jane Eyre on Stage, 1848–1898*, Aldershot: Ashgate, pp. 73–108.

Claybourne, Anna (2006) *Jane Eyre: Usborne Classics Retold*, London: Usborne.

Donaldson, Elizabeth J. (2002) 'The corpus of the madwoman: toward a feminist disability studies theory of embodiment and mental illness', *NWSA Journal*, 14:3, 99–119.

Erwin, Sherri Browning (2010) *Jane Slayre*, London: Simon & Schuster.

Fforde, Jasper (2001) *The Eyre Affair*, London: Hodder & Stoughton.

Foucault, Michel (2001) *Madness and Civilization*, London and New York: Routledge.

Gerver, Jane E. (1997) *Eyre: Stepping Stones Classic*, New York: Random House.

Gilbert, Sandra M. and Susan Gubar (1984) *The Madwoman in the Attic: The Woman Writer and the Nineteenth-Century Literary Imagination*, New Haven, Conn.: Yale University Press.

Gilman, Charlotte Perkins (1997) *The Yellow Wallpaper*, Mineola, NY: Dover.

Heilman, Robert (1960) 'Charlotte Brontë, reason, and the moon', *Nineteenth-Century Fiction*, 14:4, 283–302.

Hollyer, Belinda (2002) *Charlotte Brontë's Jane Eyre*, London: Hodder & Stoughton.

Jane Eyre (1934), dir. Christy Cabanne, Monogram Pictures.

Jane Eyre (1943), dir. Robert Stevenson, Twentieth Century Fox Film Corporation.

Jane Eyre (1997), dir. Robert Young, A&E Television Networks and London Weekend Television.

Jane Eyre (2006), dir. Susanna White, BBC Television and WGBH.

Lerner, Laurence (1989) 'Bertha and the critics', *Nineteenth-Century Literature*, 44:3, 273–300.

Paul, T.H. (2007) '*Jane Eyre*', in Patsy Stoneman (ed.), *Jane Eyre on Stage, 1848–1898*, Aldershot: Ashgate, pp. 344–72.

Pearson, Maggie (2011) *Jane Eyre: Classics Retold*, London: Franklin Watts.

Poon, Angelia (2008) *Enacting Englishness in the Victorian Period: Colonialism and the Politics of Performance*, Aldershot: Ashgate.

Rego, Paula (2004) *Jane Eyre*, London: Enitharmon Press.

Rhys, Jean (1969) Interview, *Observer Magazine*, 1 June, p. 5.

Rylance, Rick (2002) '"Getting on": ideology, personality and the Brontë characters', in Heather Glen (ed.), *The Cambridge Companion to the Brontës*, Cambridge: Cambridge University Press, pp. 148–69.

Sharpe, Jenny (1993) *Allegories of Empire: The Figure of Woman in the Colonial Text*, Minneapolis, Minn.: University of Minnesota Press.

Sinclair, Eve (2012) *Jane Eyre Laid Bare*, London: Pan.

Stoddard Holmes, Martha (2012) 'Visions of Rochester: screening desire and disability in *Jane Eyre*', in David Bolt, Julia Miele Rodas and Elizabeth J. Donaldson (eds.), *The Madwoman and the Blindman: Jane Eyre, Discourse, Disability*, Columbus, OH: Ohio State University Press, pp. 150–74.

Stoneman, Patsy (1996) *Brontë Transformations: The Cultural Dissemination of Jane Eyre and Wuthering Heights*, Hemel Hempstead: Prentice Hall/Harvester Wheatsheaf.

Stoneman, Patsy (ed.) (2007) *Jane Eyre on Stage, 1848–1898*, Aldershot: Ashgate.

Tavner, Gil (2009) *Jane Eyre*, Stroud: Real Reads.

Teale, Polly (1998) *Jane Eyre*, London: Nick Hern.

Tennant, Emma (2006) *The French Dancer's Bastard*, London: Maia.

Willing, James and Leonard Rae (2007) 'Jane Eyre; or, Poor Relations', in Patsy Stoneman (ed.), *Jane Eyre on Stage, 1848–1898*, Aldershot: Ashgate, pp. 286–336.

Woolf, Virginia (2008) 'Women and fiction'. in David Bradshaw (ed.), *Selected Essays*, Oxford: Oxford University Press, pp. 132–9.

11

Jane Eyre's transmedia lives

Monika Pietrzak-Franger

There has been more than a century of *Jane Eyre* adaptations (see Appendix). The novel's theatrical presence was soon accompanied by wide-screen adaptations: from silent movies, through classic adaptations (such as Robert Stevenson's 1943 feature film starring Orson Welles and Joan Fontaine), to more recent experimental filmic versions. Apart from its big screen afterlives, the novel has also been repeatedly adapted for television. It has returned in the form of many rewritings and intertextual echoes in fiction (for example, Jean Rhys's *Wide Sargasso Sea*, 1966; Jasper Fforde's *The Eyre Affair*, 2001; and Luccia Gray's *All Hallows at Eyre Hall*, 2014), in radio programmes, along with attracting the attention of dance, opera and performance practitioners (such as the London Children's Ballet, 1997 and 2008; and David Malouf and Michael Berkley's opera, 2000). The novel has also left its trace on the visual arts.

Jane Eyre has been remodelled for audiences with varying cultural backgrounds, thus proving the status of the novel as a Western classic. Alongside British and American screen adaptations, there have been Mexican (*El Secreto*, 1963; *El Ardiente Secreto*, 1978), Indian (*Shanti Nilayam*, 1972), Italian, Greek, Czechoslovakian (*Jana Eyrová*, 1972), Sri Lankan filmic and televisual versions (*Kula Kumariya,* 2007) and a number of internationally based productions. *Jane Eyre* has likewise travelled across genres, proving the propensity of the text to cross-reference many generic traditions, while its adaptation into a horror movie (*I Walked with a Zombie*, 1943), a BBC parody (*Jane Eyrehead*, 1982) and an erotic mash-up (*Jane Eyre Laid Bare*, 2012) highlights the novel's malleability. Faced with such variety and diversity, one could argue that the story and its protagonist have loosened themselves from their literary form to become veritable transmedia phenomena.

Recent developments support this claim by offering new ways of interpreting and 'updating' the novel. Literary mash-ups (Sherri Browning Erwin's *Jane Slayre*, 2010), graphic novels (Amy Corzine's *Jane Eyre: The Graphic Novel*, 2003) and web series (*The Autobiography of Jane Eyre*, 2013–14) have been added to the repertoire of texts that strengthen Jane's transmedia presence. As the new media climate allegedly allows for a freer way of engaging with and appropriating existing texts, one could ask: who is Jane Eyre 2.0? How has she been reinvented for the twenty-first century and to what extent is her story still relevant? Taking into consideration the independent web series *The Autobiography of Jane Eyre* (2013–14), and the media discussion it generated among the online community, I will be arguing that in contrast to popular screen adaptations of the novel, the web series disentangles the heroine from the romantic plot and repositions her within a network of relationships that encourage her growth. In this way, the series bypasses the gender critiques levelled at Brontë's text and at the majority of its mainstream adaptations. Importantly, the series' exploration of the notion of authorship and its media format allows viewers to treat the series both as an adaptation and a fictional vlog, highlighting the complex ways in which Brontë's Victorian classic continues to matter today.

Adapting Victorians: mediascapes and their tendencies

The generic hybridity of *Jane Eyre* pre-empts any stable interpretation of the novel. Summarising the complex traditions that the novel references, Delia da Sousa Correa follows a critical route that has led many scholars to assert the close intertwining of genre with gender in *Jane Eyre*. Borrowing most profusely from the traditions of autobiography, *Bildungsroman*, social-problem novel, governess novel, Gothic novel and romance, *Jane Eyre* also cross-references Romantic poetry, biblical parables and fairy tales (Da Sousa Correa, 2000a: 93–4). Oscillating between 'a story of spiritual development' and 'romantic rebellion' (Da Sousa Correa, 2000a: 96), it takes Victorian women's education, their social function and the notion of marriage as its reference points. Its 'formal plurality' and narrative polyvalence – the three narrative voices of Jane Eyre as a child, young woman and the mature Mrs Rochester – have been linked to the novel's 'resistance to patriarchy' (Da Sousa Correa, 2000a: 105). Indeed, as Cora Kaplan reminds us, 'in the 1970s *Jane Eyre* briefly attained a unique status as a positively valued "cult text" for second-wave Anglophone feminism' (2007: 7). And although there is little consensus as to its feminist characteristics, one thing that critics agree on is the novel's confrontation and questioning of long-standing gender and genre orthodoxies (see Eagleton, 1975). Despite this, readings of the novel that focus upon the overall narrative situation (i.e. the dominant voice of the second Mrs Rochester) have highlighted its rather orthodox framing (see Jordan, 1993). Similarly, scholars such as Gayatri Chakravorty Spivak and Jina Politi have pointed out the novel's problematic treatment of marginalised women and the way it intertwines imperialism with the white woman's 'assertive individualism' (Da Sousa Correa, 2000b: 127). In this context, while many critical voices have addressed the novel's treatment of Bertha Mason as Jane Eyre's uncanny 'double' and racial 'other', others have devoted their attention to the situation of Grace Poole, while others have emphasised the formative role of such female characters as Betsy, Helen Burns and Miss Temple. In Kaplan's view, '[a]s a mnemic symbol [...], *Jane Eyre*'s narrative and its mode of telling memorialise no single event but a shifting constellation of stories, images and interpretations. An iconic cultural artefact for feminism, it amplifies the dissonances within and among contemporary feminisms' (2007: 17). Kaplan's history of critical responses to the novel is also a history of affect responses, a history that highlights 'the peripatetic relation between a text like *Jane Eyre*, its audience and its interpreters, among whom the emotion that we try and fail to tie down to one or another, ceaselessly circulates' (2007: 34). This interpretative and affective plurality makes the work of the book's adapters all the more challenging.

Despite these difficulties, the past two decades have seen a deluge of Victorian adaptations and neo-Victorian texts. Indeed, neo-Victorianism, with its emphasis on contemporary texts that engage with the Victorian era in a self-reflexive way (Heilmann and Llewellyn, 2010: 4), has grown into a discipline in its own right, with its own journal.[1] Neo-Victorian critics and adaptation scholars have argued that the Victorian era offers us a version of ourselves and allows us to reconsider issues pertinent to our times. Rohan McWilliam emphasises this trend by highlighting the tendency of neo-Victorian texts to address the inarticulate of Victorian literature: 'hysteria, prostitution, consumerism, spiritualism, uppity servants, cross-dressing and [the] transgression of boundaries' (2009: 107). Yet, importantly, neo-Victorian revenants are not only younger and sexier than their nineteenth-century counterparts but also whiter and more Eurocentric. Marie-Luise Kohlke has argued that contemporary adaptations construct the Victorian era as a new Orient and sex it up for contemporary consumption (2008). At the same time, scholars and creators alike are beginning to resist the 'Anglocentricity' and 'implied imperialism' that Ann Heilmann and Mark Llewellyn cautioned against in their 2013 article 'The Victorians Now'. Indeed, Elisabeth Ho's *Neo-Victorianism and the Memory of Empire* (2012), and the 2015 special issue of *Neo-Victorian Studies* entitled 'Neo-Victorianism and Globalisation: Transnational Dissemination of Nineteenth-Century Cultural Texts', have shown that despite the prevalence of Anglo- and British-centric tendencies, a decentring of the empire is now under way both in criticism and fiction. And yet, to me, Michel Ruse's contention about the post-millennial Darwin rings true even when applied to most contemporary Victorians: they have metamorphosed from black-and-white daguerreotype traces into 'living technicolor, framed in eggshell blue and gold' (Ruse, 2003: 309). Contemporary Victorians thus offer a strikingly Disneyfied, theme-park version of the past (Ho, 2012: 140). At the same time, and in many different ways, the 'intertextual potentialities' of the Victorian past continue to 'roam across eras and genres in fantastic and dangerous liaisons' (Whelehan, 2012: 289), sometimes offering more critical versions of the Victorians.

Without doubt, the contemporary media climate fosters these intertextual potentialities. Today, literary texts are published – and globally distributed – almost simultaneously along with their multimedia adaptations and appropriations. This phenomenon has already been widely recognised and discussed in terms of convergence culture and transmedia storytelling. Markedly, Henry Jenkins regards transmedia storytelling as 'the art of world-building', where 'integral elements of a fiction get dispersed systematically across multiple delivery channels for the purpose of creating a unified and coordinated entertainment experience' (2007), the individual outcome of which, however, can never be controlled or predicted. Although transmedia storytelling is not a new phenomenon, the novel context of media convergence, understood as 'an ongoing process or series of intersections between different media systems' that defies fixation (Jenkins 2006: 282), offers new challenges and makes new demands both on literature and processes of reading and interpreting. Simultaneously, it allegedly affords unheard of possibilities for appropriating the classics.

Indeed, the past decade has also brought about the rise and fall of the enthusiastic 'Web 2.0 rhetoric of happy collaboration' (Jenkins et al., 2013: 49), along with growing accusations of sharecropping, capitalisation of free labour and exploitation. It has also seen the appearance of new (analytical) categories that promised to address these changes. Critics have been talking about the 'generation C' – the consumer generation which is 'connected, communicating, content-centric, computerized, community-oriented, always clicking' (Bruns, 2008: 4). Also, a number of categories ('prosumer', 'producer', 'pro-am') have been designed to account for new interactive potentialities. Despite the diverging foci of these categories, what all of them have in common is an emphasis on the participatory character of contemporary media, which encourages (or compels) audiences to take an active part in the creation of the final product. In this climate of alleged media productivity that celebrates intertextuality, where readers are given the chance to influence adaptations in ways hitherto unthought of, who is the contemporary Jane Eyre and to what extent is she the product of a collaborative DIY enterprise?

The Autobiography of Jane Eyre as a transmedia project

The Autobiography of Jane Eyre follows in the footsteps of *The Lizzie Bennet Diaries* (2012–13), which won an Emmy in 2013 for Outstanding Achievement in Interactive Media. Like the *Lizzie Bennet Diaries* and *Emma Approved* (2013–14), it is a transmedia project that adapts Brontë's novel for YouTube, Tumblr, Twitter, Instagram and Facebook. The series itself consists of ninety-five webisodes (web episodes – in length between two and twenty-six minutes, most no longer than four and six minutes) aired between 28 February 2013 and 21 June 2014, accompanied by Q&A sections responding to viewers' queries. The series was created by a team of students and school graduates: among them, the head writer and producer Nessa Aref, consulting producer and transmedia coordinator Kathryn Hall (who also plays Jane Eyre) and composer Daryn Cassir. Initially without a budget, the series producers started a campaign and raised approximately $11,000.

The web series as multimedia form offers unparalleled opportunities for the adaptation of Brontë's novel. This new type of seriality has, from the start, been associated with confessionality in contemporary culture and with questions of authenticity, authorship and access within a shared and sharing digital economy. Thomas Klein reminds us that the web series entered critical discourse in 2006 due to the controversies that accompanied the release of *lonelygirl15* – a YouTube blog of a sixteen-year-old girl named Bree who filmed and posted her comments on daily matters in the intimate space of her bedroom and who, it soon transpired, was a fake (Klein, 2014: 3). Debates over authenticity aside, Burgess and Greene argue that *lonelygirl15* 'legitimized vlogging as a genre of cultural production' and offered new opportunities for media self-expression

(2009: 28). Considered as 'audio-visual forms that make use of serial, fictional, and narrative devices and are first produced for the internet' (Klein, 2014: 5, n. 3), web series, like television series, are divisible into episodes and seasons. Unlike the latter, however, webisodes are much shorter and are characterised by a particular filming situation. The consistency of frontal filming and setting (usually the character's bedroom) is accompanied by a number of easily implementable variations (e.g., clothing, hairstyle, character constellations). Authenticating practices and patterns, such as the use of a hand-held cameras, or an amateurish webcam aesthetic, or medium shots are also common devices used (Näser, 2008). Unlike TV series, however, web series differ in terms of the economies of financing, promotion, production, distribution and communication economies (Klein, 2014: 5). Be that as it may, the frontal, confessional style, the young-adult context of the videos and the pseudo-interactivity they encourage all offer a sense of proximity and intimacy that appeals to adapters of the first-person narration in *Jane Eyre*.

Indeed, the series begins with Jane's self-presentation. Based in Vancouver, British Columbia, Canada, Jane Eyre is a young woman who has just finished her BA nursing degree only to continue her studies in childhood development and who will soon be employed by E. D. Rochester, the CEO of Thornfield Aluminium Exports. In the first episode, Jane describes herself as a lover of rose gardens, tea varieties and an unreserved reader of books (from *Harry Potter* and *Lord of the Rings* to *Antiques* and Margaret Atwood, as the piles on her desk make clear). She considers herself neither 'deep' nor 'mysterious' but shows her creative side and professes herself in need of a change. Curiously enough, and contradicting the form of her vlog confession, Jane states 'I'm not someone who shares things easily' (Ep. 1). This, of course, does not prevent her from revealing her heart's troubles or posting eavesdropped conversations.

Not only has the protagonist of Brontë's novel been updated to suit the demands of a contemporary internet community, other characters have undergone similar metamorphoses. In this version, Grace Poole is no longer the guardian of Bertha Mason but becomes a workaholic assistant of young Mr Rochester, who – with his youthful physique, executive role and entrepreneurial worldview – is closer to Mark Zuckerberg or Dustin Moskovitz than his literary counterpart. Key events have also been transformed to fit the requirements of the new setting and updated characters. Rochester is involved in two car accidents rather than being thrown off his horse or injured in a fire. The Rivers family are Jane's flatmates, with Mary introducing sexual diversity to the series as an open lesbian. Helen only exists in Jane's portraits and tales as her best friend who died of leukaemia. Miss Temple becomes a supportive art teacher. Blanche Ingram owns PR Ingram Consulting Ltd and describes herself in her online profile as 'a Canadian model and public relations executive with French origins' and 'the #1 "most eligible single woman in Canada"' (Anon., 2013). She is a spokesperson for a number of brands, has hosted TV shows, works as a corporate finance lawyer and occasionally appears in 'a popular network series "Vampyre"' (Anon., 2013). Last but not least, Adèle, Rochester's neglected but clever daughter, shows signs of intelligence, embodying contemporary ideas about high-end education, both in Jane's vlogs as well as on her Twitter account (@AdeleCRochester), where she often posts quirky information of general interest.

Like Adèle's Twitter account, other social-media platforms add to the experience of the series and allow for a degree of interactivity between the series' creators and its audience. In addition to Adèle's use of Twitter and Blanche's personal website, viewers can enjoy Jane's Instagram – which explores her love of photography (of tea cups, jars, glasses, pots, cans, and equally copious images of books) and add another dimension to her character – and Tumblr, the latter filled with posts containing film references, reassuring statements and handwritten wisdoms (e.g., 'I love Places that Make you Realize how tiny you and your Problems are', or 'To judge a man by his weakest link or deed is like judging the power of the ocean by one wave').[2] Viewers can also consult the programme's Facebook page, where they can interact with the series' creators (out of character) and learn about the developments within and outside the project.[3] YouTube comments also offer viewers the possibility of instantly publishing their responses to an episode or to comments posted by others. Despite the involvement of many media platforms, it remains a matter of contention whether the project can be regarded as transmedia in character. Famously, Henry Jenkins proposed a definition of transmedia storytelling as 'a process where integral elements of a fiction get dispersed systematically across multiple delivery channels for the purpose of creating a unified and coordinated entertainment experience ideally, each medium makes it [*sic*] own unique contribution to the unfolding of the story' (2011). Since the story is revealed in the vlog, and other social media only provide auxiliary information that does not contribute significantly to the narrative arc, one cannot consider *The Autobiography of Jane Eyre* an ideal type of transmedia. Yet, through the engagement of multiple media platforms it offers a transmedia experience to its audience – an experience for which issues of gender, authorship, authenticity and affect are of prime importance.

Jane Eyre's adaptations: from mother to mistress to 'a cousin, a niece, a sister, a friend'

While the form of the web series facilitates an adaptation of *Jane Eyre* that caters to the needs of contemporary young audiences in ways that traditional media platforms do not, it also responds to existing gender scripts and clearly partakes in adaptation trends. To what extent does it change the romantic entanglement of Jane Eyre in Brontë's novel and its adaptations? In their consideration of Brontë's novel, Sandra Gilbert and Susan Gubar argue that what disconcerted the Victorians about the novel was the heroine's 'anger', her 'refusal to submit to her social destiny' and their inability to accommodate her in pre-existent cultural scripts (2000: 338). This quality of Brontë's text, however, seems to be lost in its translations onto the screen. In their feminist reading of two filmic adaptations of *Jane Eyre* (Robert Stevenson in 1943 and Delbert Mann in 1970), Kate Ellis and E. Ann Kaplan argue that despite changes in women's socio-cultural situatedness, both adaptations disregard Brontë's 'ambivalence towards patriarchy' (1999: 195), while at the same time comfortably accommodating their heroine within conveniently hegemonic visual scripts. A brief glance at other film adaptations supports this contention, proving that *Jane Eyre*'s translation to screen has often elided the novel's critical potentialities.

Christy Cabanne's 1934 film bears traces both of the Motion Picture Production Code (1930) and the successful formula of 1930s romances. As a young girl, Jane Eyre is acutely aware of her situation, as her comment on the discrepancy between poetic justice in stories for children and her reality makes clear. As a young teacher in an orphanage, she is both strict and humane. Her protection of a schoolchild against the corrective actions of Mr Brocklehurst, her refusal of his 'charity' and articulation of her opinions bring about her dismissal. When at Thornfield, Jane Eyre assumes the role of a surrogate mother to Rochester's 'niece', the English-speaking Adèle, who repeatedly articulates thoughts and desires that she herself is unable to utter. Played by the 'Golden Girl' Virginia Bruce, Jane Eyre is, above all, a surrogate mother and an educator. Her character and the changing social situation are distinctively played out on the canvas of broader cultural debates of women's role in society. Sarah Berry addresses the complex gender politics of the 1930s, a time of 'retrenchment for women following the suffrage movement and the rebellious flapper era, a time when the overtly political work of first-wave feminism was diluted by economic struggles and consumer aspirations' and a time that marked 'women's negotiation of modernity and post-traditional identity' through fashion (2000: xii–xiii). The film references these debates in a complex manner. It depicts Jane Eyre as an accomplished, worldly woman: she speaks German and French, draws and sings. Unlike her literary prototype, she is intelligent, 'charming' and 'pretty', and her singing, dancing and piano-playing skills surpass the abilities of Brontë's protagonist. Her virtuosic interpretation of Schubert's serenade obliterates the novel's criticism of educational standards just as it also functions as a nod to the romance audiences of the time. Da Sousa Correa has argued that Jane's meagre skills offer her a way out of servitude to her master (she does not have to accompany him during his song) as well as contrasting her schooling and means of expression – the reflexivity of drawing – with the sophisticated education of Blanche Ingram and the propensity of mid-Victorian society to view femininity as a spectacle (2000a: 102). By contrast, the film emphasises Jane's worldly skills along with her 'discriminating taste' as she is asked to assist in the redecoration of the house for the future Mrs Rochester. This self-expression through taste in music, clothes and home decoration is accompanied by Jane Eyre's development of her own voice in writing. The film thus turns Jane Eyre into both a mother figure and a sophisticated and resourceful lady of the house.

In a similar vein, though clearly with a different emphasis, Cary Fukunaga's *Jane Eyre* (2011), as much as it emancipates the heroine, also encases her in a romantic plot. The twenty-first-century Jane Eyre is Rochester's introvert mistress, who reflects both on her formative years and her current position and considers the precarious situation of women in general. Meghan Jordan argues, however, that the film 'privileges heteronormative love for [the] subject's completion' and, like other twenty-first-century adaptations of the novel, represents 'the heroine as needing love to alleviate her dislocation from the modern world' (2014: 79). At the same time, it continues to construct her as an enjoyable commodity for our consumption.

What *The Autobiography of Jane Eyre* achieves is the decentring of the romance plot. Online community commentators have partly attributed this to practical decisions taken by the series creators following the early departure of the actor playing Rochester. What transpires is that the relationship between Rochester and Jane is framed as one among many formative relationships that shape Brontë's female protagonist. Even at the outset of the story, when she considers herself ready for a change, Jane is shown to have been formed by positive past relationships to a greater extent than by those involving cruelty and neglect. Certainly Miss

Temple, the art teacher, and Jane's late friend Helen play a considerable role in her development. Whereas in the novel Helen's views on religion and forgiveness affect Jane's sense of justice, here, the former's love of photography as a means of perceiving and responding to the world influence Jane's ways of seeing (see Ep. 8). Likewise, Jane is shown to cultivate what is initially only a cursory relationship with Grace so that when the latter suffers under the dissolution of Thornfield, Jane knows how to help her. Similarly, Diana and Mary, the Rivers sisters who offer her a home after she leaves Rochester, remain her continual companions. The most profound bond develops between Jane and Adèle. In Episode 5, Jane shows the viewers Adèle's drawings which testify not only to the girl's knowledge of fine arts but also to her imitative versatility and ability to articulate herself. At this point, Jane ruminates about the father–daughter relationship and wonders at the negligence that Adèle experiences daily. Episode 90 offers evidence of their growing attachment as Adèle talks about growing up with her addict mother and reveals her thoughts on archetypical motherhood.

Such emphases draw the audience's attention to Jane Eyre's network of friends, further supported by the anti-climactic resolution of the romantic story arc, as the relationship with Rochester at the end of the series develops off camera. The final episode highlights the myriad bonds that Jane has become part of and the plurality of the roles she inhabits and performs:

> I've made a lot of changes this past year, but some things are still the same. I still buy more books than groceries. I still drink too much tea and let my mugs pile up around me. I still miss people who can't be here anymore. I started all this because I thought I wanted something else, or to be somewhere else, but if nothing else, this year has made me re-examine who I am, who I want to be and where I want to go. Among other things, I've learned how to make my passion and my reason co-exist, instead of letting one crash the other. I've learned how to go after what I want. I've learned how to stand up for myself. I've learned how to make myself happy and in doing so, I've realized I don't need to change who I am. I am a reader, a tea drinker, a story teller, a university graduate, a new apartment inhabitant, a teacher, a soon to be business owner, a cousin, a niece, a sister, a friend. I have a family now.
>
> (Ep. 95)

This long, self-reflexive passage sheds light on the metamorphoses that Jane has undergone during that year. Although she acknowledges both the sustainability of her habits and her ability to learn, her emphasis falls upon the polymorphic identities that she inhabits daily. Next to the 'tea drinker' and 'story teller', Jane defines herself above all in relation to others: 'a cousin, a nice, a sister, a friend'. Interestingly, neither 'lover' nor a 'surrogate mother' feature on this list. This has the effect that, unlike in film and television adaptations of the story, Jane Eyre is no longer exclusively entrapped in the romantic plot. The focus, as Jane's voiceover makes clear in the last statement of the series – which cunningly echoes Jane Eyre's famous, 'Reader, I married him' – is on home: 'Dear Viewer, I made a home' (Ep. 95). Importantly, online communities have reacted to this decision in ways that foreground the complexity of the novel, its protagonist, and how they matter today.

Authorship, authenticity and affect

Like the intertwining of gender and genre, Jane Eyre's voice and her perspective – her ways of seeing – have been central to the critical reception of the novel and to its adaptations. As mentioned before, vlogging – or fictional vlogging in this case – has become the quintessence of cultural production for a younger generation and a prime site for self-expression. In this context, vlogging can be seen as a site of self-representation, identity performance and authorship for public distribution. Jane Eyre in the web series is her own creator and the creator of her story online. Apart from this, other media enable her to self-reflect and come to terms with her experiences throughout the series. She prefers reflexive arts: she draws, paints and takes photographs. Her room is always decorated by some of these, very often clearly hinting at her current mood or commenting on the situation she finds herself in. This is, for instance, the case when she moves into her own apartment and the dramatic oil diptych that accompanied her earlier episodes and could be interpreted as signalling her interim position between the love relationship with Rochester and her friendship with Simon is replaced by a canvas representing a field of flourishing sunflowers (Ep. 89 and 94). These easily decipherable motifs clearly communicate her situation and articulate her state of well-being.

Despite continuous assertions to the contrary, Jane is versatile in old and new technologies alike and knowingly uses them to disclose character traits, past events and current emotional states. Episode 32 is probably the most direct instance of this tendency as it offers a virtuoso summary of her life on a blackboard. The use of *mise-en-abyme*, a story within a story, flashbacks and, most of all, peculiar camera angles, discloses but also hides certain elements of the story, as in the highly debated reconciliation episode where the camera stays inside the room and Jane and Rochester talk on the balcony outside its reach, with only their backs visible to the viewers and no conversation to follow (Ep. 93). These and other instances highlight the degree of control on the part of its makers. Although the series attracted a rather large audience and many episodes were profusely commented upon, these discussions had but a marginal influence on the series itself. In view of the enthusiastic rhetoric that foregrounds the potentialities of participatory culture, the makers and audience continued to operate in sync with traditional understandings of the audience/author distinction – a divide that the new mediascape allegedly blurs.

In spite of the clearly adaptational character of the series and the knowledge of its literary progeny among many viewers, audience members have reacted positively to its more 'authentic' style, which they contrast to the more professional aesthetics of *The Lizzy Bennet Diaries*. Commenting on Episode 93, for instance, 'inkingideas' (the online pseudonym of Nessa Aref, series writer and producer) praises Jane for her new ways of seeing and for shedding light on the quirkiness and frustrations of life as/with a blogger:

> For Jane there's been a shift now. Instead of trying to see the world through the camera, she chooses to see it through her own eyes, walking with the lens facing down to see her steps, as if she's forgotten it's on. Now the focus is on seeing the people in her life. She doesn't hide the fact that she's filming, and I personally love that her friends accept that it's just part of who she is.
>
> (Sidenote: I feel like it's a bit the reality for many Youtubers – as their friends and family adjust, it becomes less weird and they understand that it's not about necessarily being invasive, but about the vlogger and their goals as creators.)[4]

'Inkingideas' interprets Jane's camera as a protective shield: a 'crutch' which she now discards to 'deal with personal intimate relationships head-on […] [a]nd maybe it's because we're nearing the end, but I'm really proud of Jane'.[5] Similar affective responses, like praise for the series' 'authentic' aesthetics, can be found in a number of YouTube comments on particular episodes. 'Taylor Harwood' writes under Episode 89: 'This adaptation gives all the characters a chance to show their different sides, and I love that. Good for Jane moving out on her own. She's an independent woman and can make her own decisions, especially now that she has such a strong support network'.[6]

These positive voices are accompanied by more critical declarations, such as that by 'Gabby Villalba', who expresses her disappointment: 'Honestly, I feel betrayed, disappointed with the ending. No Rochester? […] Jane, I'm glad you have a new life, a new family now, but AOJE, you disappointed me. Thank you so much for ruining the series'.[7] This comment includes a differentiation between the double tension that I have already mentioned: 'authentic' communication with the series' 'inauthentic' protagonist and an awareness of adaptation practices that have been part and parcel of the project. What is apparent here is the double contract that the viewers of the series have with its makers: on the one hand, they treat the vlog Jane as an 'authentic' vlogger, which is partly responsible for their identification with her; this is visible in their comments, where they share their experiences and outline their affective responses to the protagonist's situation. On the other hand, the second contract – the unwritten contract of knowledgeable audiences with the adapters – entitles them to comment on the changes in the series. 'Kayla Knight' metacritically responds to this issue: 'There's something I really struggle with whenever I invest myself into a series, and it is the unspoken contract between the content maker and their audience about endings. […] Was it [this ending] complete and full of the complexity we've come to expect? No. Far from it.'[8] This comment is an affective response that grows out of the violation of the code. At the same time, what is present here is the assumption that any adaptation should fulfil the expectations of readers/viewers: that it is supposed to stay true to the 'spirit' of the novel. Comments addressing the series' reinvention of the story thus betray complex and contradictory attitudes towards authorship and adaptation.

Interestingly, while addressing the altered ending of the story, online communities have ignored the final 'message' of the web series. In its last minutes, the series includes a metacommentary on the online life of the heroine and her audience, offering a pessimistic view of vlogging and online communities, and, in the end, exchanging what they offer for 'real'-life existence beyond the Internet. After her eulogy of the new family, Jane finishes with 'and the thing is, I don't need to press record to start my day. So, thank you, thank you for staying with me. Dear Viewer, I made a home' (Ep. 95). After this statement, Jane turns the camera off. Such an ending implies that her vlog diary was a way of coming to terms with her self-dissatisfaction. It accompanied her journey of self-discovery. But as soon as she finds a stable social environment, she decides to lead her life off camera. This ending also seems to comment upon the surrogate and transitory character of online communities, which, while good to have, do not seem to offer enough satisfaction to the vlog's heroine. Jane Eyre neither discloses her most intimate secrets to her audience nor does she allow it to follow her life with this new family. On a meta-level, then, the series comments on the limitations of 'authenticity' and intimacy that are possible online. It ends in favour of 'real' life, thus suggesting that the Internet is only a poor substitute for 'home' and friendship.

Jane 2.0: Victorians' posthumous lives

The discussion of *The Autobiography of Jane Eyre* and its reception shows that the relevance of Brontë's novel today seems to lie in its propensity to accommodate discussions about both gender and self-expression. It disentangles Jane Eyre from the romantic relationship as a prime site for self-definition even as it embraces the entrepreneurial 'have-it-all' of post-feminism. Nonetheless, and in contrast to prototypical expressions of the latter, the romantic relationship here is just one among many. This said, YouTube offers viewers the chance to comment upon these developments and fosters an array of contradictory responses to such modifications, thereby strengthening the sense of belonging and participation, however limited this might be. Yet it simultaneously shows that media are only a poor ersatz of intimate bonds and non-mediated relationships.

This web-series adaptation and the discussions it has raised also comment upon adaptation as a cultural praxis and on the posthumous transmedia lives of literary characters. But what does it tell us about the twenty-first-century Victorians? Clearly, if unsurprisingly, they have reached transmedia popularity. This, interestingly enough, appears as liberating as it is challenging. Although it allows contemporary young audiences to appropriate the Victorians in hitherto unheard of ways, it also seems to foster the belief that they have become our property – to be adapted, exchanged and refurbished. The danger is, of course, that their multilayered past versions will be replaced by DIY varieties much like most contemporary products for mass consumption.

Notes

1 *Journal of Neo-Victorian Studies*: www.neovictorianstudies.com (accessed 19 August 2016).
2 For Jane Eyre's Instagram account, see www.instagram.com/eyrequotes/ (accessed 19 August 2016). For her Tumblr, see http://eyrequotes.tumblr.com/ (accessed 19 August 2016).

3 For *The Autobiography of Jane Eyre*'s Facebook page, see www.facebook.com/ TheAutobiographyOfJaneEyre (accessed 28 September 2015).

4 'Inkingideas' (Nessa Aref) (2014) 'Some notes on today's episode: steps', *Inking Ideas*, Tumblr, 7 June [Tumblr], http://inkingideas.tumblr.com/ post/88102118642/some-notes-on-todays-episode-steps (accessed on 28 September 2015).

5 'Inkingideas', 'Some notes on today's episode'.

6 'Taylor Harwood' (2014) Comment on Episode 89, *The Autobiography of Jane Eyre*, www.youtube.com/watch?v=CksPH21PqW8&lc=z12iyz0qwvmcih52r 23swjl5fxuxdpbqv04 (accessed 19 August 2016).

7 'Gabby Villalba' (2014) Comment on Episode 95. *The Autobiography of Jane Eyre* www.youtube.com/watch?v=FclkWGdX4qo&lc=z12dxt0ivn3wxh52d2 2vwr3gltjbe15lx (accessed 19 August 2016).

8 'Kayla Knight' (2014) Comment on Episode 95, *The Autobiography of Jane Eyre*, www.youtube.com/watch?v=FclkWGdX4qo&lc=z12evjjpcyfbjvbis04cf vuqapr0yd04cr00k (accessed 19 August 2016).

References

Anon. (2013) 'Blanche Ingram: profile'. *Blanche Ingram* (*The Autobiography of Jane Eyre*) [WiX] http://theautobiographyofja.wix.com/blanche-ingram#!profile/ c13dn (accessed 25 September 2015).

The Autobiography of Jane Eyre (2013–14), YouTube web series, www.youtube. com/user/TheAOJaneEyre (accessed 28 September 2015).

Berry, Sarah (2000) *Screen Style: Fashion and Femininity in 1930s Hollywood*, Minneapolis, Minn.: University of Minnesota Press.

Bruns, Axel (2008) *Blogs, Wikipedia, Second Life, and Beyond: From Production to Produsage*, New York: Peter Lang.

Burgess, Jean and Joshua Greene (2009) *YouTube: Online Video and Participatory Culture*, Cambridge: Polity Press.

Da Sousa Correa, Delia (2000a) '*Jane Eyre* and genre', in Delia Da Sousa Correa (ed.), *The Nineteenth-Century Novel: Realisms*, London and New York: Routledge, pp. 87–116.

—— (2000b) '*Jane Eyre*: inside and out', in Delia Da Sousa Correa (ed.), *The Nineteenth-Century Novel: Realisms*, London and New York: Routledge, pp. 117–36.

Eagleton, Terry (1975) *Myths of Power: A Marxist Study of the Brontës*, London: Macmillan.

Ellis, Kate and E. Ann Kaplan (1999) 'Feminism and Brontë's *Jane Eyre* and its film versions', in Barbara Tepa Lupac (ed.), *Nineteenth-Century Women at the Movies: Adapting Classic Women's Fiction to Film*, Bowling Green, OH: Bowling Green State University Press, pp. 192–206.

Emma Approved (2013–14), YouTube web series, www.youtube.com/user/ PemberleyDigital (accessed 28 September 2015).

Gilbert, Sandra M. and Susan Gubar (2000) *The Madwoman in the Attic: The Woman Writer and the Nineteenth-Century Literary Imagination*, New Haven, Conn.: Yale University Press.

Heilmann, Ann and Mark Llewellyn (2010) *Neo-Victorianism: The Victorians in the Twenty-First Century, 1999–2009*, Basingstoke: Palgrave Macmillan.

Ho, Elizabeth (2012) *Neo-Victorianism and the Memory of Empire*, London and New York: Continuum.

—— (2014) 'The neo-Victorian-at-sea: towards a global memory of the Victorian', in Nadine Boehm-Schnitker and Susanne Gruss (eds.), *Neo-Victorian Literature and Culture: Immersions and Revisitations*, Abingdon and New York: Routledge, pp. 171–202.

Jane Eyre (1934), dir. Christy Cabanne, Monogram Pictures.

Jane Eyre (2011), dir. Cary Joji Fukunaga, Focus Films, BBC Films and Ruby Films.

Jenkins, Henry (2006) *Convergence Culture*, New York: New York University Press.

—— (2007) 'Transmedia storytelling 101', *Confessions of an Aca-Fan: The Official Weblog of Henry Jenkins*, http://henryjenkins.org/2007/03/transmedia_story-telling_101.html (accessed 26 September 2015).

—— (2011) 'Transmedia 202: further reflections'. *Confessions of an Aca-Fan: The Official Weblog of Henry Jenkins*, http://henryjenkins.org/2011/08/defining_transmedia_further_re.html (accessed 26 September 2015).

Jenkins, Henry, Sam Ford and Joshua Green (2013) *Spreadable Media: Creating Value and Meaning in a Networked Culture*, New York: New York University Press.

Jordan, Joh O. (1993) '*Jane Eyre* and narrative voice', in Diane Long Hoeveler and Beth Lau (eds.), *Approaches to Teaching Brontë's Jane Eyre*, New York: MLA, pp. 76–81.

Jordan, Meghan (2014) 'Dislocated heroines: Cary Fukunaga's *Jane Eyre*, romantic love and Bertha's legacy', *Neo-Victorian Studies*, 7:1, 79–103.

Kaplan, Cora (2007) *Victoriana: Histories, Fictions, Criticism*, New York: Columbia University Press.

Klein, Thomas (2014) 'Web series: between commercial and non-profit seriality', in Marcel Hartwig, Evelyne Keitel and Gunter Süß (eds.), *Media Economies: Perspectives on American Cultural Practice*, Trier: WVT, pp. 3–14.

Kohlke, Marie-Luise (2008) 'The neo-Victorian sexsation: literary excursions into the nineteenth century erotic', in Marie-Luise Kohlke and Luisa Orza (eds,), *Probing the Problematics: Sex and Sexuality*, Oxford: Interdisciplinary Press, pp. 345–56.

Leadbeater, Charles and Paul Miller (2004) *The Pro-Am Revolution: How Enthusiasts Are Changing Our Economy and Society*, London: Demos.

The Lizzie Bennet Diaries (2012–13), YouTube web series, www.youtube.com/user/LizzieBennet (accessed 28 September 2015).

McWilliam, Rohan (2009) 'Victorian sensations, neo-Victorian romances: response', *Victorian Studies*, 52:1, 106–12.

Näser, Torsten (2008) 'Authentizität 2.0: Kulturanthropologische Überlegungen zur Suche nach 'Echtheit' im Videoportal YouTube', *kommunikation@gesellschaft* (9.2). www.soz.uni-frankfurt.de/K.G/B2_2008_Naeser.pdf (accessed 27 September 2015).

Ruse, Michael (2003) 'The changing face of Darwinism', *Victorian Studies*, 45:2, 305–17.

Sconce, Jeffrey (1995) 'Narrative authority and social narrativity: the cinematic reconstitution of Brontë's *Jane Eyre*', in Janet Staiger (ed.), *The Studio System*, New Brunswick: Rutgers University Press, pp. 140–62.

Whelehan, Imelda (2012) 'Neo-Victorian adaptations', in Deborah Cartmell (ed.), *A Companion to Literature, Film and Adaptation*, Oxford: Blackwell, pp. 272–94.

12

'Reader, I [shagged/beat/whipped/f****d/rewrote] him': the sexual and financial afterlives of *Jane Eyre*

Louisa Yates

[England is] the home of Shakespeare, Austen, the Brontë sisters, Thomas Hardy. I'd like to see the places that inspired those people to write such wonderful books.

E. L. James, *Fifty Shades of Grey* (2011)

It's an updated throwback to scandalous novels of the past, including *Jane Eyre* […] *Fifty Shades of Grey* is to publishing what Spanx was to the undergarment business: an antiquated product re-imagined as innovation.

Alessandra Stanley, *New York Times* (2012)

Sex, as more than one person has observed, certainly sells. A less catchy version of the old adage might be 'Victoriana sells'. Our pleasure in consuming the Victorian – reimagined, revised, reinterpreted, rewritten, re-screened – appears insatiable. Academic writing about the neo-Victorian suggests that our desire to consume the genre is based on the pleasure generated by its knowing, winking approach to the Victorian encounter. Posing the question 'What is Neo-Victorian Studies?' Mark Llewellyn coined the term 'critical f(r)iction' to describe the 'text's play with postmodern self-reflection and self-inflection on the one hand, and the more grounded, factual, and dogmatic principles of the multidisciplinary Victorian intellectual on the other' (2008: 170). Llewellyn picks out the genre's postmodern inclinations rather than its erotic predilections, but his phrase irresistibly calls to mind the sexual frankness of the neo-Victorian genre. Indeed, neo-Victorian novels often combine the two. In Sarah Waters' first novel, *Tipping the Velvet* (1998), socially radical Victorian poetry acts simultaneously as a meta-fictional reference, resolute political gesture and playful aphrodisiac: 'it was *Towards Democracy*, the poem by Edward Carpenter; and as I turned the pages, with Florence warm beside me, I found myself growing damp' (Waters, 1999: 437). Carpenter's words are never directly quoted, creating a presence/absence that accentuates the postmodern, spectral quality of the poem's presence – and by extension, the f(r)iction between absent Victorian past and fictionalised Victorian present.

F(r)iction of all kinds is present in E. L. James's *Fifty Shades of Grey* (2011), as its protagonist Anastasia Steele coyly confesses to the man who will become her master that she is a fan of the Brontë sisters. Both the novel and its protagonist harbour literary pretensions; Steele's invocation of the English literary canon seeks to invest *Fifty Shades* with literary authority. However, although her fandom is depicted as fundamental to her character, Steele will only mention *Jane Eyre* (1847) of all the Brontës' novels, and then only once; Thomas Hardy's *Tess of the D'Urbervilles* has a much greater presence in James's novel. Why then include the Brontës at all? Alessandra Stanley, quoted at the start of this chapter, suggests the answer is simply that Charlotte Brontë sells. Stanley's analysis positions Brontë as a marketable commodity no different from a corset, an 'antiquated product' brought up to date for modern tastes and sold to contemporary consumers. *Jane Eyre* thus links the Victorian literary canon with the sexual and financial politics of the sexually explicit 'erotic makeover' novels published in the immediate aftermath of *Fifty Shades of Grey*. The erotic makeover is a small, specialised genre of erotic romantic fiction that is usually e-published and might, if very successful, have a print run (Noah, 2012). The most consistent producer of erotic makeover texts is Totally Bound, publishers of the Clandestine Classics series.[1] The series' makeovers include four Austen novels as well as *The Picture of Dorian Gray* (2013), *Tom Jones* (2013) and even *20,000 Leagues Under the Sea* (2012), but it was an echo of *Jane Eyre*'s most recognised sentence that was used to launch the series: a press release titled 'Reader, I Spanked Him…' (Anon., 2012). Crucially for my analysis, the publisher's press release specifically referenced the 'dramatic revival' in erotic romance as a result of 'the rising popularity of e-readers and record-breaking success of "mummy porn" novel *Fifty Shades of Grey*' (Anon., 2012).

This chapter's argument concerns differing discourses of appropriation that substantiate the revisionist principles of both neo-Victorian novels and erotic makeovers. These discourses emerge from the texts themselves (including their paratextual apparatus), from marketing material and reviews in both online and print media, and from within the academy. The neo-Victorian novel and the erotic makeover share a generative discourse; this chapter identifies shared financial imperatives and legitimating discourses that are proffered as an explanation for both genres' existence. Both genres employ models of silence, invisibility and absence, presented as a sexual/textual repression supposedly released by the revisionist text. As such, both forms of appropriation depend upon the survival and persistence of the same narrative of 'our repressed Victorian past' – the very narrative that both genres purport to counter and rewrite. I want to suggest, however, a new way of problematising the generative impulse. In this reading, producers of erotic makeovers appropriate the academic neo-Victorian vocabulary, wrapping the makeover's genesis in a postmodern gauze that obscures its pecuniary reasons for existence; couched in the language of the academy, its release is heralded as the product of altruistic research or an uncovering and restoration of those lost to history rather than an attempt to secure a share of a lucrative reading market. The academy, meanwhile, obfuscates the financial imperatives that shape 'literary' neo-Victoriana. Considering the two genres in this way reveals not only that 'literary', 'legitimate' revisionary fictions have produced 'non-literary', 'illegitimate' offspring but also offers a new way of contextualising neo-Victorian fictions via the erotic makeover's enterprising attempts at exacting revenue from neo-Victorian consumers. As such, this chapter focuses on two case studies, the first a 'non-literary' erotic makeover from publisher Clandestine Classics and the second a neo-Victorian novel, *Charlotte* by D. M. Thomas (2000). A comparative reading throws into relief not only their shared discourses and practices – including self-definitions from publisher and author respectively – but also their different receptions in the words of publicists, journalists and academics.

It is not hard to understand that makeovers are written for money. As we shall see throughout this chapter, however, the erotic makeover overwrites discussions of monetary gain with a purposeful, postmodern conflation of Charlotte Brontë with *Jane Eyre*, in order to position itself as a sexual/textual release – a 'revelatory' process which is a variation of academic neo-Victorian discourses of concealment/revelation, or silence/

speech,[2] and which I define as follows: the deliberate creation of erotic desires, assigned to a particular author (or, as often found, an entire historical epoch); the assumption that such desires were repressed by the author but present in her literature via meaningful elisions or allusive images. There is a further assumption that these desires are available to the attentive reader and, most crucially, that these desires can be given life in a revisionary text. The sexual/textual release is characterised entirely as creative, beneficial and therapeutic. There is therefore tension at the centre of the erotic makeover's production, generated by the sharp contrast between the postmodern vocabulary of sexual/textual release used by Clandestine Classics and the potential financial gains that stand to be made from republishing works in the public domain with the small number of changes needed to establish copyright. *Fifty Shades of Grey* was originally *Twilight* fan fiction,[3] rewriting Stephanie Meyer's young-adult vampire phenomenon; increasingly, claims of artistic originality or altruistic research such as those made by Clandestine Classics (discussed below) falter in the face of the rewriting made possible by computer software and e-publishing as well as the growing contribution that online fan fiction communities make as authors and readers. In turn, any discussion of profits to be made from our fervour for the Victorian must incorporate our wider enthusiasm for consuming 're-visionary' forms. As well as erotic makeovers, UK and US television shows such as Sky's *Penny Dreadful* (2014–16) or the BBC's *Sherlock* (2010–), fan-fiction forms or neo-Victorian literature all form a range of revisionist fictions that – alongside statements explaining their production – initiate a complex conversation across the topics of authorship, fan fiction, copyright law, originality and Victoriana.

D. M. Thomas's *Charlotte* is an unusual example of neo-Victorian re-visionary fiction in that its genesis is attributed to many of the same financial and creative stimuli as the Clandestine Classics *Jane Eyre* (2012). Both Thomas and Clandestine Classics cite Charlotte Brontë, rather than her novel, as a catalyst for their fiction. Although superficially quite different – the former 'literary', the latter 'non-literary', with all the differences in marketing, presentation and audience this entails – both the novel and erotic makeover blend cultural capital with financial potential in a way that prompts this chapter to reconsider both the erotic makeover and the neo-Victorian novel in the context of postmodern presentations of history, as well as fandom, fan fiction and literary tourism. In this context, Brontë's celebrity is as much a commodity as her text.

'It has always been something I wanted to do': the origins of the erotic makeover

It is worth pausing to elaborate on the form and narrative of Clandestine Classics' *Jane Eyre*. It was the first of Totally Bound's erotic makeovers, establishing the formula for the series. The makeover has a curious joint authorship, being credited to 'Charlotte Brontë and Sierra Cartwright'. Yet Cartwright adds very little original material. With the exception of simplified punctuation and updated spelling – semi-colons become commas, while John Reed's 'shew the book' becomes 'show the book' – the original *Jane Eyre* print edition remains untouched. The only additions to the original text are those that add explicit sexual encounters to the relationship between Jane and Edward Rochester. Particularly explicit are the instances that come after the visit and injury of Richard Mason and which establish the relationship between the two:

> 'I'm not an easy master, Jane. Moody, demanding. My tastes may be offensive to one as delicate as you.'
> Scoffed I, 'Dear sir, only you find me delicate. I assure you I am not.'
> 'Then lift your dress.' […] 'Lift your dress,' repeated he. 'I will help you with your undergarments, but if you've a desire to explore with another, this is your opportunity. I will force you into nothing – that is not my way. You must always show me your willingness else I shall send you back to your room and encourage you to throw the bolt. What I offer you is the most glorious of all freedoms, the opportunity to be always at choice, to accept my instructions or deny completely – thus you are the one with the upper hand.
> 'If you opt to stay, Miss Eyre, heed my warning, my desires are unusual.'
> (Brontë and Cartwright, 2012: 136)

Edward's suggestion to Jane that she 'opt to stay' and become a submissive partner to his experienced dominant clearly demonstrates the erotic makeover's debt to *Fifty Shades of Grey*. Subsequent encounters introduce sex toys and spankings that make little encroachment on the original novel but that clearly adapt *Fifty Shades*. Jane replicates the distinctive stress position in which Christian Grey trains Anastasia Steele:

> When I tell you to come in here, I expect you to kneel over there […] place your hands and forearms flat on your thighs. Good. Now part your knees. Wider. Wider. Perfect. Look down at the floor.
> (James, 2012: 320)

> Kneel for me – my sweet submissive Jane – in the position I prefer, your thighs as far apart as you can manage. When I instruct you to kneel thus,

I wish you to have your eyes downcast, your hands on your thighs with the palms facing upward.

(Brontë and Cartwright, 2012: 432)

Erika Kvistad notes that *Jane Eyre* substantially precedes the specific vocabulary of BDSM (bondage discipline sado-masochism – the first recorded use of both 'sadism' and 'masochism' are dated to 1886, while 'kink' and BDSM are 1965 and 1991 respectively). Kvistad persuasively suggests that 'the worlds of need, devastation, experimentation, and force' found in Brontë's novels are an indirect source of sexual power dynamics (2013). Kvistad's analysis of *Jane Eyre* as a BDSM novel that did not yet have the vocabulary encourages us to consider *Jane Eyre* (2012) as a textual release brought about by more articulate times. Intriguing as this is, I want to suggest that the erotic makeover has a much more obvious catalyst for existence: the financial success of *Fifty Shades of Grey*.

E. L. James's *Fifty Shades of Grey* brought about a revolution in publishing that was not just financial. First published as an e-book before the rights were acquired by Vintage in March 2012, critical reception of the book was poor. Salman Rushdie stated that 'I've never read anything so badly written that got published. It made *Twilight* look like *War and Peace*' (Irvine, 2012). Coining the word 'spankbuster', the *London Review of Books* identified the novel's desire for money from writing sex: 'a great deal of fun can be had by noting the many comforts offered for a life of mild depravity [...] the specificity [O'Hagan refers here to brand names such as Audi and Apple over details of sex acts] implies a desire much larger than any desire people might have for kinky sex' (O'Hagan, 2012: 29). The popular audience was less critical, with combined e-book and paperback sales reaching 100 million by early 2014 (Flood, 2014) and the film adaptation taking over $350 million in its first two weeks of release (Anon., 2015). *Fifty Shades'* gargantuan financial success prompted three main strands of discussion in the mainstream and online media. The first asked what the BDSM relationship between the novel's main characters revealed about the sexual tastes of its readers. The second linked *Fifty Shades'* success to the anonymity of new e-reading technologies and online retailers, imagining a reader of erotic and/or romantic fiction whose taboo reading practices could now be indulged but also concealed. The third strand consisted almost entirely of versions of and reactions to a Clandestine Classics press release announcing the racy makeover of classic novels. The press release parlayed the neo-Victorian discourse of concealment and revelation into marketing the series as a modern corrective to the repressed novels of yesteryear.

The Clandestine Classics *Jane Eyre* replicates *Fifty Shades'* high-media, low-critical reception. The print and online media reaction was intense but short-lived; almost all media pieces were published in the third week of July 2012, and almost all were the Clandestine Classics press release thinly disguised. In the UK, the *Daily Mail*, *Sun*, *Independent*, *Telegraph*, *Guardian* and *Times* all covered the story; in the United States, *Time* magazine featured the makeover, as did the French newspaper *Le Monde*. Two Brontës occupy central positions:

> Classic novels including *Jane Eyre, Pride and Prejudice* and *Northanger Abbey* are to get a steamy 18-certificate makeover from some of the world's leading erotic fiction writers [...]. The much-loved works of literature by famed authors including Charlotte and Emily Brontë, have been re-imagined for the very first time as works of adult fiction [...] complete with graphic sex and fetish scenes. [...] The re-worked versions of the classics include the full text of the original books with a series of specially written scenes featuring adult content to provide a seamless reading experience. While 19th century [*sic*] society demanded that novels only went so far when it came to depicting the true passionate nature of love and romance, the new series [...] invites readers to put the old-fashioned pleasantries to one side and enjoy the sensual scenes that were only ever alluded to in the original versions.
>
> (Anon., 2012)

The neo-Victorian vocabulary of revelation is certainly present here, but it is the press release's confusion of textual silence with repressed authorial desires that speaks most clearly to the makeover's origins. Novels that 'only go so far' and can only 'allude' to explicit sex are positioned as revealing the 'true passionate nature' of the women who wrote them. Initially, the 'specially written scenes' are presented as a 're-imagining' of 'graphic sex and fetish scenes', a turn of phrase that not only conflates Charlotte and Emily Brontë with their literary works but that specifically suggests that revisionary writers are able to 'read' the psychological sexual landscape of Charlotte and Emily. The press release's air of irrefutability affirms conflation: references to the 'full text' and 'original versions' encourages an assumption of careful research, while the blithe pronouncement of what nineteenth-century society 'demanded' works hard to create an impression of Victorian literary expertise. Imagining and reading are creative mental processes, and, as we shall see in the next section, reading and imagining are linked in neo-Victorian discourse, the latter becoming a creative (fictional) response to elisions in (historical) documents. But the prefix in 'reimagined' indicates a return, a second process, a realisation of what was present but buried. This is reinforced with 're-work', which again suggests a remodelling of extant material, returning again to the notion that these explicit scenes originated not with Sienna Cartwright but with Charlotte Brontë. The 'graphic sex and fetish scenes' are therefore positioned as a corrective to the original 'classic work', despite claims of a 'seamless reading experience'. Once again, we return to an image of the erotic makeover 'reading' a sexually repressed Charlotte Brontë.

Written sex, therefore, is not only a release, it is a psycho-sexual/textual process, and a sexually explicit afterlife is conjured via the conflation of Charlotte Brontë with the words of her novel. Unnamed readers (one might also say 'consumers') of 'graphic sex and fetish scenes' are prompted to exercise their imaginative faculties by reading not only *Jane Eyre* but also Charlotte Brontë. The 'allusions' in the original novel are directly linked to imagery of repressive nineteenth-century sexual discourses which permitted only 'old-fashioned pleasantries' rather than the 'true passionate nature of love'. The implication is clear: Charlotte's sexual nature was repressed by Victorian society, ergo her *Jane Eyre* must be in need of an explicit reimagining. Tracing this to its logical conclusion, the additions to the Clandestine Classics *Jane Eyre* are shaped as an unambiguous shout of freedom, a declaration of everything that Brontë was prevented from writing. Representations of explicit sex are positioned as a textual release for a long-dead patient: a Freudian writing cure. The curious co-authorship becomes something of an analyst–patient relationship, with a ghostly Charlotte on the couch. Diagnosing Brontë – and, by extension, the Victorians – as sexually repressed lends a new reading to Claire Siemaszkiewicz's statement that 'whenever I read classics from authors like Jane Austen, I often think about the potential "uncensored versions" that the original authors were unable – or unwilling – to include' (Anon., 2012). Intriguingly, Siemaszkiewicz replaced Austen with Brontë when she reworked this statement for *The Guardian* (Siemaszkiewicz, 2012). Whether Austen or Brontë, Siemaszkiewicz's statement silences both individual author and written expression, conjuring an image of a repression of the individual sexual psyche as well as a text suppressed by a ghostly social censor. The result is a novel that relies upon a sexually silent nineteenth century in order to present its textual inventions as a clairvoyant restorative.

Miriam Burstein has written of the problems of equating 'sex' with unambiguous written descriptions of 'erotic' sexual acts. Considering

Clandestine Classics' rhetorical statement, 'you didn't really think that these much loved characters only held hands and pecked cheeks, did you?', Burstein drily notes that 'one is tempted to suggest that for those of us who have actually read the books in question, the answer to that question is…no, we *didn't*, actually' (2012, italics in the original). To read Charlotte as repressed, silenced and in need of release is to turn a blind eye to long-standing traditions of reading her work in terms of free expression, resistance and transgression. Sandra M. Gilbert wrote persuasively of the '"hunger, rebellion and rage" fostered in both Charlotte Brontë and her heroines by a coercive cultural architecture' and the 'subversive strategies through which author and characters alike sought to undermine the structures of oppression' (1998: 353). It is worth noting that the 'hunger, rebellion and rage' of which Gilbert writes so approvingly are an echo of a disapproving Matthew Arnold's judgement of *Villette*, showing how keen both Moderns and Victorians have been to read Brontë's passions in the words of her novels.[4] Today, journalist Tanya Gold sees the 'real Charlotte' as a 'filthy bitch, grandmother of chick-lit, and friend'; in *Jane Eyre*, Brontë 'dared, baldly, to state her lust' (Gold, 2005). Gold foreshadows the vocabulary of Clandestine Classics as well as the publisher's depiction of a tussle between Eros (a creative, life-producing force) and Thanatos (often known as Freud's death drive) – the censor in this example is the 'literary criminal' Elizabeth Gaskell, charged with stripping 'Charlotte of her genius' and transforming 'her into a sexless, death-stalked saint' (Gold, 2005). Nevertheless, Gold's Brontë retains the sexual life denied her by Clandestine Classics. The 'filthy bitch' is a close relation to Gilbert's hungry, angry, rebellious writer. Siemaszkiewicz's wan, repressed Brontë wavers, becomes indistinct; the 'revelations' of her *Jane Eyre* lose their authority.

A repressed Charlotte, therefore, makes for an odd afterlife for both Brontë and *Jane Eyre*. Clandestine Classics require that readers fail to see any of the sex, sensuality and sadomasochism that some readers see in Brontë's novel. But a refusal to see – no matter how artificial – has some advantages when attempting to reveal the origins of the erotic makeover. Reading Cartwright's additions to *Jane Eyre* reveals a litany of assumptions of what comprises erotic liberation. Armed with a pair of scissors, a reader could transform *Jane Eyre* (2012) into *Jane Eyre* (1847) with just a few snips. The source text would remain almost entirely untouched. An addition made to the immediate aftermath of Bertha Mason's attack on her brother reveals much about the prosaic methods, rather than any postmodern playfulness, of the erotic makeover:

I went; sought the repository he had mentioned. *I found the task terribly intimate, of a sort a husband would demand of his wife. My master requiring me to do odd things was becoming a habit. I frowned when my hand found a smooth, wooden pole of sorts. I took it out and looked at it. I knew instantly what it was! I had seen such a phallus in the book that resided in my drawer. I had imagined something like this pressing inside my genitalia, held in Mr Rochester's loving grip. I had no doubt now that he knew I had the book. Indeed, I imagine he hoped I would take it. I shook myself from my thoughts. I dare not tarry!* I found the articles named, and returned with them.

(Brontë and Cartwright, 2012: 313, emphasis mine to indicate Cartwright's additions)

As seen above, Clandestine Classics' claims of a 'seamless reading experience' characterises the Brontë–Cartwright relationship as though it were a mutually beneficial, collaborative process between patient and therapist. The quoted section intends to render this collaboration graphically, with the new material inserted between two original and untouched sentences. Yet in both form and content the italicised section maintains a discrete distance from the original *Jane Eyre*. Most obviously, the addition offers an oddly decontextualised reading experience. In the original text, Richard Mason has been attacked by Bertha; Jane's discovery of a dildo among Rochester's clean shirts and neckties is a bathetic contrast to the trauma and shock of the moment. As Burstein has noted, 'this version's sex scenes, far from illuminating the text or filling in a gap, jar harshly against the rest of the narrative' (2012). Similarly jarring to scholars is the new material's assumptions about sexual attitudes in the mid nineteenth century. Simply compiling a list of the makeover's questionable historical assumptions is not my intention; nevertheless, it is worth noting that sex toys and their use are among the more contentious areas of Victorian Studies, while 'the book' to which Jane refers is likely an anachronism.[5] Jane describes the book as having 'little text' and many images of 'positions, sexual positions!' (Brontë and Cartwright, 2012: 213). Jane's anonymising of the text stems not from primness on her part but probably from the author's lack of research. Henry Spencer Ashbee's expansive bibliography *Forbidden Books of the Victorians* (1877–85) makes it clear that while illustrations were commonly included, they were actually few in number, perhaps six or eight per book (Ashbee, 1970). Far from an image of careful, altruistic research, Rochester's picture-filled book is an amalgamation of sex manuals more modern than Victorian.

Leaving accuracy aside, postmodernism would be the more usual scholarly context for a discussion of Cartwright's additions. Mark

Llewellyn's notion of critical f(r)iction highlights the postmodern context of neo-Victorian fiction, while in her seminal *A Poetics of Postmodernism* (1988) and *The Politics of Postmodernism* (1989), Linda Hutcheon defines historiographic metafiction as 'those well known and popular novels which are both intensely self-reflexive and paradoxically lay claim to historical fictions and personages' (1988: 5). Although erotic makeovers struggle with self-reflexivity, they certainly lay claim to Brontë, Austen, Wilde and others; postmodernity therefore remains a useful discourse for a discussion of neo-Victorian rewriting. Nevertheless, it is my contention that the erotic makeover is more an expression of the desire for money than it is the liberation of Brontë's desires or the realisation of the contingency of history. Indeed, twenty years after coining the term 'historiographic metafiction', Hutcheon's ongoing discussion of desire and adaptation introduced 'the capitalist desire for gain' as a prime catalyst for some adaptations. Considering the threat that adaptations can pose 'to the ownership of cultural and intellectual property', Hutcheon notes that postmodern appropriation – that is, work that 're-functions' original material (another name for 're-vision', the process I draw on here) – is often legally permitted as 'critical commentary' rather than 'illegal copying' (Hutcheon, 2012: 89). In this context, Clandestine Classics' vocabulary of desires released starts to look like legal safewording. Copyright law is labyrinthine and varies by country, but by every applicable measure the text of *Jane Eyre* is in the public domain.[6] Any additions, however, whether in the form of Cartwright's additions to *Jane Eyre*, or a scholarly introduction to the novel of the type published by Penguin or Oxford University Press, are protected under copyright.[7] In the simplest terms, publishers are able to sell copies of *Jane Eyre* that have cost them nothing for the source text. Self- or e-publishing, meanwhile, along with the rise of the Internet, has considerably reduced the cost of bringing a text to market. Although figures are unobtainable (when asked for this piece, Totally Bound declined to discuss sales figures), *Jane Eyre* has great financial potential as an erotic makeover and Charlotte Brontë has a vigorous financial afterlife. Charlotte's 'liberation' by Cartwright's pseudo-postmodern therapeutic intervention, clarified above, is revealed as nothing more than a sleight of hand to distract us from the fact that she has been resurrected in order to function as an out-of-copyright unique selling point.

The makeover, however, offers only one way of reimagining the Victorian. Kate Harrad's *James Eyre and Other Genderswitched Stories*

(2012) is a striking example of revising the nineteenth century without recourse to a wider postmodern framework. Like Clandestine Classics, Harrad makes very few changes to literary works in the public domain. She simply switches genders, renaming male protagonists as female, and female as male: Jane becomes James Eyre, appointed by Miss Rochester as a tutor to little Auguste. Unlike Clandestine Classics, however, Harrad's re-visioning technique openly acknowledges the need to use works that are 'out-of-copyright' (Harrad, 2012: 2), and her introduction to the anthology has a practical editorial tone that eschews Clandestine Classics' pseudo-postmodern vocabulary of restriction and release. Harrad's description is very much that of a writer in the online age: 'Creating a first draft is easy: I use gutenberg. org to acquire the text, then regender.com to do a rough gender swap. However, some editing is required after. For example, references to women having beards and men having babies have to be removed or at least made more ambiguous' (Harrad, 2012: 2–3). The regendering process – a simple 'find and replace' automatically processed by reg-ender.com – is to some extent removed from the complex transmedia processes occurring elsewhere in fan fiction. Nevertheless, Harrad's tone offers a new discursive context for discussing Victorian after-lives, one that acknowledges commercial as well as creative motiva-tions and offers a more honest assessment of appropriation. Unlike Cartwright's co-authorship, Harrad describes herself as the editor of her text, minimising her creative input and imparting a sharp contrast to Clandestine Classics' attempt at academic authority. Both Harrad's approach and the analysis in this chapter suggest that a new origin for the neo-Victorian should be considered, one that applies the generative explanations of the erotic makeover – financial, legal, postmodern – to the neo-Victorian novel. Like the makeover, the neo-Victorian refuses to abandon, as Harrad does, pretensions to authorial originality; this has interesting ramifications in relation to the commercial possibilities of Charlotte Brontë.

'Erotic makeover' vs. 'neo-Victorian adaptation': a shared commercial impulse

Suggesting that the pleasure in the neo-Victorian encounter – in any media form – has financial origins is very different to the usual approach to the neo-Victorian. Long before *Fifty Shades* made Anastasia a neo-Victorian consumer, critical responses explaining re-visions of the nineteenth century were resolutely literary in tone. One of the most persuasive is 're-visionary' fiction, defined not only as postmodern (due to the slippage inherent in the term, discussed above) but as having an impeccable literary heritage, being 'novels which "write back to" – indeed, "rewrite" canonical texts from the past, and hence call to account formative narratives that have arguably been central to the construction of "our" consciousness' (Widdowson, 2006: 491). Jean Rhys's *Wide Sargasso Sea* (1966) is 'the best known and prototypical' re-visionary novel, due to its 'attempts to revoice those silenced by previous fiction and thus written out of "history"' (Widdowson, 2006: 497). *Jane Eyre* is therefore a formative text par excellence, as Rhys's novel is accepted as a literary revision of the Victorian which has a particularly vibrant life in both critical and commercial UK culture. Neo-Victoriana has a claim on our hearts and minds; Cora Kaplan has written of the emotions triggered by Victorian novels, and particularly *Jane Eyre*, in the context of neo-Victorian novels 'condensing in their images or stories traumatic tropes and narratives which surprisingly continue to trigger strong affective responses which seem strangely excessive in relation to their catalyst' (2007: 16). Strong affective responses, however, not only allow Clandestine Classics to position the erotic makeover as re-visionary commentary but have also worked to muffle discussion of the commercial appeal of neo-Victorian fiction. Neo-Victorian novels sell in considerable numbers – the works of Sarah Waters and A. S. Byatt spring to mind – but there is little discussion of the genre's participation in the models of commerce described by Linda Hutcheon. Famous Victorian cultural figures of the type that Widdowson calls 'literary', such as Charles Dickens, Walter Scott, William Wordsworth, Thomas Carlyle and, specifically, Charlotte Brontë, possess a vast cultural capital and a strong commercial appeal. All of the authors mentioned have houses which are now preserved as chargeable tourist attractions; the Brontë parsonage at Haworth offers visitors 'everything from Brontë Original Unique Yorkshire Liqueur to Brontë fudge' (Watson, 2006: 107), just one of the literary spaces (others are Dickens World [now closed], Dove Cottage or Carlyle's House) in which canonical authors are simultaneously commercialised and memorialised. Yet neo-Victorian novels derived from the works of these figures are not understood to be commercial ventures. Understandably, in the context of literary criticism, academic assessment of the neo-Victorian makes little comment on the socio-economic circumstances of the genre's existence. At most, the academy refers to the genre's 'popular appeal' before contextualising neo-Victorian analyses in the postmodern terms of 'concealment/revelation' that Siemaszkiewicz borrows to discuss *Jane Eyre* (2012).[8]

It is rare to find a truly re-visionary neo-Victorian novel, however, as most draw on common perceptions of 'the Victorian', the 'crinolines, [...] bonnets, orphans or moustaches so big you can twirl them for hours', as one journalist had it (Ravenhill, 2009), rather than any one specific pre-textual nineteenth-century historical or fictional document.[9] D. M. Thomas's *Charlotte* is therefore unusual, drawing very specifically on *Jane Eyre*, and this 'reimagining' of a single specific Victorian text therefore provides an initial link between Thomas's *Charlotte* and the erotic makeover of *Jane Eyre*. *Charlotte*'s plot is multilayered and deliberately bewildering but can be teased out into four loose strands, the first involving a 'lost' manuscript purporting to be the work of Charlotte Brontë. Academic Miranda Stevenson narrates the second strand while visiting Martinique, during which she reveals she is the author of the 'lost' manuscript, written for her father when she was a teenager; 'an increasing urge to escape from reality into fiction' means that Miranda 'becomes' Brontë, scribbling into notebooks in Martinique bars (Thomas, 2001: 128). A third section, narrated by Miranda's father, gives way to a fourth strand – or perhaps just a rekindling of the first – a letter from the son of Edward Rochester and Bertha Mason, announcing the death of his lover, Jane Eyre. Both makeover and novel position 'Victorian' protagonists in sexually explicit episodes; both draw upon the same self-reflexive vocabulary of concealment and revelation, silence and speech, in their engagement with the long nineteenth century. As seen above, Clandestine Classics draws upon the vocabulary of the neo-Victorian re-visionary in order to lend intellectual gravitas to the erotic makeover's use of its pre-text. In turn, *Charlotte* uses the conceit of forged Brontë letters to deliver a postmodern swipe at concepts of literary genius. *Charlotte* fictionalises not only the conflation of author with text that I outlined above but also demonstrates a form of commercial re-vision in which Brontë was given a lively, sexually inclined afterlife well before any such generative discourse was given to justify the erotic makeover's appropriation of Charlotte's novels and desires.

Cartwright's appropriation of Brontë's authorial/textual/sexual identity is further complicated in *Charlotte*. Thomas does not assign himself a position of co-author or even editor. Unlike many other neo-Victorian novels, Thomas does not append an afterword explaining his motivation for revising the Victorian.[10] Nevertheless, the cover of both the first and second editions juxtaposes an intimate form of Brontë's name with Thomas's. Both covers use images of wind and surf to generate a sense of travel and transition. However, while the first edition depicts a decidedly equivocal windswept Victorian woman who could be either Jane Eyre or Charlotte, the second cover shows the torso of a topless woman in a string bikini.[11] The latter's holiday tone renders 'Charlotte' as tourist destination, an alternative to Haworth. As its title suggests, *Charlotte* is a neo-Victorian novel that conflates author with text and, in re-visionary terms, Thomas's novel keeps both its pre-texts in clear sight: both Brontë and *Jane Eyre* are textually present throughout. The first edition of the novel was titled *Charlotte: The Final Journey of Jane Eyre* (the subtitle was omitted from the second edition); *Charlotte*'s first line is 'Reader, I married him.' *Charlotte*'s constant commingling of authors, characters and texts is a persuasive commentary on the profitable pleasure of writing sex into the nineteenth century. I turn now, however, to the problematic aspects of commercialising an author's afterlife.

Charlotte is relatively unusual in that it is literary fiction with acknowledged commercial origins. Thomas makes no claims to the realisation of Brontë's repressed desires or the desire to revise the nineteenth century. Instead, his website explains that he 'was invited by a publisher to write an unorthodox continuation of *Jane Eyre*'.[12] 'Unorthodox' in this context occupies the same ground as Clandestine Classics' 'sex and fetish scenes'. In similar sexually charged tones to Clandestine Classics, the back matter presents re-visionary sexual encounters as *Charlotte*'s unique selling point: 'Both remarkable and surprising, it offers a darker, alternative ending to the story of Jane and Mr Rochester in the classic *Jane Eyre*' (Thomas, 2001: back matter). Explicit sex in the context of a neo-Victorian novel, however, is accepted as critical commentary on the Victorian, and *Charlotte* received positive critical reactions of the kind that would elude the Clandestine Classics *Jane Eyre*. Reviewers noted that 'Thomas skilfully pulls back the tissue of each life to reveal the layers beneath', and that his novel was 'much, much more than a sequel' as well as 'a wickedly irreverent antidote to earnest study' (quoted in Thomas, 2001: front matter). No mention is made of Thomas's commercial motive, though it is important to note that this silence emanates from critical quarters rather than the novelist. Textually, the erotic makeover's minimal additions are strikingly different from other neo-Victorian appropriative fictions – A. S. Byatt's *Possession* (1990), Will Self's *Dorian* (2002) or *Rustication* (2013) by Charles Palliser, for example – which mediate their engagement with the Victorian through a variety of parodic textual strategies, including the relocation of characters, the use of archetypes and intertextuality. These are the signals of both 'literary' historical

fiction and a postmodern writing back. As such, Thomas's novel is marketed in the postmodern terms to which Clandestine Classics aspires.
Indeed, *Charlotte* has been characterised as a palinode, or 'a text which
retracts, negates or contradicts that which has previously been stated',
and elsewhere Thomas is specifically positioned as a re-visionist invoking 'pathologies of sexuality, empire and slavery' (Gutleben, 2002: 11).
I do not mean to suggest that these readings are mistaken, just that they
shy away from acknowledging the commercial considerations of using
Brontë and her most famous novel as a stimulus for literary production.

Calling to mind Clandestine Classics' 'seamless reading experience',
Charlotte's re-vision of *Jane Eyre* includes a sexually active relationship
between Jane and Edward. Although refusing 'to draw a veil over the inti-
macies which transpire between a man and his wife' (Thomas, 2001: 16),
the narrative's tone gestures to the nineteenth century with euphemisms
such as 'union' and 'passionate embrace' in place of the BDSM-infused
vocabulary of the erotic makeover. Despite its knowing primness, the
novel nevertheless works within the neo-Victorian discourse that would
later be appropriated by Clandestine Classics: Victorian repression, elim-
inated by neo-Victorian release. Thomas's Jane realises that Edward is
impotent, and the intercourse they have had has been with his hands
and fingers, explaining her failure to conceive. *Jane Eyre*'s description of
Jane placing their firstborn into Rochester's arms is rewritten as 'romantic' wish fulfilment: 'Reader, this is a very different picture of my marriage from that which you were presented with in what I would call my
"romantic" version' (Thomas, 2001: 52). Jane's tacit acknowledgement that
she has deceived her reader has more than an echo of Siemaszkiewicz's
assertion as to what the Victorians would and would not permit. Jane's
sexual naivety is as Victorian for Thomas as it is for Siemaszkiewicz, a
shared conceit that allows both genres to position themselves as a sexual/
textual release.

Charlotte's Mr Rochester dies, and Jane leaves England in search of
her late husband's child. Rather than continue Jane's release via sexually explicit encounters – adopting the more familiar 'hidden history'
model of the re-visionary neo-Victorian (Widdowson, 2006: 492) – the
novel introduces what is apparently Brontë herself into the dialectic
encounter:

> I set about arranging our voyage; bought us both suitable clothes for the
> tropics; left all in the hands of Edward's agent. On a morning of good,
> sweet English rain, we crossed the English Channel to Calais, the first
> stage of our long journey to Martinique. [...]

> Soon after arrival on the island, I was sitting at a table opposite a plain, bespectacled Martinique girl nervously checking a list. 'Charlotte Brontë?' she asked, and I nodded.
>
> (Thomas, 2001: 79, 81)

Charlotte presents us with a disorientating re-visionary transmutation. The first quotation is undoubtedly the voice of Jane and the end of the revised *Jane Eyre*. How to explain, then, the arrival of Charlotte on Martinique? Her surroundings give no clue: the 'coach journey', 'hotel', even the 'juice and coffee in the restaurant' are oddly ahistorical (Thomas, 2001: 81, 83). Neo-Victorian scholarship might well consider this a postmodern collapse of the historical distance between Victorians and Moderns, an example of Victoriana's vigorous afterlife.[13] This does not necessarily take into account the pleasure generated by appropriating Brontë's identity in a sexual context. Appropriation is complicated by 'Charlotte's' explicit sex with Jerry, a beach waiter, where she speaks in a West Country accent that cannot belong to one born in Yorkshire: 'that's right, fuck me, my 'andsome! Get it right in there … Bite my neck, my breasts, my lover … I d'like [*sic*] that…' (Thomas, 2001: 83). 'Charlotte' is Miranda Stevenson, a personification of a complex reading relationship with a celebrity author. Visiting Martinique for an academic conference, bureaucratic confusion on the part of the 'bespectacled Martinique girl' with the list leads to Miranda checking into her hotel as Charlotte Brontë. An academic who studies Brontë, she is attending a conference on 'Liberated Women of Europe' (*L'Europe des Femmes Libérées*), and her paper addresses not *Jane Eyre* but asks, 'Who is this Charlotte Brontë?' (Thomas, 2001: 138). Through both sex and text, it is Brontë's celebrity and cultural capital rather than her novel which are the generating power of Thomas's novel. *Charlotte's* sex scene appears to give readers what they want (certainly what Clandestine Classics insist that they want) before revealing that the desired living, breathing Victorian-but-modern Charlotte has always been plain old modern Miranda. *Charlotte* appears to offer a clairvoyant communication with Charlotte but was always a jab at those readers who want to see long-dead authors resurrected with modern desires and motivations. Thomas could not consciously have foreseen the Clandestine Classics *Jane Eyre*; his novel, however, summarises the socio-economic conditions that allow the erotic makeover to attempt a commercial afterlife.

In many ways, this chapter is less a discussion of the afterlives of Charlotte Brontë, Jane Eyre or *Jane Eyre*, and more about the motivations and rewards in reimagining the Victorian. Brontë functions as a source of income and profit as well as pleasure. My reading here suggests that Thomas's narrative conflation of Miranda Stevenson with Brontë serves as a commentary on the commercial imperatives of the afterlife. Stevenson not only has sex as Charlotte but writes as her, too, in moments that acknowledge the financial gains to be made from Brontë's cultural capital. *Charlotte*'s first strand, the alternate ending of *Jane Eyre*, is revealed as a forgery created by a teenage Miranda angry at her widowed father's new romantic relationship. The forged 'Brontë original' is kept by Miranda's father in his safe, a nod by the novel to the commercial market for these Victorian authors. Indeed, when Brontë's letters to fans of *Jane Eyre* sell for thousands, one can only speculate at the lucrative potential of Miranda's talent for mimicry (Anon., 2013).[14] To return to my opening pages, however, Miranda's urge to imitate cannot be explained simply as 'Brontë sells'; the psycho-textual process that I defined earlier returns at this moment, as Miranda suggests 'creating alternative endings to nineteenth-century novels – to bring out some of the repressed issues' (Thomas, 2001: 174). Like Clandestine Classics, Brontë's afterlife starts to be offered as a distinctly therapeutic process for both writer and reader. As both adult and teenager, Miranda seeks to place Charlotte back on the couch in order to provide both money and psychological balm. *Charlotte* precedes the development of the erotic makeover by some years, but the simultaneously commercial, therapeutic and historicising fictions that she wants to write, and the discourses that are used to explain them, have the potential to illuminate the shared commercial origins of both the erotic makeover and the neo-Victorian novel, an origin that rarely features in the scholarship of 'legitimate' neo-Victoriana. In considering a tiny proportion of the numerous *Jane Eyre* adaptations (see Appendix), this chapter can only ever be a starting point in considering the commercial afterlife of the Victorian. Nevertheless, it is clear that emerging adaptive literary forms, and growing transmedia creation and distribution, such as the erotic makeover and fan fiction like *Fifty Shades of Grey*, has significant potential to inform our readings of both the neo-Victorian and its accompanying scholarly discourses. The erotic makeover may be of limited literary value in and of itself, and its claims of sexual/textual release remain unconvincing; nevertheless, by initiating a discussion of Victoriana's commercial underpinnings, it raises awareness of the wider economic impulses at work in contemporary literary culture.

Notes

1 'Total E-Bound Publishing' became 'Totally Bound' during the writing of this chapter, and the book series became 'Classics Exposed'. Founder Claire Siemaszkiewicz's *Guardian* profile, created in July 2012, credits her as the founder of 'Total E-Bound Publishing, the UK's largest publisher of erotic romance fiction'. 'Profile: Claire Siemaszkiewicz', *The Guardian*, July 2012, www. theguardian.com/profile/claire-siemaszkiewicz (accessed 15 September 2014).

2 Almost all neo-Victorian critiques, popular and academic, function in this way, but specific examples are the three significant monographs on the genre: Heilmann and Llewellyn (2010), Boehm-Schnitker and Gruss (2014) and Kohlke and Gutleben's series on the neo-Victorian, published by Rodopi/ Brill.

3 Added to the *Oxford English Dictionary* in 2004, fan fiction is defined as 'fiction, usually fantasy or science fiction, written by a fan rather than a professional author, *esp.* that based on already-existing characters from a television series, book, film, etc.'

4 Arnold's conflation of author and text is clear: 'Why is *Villette* disagreeable? Because *the writer's mind* contains nothing but hunger, rebellion, and rage, and therefore that is all she can, in fact, put into her book' (Arnold, 1901: 33, emphasis mine).

5 The website of Lesley A. Hall, a noted historian in the field of gender and sexuality, gives an excellent overview: www.lesleyahall.net (accessed 25 September 2014).

6 For a recent discussion, see Schwabach (2011).

7 With thanks to the Intellectual Property Office's clarification of the Copyright, Designs and Patents Act 1988. The 1847 printed copy of *Jane Eyre* remained in copyright for seventy years after Brontë's death; copyright of the manuscript would have been retained by any beneficiaries of Brontë's estate but again, for seventy years.

8 The academic response that comes closest to exploring financial generative impulses is Palmer (2008).

9 For a definition of 'pre-text', see Humpherys (2002).

10 Neo-Victorian novels commonly include either a fore- or afterword giving details of authorial motivation and, frequently, research activities: Sarah Waters' *Fingersmith* (2002), Margaret Atwood's *Alias Grace* (1996), Michel Faber's *The Crimson Petal and the White* (2002) and A. S. Byatt's *The Children's Book* (2009) are all popular examples.

11 The image is *The Beach Is Our Shop Window* (1992) by photographer Christopher Pillitz, www.christopherpillitz.com/projects/brazil_incarnate/ (accessed 17 December 2015).

12 D. M. Thomas, 'Novels: Charlotte', www.dmthomasonline.net/articles_ 123642.html (accessed 5 October 2014).

13 See Kucich and Sadoff (2000) and Llewellyn (2008).
14 In 2015, the Brontë Society discovered a short story and poem authored
    by Charlotte Brontë. These unpublished works were found inside a novel
    owned by Maria Brontë, which the society had purchased for over £200,000
    (Flood 2015).

References

Anon. (2012) 'Reader, I spanked him …: classic novels get steamy 21st century
    make-over', *Clandestine Classics*, 17 July, http://clandestineclassics.blogspot.
    co.uk/p/press.html (accessed 12 April 2014).
Anon. (2013) 'Charlotte Brontë letter sells for £24,000', *The Telegraph*, 4 September,
    www.telegraph.co.uk/history/10286358/Charlotte-Bronte-letter-sells
    -for-24000-at-auction.html (accessed 5 January 2014).
Anon. (2015) '*Fifty Shades of Grey* is most successful 18-rated film ever', *The
    Telegraph*, 24 February, www.telegraph.co.uk/culture/film/film-news/11431297/
    Fifty-Shades-of-Grey-is-most-successful-18-rated-film-ever.html (accessed 20
    August 2016).
Arnold, Matthew (1901) *The Letters of Matthew Arnold, 1848–1888*, ed. George
    W. E. Russell, 2nd edn, London: Macmillan.
Ashbee, Henry Spencer (1970) *Forbidden Books of the Victorians*, ed. Peter Fryer,
    London: Odyssey Press.
Boehm-Schnitker, Nadine and Susanne Gruss (eds.) (2014) *Neo-Victorian
    Literature and Culture: Immersions and Revisitations*, Abingdon and New York:
    Routledge.
Brontë, Charlotte and Sierra Cartwright (2012) *Jane Eyre*, Lincoln: Total-E-Bound.
Burstein, Miriam (2012) 'Clandestine Classics: *Jane Eyre*', *The Little Professor*, 5
    October, http://littleprofessor.typepad.com/the_little_professor/2012/10/
    clandestine-classics-jane-eyre-.html (accessed 12 May 2014).
Flood, Alison (2014) '*Fifty Shades of Grey* trilogy has sold 100m copies world-
    wide', *The Guardian*, 27 February, www.theguardian.com/books/2014/feb/27/
    fifty-shades-of-grey-book-100m-sales (accessed 4 March 2014).
—— (2015) 'Unseen Charlotte Brontë story and poem discovered', *The Guardian*,
    12 November 2015, www.theguardian.com/books/2015/nov/12/unseen-
    charlotte-bronte-story-and-poem-discovered (accessed 14 November 2015).
Gilbert, Sandra M. (1998) '*Jane Eyre* and the art of furious lovemaking',
    Novel: A Forum on Fiction, 31:3, 351–72.
Gold, Tanya (2005) 'Reader, I shagged him: why Charlotte Brontë was a filthy
    minx', *The Guardian*, 25 March, www.theguardian.com/books/2005/mar/25/
    classics.charlottebronte (accessed 20 May 2014).
Gutleben, Christian (2002) 'Palinodes, palindromes and palimpsests: strategies
    of deliberate self-contradiction in postmodern British fiction', *Miscelánea*,
    26, 11–20.

Harrad, Kate (2012) *James Eyre and Other Genderswitched Stories*, CreateSpace Independent Publishing Platform.

Heilmann, Ann, and Mark Llewellyn (2010) *Neo-Victorianism: The Victorians in the Twenty-First Century, 1999–2009*, Basingstoke: Palgrave Macmillan.

Humpherys, Anne (2002) 'The afterlife of the Victorian novel: novels about novels', in Patrick Brantlinger and William B. Thesing (eds.), *A Companion to the Victorian Novel*, Oxford: Blackwell, pp. 442–57.

Hutcheon, Linda (1988) *A Poetics of Postmodernism: History, Theory, Fiction*, London and New York: Routledge.

—— (1989) *The Politics of Postmodernism*, London and New York: Routledge.

—— (2012) *A Theory of Adaptation*, 2nd edn, London and New York: Routledge.

Irvine, Chris (2012) 'Sir Salman Rushdie: "*Fifty Shades of Grey* makes *Twilight* look like *War and Peace*"', *The Telegraph*, 9 October, www.telegraph.co.uk/culture/books/booknews/9596577/Sir-Salman-Rushdie-Fifty-Shades-of-Grey-makes-Twilight-look-like-War-and-Peace.html (accessed 1 March 2014).

James, E. L. (2012) *Fifty Shades of Grey*, London: Arrow Books.

Llewellyn, Mark (2008) 'What is Neo-Victorian Studies?' *Neo-Victorian Studies*, 1:1, 164–84.

Kaplan, Cora (2007) *Victoriana: Histories, Fictions, Criticisms*, Edinburgh: Edinburgh University Press.

Kohlke, Marie-Luise (2014) 'Mining the neo-Victorian vein: prospecting for gold, buried treasure and uncertain metal', in Nadine Boehm-Schnitker and Susanne Gruss (eds.), *Neo-Victorian Literature and Culture: Immersions and Revisitations*, Abingdon and New York: Routledge, pp. 21–37.

Kucich, John and Dianne F. Sadoff (eds.) (2000) *Victorian Afterlife: Postmodern Culture Rewrites the Nineteenth Century*, Minneapolis, Minn.: University of Minnesota Press.

Kvistad, Erika (2013) 'Scenes of unveiling: reading sex writing in Charlotte Brontë', *Writing from Below*, 1:2, 31–8, www.lib.latrobe.edu.au/ojs/index.php/wfb/article/view/426 (accessed 20 August 2016).

Noah, Sherina (2012) 'Oh Mr Darcy! *Pride and Prejudice* among classic novels to receive erotic makeover', *The Independent*, 17 July, www.independent.co.uk/arts-entertainment/books/news/oh-mr-darcy-pride-and-prejudice-among-classic-novels-to-receive-erotic-makeover-7946364.html (accessed 25 September 2014).

O'Hagan, Andrew (2012) 'Travelling southwards', *London Review of Books*, 34:14, 29–31.

Palmer, Paulina (2008) '"She began to show me the words she had written, one by one": lesbian reading and writing practices in the fiction of Sarah Waters', *Women: A Cultural Review*, 19:1, 69–86.

Ravenhill, Mark (2009) 'So the Victorian TV drama has gone out of fashion? Don't be fooled. The bonnet will be back', *The Guardian*, 19 July, www.theguardian.com/culture/2009/jan/19/television-bbc (accessed 26 October 2015).

Schwabach, Aaron (2011) *Fan Fiction and Copyright: Outsider Works and Intellectual Property Protection*, Farnham: Ashgate.

Siemaszkiewicz, Claire (2012) 'Why we're putting the "missing" sex scenes back into Charlotte Brontë', *The Guardian*, www.theguardian.com/commentisfree/2012/jul/17/missing-sex-scenes-charlotte-bronte (accessed 26 September 2014).

Stanley, Allessandra (2012) 'Glass slipper as fetish', *New York Times*, 2 April, www.nytimes.com/2012/04/03/books/fifty-shades-of-grey-s-and-m-cinderella.html (accessed 24 September 2014).

Thomas, D. M. (2001) *Charlotte*, London: Duckbacks.

Waters, Sarah (1999) *Tipping the Velvet*, London: Virago.

Watson, Nicola J. (2006) *The Literary Tourist*, Basingstoke: Palgrave Macmillan.

Widdowson, Peter (2006) 'Writing back: contemporary re-visionary fiction', *Textual Practice*, 20:3, 491–507.

Appendix: Charlotte Brontë's cultural legacy, 1848–2016

Kimberley Braxton

This appendix builds upon and extends the works of D. M. Nudd (1991), Patsy Stoneman (1996, 2007 and 2013), H. Philip Bolton (2000), Lucasta Miller (2001), Christine Alexander and Margaret Smith (2003), and Patricia Ingham (2006). My research also draws upon the following online resources: the Internet Movie Database (www.imdb.com), the British Film Institute website (www.bfi.org.uk), Amazon (www.amazon.co.uk) and the extensive online library of Chawton House (http://chawtn.cirqahosting.com).

Tracing attributions and influence across 169 years, from the publication of *Jane Eyre* (1847) to Charlotte Brontë's bicentenary in 2016, is a difficult task, and there will inevitably be omissions and overlooked works in what follows. These lacunae are, presumably, most numerous in my account of early stage and film adaptations, where the archival record is less complete and certain. In the case of our contemporary moment, omissions are due to the proliferation of self-published works and fan fiction that respond to the Brontës' life and work. But there has been an attempt to capture this wide variety. Brontë bicentenaries, spanning 2016 to 2020, have produced a continuous stream of publications and productions inspired by the family. Therefore, this appendix can only hope to offer a snapshot of what is available at this time of reflection and change in the Brontës' legacies and afterlives.

I: Inspired by Charlotte Brontë's work

Film

Jane Eyre (1909) Italian silent film (see Stoneman, 2008).
Jane Eyre (1910) Italian silent film (see Stoneman, 2008).

Jane Eyre (1910), dir. Theodore Marston, Thanhouser Film Corporation. Notes: There is some debate about the directorial credit for this film. However, Marston is supported by Ingham and Stoneman.

Jane Eyre (1914), dir. Frank H. Crane, Imp-Universal Pictures.

Jane Eyre (1914), dir. Martin Faust, Whitman Features Company.

The Castle of Thornfield (1915), Savoia Film.

Jane Eyre (1915) Alan Hale as Rochester.

Jane Eyre (1915) Richard Tucker as Rochester.

Jane Eyre (1915) Conway Teale as Rochester.

Jane Eyre (1915), dir. Travers Vale, Biograph Company.

Jane Eyre (1918), dir. Riccardo Tolentino.

Woman and Wife (1918), dir. Edward José, Select Pictures.

The Orphan of Lowood (1920) Hungarian silent film.

Jane Eyre (1921), dir. Hugo Ballin, Hugo Ballin Productions and W. W. Hodkinson Corporation.

Shirley (1922), dir. A. V. Bramble, Ideal.

Die Waise von Lowood (1926), dir. Curtis Bernhardt, Sternheim Film.

Jane Eyre (1934), dir. Christy Cabanne, Monogram Pictures.

South Riding (1937), dir. Victor Saville, Victor Saville Productions and London Film Productions. Note: Winifred Holtby's original novel, and this subsequent adaptation, are heavily influenced by *Jane Eyre*.

Intermezzo (1939), dir. Gregory Ratoff, Selznick International Pictures. Note: Released in UK as *Escape to Happiness*.

Jane Eyre (1939), dir. Edward Sobol, NCB.

When Tomorrow Comes (1939), dir. John M. Stahl, Universal Pictures.

Rebecca (1940), dir. Alfred Hitchcock, Selznick International Pictures.

I Walked With a Zombie (1943), dir. Jacques Tourneur, RKO Radio Pictures.

Jane Eyre (1943), dir. Robert Stevenson, Twentieth Century Fox Film Corporation.

The Seventh Veil (1945), dir. Compton Bennett, Ortus Films and Sydney Box Productions.

Sangdil (1952), dir. R. C. Talwar, Talwar Films.

Jane Eyre (1952), dir. Jack Gage, CBS.

Serenade (1956), dir. Anthony Mann, Warner Bros.

Interlude (1957), dir. Douglas Sirk, Universal International Pictures.

Jane Eyre (1968), dir. Giorgos Lois.

Interlude (1968), dir. Kevin Billington, Columbia Pictures Corporation and Domino Films.

Jane Eyre (1970), dir. Delbert Mann, British Lion Pictures.

Orlando (1993), dir. Sally Potter, Adventure Pictures, Lenfilm Studio and Mikado Film. Note: Stoneman (1996) identifies a *Jane Eyre* sequence in this adaptation of Virginia Woolf's novel.

Wide Sargasso Sea (1993), dir. John Duigan, Laughing Kookaburra Productions and Sargasso Productions.

Jane Eyre (1996), dir. Franco Zeffirelli, Cineritino S.r.L., Flach Film and Mediaset.
Jane Eyre (2011), dir. Cary Joji Fukunaga, Focus Films, BBC Films and Ruby Films.

Television, radio, etc.

Jane Eyre (1931), prod. Howard Rose, BBC Radio.
Jane Eyre (1956), prod. Campbell Logan, BBC Television.
Jane Eyre (1957), dir. Lamont Johnson, NBC.
Villette (1957), prod. Barbara Burnham, BBC Television.
Jane Eyre (1957), dir. Anton Giulio Majano, RAI Radiotelevisione Italiana.
Jane Eyre (1958), dir. Peter Hoen, Nederlandse Christlijke Radio-Vereniging.
Jane Eyre (1961), dir. Marc Daniels, CBS.
Jane Eyre (1963), dir. Rex Tucker, BBC Television.
Villette (1970), dir. Moira Armstrong, BBC Television.
Jane Eyre (1970), dir. Delbert Mann, Omnibus Productions and Sagittarius Productions.
Jane Eyre (1973), dir. Joan Craft, BBC Television.
Jane Eyre (1983), dir. Julian Amyes, BBC Television.
A Consoling Blue (1985) by Michelene Wandor, prod. Cherry Cookson, BBC Radio.
Star Trek: Voyager (1995), Season 1, Episodes 13 ('Cathexis') and 16 ('Learning Curve'), and Season 2, Episode 8 ('Persistence of Vision'), dir. Kim Friedman, David Livingston and James L. Conway. Paramount Pictures. Note: in these episodes, Captain Janeway participates in a 'holonovel' (simulated on the ship's holodeck, filename 'Janeway Lambda 1') inspired by *Jane Eyre* and other Victorian novels.
Jane Eyre (1997), dir. Robert Young, A&E Television Networks and London Weekend Television.
Villette (1999), dir. Catherine Bailey, by James Friel, BBC Radio 4.
Jane Eyre (2006), dir. Susanna White, BBC Television and WGBH.
Wide Sargasso Sea (2006), dir. Brendan Maher, BBC Wales and Kudos Film and Television.
Villette (2009), dir. Tracey Neale, by Rachel Joyce, BBC Radio 4.
The Autobiography of Jane Eyre (2013–14) Transmedia web series.
Shirley (2014), by Rachel Joyce, BBC Radio 4.
A Very British Romance with Lucy Worsley (2015) Episode 2, dir. Rachel Jardine, BBC Television.

Novels, poetry, etc.

Barry, Jane (n.d.) 'Mr Rochester' (quoted in Stoneman, 2008).
Brontë, Anne (1849) *The Tenant of Wildfell Hall*.
Craik, Dinah Mulock (1850) *Olive*.

Craik, Dinah Mulock (1853) *Agatha's Husband.*
Kavanagh, Julia (1853) *Daisy Burns.*
Gaskell, Elizabeth (1855) *North and South.*
Kavanagh, Julia (1855) *Grace Lee.*
Browning, Elizabeth Barrett (1857) *Aurora Leigh.*
Kavanagh, Julia (1858) *Adèle: A Tale.*
Braddon, Mary Elizabeth (1862) *Lady Audley's Secret.*
Warboise, Emma (1865) *Thorneycroft Hall.*
Broughton, Rhoda (1867) *Cometh Up As a Flower.*
James, Henry (1898) *The Turn of the Screw.*
Dane, Clemence [Winifred Ashton] (1917) *Regiment of Women.*
von Arnim, Elizabeth (1921) *Vera.*
Holtby, Winifred (1936) *South Riding.*
Lehmann, Rosamond (1936) *The Weather in the Streets.*
Du Maurier, Daphne (1938) *Rebecca.*
Allingham, Margery (1945) 'Wanted: someone innocent'. In *Deadly Duo.*
Taylor, Elizabeth (1945) *At Mrs Lippincote's.*
Taylor, Elizabeth (1946) *Palladian.*
Towers, Frances (1949) *Tea with Mr Rochester.*
Brand, Christianna (1950) *Cat and Mouse.*
Holt, Victoria (1961) *Mistress of Mellyn.*
Murdoch, Iris (1963) *The Unicorn.*
Rhys, Jean (1966) *Wide Sargasso Sea.*
Drabble, Margaret (1969) *The Waterfall.*
Angelou, Maya (1969) *I Know Why the Caged Bird Sings.*
Spark, Muriel (1971) *Not to Disturb.*
Lessing, Doris (1972) *The Four-Gated City.*
Jhabvala, Ruth Prawer (1975) *Heat and Dust.*
Naipaul, V. S. (1975) *Guerillas.*
Greenwald, Sheila (1980) *It All Began with Jane Eyre or The Secret Life of Franny Dillman.*
Weldon, Fay (1983) *The Life and Loves of a She-Devil.*
George, Catherine (1984) *Devil Within.*
Comyns, Barbara (1985) *The Juniper Tree.*
Winterson, Jeanette (1985) *Oranges Are Not the Only Fruit.*
Dangarembga, Tsitsi (1988) *Nervous Conditions.*
Swindells, Robert (1989) *Follow A Shadow.*
Byatt, A. S. (1990) *Possession.*
Kydd, Robbie (1991) *The Quiet Stranger.*
Power, Maggie (1994) *Lily.*
Dedeaux, P. N. (1996) *An English Education.*
Thomas, D. M. (2000) *Charlotte: the Final Journey of Jane Eyre.*
Braddon, Mary Elizabeth and Jennifer Carnell (2001) *One Fatal Moment and Other Stories and at the Shrine of Jane Eyre.*

Fforde, Jasper (2001) *The Eyre Affair*.

Tennant, Emma (2002) *Thornfield Hall: Jane Eyre's Hidden Story*.

Faber, Michel (2002) *The Crimson Petal and the White*.

Rego, Paula (2002) *Jane Eyre*.

Boylan, Clare (2003) *Emma Brown*.

Tennant, Emma (2003) *Adèle: Jane Eyre's Hidden Story*.

Jones, Gail (2004) *Sixty Lights*.

Vandever, Jennifer (2005) *The Brontë Project*.

Brontë, Charlotte, Anna Claybourne and Bob Harvey (2006) *Jane Eyre: Usborne Classics Retold*.

Tennant, Emma (2006) *The French Dancer's Bastard: The Story of Adèle from Jane Eyre*.

Brontë, Charlotte and Amy Corzine (2008) *Jane Eyre: The Graphic Novel*.

Moise, Claire (2009) *Adele, Grace and Celine: The Other Women of Jane Eyre*.

Newark, Elizabeth (2009) *Jane Eyre's Daughter*.

Jeschke, Melanie M. (2009) *Jillian Dare*.

Woodward, Kay (2009) *Jane Airhead*.

Bennett, Kimberley A. (2010) *Jane Rochester*.

Brontë, Charlotte and Sherri Browning Erwin (2010) *Jane Slayre*.

Kohler, Sheila (2010) *Becoming Jane Eyre*.

Bradley, Tara (2011) *Jane Eyre's Husband – The Life Edward Rochester*.

Holland, Clair (2011) *Jane Eyre's Rival: The Real Mrs Rochester*.

Jones, Ken (2011) *The Memoirs of Edward Rochester*.

Keffer, Chrissy Breen (2011) *An American Heir: A Modern Retelling of Jane Eyre*.

Niemann, J. L. (2011) *Rochester: Consummation – The Continuing Story Inspired by Charlotte Brontë's 'Jane Eyre'*.

Bailey, Hilary (2012) *Mrs Rochester*.

Brontë, Charlotte and Eve Sinclair (2012) *Jane Eyre Laid Bare*.

Brontë, Charlotte and Karena Rose (2012) *Jane Eyrotica*.

Brontë, Charlotte and Sierra Cartwright (2012) *Clandestine Classics: Jane Eyre*.

Adam, Jennifer (2012) *Little Miss Brontë: Jane Eyre*.

Slan, Joanna Campbell (2012) *Death of a Schoolgirl (Jane Eyre Chronicles)*.

Livesey, Margot (2012) *The Flight of Gemma Hardy*.

Slan, Joanna Campbell (2013) *Death of a Dowager (Jane Eyre Chronicles)*.

Ashworth, A. J (ed.) (2013) *Red Room: New Short Stories Inspired by the Brontës*.

Niemann, J. L. (2013) *Rochester: Redemption – The Continuing Story Inspired by Charlotte Brontë's 'Jane Eyre'*.

Ilkley and Calderdale Young Writers (2013) *Inspired by the Brontës*.

Rigel, L. K. (2013) *My Mr. Rochester: Mesrour (Jane Eyre Retold, vol. 1)*.

Rigel, L. K. (2014) *My Mr. Rochester: Master (Jane Eyre Retold, vol. 2)*.

Rigel, L. K. (2014) *My Mr. Rochester: Trickster (Jane Eyre Retold, vol. 3)*.

Rigel, L. K. (2014) *My Mr. Rochester: Lover (Jane Eyre Retold, vol. 4)*.

Rigel, L. K. (2014) *My Mr. Rochester: Liberator (Jane Eyre Retold, vol. 5)*.

Gray, Luccia (2014) *All Hallows at Eyre Hall.*
Stubbs, Jane (2014) *Thornfield Hall.*
Carrie Sessarego (2014) *Pride, Prejudice and Popcorn: TV and Film Adaptations of Pride and Prejudice, Wuthering Heights, and Jane Eyre.*
Carrie Sessarego (2014) *Jurassic Jane Eyre: The Dinosaur Turned Me Lesbian.*
Gray, Luccia (2015) *Twelfth Night at Eyre Hall.*
Ortberg, Mallory (2015) *Texts from Jane Eyre: And Other Conversations with Your Favourite Literary Authors.*
Reay, Katherine (2015) *The Brontë Plot.*
Chevalier, Tracy (ed.) (2016) *Reader, I Married Him – Stories Inspired by Jane Eyre.*
Cory, Charlotte (2016) *A Visitorian Jane Eyre.*

Stage plays, musicals, operas, etc.

Turner, Joseph W. (1848) 'The Little Orphans Song'.
Courtney, John (1848) *Jane Eyre or The Secrets of Thornfield Manor*, London: Victoria Theatre.
Brougham, J. (1849, 1856) *Jane Eyre*, New York.
Jane Eyre (1850) New York City: Bowery.
Birch-Pfeiffer, Charlotte (1854) *Jane Eyre.*
Die Waise Von Lowood (1854) New York City: Stadt Theatre.
Bell, Currer (1866) *Jane Eyre*, St Louis: Olympic Theatre.
Tayleure, Clifton W. (1867, 1871, 1874) *Jane Eyre; or, The Orphan of Lowood.*
Brougham, J. (1867, 1868) *Jane Eyre*, London: New Surrey Theatre.
Birch-Pfeiffer, Charlotte (1870) *Jane Eyre; or, The Orphan of Lowood*, New York, Fourteenth Street Theatre.
Jane Eyre (1871) New York City, New Stadt Theatre.
Jane Eyre (1872) Chicago, McVicker's Theatre.
Thompson, Charlotte (1873) *Jane Eyre*, New York City: Union Square Theatre.
Houghton, J. S. (1874) *Jane Eyre*, Philadelphia.
Jane Eyre (1874) New York City, Union Square Theatre.
Jane Eyre (1874) New York City, Mrs Conway's.
Jane Eyre; or, The Orphan of Lowood (1875) Boston Theatre, Boston, MA.
Jane Eyre (1875) St Louis, De Bar's Grand Opera House.
Thompson, Charlotte (1875) *Jane Eyre*, New York City, Globe.
Jane Eyre (1875) New York City, Union Square Theatre.
Jane Eyre (1876) New York City, Brooklyn Theatre.
Thompson, Charlotte (1876) *Jane Eyre*, Buffalo and New York City: Academy of Music.
Die Waise Von Lowood (1876–77, 1878) New York City, Germania.
Clarendon Dramatic Society (1876) *Jane Eyre.* New York City, Central Hall.
Dickinson, Anna (1876) *Jane Eyre*, New York.
von Hering, Heringen (1877) *Jane Eyre*, Coventry.
Jane Eyre (1877) New York City: Academy of Music.

Jane Eyre (1877) New York City: Wallack's National Theatre.
The Governess (1878) New York City: Broadway.
Paul, T. H. (1879) *Jane Eyre*, Oldham: Adelphi.
Die Waise Von Lowood (1879) New York City: Brooklyn Athenaeum.
Willing, James, J. T. Douglass and Leonard Rae (1879, 1882) *Jane Eyre or Poor Relations.*
Jane Eyre (1880, 1882–85, 1897) New York City: Grand Opera House.
Wills, W. G. (1882) *Jane Eyre*, London: Globe Theatre.
Jane Eyre (1883) New York City, Mount Morris Theatre.
Thompson, Charlotte (1883) *Jane Eyre*, New York, 23rd Street Theatre.
Thompson, Charlotte (1884) *Jane Eyre*, New York City, Star.
Jane Eyre (1884) New York City, Thalia Theatre.
Thompson, Charlotte (1885) *Jane Eyre*, Iowa: Fort Madison.
Jane Eyre (1886) Harlem, Theatre Comique.
Thompson, Charlotte (1887) *Jane Eyre*, New York City, Forepaugh's Theatre and Museum.
Jane Eyre (1888) New York City, Lee Avenue Academy of Music.
Jane Eyre (1888) New York City, Star.
Jane Eyre (1888) New York City, People's Theatre.
Jane Eyre (1888) New York City, Fourteenth Street.
Jane Eyre (1889) New York City, Brooklyn Theatre.
Jane Eyre (1889) New York City, Jacob's Lyceum.
Die Waise Von Lowood (1889) New York City, Amberg.
Jane Eyre (1890) New York City, Amphion Academy.
Lewis, Mrs Walter (1900) *Jane Eyre.*
Jane Eyre (1905) New York City, Academy.
Leffingwell, Miron (1909) *Jane Eyre.*
Blaney, Charles E. (1910) *Jane Eyre.*
Haswell, Percy (1914) *Jane Eyre.*
Jane Eyre (1915) New Orleans.
Kirkbride, W. H. C. (1915) *The Master of Thornfield.*
Shomer, Rose Bachelis and Miriam Shomer-Zunser (1920) *The Master of Thornfield.*
Stone, P. M., arr. (1929) *Dramatic Readings from 'Jane Eyre' (Charlotte Brontë).*
Stone, P. M., arr. (1929) *Dramatic Readings from 'Villette' (Charlotte Brontë).*
Birkett, Phyllis (1929, 1931) *Jane Eyre*, Keighley.
Stone, Phyllis M. (1929) *Parish Plays.*
Carleton, Majorie Chalmers (1936) *Jane Eyre by Charlotte Brontë: A Dramatisation in Three Acts.*
Jerome, Helen (1936, 1937, 1938, 1940, 1942, 1943) *Jane Eyre: A Drama of Passion in Three Acts.*
Carleton, Marjorie (1938) *Jane Eyre*, New York City, Friends' Meeting House.
Phelps, Pauline (1941) *Jane Eyre*, Iowa.

Brandon, Dorothy (1944) *The Master of Thornfield*, Oxford.
Kendall, Jane and Anne Martens (1945) *Jane Eyre*, Chicago.
Tyler, Brian (1954) *Jane Eyre*, England Touring Production.
Jane Eyre (1955) Oakwell Hall, Dewsbury Pioneers Amateur Operatic Society.
Hartford, Huntingdon (1956) *Jane Eyre*, New York.
Cox, Constance (1959) *Jane Eyre, A Play from the Novel by Charlotte Brontë.*
Jane Eyre (1959) Hollywood Playhouse.
Shaper, Hal and Roy Harley Lewis (1961) *Jane*, London: Theatre Royal.
Jepson, Alfred (1962) 'Rochester's Song to Jane Eyre'.
Holroyd, George Henry (1964) *Plays from Literature ... Jane Eyre from the Novel by Charlotte Brontë.*
Cannon, John (1973) *Jane Eyre*, Crewe.
Robinson, Noel (1974) *Glasstown: A Play.*
Crompton, Margaret (1978) *Shadows of Villette*, Macclesfield, New Playwrights' Network.
Kontaibo, Kazue (1978) *Jane Eyre*, Japan.
Hamilton, Lionel (1978) *Jane Eyre.*
Martin, Christopher (1983) *Jane Eyre*, Stoke-on-Trent, Victoria Theatre.
Myerson, Jonathan (1984) *Jane Eyre*, Harrogate and York.
Davis, Ted (1984) *Jane Eyre*, Maine, Theatre Monmouth.
Haughey, Sheila (1985) *Jane Eyre*, Cheltenham.
Vance, Charles (1985) *Jane Eyre*, England Touring Production.
Wharton, Sylvia (1985) *The Childhood of Jane Eyre*, Belgrade Theatre, Coventry Studio Production, Keighley Playhouse.
Coe, Peter (1986) *Jane Eyre*, Chichester Festival.
Weldon, Fay and Helena Kaut-Howson (1986) *Jane Eyre*, Birmingham Repertory Theatre.
Reade, Paul (1987) *Jane Eyre.*
Coe, Peter (1987) *Jane Eyre.*
Lucas, Valerie and David Cottis (1988) *Shadow in the Glass*, Cardiff: Sherman Arena.
Marten, Annette (1989) *Jane Eyre*, Eastern Michigan University Theatre Production.
Yordon, Judy (1989) *Jane Eyre*, Indiana, Ball State University Theatre Production.
Shewell, Debbie (1990) *More Than One Antoinette*, Young Vic Theatre.
Calvit, Christine (1991) *Jane Eyre*, Chicago, Lifeline Theatre.
Shelmerdine, Roger (1991) *Jane Eyre: The New Musical*, Altrincham, Sale Civic Theatre.
The Haunting of Jane Eyre (1991) Loki Theatre Co-operative.
Vigeland, Nils and Charlotte Brontë (1992) *False Love/ True Love*, London, Almeida Theatre.
Hall, Willis (1992) *Jane Eyre*, Sheffield, Crucible Theatre.
Hunt, Sally (1993) *Jane Eyre*, Leeds, Civic Theatre.
Jones, Nick (1993) *Jane Eyre*, Cheltenham, Everyman Theatre.

Postma, Melanie, Sally Dunbar and Timothy Clarke (1993) *The Glasstown Confederacy.*

Portrait of a Governess, Disconnected, Poor and Plain (1994) Yorkshire, Brontë Society and Gondal Theatre.

Gomelskaya, Julia (composer) and Polyanna Buckingham (choreographer) (1997) *Jane Eyre*, London Children's Ballet.

Joubert, John (1997) *Jane Eyre.*

Adams, Judith (playwright) (1997) *Villette*, Sheffield, Crucible Theatre.

Malthaner, Michael, Charles Corritore and David Matthews (1998) *Jane Eyre*, Erie, PA, Erie Playhouse.

Hall, Willis (1998) *Jane Eyre*, Sheffield, Crucible.

Teale, Polly (1999) *Jane Eyre*, Leeds, West Yorkshire Playhouse, Shared Experience Theatre Company.

Berkeley, Michael and David Malouf (2000) *Jane Eyre*, Chandos.

Stout, Mary, Paul Gordon, Marla Schaffel, James Barbour and John Caird (2000) *Jane Eyre, The Musical*, Sony BMG.

Evans, Lisa (2005) *Villette.*

Bullard, Therese and Max Reger (2007) *Jane*, Michigan, Kalamazoo Ballet Company.

Race, Debby, Jana Smith, Wayne R. Scott and Brad Roseborough (2008) *Jane Eyre*, Redlands, CA, Lifehouse Theatre.

Gomelskaya, Julia and Nicola Tongue (2008) *Jane Eyre*, London Children's Ballet.

Bosc, Michel (2009) *A Symphony (7th).*

Lazy Bee Scripts (2013) *Jane Eyre.*

Cookson, Sally (2015) *Jane Eyre*, Bristol Old Vic.

Marshall-Griffiths, Linda (2016) *Villette*, Leeds, West Yorkshire Playhouse.

II: Inspired by Charlotte Brontë's life

Biographical studies

Gaskell, Elizabeth (1857) *The Life of Charlotte Brontë.*

Reid, T. Wemyss (1877) *Charlotte Brontë: A Monograph.*

Swinburne, A. C. (1877) *A Note on Charlotte Brontë.*

Leyland, Francis (1886) *The Brontë Family with Special Reference to Patrick Branwell Brontë.*

Birrell, Augustine (1887) *Life of Charlotte Brontë.*

Shorter, Clement (1896) *Charlotte Brontë and Her Circle.*

Harland, Marion (1899) *Charlotte Brontë at Home.*

Kinsley, William W. (1899) *The Brontë Sisters.*

Shorter, Clement K. (1905) *Charlotte Brontë and Her Sisters.*

Crookshank, Richard (n.d.) *The Life of the Brontës.*

Shorter, Clement K. (ed.) (1908) *The Brontës: Life and Letters.*

Clare, Maurice (May Byron) (n.d.) *A Day with Charlotte Brontë.*

Sinclair, May (1912) *The Three Brontës.*

Masson, Flora (1912) *The Brontës.*

Chadwick, Esther (1914) *In The Footsteps of the Brontës.*

Macdonald, Frederika (1914) *The Secret of Charlotte Brontë.*

Goldring, Maude (1915) *Charlotte Brontë: The Woman.*

Wood, Butler (ed.) (1917) *Charlotte Brontë, 1816–1916: A Centenary Memorial.*

Wright, J. C. (1925) *The Story of the Brontës.*

Clarke, Isabel C. (1927) *Haworth Parsonage: A Picture of the Brontë Family.*

Dimnet, Ernest (1927) *The Brontë Sisters (originally Les Soeurs Brontë, 1910).*

Sugden, K. A. R. (1929) *A Short History of the Brontës.*

Wise, T. J. and John Alexander Symington (ed.) (1932) *The Brontës: Their Lives, Friendship and Correspondence in Four Volumes.* Shakespeare Head Brontë.

Benson, E. F. (1932) *Charlotte Brontë.*

Willis, Irene Cooper (1933) *The Brontës.*

Delafield, E. M. (1935) *The Brontës: Their Lives Recorded by Their Contemporaries.*

Bentley, Phyllis (1947) *The Brontës.*

Hinkley, Laura L. (1947) *The Brontës: Charlotte and Emily.*

Millmore, Royston (1947) *Brief Life of the Brontës.*

Hanson, E. M. and L. Lawrence (1949) *The Four Brontës: The Lives and Works and Charlotte, Branwell, Emily and Anne Brontë.*

Bailey, Priscilla (1953) *Charlotte Brontë.*

Lane, Margaret (1953) *The Brontë Story.*

Crompton, Margaret (1955) *Passionate Search: A Life of Charlotte Brontë.*

Gérin, Winifred (1967) *Charlotte Brontë: Evolution of Genius.*

Pollard, Arthur (1968) *Charlotte Brontë.*

Morrison, N. Brysson (1969) *Haworth Harvest: The Lives of the Brontës.*

Bentley, Phyllis (1969) *The Brontës and their World.*

Winnifrith, Tom (1973) *The Brontës and their Background.*

Wilks, Brian (1975) *The Brontës.*

Peters, Margot (1975) *Unquiet Soul: A Biography of Charlotte Brontë.*

Moglen, Helene (1976) *Charlotte Brontë: The Self Conceived.*

Nestor, Pauline (1987) *Charlotte Brontë.*

Fraser, Rebecca (1988) *Charlotte Brontë.*

Winnifrith, Tom (1988) *A New Life of Charlotte Brontë.*

Gardiner, Juliet (1993) *The Brontës at Haworth.*

Barker, Juliet (1994) *The Brontës.*

Guzzetti, Paula (1994) *A Family Called Brontë.*

Orel, Harold (1996) *The Brontës: Interviews and Recollections.*

Sellars, Jane (1997) *Charlotte Brontë.*

Wilks, Brian (1998) *Charlotte in Love: The Courtship and Marriage of Charlotte Brontë.*

White, Kathryn (1998) *The Brontës.*

Miller, Lucasta (2001) *The Brontë Myth*.
Gordon, Lyndall (2008) *Charlotte Brontë: A Passionate Life*.
Cox, Jessica (2011) *Brief Lives: Charlotte Brontë*.
Harman, Claire (2016) *Charlotte Brontë: A Life*.

Novels, poetry, etc.

Carter Holloway, Laura (1883) *An Hour with Charlotte Brontë; or, Flowers from a Yorkshire Moor*.
Arnold, Matthew (1855; rev. 1890) 'Haworth Churchyard'.
Johnson, Lionel (1890) 'Brontë'.
Spofford, Harriet (1897) *In Titian's Garden and Other Poems*.
Woolf, Virginia (1904) 'Haworth November 1904', *The Guardian*.
Sinclair, May (1914) *The Three Sisters*.
Graves, C. L. (1917) 'To Charlotte Brontë'.
Mackereth, J. A. (1927) *Storm-Wrack: A Night with the Brontës*.
Woolf, Virginia (1929) *A Room of One's Own*.
Ferguson, Rachel (1931) *The Brontës Went to Woolworths*.
Cook, E. Thornton (1935) *They Lived: A Brontë Novel*.
Jarden, Mary Louise (1938) *The Young Brontës: Charlotte and Emily, Branwell and Anne*.
Cornish, Dorothy H. (1940) *These Were the Brontës*.
Ratchford, Fannie Elizabeth (1941) *The Brontës' Web of Childhood*.
Taylor, Elizabeth (1949) *A Wreath of Roses*.
Braithwaite, William Stanley (1950) *The Bewitched Parsonage: The Story of the Brontës*.
Wallace, Kathleen (1951) *Immortal Wheat*.
Dickinson, Emily (1955) *The Poems of Emily Dickinson*.
Lee, Austin (1956) *Miss Hogg and the Brontë Murders*.
White, Hilda (1957) *Wild Decembers: A Biographical Portrait of the Brontës*.
Bentley, Phyllis (1960) *The Young Brontës*.
Forest, Antonia (1961) *Peter's Room*.
Clarke, Pauline (1962) *The Twelve and the Genii*.
Clarke, Pauline (1963) *The Return of the Twelves*.
Kyle, Elizabeth (1963) *Girl with a Pen*.
Vipont, Elfrida (1966) *Weaver of Dreams: The Girlhood of Charlotte Brontë*.
Byatt, A. S. (1967) *The Game*.
Maurat, Charlotte (1967) *The Brontës' Secret*.
Amster, Jane (1973) *Dream Keepers: The Young Brontës: A Psycho-Biographical Novella*.
Banks, Lynne Reid (1976) *Dark Quartet: The Story of the Brontës*.
James, Donna (1977) *Brontë Life*.
Lane, Margaret (1980) *The Drug-Like Brontë Dream*.

Long, Freda M. (1980) *Haworth Harvest*.

Sturges, Florence M. (1981) *A Brontë Tapestry*.

Barnard, Robert (1983) *The Missing Brontë: A Perry Trethowan Novel*.

Barnes, Julian (1984) *Flaubert's Parrot*.

Urquhart, Jane (1990) *Changing Heaven*.

Brighton, Catherine (1994) *The Brontës: Scenes From the Childhood of Charlotte, Branwell, Emily and Anne*.

Kilworth, Garry (1995) *The Brontë Girls*.

Barraclough, June (1995) *Daughter of Haworth*.

Hughes, Glyn (1996) *Brontë*.

Tully, James (1999) *The Crimes of Charlotte Brontë: The Secret History of the Mysterious Events at Haworth*.

Rowland, Laura Joh (2008) *The Secret Adventures of Charlotte Brontë: A Novel*.

James, Syrie (2009) *The Secret Diaries of Charlotte Brontë*.

Morgan, Jude (2009) *The Taste of Sorrow*.

Gael, Juliet (2010) *Romancing Miss Brontë*.

Carter, Michele (2011) *Charlotte Brontë's Thunder: The Truth Behind The Brontë Sisters' Genius*.

Rowland, Laura Joh (2013) *Bedlam: The Further Secret Adventures of Charlotte Brontë*.

Stevenson, Ellie (2013) *Watching Charlotte Brontë, and Other Surreal Stories*.

Lower, Becky (2014) *Blame it on the Brontës*.

Janzing, Jolien (2015) *Charlotte Brontë's Secret Love*.

Reef, Catherine (2015) *The Brontë Sisters: The Brief Lives of Charlotte, Emily and Anne*.

Jackson, Mick (2016) *Yuki Chan in Brontë Country*.

Manning, Mick and Brita Granström (2016) *The Brontës – Children of the Moors: A Picture Book*.

Plays, ballets, operas, musicals, etc.

Linton, M. B. (1926) *The Tragic Race: A Play about the Brontës*.

Firkins, Oscar (1932) *Empurpled Moors: In the Bride of Quietness, and other plays*.

Dane, Clemence [Winifred Ashton] (1932) *Wild Decembers: A Play in Three Acts*.

Sangster, Alfred (1932) *The Brontës*, Sheffield Repertory Theatre.

Ferguson, Rachel (1933) *Charlotte Brontë: A Play in Three Acts*.

Sheridan, Mary D. (1933) *The Parson's Children*.

Sheridan, Mary D. (1933) *The Parson's Wife*.

Davison, John (1933) *The Brontës of Haworth Parsonage: A Chronicle Play of a Famous Family*, Birmingham Repertory Theatre.

Moorhouse, Ella (1933) *Stone Walls: A Play about the Brontës*. Bradford Civic Playhouse.

Totheroh, Dan (1934) *Moor Born: A Play*.

Purchase, Edward (1937) *The White Flame.*

Goudge, Elizabeth (1939) *Three Plays: Suomi; The Brontës of Haworth; Fanny Burney.*

Graham, Martha (1943) *Deaths and Entrances*, New York, Graham Dance Company.

Gérin, Winifred (1955) *My Dear Master.*

Gittings, Roberts (1957) *The Brontë Sisters*, National Federation of Women's Institutes Drama Festival.

de Zogheb, Bernard (1963) *Le Sorelle Brontë.*

Hynd, Ronald (1974) *Charlotte Brontë*, Bradford, Royal Ballet, Alhambra Theatre.

Crane, Richard (1976) *Thunder: A Play of the Brontës.*

Cross, Beverley (1978) *Haworth.*

Jackson, Douglas (1980) *Episode: A Moment in the Lives of the Brontës*, Macclesfield, New Playwrights' Network.

Armistead, Donna (1984) *The World Within*, Nottingham, Nichols School Dance Department.

Hunt, Anthony (1985) *Brontë Seasons.*

Alexander, Lesley (1988) *A Tender Fire.*

Bollinger, Lee (1989) *The Gales of March.*

Kershaw, Noreen (1989) *Withering Looks.*

Gable, Christopher, Gillian Lynne and Dominic Muldowney (1995) *The Brontës*, Leeds, Northern Ballet Theatre, Grand Theatre.

Teale, Polly (2005) *Brontë*, Guildford, Yvonne Arnaud Theatre, Shared Experience Theatre Company.

Morrison, Blake (2011) *We Are Three Sisters*, Halifax, Viaduct Theatre Northern Broadsides.

Ash, Christopher and Carl Miller (2016) *Wasted*, Leeds, West Yorkshire Playhouse.

Film, television, radio, etc.

Three Sisters of the Moors (1944), dir. John Larkin, Twentieth Century Fox Film Corporation.

Devotion (1946), dir. Curtis Bernhardt, Warner Bros.

The Brontës (1947), prod. Harold Clayton, BBC Television.

The Brontë Family (1951), prod. Pamela Brown, BBC Television.

The Loretta Young Show (1953) Season 1, Episode 9 ('The Brontë Story'), dir. Robert Florey, Lewislor Productions.

The Brontës of Haworth (1973), dir. Marc Miller, Granada and Yorkshire Television.

Les Sœurs Brontë (1979), dir. André Téchiné, Action Films.

Blue Peter Special Assignment: The Brontës at Haworth (1979), dir. Dorothea Brooking, BBC Television.

Brontë (1983), dir. Delbert Mann, Sonny Fox Production.

In the Shadows of the Brontës (1990), dir. Peter Harker, Classic Productions.

A Wild Workshop: Yorkshire and the Brontës (1992), dir. Richard Spanswick, Videolink.

Famous Authors: The Brontë Sisters (1996), prod. Malcolm Hossick.

Great Women Writers: The Brontë Sisters (2000), dir. Dominique Mougenot, Kultur Video.

In Search of the Brontës (2003), dir. Samira Osman, BBC Television.

The Brontë Sisters (2004), dir. Laura Sobel, Working Dog Productions.

The Other Brontë Sister (2010), dir. Jamie Hawkins-Gaar, Bland Hack Pictures.

Perspectives (2011) Episode 3 ('Shelia Hancock: The Brilliant Brontë Sisters'), dir. Gareth Williams, Blakeway North.

Psychobitches (2013) Season 1, Episode 1, and Season 2, Episode 2, dir. Jeremy Dyson, Sky Arts.

Sex with the Brontës (2014), dir. Nora Gruber and Kate Hacket, www.funnyordie. com (accessed 11 August 2016).

Finding Gondal: The Story of the Brontë Family (2015), dir. Morgan Rauscent, Reino Unido.

Walking through History (2015) Season 3, Episode 1 ('Brontë Country'), dir. James Franklin, Channel 4 and Wildfire Television.

Charlotte Brontë in Babylon (2016), dir. Charlotte Riches, BBC Radio 4.

Being the Brontës (2016), dir. Linda Sands, BBC Television.

To Walk Invisible (2016), dir. Sally Wainwright, BBC Television.

The Brontës (pre-production).

The Secret Diary of Charlotte Brontë (in development).

References

Alexander, Christine and Margaret Smith (2003) *The Oxford Companion to the Brontës*, Oxford: Oxford University Press.

Bolton, H. Philip (2000) *Women Writers Dramatized: A Calendar of Performances from Narrative Works Published in English to 1900*, London and New York: Mansell.

Ingham, Patricia (2006) *The Brontës*, Oxford: Oxford University Press.

Miller, Lucasta (2001) *The Brontë Myth*, London: Jonathan Cape.

Nudd, D. M. (1991) 'Bibliography of Film, Television and Stage Adaptations of Jane Eyre', *Brontë Society Transactions* (20.3). 169–72.

Stoneman, Patsy (1996) *Brontë Transformations: The Cultural Dissemination of Jane Eyre and Wuthering Heights*, Hemel Hempstead: Prentice Hall/Harvester Wheatsheaf.

—— (2007) *Jane Eyre on Stage, 1848–1898*, Aldershot: Ashgate.

—— (2008) 'Jane Eyre's Other: the emergence of Bertha'. *The Brontës in the World of the Arts*, ed. Sandra Hagan and Juliette Wells, Aldershot: Ashgate. 197–211.

—— (2013) *Charlotte Brontë*. Tavistock: Northcote House.

Index

Note: an 'n' after a page reference indicates the endnote number

Adams, Francis William
  Lauderdale 99
Adams, Judith 183, 187–8, 191, 193,
  194n.4
adaptations 3, 25, 31–3, 116, 125, 130,
  139, 165, 182–3, 185–94, 200,
  207, 221–5, 229–36, 237n.1,
  241–54, 258–75
  historiographic metafiction 268
  makeovers 260, 267–9, 271
    erotic makeovers 34, 259–75
  mash-up fiction 222, 224, 241–2
  prequels 32, 197, 202, 207
  revisions 260–1, 264, 268, 270–4
  sequels 32, 197
  transmedial 183, 186
Adorno, Theodor 120, 136
Africa 60
Agnes Grey 137
Alexander, Christine 14, 146, 148
Allott, Miriam 105
Alps 28, 60, 66, 74–6
America 62–3, 90–1
Anglo-French Wars 62
Angria 60, 149
archives 116–18, 121–5, 139
Aref, Nessa 245, 252
Arias, Rosario 113n.1
Armitt, Lucie 192

Arnold, Matthew 46, 50, 98–9,
  100–11, 184, 266, 276n.4
Ashbee, Henry Spencer 267
Atkins, Finn 24
Atwood, Margaret 276n.10
Austen, Jane 52, 150–1, 259, 265
Australia 63, 212, 215
Australian Brontë Association 16
autobiography 28, 31, 104, 146, 165,
  173, 183, 204, 206

Babbage, Frances 130
Bailey, Catherine 192
Bailey, Hilary 224, 237
Baldick, Chris 211
Barker, Juliet 15, 104
Barlow, George 99–104
Barrett Browning, Elizabeth 172
Bedford, F. D. 233, 238n.18
Bell, Currer 6, 9, 45–6, 55, 109–10,
  124, 183
Benson, Arthur C. 2
Bentley, Phyllis 69, 77n.1, 173
Berglund, Birgitta 10
bicentenary of Charlotte Brontë 1, 3,
  24–5, 93
Bildungsroman 214, 242
biodramas 29–30, 116–18, 125–9,
  131, 137–9

biofiction 97–8, 101–4, 111–12, 200
biographies 26, 29, 43–4, 47, 56, 81,
    87, 93n.2, 97, 99, 102–7, 110,
    119–28, 130–4, 139, 146, 166,
    169, 171, 173, 179, 193, 198,
    206, 223
    psychobiography 167
Birch-Pfeiffer, Charlotte 33, 224
Bloomsbury 166
Bluebeard 194n.3, 206
body, the 46–7
Bonnell, Henry Houston 119–21,
    137, 139n.2
Boone, Joseph A. 187, 189–90
Bostridge, Mark 186
Bowen, Elizabeth 167
Bower, Benji 162
Boyde, Carole 194n.7
Bradby, Godrey Fox 135–6
Braddon, M.E. 222, 226
Bramwell, Bill 88
Branwell, Elizabeth 79, 126, 170
Brittain, Vera 31, 77n.1, 165,
    169, 173
Brock, C.E. 10
Brontë, Anne 2–3, 5, 25, 67, 107–8,
    110–11, 127–9, 136
Brontë, Branwell 9, 13–16, 21, 97,
    99–104, 113n.2, 120, 125
Brontë, Emily 2–3, 5, 13, 15, 48,
    77n.3, 79–80, 86–7, 96, 101,
    105, 107–8, 110–11, 126–7,
    130–2, 134–8, 140n.6, 147–8,
    165, 167, 176, 224, 264
Brontë, Patrick 5–7, 21, 48, 55, 99,
    103, 113n.2, 118–20, 125–7,
    134, 136, 169, 172
Brontë Society 1, 15, 18, 27, 43, 79,
    91, 116–19, 121, 124–5,
    132–4, 137, 276n.13
Brontëana 119, 133
Brotherton, Edward, Lord 121
Brougham, John 226

Brown, Martha 17
Bruce, Virginia 248
Brussels, Belgium 15, 26, 28, 32,
    48, 52, 60, 77n.3, 79–93,
    123–8, 131, 137, 166, 170–1,
    183–5, 191
Brussels Brontë Group 91
Bulwer-Lytton, Edward 184
Burgess, Jean 245
Burns, Robert 155–6
Butterfield, Rosse 121
Byatt, A. S. 270, 272, 276n.10
Byrne, Georgina 102

Cabannne, Christy 33, 223, 229–30,
    234, 236, 248
Canada 63, 246
Cannon, John 238n.12
capitalism 64
Cappleman, Joolia 229
Carlyle, Thomas 124, 270
Caroline Vernon 149
Cartwright, Sierra 262, 265–9, 271
Cassir, Daryn 245
Cecil, David 184
Celts 49
centenary of Charlotte Brontë 1
Chadwick, Esther 19–20, 119
Chappel, Alonzo 10, 13, 21
Chartism 71, 74, 200
Chekov, Anton 175
Chesterton, G. K. 1–2
Clandestine Classics 259–75
Clarke, Michael M. 186
Claybourne, Anna 228
Clayton, Jay 212
Clive, Colin 223, 229
clothes 54
    corsets 10, 24
Colburn, Henry 124
Colby, Robert A. 184
Collins, Wilkie 202, 213
colonialism 60

Communist Manifesto, The (Karl Marx and Friedrich Engels) 200
'Condition of England' debates 62–3, 71
Cooke, W. H. 50–1
Cookson, Sally 162
copyright 268
  copyright law 21, 268
Cornhill Magazine 19
Correa, Delia da Sousa 242
Cory, Charlotte 21, 23, 25
Cory, William 51
Corzine, Amy 241
cosmopolitanism 80, 82, 92–3n.2
Courtney, John 33, 200, 222, 225
Cowper, William 157
cults 27, 29, 43, 47–8, 51, 54, 56, 81, 132
Cumberland, Gerald 83, 85–6
Cust, Lionel 19

Da Sousa Correa, Delia, 249
Daily Mail 264
d'Albertis, Deirdre 57n.2
Dalton, Timothy 229
Dane, Clemence 116, 131
Darwin, Charles 244
Davies, Andrew 191
Davison, John 116
Derrida, Jacques 185
Deutsch, Helen 27, 44, 53
Dickens, Charles 202, 270
Dickens World 270
Dickinson, Emily 50, 99, 109–10
Dinsdale, Ann 16
Disney, Walt 244
Dixon, Ella Hepworth 168
Dixon, Mary 17–18
domestic fiction 156
domesticity 13, 31, 48, 56, 61–2, 69, 73, 81, 90, 122, 157, 165, 167–8, 170–1, 174, 179

Douglas-Fairhurst, Robert 147, 149
du Maurier, Daphne 178
Duthie, Enid 93n.2, 104

Easson, Angus 104
Eco, Umberto 211
Edgerley, C. Mabel 15, 116
editing 121–2, 130, 138
education 70, 130, 183, 188
Eliot, George 48, 107
Ellis, Kate 248
Emery Walker Collection 18
emigration 65–6, 68, 70–1
Emmy Awards 245
empire 215
employment, women's 67
English Woman's Journal 65
Englishness 3, 28
Erwin, Sherri Browning 199, 224, 227–8, 242
ethics 197–9, 205–8
Europe 60, 63, 200
Evans, Linda 183

Faber, Michel 276n.10
fairy tales 47, 198, 242
family 3, 31, 46, 97–8, 105–6, 165, 167–9, 174, 179
fandom 259
  fan art 21
  fan fiction 199, 224, 261, 269, 275, 276n.3
Fassbender, Michael 223
Favret, Ann 149–50
Fawcett, Millicent 56
feminism 3, 31, 56, 60–5, 69–70, 77, 157, 164–6, 169–71, 174, 178–9, 210, 221, 243, 248, 254
femininity 3, 13, 26, 30, 69, 81–2, 90, 227, 234, 249
Ferguson, Rachel 30, 98, 101–4, 111, 118, 130–9

Fforde, Jasper 32, 197–200, 204,
    207–12, 214, 217, 224, 227–8,
    236–7, 241
film 33, 182, 186, 222, 229,
    233, 249
  Dangerous Minds (1995) 194n.5
  Dead Poets' Society (1989) 194n.5
  Goodbye Mr Chips (2002) 194n.5
  Hollywood 182
  I Walked With a Zombie (1943) 241
  Motion Picture Production
    Code 248
  School of Rock (2003) 194n.5
  silent films 223, 241
  Woman and Wife (1918)
Firkin, Oscar 116
Fitzgerald, Edward 3
folk tales 29, 205
Fontaine, Joan 241
forgeries 19–20
Foucault, Michel 122
Freedgood, Elaine 215
Freud, Sigmund 177, 187, 265–6
friendship 70, 74, 173
Fuest, Robert 229
Fukanago, Cary 223, 231, 236, 249

Gabain, Ethel 233–4, 238n.17
Galloway, F. C. 118–19
Garrett, Edmund 234
Gaskell, Elizabeth 2–3, 5–6, 9–10,
    13–14, 23–4, 26, 28–9, 31,
    43–9, 53, 55, 59–61, 79,
    81, 97–8, 103–7, 110,
    112, 113n.2, 117, 121–30,
    140n.5, 146–7, 164, 166,
    168–74, 179, 185, 266
gaze, male 187
genius 1, 3, 13, 26, 44–6, 52, 55–6, 63,
    164, 174, 271
Gerver, Jane E. 228
Giardina, Denise 97
Gibbons, Stella 140n.3

Gilbert, Sandra 32, 223, 233, 248, 266
Gill, Stephen 151
Gilman, Charlotte Perkins 175–6,
    222, 226
Glen, Heather 148, 186, 201
global space 59, 61–4, 76–7
Goffman, Erving 6
Gold, Tanya 266
Gordon, Lyndall 55
Gosse, Edmund 1–2
gothic 33, 51, 85, 97, 105, 156, 178,
    192–3, 194n.8, 221, 224,
    226–7, 229, 242
Goudge, Elizabeth 116
governesses 16, 167, 204
graphic novels 242
grave, Charlotte Brontë's 50,
    99–100
Gray, Luccia 241
Green, Alice Boyd 19
Greene, Joshua 245
Greenwood, John 15
Gronzy, James Gorin Von 16
Guardian, The 43, 264–5
Gubar, Susan 32, 223, 233, 248

Haire-Sargeant, Lin 198, 224
Haley, Robert 17
Hall, Kathryn 245
Hardy, Thomas 210, 259
Harland, Marion 28, 52–3, 83–4, 87,
    90, 119
Harman, Claire 2, 15, 17
Harper, Janet 83, 86
Harrad, Kate 268–9
Hatfield, C. W. 146
Hattaway, Meghan Burke 46
Haworth 24, 26–9, 43, 45, 47–51,
    53–6, 59–60, 66, 79–82, 90–1,
    93, 96, 99, 106, 119, 124–6,
    130, 134–5, 169, 171, 173, 175,
    191, 272
  see also Yorkshire

Haworth Parsonage 26, 29, 50–2, 54,
    56, 79–80, 82, 86, 112, 116–17,
    119, 125
Hazelgrove, Jenny 102
Heger, Claire Zoe 128–9
Heger, Constantin 28, 30, 32,
    77n.3, 80, 83, 93n.2, 93n.5,
    123–31, 140n.5, 153, 171,
    173, 185
Heger, Madame 82, 128
Heger, Paul 19–20, 123
Heilman, Robert 238
Heilmann, Ann 102, 197, 244
Heilmann, Robert B. 194n.8
Hemans, Felicia 157
Henry Hastings 149
heritage 27, 30, 81, 85, 117, 125
Hinds, Ciaran 229
Hirst, Grace 74, 76
historical fiction 197–8
Ho, Elizabeth 244
Hollyer, Belinda 228, 236
Holmes, C. J. 20
Holtby, Winifred 31, 165,
    173–4, 177–9
Hopewell, Donald 121
Horner, Avril 178
Household Words 105
Hubbard, Kate 194n.2
Humble, Nicola 111
Humphreys, Anne 203
Hutcheon, Linda 268, 270
Hutchins, B. L. 170

illustration 233–4
Independent, The 264
India 213, 215
influence 26, 147
intertextuality 199–200, 203, 211, 217,
    222, 244–5, 272
Ireland 49, 55–6
    Irish Famine 60
Italy 63

James, E. L. 34, 258, 263
Jameson, Storm 173
Jane Eyre 16, 21, 30–3, 49, 70, 102,
    105–7, 112, 116, 146, 148–
    50, 152–3, 155, 157, 161–2,
    165, 178, 182, 186, 190, 192,
    194n.2, 194n.3, 197–204,
    207–8, 210–17, 221–8, 232–3,
    237, 242, 245–6, 248–9, 251,
    258–263, 265–6, 268, 270,
    272–3, 275
Jenkins, Henry 222, 244, 247
Jerwood Vanbrugh Theatre 187
Jex-Blake, Sophia 172
John, Juliet 85
Johnson, Claudia L. 44, 52
Johnson, Lionel Pigot 108–9, 111
Johnson, Samuel 46, 99
Jones, Gail 32, 197–200, 204, 210–17
Jones, Lloyd 211
Jordan, Meghan 249
Joyce, Rachel 190–1
juvenilia, Charlotte Brontë's 29–30,
    60, 117, 147–8

Kaplan, Cora 166, 201, 242–3, 270
Kaplan, E. Ann 248
Kingsley, Charles 45
Kirchknopf, Andrea 210
Klein, Thomas 245
Kohler, Sheila 198
Kohlke, Marie-Louise 243
Kontou, Tatiana 113n.1
Kvistad, Erika 263

Lamonica, Drew 164
Landon, Laetitia Elizabeth 148
landscape 24, 68, 75, 88–90
Landseer, Edwin 16
Law, Jude 232
Lawrence, Margaret 171–2
Leitch, Thomas 182–3
Letissier, Georges 203

letters, Charlotte Brontë's 3, 18, 27–8, 53, 55, 66–71, 83, 117, 122–9, 131, 139, 150, 165, 168–71, 173, 175, 193, 275
Lewes, G. H. 104, 150–1, 154, 189
libraries 117
Lindner, April 199, 225
Linton, M. B. 101, 108
literary reputation, Charlotte Brontë's 3, 47
Litvak, Joseph 190
Llewellyn, Mark 102, 197, 244, 258, 268
London Children's Ballet 233, 241
London Review of Books 263
Luddites 62, 69, 106
Lutz, Deborah 140n.3
Lynch, Deirdre 44

Macdonald, Frederika 83
MacEwan, Helen 83, 91
Malone, Catherine 185
Mann, Delbert 248
Marcus, Sharon 172
Married Women's Property Act (1882) 200
Martineau, Harriet 46, 48–9
Matthews, Samantha 99, 103
Maxwell-Martin, Anna 165, 191–2
Mayor, F. M. 174
McCormack, Catherine 192
media 17, 24, 26, 33
    BBC 24, 125, 165, 191–3, 241
melodrama 30, 33, 130, 204, 226
Meyer, Stephanie 261
middlebrow fiction 111
migration 60–5, 67
Milbank, Alison 186
Millais, John Everett 25, 234
Miller, Lucasta 56, 60, 80–1, 93n.2, 96, 104, 125, 166, 182–3, 185, 198, 203
Milton, John 148

mobility 59–64, 67–9, 70, 72, 76, 89
modernism 165–7, 170–2, 174, 179, 199
Molloy, Seamus 17
Monde, Le 264
Moorhouse, Ella 116
mourning 56
Mozley, Ann 45–7, 184
Murray, Janet Horowitz 70–1, 77n.2
museums 24–6, 56, 118–25, 132, 136, 139
    Brontë Parsonage Museum, Haworth 15–18, 21, 24–5, 27, 29–30, 53, 56, 79, 81, 96, 116–17, 119–25, 130–3, 191, 211, 270
        Wade extension 24
    Dove Cottage, Lake District 270
    Sir John Soane's Museum, London 25
myth 26, 28–31, 44, 55–6, 60–4, 80–2, 88, 90, 92–3, 109, 118, 131–2, 134, 139, 165, 179, 185, 198, 211

narrator, unreliable 190–1
national identity 82, 90
National Portrait Gallery 10, 13, 15–18, 20
Neilson, Marion Sellers 74, 76
neo-Victorian fiction 26, 32–4, 102, 165, 171, 174, 197–203, 205–6, 208, 212–13, 216–17, 217n.2, 218n.5, 243, 258–61, 263–4, 268–75, 276n.2, 276n.10
Nerval, Monsieur de 205
Newby, Thomas 137
New Woman 165, 168
New York Post 116
Nicholls, Arthur Bell 6, 9, 13–14, 18, 24, 51, 55, 103, 111, 122, 137, 173
nostalgia 32, 85, 87, 198, 200–1, 226

Nussey, Ellen 6, 9, 15–16, 18, 46, 65, 70, 103, 122, 128–9, 172–3

obituaries 26–7, 48, 56
Oehler, Bernice 234, 238n.20
Oliphant, Margaret 166–7
Ophelia (*Hamlet*) 234
orient 243
Orr, Aviva 97
Ovid 109

Palliser, Charles 272
Parker, Cornelia 96–7
Pascal, Julia 183, 191, 193
Paul, T. H. 226
Pearson, Maggie 225
Pease, Alison 175
Pensionnat Heger 28, 48, 79–80, 82–5, 87–91, 126, 128, 130, 171, 185
Peterson, Linda H. 44, 55
photography 9, 13, 15, 17–18, 23–4, 29, 108, 206, 214–16
Photoshop 21
phrenology 7
Picardie, Justine 96–7
Pierpont Morgan Library 133
Plasa, Carl 60
Plotz, John 211
Poems by Currer, Ellis and Acton Bell 1, 145–6, 149, 158–9
'Pilate's Wife's Dream' 146–7
poetry 26, 29–30, 146
Politi, Jina 243
Poon, Angelia 235
pop art 21
portraiture 5–7, 13, 15, 17, 19–21, 25, 124
Gun Group, The 13–15
Pillar Portrait, The 13–14, 20
Richmond, George 5–7, 9–10, 14–15, 20–1

self-portrait, Charlotte Brontë's 15–16, 215
postmodernism 267–74
Power, Maggie 198
Priestley, J. B. 173
Professor, The 30, 79, 88, 133, 149, 152–4, 157, 161, 185–6, 189, 192
provincialism 175
Punch 130
Pusham, Patricia
Puttnam's Monthly Magazine 186

race 33, 201, 225, 227, 232
Rachel 218n.4
Radcliffe, Ann (*The Italian*) 150, 156–7
radio plays 31, 183, 186, 188, 191–3, 241
Rae, Leonard 226
Raitt, Suzanne 170
Rego, Paula 234
Reid, T. Wemyss 55–6
relics 14, 27, 29, 54–5, 81, 87, 111, 117–25, 132–3, 136, 138–9
mementoes 104
memorabilia 53, 56
souvenirs 1, 87, 93n.7, 120
Rhys, Jean 32, 202, 205, 207, 221, 223, 226, 236, 241, 270
Rich, Adrienne 202
Rigby, Elizabeth 46
Rigel, L. K. 199
Roberts, Michèle 171
Roberts, Sir James 119
Robinson, A. Mary F. 125
Rodenberg, Patsy 183, 191, 193
Roe Head School 48, 65
Romanticism 148–53, 155, 157, 242
Roses, Karena 224
Ross, Marion Pollock 74
Rowland, Laura Joh 199
Ruse, Michael 244

Rushdie, Salman 263
Rye, Maria S. 65
Rylance, Rick 222

Salmon, Richard 55
Sand, George 150
Sangster, Alfred 30, 117,
    125–31, 138–9
Scott, Sir Walter 154–5, 270
Self, Will 272
Sellars, Jane 9, 14
sentimentality 151
Seton-Gordon, Elizabeth 18
Sewell, Helen 234, 238n.19
Sex Disqualification Removal Act
    (1919) 170
sexuality 3, 33–4, 167, 172, 212,
    224–5, 227, 229, 231–2, 258,
    262, 266, 273
  BDSM 263, 273
  lesbianism 172, 247
  masochism 263
  sadism 263
Shakespeare Head edition of the
    Brontës' works 29, 117,
    121, 124–9, 138, 140n.4,
    140n.6, 146
Sharpe, Jenny 228
Shaw, Margaret L. 187, 190
Shelley, Mary 211
Shiller, Dana 201
Shirley 19, 23, 27, 30, 59–64, 66–7,
    70–2, 74–7, 77n.1, 93n.2, 102,
    134, 156–7, 159, 161, 177
Shorter, Clement 19, 112, 122–30,
    140n.4, 146
Shuttleworth, Sally 60, 175
Siemaszkiewicz, Claire 265–6, 271,
    273, 276n.1
Sinclair, Eve 224, 231
Sinclair, May 31, 164–6, 170–1,
    173–7, 179
sisterhood 164, 175

Smith, Elder 19, 146, 151, 185
Smith, George 5, 7, 9, 13, 18, 67,
    122, 140n.5
Smith, Margaret 140n.4
spinsters 67, 164–5, 167–8,
    170–2, 174–9
Spivak, Gayatri Chakravorty 33, 243
Spofford, Harriet Prescott 99, 110–12
Stanley, Alessandra 258–9
Stephen, Leslie 49
Stevens, Joan 66
Stevenson, Juliet 194n.7
Stevenson, Robert 229, 233, 236,
    241, 248
Stewart, Susan 93n.7
Stoddart Holmes, Martha
    223, 238n.7
Stowe, Harriet Beecher 107
Stubbs, Jane 224
Sun, The 264
supernatural 102–6, 112
  ghosts 29, 49, 52, 56, 84–6, 96–9,
    100–12, 130, 149, 203, 221,
    227, 232–4, 237, 265
  hauntings 49, 59, 61, 85, 98–9, 102,
    105, 149, 221, 226
  séances 29, 96–7, 101–2, 107
  spiritualism 29, 96, 102, 107, 110
surveillance 183
Sutcliffe, Halliwell 2
Sweet, Matthew 197
Swinburne, Algernon 48
Symington, J. A. 119–30

Taylor, Mary 27, 46, 48, 59–60, 64–5,
    77, 103, 168, 173
Tavner, Gill 228
teaching 167, 189
Teale, Polly 223, 238n.5
Telegraph, The 264
television 222–3, 229, 233, 236,
    241, 246
  Glee (Fox, 2011–15) 194n.5

television (*cont.*)
   Penny Dreadful (Sky, 2014–16) 261
   Saturday Night Live (NBC, 1975–) 232
   Sherlock (BBC, 2010–) 261
   South Riding (BBC, 2011) 165
   White, Suzanne 230–4, 236
Tenant of Wildfell Hall, The 146
Tennant, Emma 32, 197–200, 203–7, 217, 218n.4, 226, 236
Tetley, Sara 88
Thackeray, William Makepeace 25, 46, 137, 150–1
theatre 117, 125, 130, 138, 183, 187–8, 222–3, 241
   Frantic Assembly 191
   opera 223, 241
   Royalty Theatre, London 125
   Sheffield Crucible Theatre 187, 194n.4
   Sheffield Repertory Theatre 125
   Stephen Joseph Theatre, Scarborough 187
   West Yorkshire Playhouse, Leeds 183
   see also London Children's Ballet
Thomas, D. M. 198, 260–1, 271–5
Thompson, J. H. 9–10, 13, 24
Time 264
Times, The 13, 19–20, 123, 171, 264
Totally Bound 259, 262, 268, 276n.1
tourism 26–8, 30, 43, 55, 60, 79–81, 83–90, 99, 117, 119, 125, 131–4, 136, 138, 173, 207, 270, 272
   Brontë Country 80–1, 93n.4, 93n.7
   see also Haworth
   literary pilgrimages 25–8, 44–5, 49, 51–2, 54, 81, 87, 91, 99, 119, 130–4
   TripAdvisor 23
Trafton, Adeline 83–5, 87, 89–90

Transactions (Brontë Society Journal) 118–19
transmedia 33, 241–2, 244–5, 247, 254, 269, 275
travel writing 28
Trott, Sophie 24
Tully, James 199
Turner, J. Horsfall 13, 15
Turner, Nick 203

Uglow, Jenny 104–5
Urquhart, Jane 97

vampires 226, 228, 261
Victoria Magazine 65, 77n.4
Victoriana 258, 260–1, 270, 275
Villette 19, 26, 28, 31, 52, 79–80, 82–5, 88, 90, 100, 105, 123, 157, 161–162n.1, 164–8, 177, 179, 182–7, 189–94, 194n.2, 194n.3, 194n.4, 218n.4, 266, 276n.4

Wade, John 119
Wainwright, Sally 24
Waldorf, Willela 116
Ward, (Mary) Mrs Humphry 1–2, 49
Wasikowska, Mia 223
Waters, Sarah 259, 270, 276n.10
Watson, Nicola J. 51, 81, 85, 88
web 224, 253, 268
   eBay 17
   e-publications 259, 261, 263, 268
   Facebook 245, 247
   Google Images 20–1
   gutenberg.org 269
   Instagram 245, 247
   online communities 17, 33, 242, 246, 249, 251, 253, 261
   regender.com 269
   social media 247
   Tumblr 245, 247
   Twitter 245, 247

Vlogs 242, 246–7, 251, 253–4
YouTube 245, 247, 252, 254
web series 33, 224, 238n.10, 242,
    245–6, 248, 251, 254
    Autobiography of Jane Eyre (2013–
    14) 33, 224, 238n.10, 242, 245,
    247, 249, 254
    Emma Approved (2013–14) 245
    Lizzie Bennet Diaries 245, 252
    lonelygirl15 245
Wehrmann, Jürgen 210
Welldon, J. E. 56
Welles, Orson 229, 241
Wellesley, Arthur, Duke of
    Wellington 5
Wellington, New Zealand 27–8, 65–6,
    71, 73–4, 76–7n.4
Wells, Juliette 209
West Indies 226
Westminster Review 150, 189
Wheelwright, Laetitia 123
Widdowson, Peter 202, 270
Wilde, Oscar 268
Williams, W. S. 23, 151
Willing, James 226
Wills, W. G. 200
Wilmot, Thomas Slaney 107
Windsor, Valerie 189
Winnifrith, Tom 146, 148–9, 153
Wise, T. J. 124, 130
Wolfe, Theodore 83, 85–8, 90
women's rights 67
    employment 67, 167

female education 174
feminism 3, 31, 56, 60–5, 69–70,
    77, 157, 164–6, 169–71,
    174, 178–9, 210, 221, 243,
    248, 254
Langham Place Group 65
'redundant' women 65, 167–8
working women 67, 70, 72, 167,
    174–5, 177, 179
Wooler, Margaret 48, 66
Woolf, Virginia 27, 30–1, 43–4, 53–4,
    56, 120, 136, 165–7, 170, 172,
    174, 179, 201, 209, 221
Wordsworth, William 150–5, 157,
    159–60, 270
World War I 175
Wroot, Herbert, C. 93n.2
Wuthering Heights 81, 96–7, 101–2,
    105, 137, 146, 165, 168, 182

Yorkshire 3, 24, 26, 29, 43, 49–50,
    54–5, 63, 66–8, 81, 91,
    173, 191
    see also Haworth
Yorkshire Penny Bank 27, 43,
    52–4, 118–20
Young Adult fiction 222, 225
Young, E. H. 174
Young, Robert 229–30, 234–6

Zamorna 149
Zefferelli, Franko 231
Zlosnik, Sue 178